THE SOURCES OF THE MESSAGE

Illuminating the teachings of Jesus as given in the synoptic gospels
by reference to the Old Testament and other Jewish literature

A. R. Tindall

The Alethinos Press
P.O. Box 280
Hastings TN34 9DF
U.K.
www.alethinospress.co.uk

Tindall, A. R. (Alex. R.)

THE SOURCES OF THE MESSAGE
Includes bibliographical references and indices.

1. Synoptic gospels.   2. Christianity.   3. Judaism.

ISBN 978-0-9552223-0-6

Printed by PABA Ltd., Bruninieku Street 10a, Riga, LV-1001, Latvia, e-mail info@paba.lv, phone +371 7310002, fax +371 7315266

CONTENTS.

PREFACE

The statistics relating to the numbers of people reading the bible are clear: the majority never open it, and only a tiny minority read it regularly. There are many reasons for this; simple indifference and apathy is obviously wide-spread, but the bible is not always easy to grasp, the language is sometimes unusual and complex, while the ethics and morality seem to be either quite foreign to the modern mind or hopelessly idyllic and unattainable. The contradictions amongst the gospels, and the so-called miracle stories, are other things to which many respond negatively. Uncertainty about the history of the bible, especially of the N.T., and the emphasis on the Jesus of the faith of the early church, are problems for many. Such a Jesus easily becomes a remote theological abstraction, a third of an incomprehensible Trinity, rather than a man who lived in Palestine two thousand years ago.

To discover what the gospels really say and mean is the work of full-time study. One must attain familiarity with several ancient languages; the laws and cults of the Hebrew, Roman and other societies of the time; analysis of the text; as well as archaeological study of remains and graves. It is not surprising that few can achieve the necessary competence. Nevertheless, there are scholars who cover a great deal of the required subjects but they publish their findings in learned journals which are not easy for the uninitiated to understand. This book attempts to present some of the discoveries of the experts in a form that the rest of us can understand so that we can answer the question: "What would Jesus' listeners have made of what he was teaching and preaching? How did they understand him?" What the message is for us today is left to the reader to decide but it is hoped any judgement will be based on a better understanding of the gospel texts.

Judaism was the culture in which Jesus, the disciples and apostles lived. It was a world in which the laws, customs, habits, aspirations and hopes of Judaism determined almost all conduct. They were Jews, as were the authors of the gospels and most of those who listened to Jesus. The lack of even a superficial acquaintance with Judaism on the part of today's Christians is a severe handicap to grasping the mode of thought of the evangelists and the society Jesus and his fellow Jews experienced.

The whole of Jesus' ministry can be perceived as the embodiment of Judaism as it should be. Flusser has written: "I have never found any aspect of Jesus' teaching which would have caused his hearers to suspect him of heresy." The endless complications imposed by the scribes, elders, sages and other religious leaders meant that, according to them, only the most single-minded dedication could hope to bring a person to salvation. By returning to the relative simplicity of the Law, based on the commandment to love God and other people, Jesus cleared the way for all but the recalcitrant to live in God's realm and obey his rules.

Much of Jesus' teaching seems obscure to us today, but at the time those hearing him would have immediately made associations with other passages which would have made Jesus' message very much more effective. Here is one example of thousands which could be mentioned. It is found in a rabbinical work as a comment on Lam. 1:21 and it begins:

> It is like a queen to whom the king said, "Do not lend anything to your neighbours, and do not borrow anything from them." One time the king became angry with her and drove her out of the palace. She went to all her neighbours, but none received her, so she returned to the palace. The king said to her, "You have acted impudently!" She said to him, "You are the one who has done it because you told me to neither lend nor borrow anything from our neighbours. If I had lent them an article or borrowed one from them, and if one of them had seen me outside her home, would she not have received me?"

No unspoken implications occur to us in connection with this odd passage, but to those at the time who had memorised vast amounts of Jewish religious literature it would have reminded them of:

> "If a man places his wife under a vow not to lend nor to borrow a sieve, a basket, a millstone, or an oven, [and she does] he must divorce her and give her marriage dowry back to her because he causes her to have a bad name among her neighbours" (b.Ket. 72a).

Thus those hearing the story would know at once the implications for the king's character. It was not necessary to state explicitly that he did not deserve to keep his queen if he treated her so improperly.

Most, if not all, of the parables and stories of Jesus would similarly have reminded his hearers of associated passages and, unless we know something of this background, we get only a limited, distorted or even misleading understanding of the meaning of Jesus' teaching. It is hoped that this book will help to eliminate such misunderstandings and stimulate others to read for themselves the rich Jewish literature of which only a small fraction has been included here. You do not have to be a Jew in order to read and enjoy Jewish books, even the earliest ones.

In ancient times, it was not in any way considered improper to put the writer's own words into the mouth of a famous person. There was little concern for historical accuracy, nor of reporting events dispassionately. The aim was to tell a convincing story. Moreover, the standard mode of recording was by memorising the parables, stories and sayings, especially perhaps, those originally in verse, probably supported by the apostles' notes. It is well known that oral transmission by poetry and stories is effective, and often preserves the essential meaning without serious distortion. Nevertheless, the reader should bear in mind all the time that no-one can legitimately assert, 'Jesus said', so and so. The most one can do is to say that one or more of the writers of the N.T. tell us that he said so and so, although to avoid cumbersome circumlocutions, the simpler, direct statement has usually been used here as elsewhere.

The arrangement of each gospel is secondary. Most scholars believe that they began as collections of short passages which were built up into the gospels. The evangelists wrote with their own particular purposes in mind. For example, many think that Mark's gospel follows the pattern of the O.T. stories of the Exodus from Egypt, the Passover, the conquest of Canaan, the faithfulness of Moses, Aaron, Joshua and Caleb, the intransigent wickedness of the Israelites and God's wrath, patience and love. Matthew probably wrote for those who saw Christianity as a form of Judaism, and created his gospel on the pattern of the five books of the Torah, while Luke perhaps tailored his gospel to the needs of converts from non-Jewish beliefs. They did not hesitate to vary the basic forms of the stories they had received. There was no thought of direct quotation; the passage would be freely reproduced or adapted in some way and it was more a case of using the saying rather than transmitting it.

It has to be admitted that it is a very delicate task to tease out the original stories and sayings from the gospels as we now have them, but it is one of the triumphs of biblical scholarship that so much has been achieved. By this research it is possible to make plain much of Jesus' teaching. At first it looks as though there are so many differences in the three synoptic gospels that the exercise cannot be justified, but it must be remembered that it was common practice to use the same saying for different purposes. Also, many of the passages are typically admonitions, explanations and exhortations which allow a greater laxity of expression than statements of the law, which require the utmost precision. It is a fascinating study to trace the changes in the texts which have resulted from faulty memorisation, inaccurate or unclear notes, mistakes in writing them from dictation, wrong translations and sometimes even deliberate corruption of the text to suit the dogmas of the church, but that is not the purpose of the present book.

At the same time new discoveries are being made every year, and there is still much that needs to be elucidated. This is perhaps disappointing, but it is much better to be disappointed than misled. Regrettably churches and religious circles have not always appreciated this. Many like to be dogmatic and give solutions to the uncertainties, but those peddling them should be treated as 'false prophets'. If Christians overlook a proper understanding of the teaching of Jesus given in the gospels, they may practise the partly false religion of 'Christianity'as manifest in churches, and they may have faith in Jesus, but they are not practising the faith of Jesus.

The gospel of John stands out as very different from the other three gospels of Matthew, Mark and Luke (the synoptic gospels). In a recent study, Casey has shown how the gradual separation from Judaism of the early community of Jesus' followers, (at first forming a subdivision of Judaism), led to increasing emphasis on the differences between the mother religion and its offshoot. Those writing about Jesus began to proclaim him as a divine being sent from heaven, "God's Son". This came to influence N.T. writings from Paul onwards and culminated in the books of John. The gospel of John is a work of theology based on many concepts not found in the teaching of Jesus and does not belong to a proper study of Jesus' teaching.

Judaism

Judaism had many strata and subdivisions with a wide range of attitudes, from a legalistic or rigorous pharisaism to apocalyptic visionaries and mystics; from an attractive religious humanism to an unattractive fanatical dogmatism. Among the various factions of Jews of Jesus' time, were Pharisees, Sadducees, doctors of the Law, scribes, elders and so forth, but as there is no certain way of distinguishing these various groups properly, they are usually referred to here as religious leaders. After the war of 66-70 C.E., the Pharisees became the dominant group.

Some of the topics which naturally arise in the minds of Christians are dealt with in the Jewish literature of the time, and some examples are given here.

1.   Why did God command the building of the Tabernacle, and sanction the building of the Temple? Surely he requires no dwelling-place. "Behold the heavens cannot hold him. Does not God fill heaven and earth? It must be in honour of his people that He appointed the place of meeting. ... When Israel was in Egypt, the nation was yet young: "When Israel was a child I loved him; from Egypt did I call my son" (Hos. 11:1) and at Sinai, "Face to face the Lord spake with you" (Dt. 5:4). But from the time when they accepted the Torah, with the words: "All that the Lord hath spoken we will do, and we will hear", they were a fully-developed nation. Then he said, "It is not seemly for my children that I should speak to them and correct them in public, or, when I have hard words to say to them that all the world should hear; but let them build a Tabernacle, and when I have to speak to them I will speak from the Tabernacle." (Num.R. 12).

2.   King Solomon has said, "The day of one's death is better than that of his birth. When a human being is born all rejoice, and when he dies all weep. But it should not be so. Rather at one's birth no one has yet cause to rejoice; for no one knows to what future the babe is born, what will be the development of his intellect or of his soul, and by what works he will stand; whether he will be a righteous man or a wicked man, whether he will be good or evil; whether good or evil will befall him. But when he dies, then all ought to recognise if he has departed leaving a good name and has gone out of this world in peace" (Koh.R. on Ecc. 7).

3.   Why did not God give the whole law to all the peoples since all belong to God? God gave some laws to Adam, more still to Noah, still more to Abraham. He gave to all peoples such laws as they needed and could keep, and worldly prosperity as well. The laws of right-conduct, morality and mercy were given for all men; but on Mount Sinai Israel said, "All that the Lord says we will do and we will hear." Therefore he showed them the distinction between clean and unclean, between holy and profane, and gave them the Law of Holiness. (Ex.R. 30).

As the reader reads through the passages it will quickly become clear that the Jewish scholars were extremely adept in finding interpretations, usually through intricate argument - the main entertainment for at least the educated Jews, then as now - some of which seems to us to be very far-fetched. If some of the stories seems

Bibliography.

Reference books.

Aland, K. Synopsis of the four gospels: Stuttgart, German Bible Society, 1989.
Arnt W.F. and Gringrich F.W. A Greek-English lexicon of the New Testament: Chicago, University Press, 1957.
Bowker, J. The Targums and rabbinic literature. Cambridge: University Press 1969.
Brenton, L.C.L. The Septuagint version: Greek and English. Grand Rapids: Zondervan (n.d.)
Charles, R.H. The Apocrypha and Pseudepigrapha of the Old Testament. Oxford: Clarendon Press, 1913.
Danby, H. The Mishnah. Oxford: University Press. 1933.
Freedman, H. (ed.) Mishnah Rabbah. London: Soncino Press 1983.
Glatzer, N. (ed.) The Passover haggadah. New York: Schocken Books 1979.
Lake, K. The apostolic fathers. London: Heinemann Press 1977.
Montefiore, C.G. Rabbinic literature and gospel teachings. London: Macmillan 1930.
Montefiore, C.G. and Loewe, H. A rabbinic anthology. London: Macmillan 1938.
Robinson, J.M. (ed.) The Nag Hammadi library in English. Leiden: Brill 1977.
Stenning, J.F. (ed.) The Targum of Isaiah. Oxford: Clarendon Press 1949.
Schuerer E., Vermes G., Millar F. and Goodman M. The history of the Jewish people in the age of Jesus Christ. Edinburgh 1986.
Tanakh: a new translation of the Holy Scriptures. Philad. and Jerusalem 1985.
Vermes, G. The Dead Sea Scrolls in English. Harmondsworth, Penguin 1995.

Other books.

Bammel E. and Moule C.F.D. *Jesus and the politics of his day.* Cambridge: University Press 1984.
Barrett C.K. *The New Testament background: selected documents.* London: SPCK 1956.
Barrett C.K. *Jesus and the gospel tradition.* London: SPCK 1967.
Beckwith R. *The Old Testament canon of the New Testament church.* London: SPCK 1985.
Bernfeld, S. *Der Lehren des Judentums.* Berlin: Schwestschke. 1922.
Best E. and Wilson R. McL. (eds.) *Text and interpretation.* Cambridge: University Press 1979.
Black M. *An Aramaic approach to the Gospels and Acts.* Oxford: Clarendon Press, 1967.
Boeker H.J. *Law and the administration of justice in the Old Testament and ancient east.* London: SPCK 1980.
Booth R.P. *Contrasts - gospel evidence and Christian beliefs.* Bognor Regis: Paget 1990.
Bornkamm G. *Jesus of Nazareth.* London: Hodder and Stoughton, 1973.
Bruce F.F. *Jesus and Christian origins outside the New Testatment.* London: Hodder and Stoughton, 1984.

Bultmann R. *Primitive Christianity.* London: Thames and Hudson 1956.

Burney C.F. *The poetry of our Lord.* Oxford: Clarendon Press 1925.

Cadoux A.T. *The parables of Jesus.* London: James Clark n.d.

Carmignac, J. *La naissance des évangiles synoptiques.* Paris: O.E.I.L. 1984.

Casey, M. *From Jewish prophet to Gentile God.* Cambridge, Clark 1991

Charlesworth J.H. *Jesus within Judaism.* London: SPCK 1988.

Compendium Rerum Judaicarum ad Novum Testamentum. Assen, Van Gorcum, 1984.

    Mikra II/1 *Text, translation, reading and interpretation of the Hebrew bible in Judaism and early Christianity.* (ed. Mulder M.J.)

    Mikra II/2 *Jewish writings in the Second Temple period.* (ed. Stone M.E.)

Dahl N.A. *Jesus in the memory of the early church.* Minniapolis: Augsburg Publishing House 1976.

Daube, D. *The New Testament and rabbinic Judaism.* Salem: Ayer 1984.

Davies W.D. *Paul and rabbinic Judaism.* London: SPCK 1962.

Davies W.D. and Daube E. (eds.) *The background of the New Testament and its eschatology.* Cambridge: University Press 1964.

Derrett J.D.M. *Law in the New Testament.* London: Darton, Longman and Todd 1970.

Derrett J.D.M. *Studies in the New Testament. Vols. 1-5.* Leiden: Brill 1977-1989.

Derrett J.D.M. *The Anastasis: the resurrection of Jesus as an historical event.* Shipstone-on-Stour: Drinkwater 1982.

Derrett J.D.M. *The making of Mark.* Shipstone-on-Stour: Drinkwater 1985.

Derrett J.D.M. *New resolutions of old conumdrums: a fresh insight into Luke's gospel.* Shipstone-on-Stour: Drinkwater 1986.

Didrichsen B.K. *Den markianske skilsmisseperikope.* Oslo: Gyldendal Norsk Forlag 1962.

Dodd C.H. *The parables of the kingdom.* Glasgow: Collins 1978.

Dschulnigg, P. *Rabbinische Gleichnisse und das Neue Testament.* Bern, Lang 1988.

Epp E.J. and Fee G.D. *New Testament textual criticism.* Oxford: Clarendon Press 1981.

Feldman A. *The parables and similes of the rabbis.* Cambridge: University Press 1937.

Fletcher B. *The Aramaic sayings of Jesus.* London: Hodder and Stoughton 1967.

Garbini G. *History and ideology in ancient Israel.* London: SCM 1988.

Gerhardsson B. *Memory and manuscript.* Copenhagen: Gleerup 1964.

Ginsburg L. *Legends of the Jews.* Philadelphia: Jewish Publication Society of America, 1909, 1907.

Harvey A.E. (ed.) *Alternative approaches to New Testament study.* London: SCPK 1985.

Hendrickx H. *The parables of Jesus.* London: Geoffrey Chapman 1986.

Hengel M. *Between Jesus and Paul.* London: SCM 1983.

Jeremias J. *Unknown sayings of Jesus.* London: SPCK 1964.

Jeremias J. *The central message of the New Testament.* London: SCM 1965.

Jeremias J. *Jerusalem in the time of Jesus.* London: SCM 1969.

Jeremias J. *The parables of Jesus.* London: SCM 1972.

Jervell J. *Historiens Jesus.* Oslo: Gyldendal Norsk Forlag 1978.

Kee H.C. *Community of the New Age: studies in Mark's gospel.* London: SCM 1977.

Kvalbein H. (ed.) *Blant skriftlaerde og fariseerne.* Oslo: Verbum Forlag 1984.

Lach S.T. *A rabbinic commentary on the New Testament.* Hoboken, N.J.: Ktav Publishing House 1987.

Leaney A.R.C. *The Jewish and Christian world, 200 BC to AD 200.* Cambridge: University Press 1984.

Lindars B. and Smelley (eds.) *Christ and spirit in the New Testament.* Cambridge: University Press 1973.

Maccoby, H. *Judaism in the first century.* London: Sheldon Press 1989.

Mackey J.P. *Jesus - the man and the myth.* London: SCM 1979.

Manson T.W. *The teaching of Jesus.* Cambridge: University Press 1943.

Manson T.W. *The sayings of Jesus.* London: SCM 1949.

Metzer B.M. *A textual commentary on the Greek New Testament.* Stuttgart: United Bibleocieties 1971.

Meyers E.M. and Strange J.F. *Archaeology, the rabbis and early Christianity.* London: SCM 1981.

Moule C.F.D. *Essays in New Testament interpretation.* Cambridge: University Press 1982.

Neill S. *The interpretation of the New Testament 1861-1961.* Oxford: University Press 1966.

Neusner J. *Way of Torah - an introduction to Judaism.* Belmont 1979.

Neusner J. *Judaism - the evidence of the Mishnah.* Chicago and London: University of Chicago Press 1981.

Neusner J., Green W.S. and Frerichs E.S. (eds.) *Judaisms and their Messiahs at the turn of the Christian era.* Cambridge: C.U.P. 1990.

Nineham D.E. (ed.) *Studies in the gospels.* Oxford: Blackwell 1955.

Oesterley W.O.E. *The gospel parables in the light of their Jewish background.* London: SPCK 1936.

Pagels E. *The gnostic gospels.* Harmondsworth: Penguin 1982.

Riches J. *Jesus and the transformation of Judaism.* London: Darton, Longman and Todd 1980.

Robinson J.A.T. *Twelve New Testament studies.* London: SCM 1962.

Robinson T. *The evangelists and the Mishna.* London: Nisbet, 1859.

Sanders E.P. *Paul and Palestinian Judaism.* London: SCM 1977.

Sanders E.P. *Jesus and Judaism.* London: SCM 1985.

Sandmel S. *A Jewish understanding of the New Testament.* London: SPCK 1977.

Sigal P. *The halakah of Jesus of Nazareth according to the gospel of Matthew.* Lanham: University Press of America 1986.

Smith M. *Tannaitic parallels to the gospels.* Philadelphia: Society for Biblical Literature 1968.

Smith M. *The secret gospel.* Clearlake: The Dawn Horse Press 1982.

Stern D. *Parables in Midrash.* Harvard University Press, Cambridge Mass. 1991

Taylor V. *The gospel according to St. Mark.* London: Macmillan 1966.

Tresmontant C. *Le christ hébreu.* Paris: O.E.I.L. 1983.

Trosme E. *Jesus and his contemporaries.* London: SCM 1973.

Vermes G. *Scripture and tradition in Judaism.* Leiden. Brill 1961

Vermes G. *Jesus the Jew.* London: Collins 1973.

Vermes G. *Jesus and the world of Judaism.* London: SCM 1983.

Walker T. *The teaching of Jesus and the Jewish teaching of his age.* London: Allen and Unwin 1923.

Walker T. *Jewish views of Jesus.* London: Allen and Unwin 1931.

Walker T. *Hebrew religion between the testaments.* London: Clarke 1937.

Walton, J.H. *Ancient Israelite literature in its cultural context.* Grand Rapids: Zondervan 1989

Wiles M. and Santer M. *Documents in early Christian thought.* Cambridge: Univesity Press 1975.

Wilson R. McL. *Studies in the gospel of Thomas.* London: Mowbray 1960.

In addition numerous articles in journals of biblical research have been consulted.

Rabbinical and other Jewish Literature:

b.	Babylonian Talmud	Ned.	Nedarim
D.E.Z.	Derek Erez Zutta	Nez.	Nezikin
j.	Jerusalem Talmud	Pes.	Pesharim
m.	Mishna	Pis.	Piska
MDR	Midrash Debarim Rabbi	RSh.	Rosh ha-Shanah
Mek.	Mekilta (Rabbi Ishmael)	Sanh.	Sanhedrin
Midr.	Midrash	Shab.	Shabbath
O.	Onchelos	Shebi.	Shebi'ith
p.	Pesher	Shebu	Shebuoth
PB	Prayer Book	Shir.	Shirata
PRE	Pirkei de R. Eliezer	Sot.	Sotah
PK	Pesikta Kahana	Suk.	Sukkah
PO	Oxyrhynchus papyri	Ta'an	Ta'anith
PR	Pesikta Rabbati	Tam.	Tamid
Ps-J.	Pseudo-Jonathan	Tem.	Temurah
R.	Rabbah	Vay.	Vayassa
Sif.	Sifra or Sifre	Yeb.	Yebamoth
t.	Tosephta	Yom.	Yoma
Tanh.B	Tanhuma (Buber)	Zeb.	Zebahim
T.e.D.	Tanna debe Eliyahu		
Tg.	Targum		

Tractates:

Ama.	Amalek
ARN	Avot Rabbi Nathan
Bah.	Bahodesh
A.Z.	Abodah Zarah
B.B.	Babba Bathra
Bek.	Berakoth
Besh.	Beshallah
Bez.	Betzah
Bikk	Bikkurim
B.K.	Babba Kamma
B.M.	Babba Metzia
Erub.	Erubin
Git.	Gittin
Hag.	Hagagah
Hor.	Horayoth
Hull.	Hullin
Kas.	Kaspa
Ket.	Ketuboth
Kid.	Kiddushin
Meg.	Megillah
Men.	Menahoth

Abbreviations

B.C.E.	Before Common Era (B.C.)	Bar.	Baruch
C.E.	Common Era (A.D.)	Did.	Didache
DSS	Dead Sea Scrolls	En.	Enoch
I.T.	Intertestamentary books	Esd.	Esdras
LXX	Septuagint (Greek O.T.)	Ezr.	Ezra
N.T.	New Testament	J.A.	Joseph and Asenath
O.T.	Old Testament	Jub.	Jubilees
		Jud.	Judith
O.T. books:		L.A.	Letter of Aristeas
Am.	Amos	Mac	Maccobees
Cant.	Canticles	P.Az	Prayer of Azariah
Chr.	Chronicles	P.M.	Prayer of Manasseh
Dan.	Daniel	P.P.	Pseudo-Philo
Ecc.	Ecclesiastes	P.Ph	Pseudo-Phycylides
Ex.	Exodus	P.S.	Psalms of Solomon
Ezk.	Ezekiel	Sir.	Sirach
Gen.	Genesis	S.O.	Sibylline Oracles
Hab.	Habakkuk	T.Ash.	Testament of Asher
Hag	Haggai	T.Ben.	Testament of Benjamin
Ho.	Hosea	T.Dan	Testament of Dan
Is.	Isaiah	T.Gad	Testament of Gad
Jdg.	Judges	T.Iss	Testament of Issachar
Jer.	Jeremiah	T.Jos.	Testament of Joseph
Jl.	Joel	T.Jud.	Testament of Judah
Jon.	Jonah	T.Lev.	Testament of Levi
Jos.	Joshua	T.Nap	Testament of Naphtali
Kgs.	Kings	T.Reu	Testament of Reuben
Koh.	Kohelet; see Ecc.	T.Sim	Testament of Simeon
Lam.	Lamentations	T.Zeb	Testament of Zebulun
Lev.	Leviticus	Tob.	Tobit
Mal.	Malachi	W.S.	Wisdom of Solomon
Mic.	Micah	Zad.	Zadokite fragment
Nah	Nahum		
Neh.	Nehemiah	Dead Sea Scrolls:	
Num.	Numbers	C.Is.	Commentary of Isaiah
Obd.	Obadiah		(4Q 161-4)
Ps.	Psalms	C.R.	Community Rule (1QS)
Pvb.	Proverbs	D.R.	Damasus Rule (CD)
Rut.	Ruth	H.	Thanksgiving Hymns (1QH)
Sam.	Samuel	Hor.	Horoscope (4Q 186)
S.S.	Song of Solomon	L.F.	Liturgical fragments or
			prayers (1Q34)
Intertestamentary books:		W.R.	War Rule (1QM, 4QM)
Ahk.	Story of Ahikar		
A.M	Assumption (Testament) of		
	Moses		

Section A. Beginnings.

A 1. John the baptizer - Mt.3:1-12. Mk. 1:2-8. Lk. 3:2-17.

      The O.T. is full of various prophecies, including several foreseeing the coming of the Messiah, and the evangelists have described the activities of John, the one baptizing in the wilderness, such that he appears as the forerunner of the Lord's coming to earth on the day of Judgement:

> `In the prophets it is written:
> I will send my herald before your face
> and he will prepare your way for you";
> and:
> "A voice crying in the wilderness:
> Prepare a way for the Lord:
> Make straight his paths
> And every mountain and hill levelled:
> Every ravine shall be filled in,
> The crooked place shall be straightened,
> And the rough ways made plains:
> And all mankind shall see God's deliverance."

      Thus it was that John travelled all over the Jordan valley, dressed in a rough coat of camel's hair, with a leather belt round his waist, saying, "Repent for the kingdom of God is near." His food was locusts and wild honey and he proclaimed a baptism of repentance for the forgiveness of sins. Many flocked to him and were baptized in the river Jordan, confessing their sins, but to some of the religious leaders he called out, "You offspring of vipers, who warned you to escape from the coming retribution? You must show by the fruit it bears that your repentance is genuine. Do not begin by saying to yourselves, 'We have Abraham for our father'. God could make children for Abraham of these stones here. Already the axe is laid at the roots of the tree, and every tree that does not produce good fruit is cut down and thrown on the fire."

      "I baptize you with water," proclaimed John, "but there is one coming mightier than I. I am not fit to untie his sandals: he will baptize you with the Holy Spirit and with fire. His fan is in his hand ready to winnow his threshing floor and thoroughly clean it out. He will gather the wheat into his granary, but the chaff will be burnt on an everlasting fire."

      The people asked him what they should do. John told them: "The man with two shirts must share with him who has none, and those with food must do the same." To a tax-gatherer he said, "Take no more than the correct assessment"; and to some soldiers he said, "No more bullying, no blackmail and no extortion - make do with your pay."

The initial quotations in this passage are from the O.T.: 'Behold I send an angel before you to guard you on the way and to bring you to the place which I have prepared' (Ex. 23:20); 'Behold, I send my messenger to prepare the way before me and the Lord whom you seek will suddenly come to his temple; the messenger of the covenant in whom you delight is coming, says the Lord' (Mal. 3:1); 'A voice cries in the wilderness, "Prepare the way of the Lord, make straight in the desert a highway for our God. Every valley shall be filled and every mountain and hill made low, the uneven ground shall become level and the rough places a plain. And the glory of the Lord shall be revealed and all mankind together shall see it, for the Lord has spoken it"' (Is. 40:3-4). In I.T.: 'God has appointed that every mountain ... should be made low, and the valleys filled up, that Israel may go safely in the glory of God' (II Bar. 5:7). Some scholars think that the 'path' was the study of the Law (DSS, CD 8:15-16). Others see this passage as meaning that God will lead his people through the wilderness in a holy war to redemption and the Israelites' homeland: 'I [the Lord] will lay waste the mountains and hills and dry up all their herbage ... I will lead the blind by a road they do not know; by paths they have not known I will guide them. I will turn the darkness before them into light, the rough places into level ground' (Is. 42:15-16).

The tenor of the passage echoes: 'The great day of the Lord is near ... a day of wrath is that day, a day of distress, anguish, ruin, devastation...' (Zph. 1:14-15) and '... because of your evil deeds, my Word shall destroy you, as the whirlwind the chaff, and the nations shall be as the burning of fire' (Tg.Is. 33:11). Although there are many passages in the rabbinical literature which call for repentance in the N.T. sense, that is to return to living within God's laws as well as regretting past sins, it is striking that there are few in the O.T. Jeremiah and Ezekiel call directly for repentance: 'Now therefore amend your ways and your deeds and obey the voice of the Lord your God and he will repent of the evil he has pronounced against you' (Jer. 26:13) and 'Repent and turn from all your transgressions, lest iniquity be your ruin.' (Ezk. 18:30).

In I.T. writings, calls for repentance are more common: 'Have mercy on all men ... and overlook the sins of men, that they may repent.' (W.S. 11:23); 'God cleanses from sin the soul of one who makes confession ... and his goodness is upon them that sin, if they repent.' (P.S. 9:12,15); 'Turn to the Lord and forsake sins; supplicate before his face ... How great is the mercy of the Lord and his forgiveness to them that turn to him.' (Sir. 17:25,29); 'None who transgresses wilfully any commandment, shall be believed as a witness against his neighbour ... until he is cleansed through repentance.' (DSS, DR 10).

Repentance is widely acknowledged as important in rabbinical literature: 'God says: "My hands are stretched out towards the penitent. I reject no one who gives me his heart in penitence;" but not invariably: 'However many sins a man may have committed, if he return to God all are forgiven: ... but if he does not return, God warns him once, twice, thrice. Then if he does not return, God exacts punishment'

(Tanh.B. 47b); 'After God has waited for the wicked to repent and they do not, then if finally they wish to repent, God takes away from them the power to do so. Even if they wish to turn back to the Lord, they cannot, for he has bound them and barred the way before them.' (Ex.R. 11:1).

The baptism John gave was of water and he said that another coming after him would baptize with fire. O.T. passages describing baptism by fire and water may lie at the back of the evangelists' accounts of the baptism of John: 'On that day ... I the Lord shall wash away the filth of the sons and daughters of Zion, and shall purge the blood from among them with the spirit of judgement and spirit of burning.' (Is. 4:2-4 LXX). In rabbinical thought the Torah is like fire or, as some said, it was proclaimed between fire and water (Mek. Bah. 4 on Ex. 19:17-18). The two baptisms - of water and of fire were well known in Judaism: '...wash your whole bodies in ever-running rivers.' (Sib. Or. 4:165) Water cleansed and fire purified.

The imagery of the retribution to come, being blown away or cast in the fire occurs in Jewish literature: 'For their worms will not die; their fire shall not be quenched and they be an abhorrence to all flesh' (Is. 66:24); 'Because of your evil deeds my Word shall destroy you as the whirlwind the chaff, and the nations ... as thorns cut down ... shall be burnt in the fire' (Tg.Is. 33:11-12)

It was common at the time for prophets and ascetics to have minimal coarse clothing and have the kind of diet described in this passage, but John's clothing is also like that of Elijah: 'He wore a garment of haircloth, with a girdle of leather about his waist. And he said, "It is Elijah, the Tishbite"' (II Kgs. 1:8). This is one reason for the idea that John was Elijah returned to earth from heaven. (See also H 10).

To take off sandals is to take on the role of a foreign slave. A Hebrew slave did not have to stoop so low: 'A Hebrew slave must not wash the feet of his master nor put his shoes on him, nor carry his things before him to the bathhouse' (Mek. Nez.1) and the evangelists portray John as subordinate and in this way emphasise that they see Jesus as the master.

* * *

3

A 2. Jesus' baptism - Mt. 3:13-17. Mk. 1:9-11. Lk. 3:21-22.

A voice from heaven was not unknown in Judaism. It was believed that the voice could be heard directly or indirectly, that is from another person, even accidentally. This concept was extended to prophecy when it was believed the Spirit was present and where the divine element was a true characteristic of the prophet (b.Sot. 48b).

A voice bearing witness to the person's righteousness was by no means particularly strange in the first century. There are several examples: 'He said to me, "You are my son, today I have begotten you"' (Ps. 2:7); 'Jacob is my servant, I will help him. Israel is my chosen, my soul has accepted him; I have put my Spirit upon him; he shall bring forth judgement to the nations' (Is. 42:1 LXX); 'Israel is my son, my first-born. Behold my servant whom I uphold; my elect in whom my soul delights' (Midr.Ps. 2:9) and 'Israel is my servant, Jacob, with whom I am well pleased; ... you whom I have chosen ... the seed of Abraham my friend ...' (Tg. Is. 41:8).

The idea that the messiah would be confirmed by God's voice from heaven was believed by many Jews and the servant referred to was the messiah: '...my servant the messiah ... I am well pleased with him...' (Tg.Is. 43:10). In I.T. books too: 'The heavens were opened and I saw, and power was given to me and a voice was heard from on high...' (II Bar. 22:1); 'The heavens shall be opened to him to pour out the spirit, the blessing of the Holy Father.' (T.Jud. 24:2). The evangelists ascribe to Jesus' baptism similar significance.

Jesus of Nazareth came from Galilee and was baptised with others by John in the Jordan river. Straight away, when Jesus came up out of the river and was praying, the heavens opened and the Spirit descended on to him like a dove. A voice from heaven echoed on earth: "You are my son, my chosen, today I have brought you forth."

The language used suggests the translation (from an Aramaic original) should be not "the spirit descended like a dove" but "the spirit at once coming down on him."

'Going up' has several associations. Firstly, to rise from the grave, from death to life. In Jewish thought, as in Christianity, conversion was conceived as changing from being dead to being alive, by a new birth and liberation from former sins. After his immersion, the Jew does not become ritually 'clean' before the sun has gone down: 'When the sun has gone down, he shall be clean' (Lev. 22:7) but Jesus is portrayed as receiving the Holy Spirit immediately which is intended to imply that he must have been without sin and therefore the Lord himself.

Secondly, going up signifies the Exodus from Egypt and the story is intended as a repetition of the crossing of the Jordan from the wilderness into the promised land by the children of Israel. Jesus, like his namesake, Joshua, crossed the river Jordan into a new promised land, but this time there would be no idolatry. The kingdom of God was nigh, and the New Israel would be pure and unpolluted: 'The Lord said to Joshua, "... now arise, go over this Jordan ... into the land which I am giving to the people of Israel'" (Jos. 1:1-2); 'And Joshua said to the people, "Sanctify yourselves; for tomorrow the Lord will do wonders among you ..."' (Jos. 3:5). The time was like that when, 'They remembered the days of old of Moses his servant. Where is the one who brought them up out of the sea ... where is the one who put within them his holy spirit? ... Thus you led your people, to make for yourself a glorious name' (Is. 63:11-14).

The evangelists, and Mark in particular, write in a way which shows they were probably aware of the Jewish notion that Isaac was killed by Abraham but revived or was resurrected by an angel. This was the result of the faith of Abraham and of Isaac himself in their obedience to God's testing. Jesus is portrayed not only as God's beloved servant, but also as a second Isaac, one who must be obedient to his faith and be the new redeemer: 'The heavens shall be opened and from the temple of glory shall sanctification come on him, with the Father's voice, as from Abraham to Isaac.' (T.Lev. 18:6), that is as God's son, the Messiah, as Isaac heard his father's voice.

Matthew adds that when Jesus came to John to be baptised, John tried to dissuade him;

"Do you come to me?," he said. "I need rather to be baptised by you." But Jesus replied, "For the moment we should conform in this way with righteousness."

The import of this remains unclear, but two points may have a bearing. There is some evidence for the belief that there were groups in the time of Jesus who thought that the baptism of John the baptiser was sufficient; also, there was a belief that if one lived a life in exact accordance with the Law from one's baptism, one would be the Messiah.

There were detailed rules in Judaism about the water which may be used for baptism, the most suitable being running water in rivers or the sea.

* * *

5

Moses was given the message that God had come down to the mountain to instruct Israel: 'The Lord said to Moses, "Go to the people and consecrate them today and tomorrow ... and on the third day the Lord will come down upon Mt. Sinai in the sight of all the people."' (Ex. 19:10-11). Likewise, Jesus began on his attempt to persuade the Jews to repent and turn again and accept God's rule. The kingdom he could offer was not material, but that which the gospel proclaimed. It was near, it was upon them: 'Happy are all who take refuge in him' (Ps. 2:11).

After John had been arrested, Jesus, armed with the power of the Spirit, came to Galilee proclaiming: "The time has come; the kingdom of God is near at hand, repent and believe the gospel." He said, "I give the good news of the kingdom of God to other towns also, for that is what I was sent to do." So he proclaimed the gospel in the synagogues.

Matthew includes:

Jesus settled in Capernaum on the sea of Galilee, in the district of Zebulun and Naphtali. This was in fulfilment of the prophecy of Isaiah: "Land of Zebulun, and of Naphtali, on the road by the sea, across the Jordan, heathen Galilee. The people that lived in darkness saw a great light; light dawned on the dwellers in the land of death's dark shadow."

The quotation is based on Isaiah (9:1-2) and the names, Zebulun and Naphtali, may be significant; zebul meant a sanctuary and great learning, while naphtali could mean service of the Torah. Naphtali was renowned for the exceptional honour he accorded his father Jacob, by being the quick and reliable bearer of Jacob's messages. 'Naphtali is a hind let loose that bears beautiful words.' (Gen. 49:21).

The land of these two tribes was in the area of Galilee and associated with the sea: 'Zebulun shall dwell on the shore of the sea and his border shall be Sidon.' (Gen.49:13). This land had been destroyed before, but it would flourish again: 'In the former time God brought into contempt the land of Zebulun and Naphtali, but in the latter time he will make glorious the way of the sea, the land beyond Jordan, Galilee of the Gentiles.' (Is. 9:1); 'Naphtalim is a spreading stem, bestowing beauty on its fruit.' (Gen. 49:21 LXX). According to some rabbinical literature, 'Miracles were performed ... through the tribes of Zebulum and Naphtali.' (Mek.Besh. 6)

By such hints and references, the evangelists indicate that they believe Jesus to be connected with O.T. prophecies. Perhaps Jesus did settle in Capernaum - it is said to have had a good library - but the implications of the evangelists are additional to the simple historical statement. In fact Capernaum was in the district of Naphtali not Zebulun, and in the Aramaic version of Isaiah, the sense of this passage is the opposite to that given by Matthew: 'For none who come to oppress them shall be wearied. As at the former time, the people of the land of Zebulun and the people of the land of Naphtali have been carried into exile; and their remnant shall a mighty king carry into exile, because they remembered not the mighty act which was done at the sea, the miracles of Jordan ....' (Tg.Is 8:23).

* * *

The evangelists now report the beginning of Jesus' preaching, in his home town, which astonished those listening. He proclaimed a new start, a new Israel, but they all knew him too well and he was unable to heal many there. The accounts given in the gospels of Matthew and Mark are not the same as in Luke. In Luke, the congregation are so angry they threaten the life of Jesus. In the first two gospels, Jesus was unable to help the people because of their lack of faith.

Matthew and Mark:

Jesus, with his disciples, returned to Nazareth, his home town, and on the sabbath he began to teach the people in the synagogue. They were astonished: "What wisdom has been given him; where does he get it from? And the powerful deeds we have heard about - how can they be? Is he not the craftsman, son of Mary, brother of James and Joseph, Judas and Simon and of his sisters, too?"
Jesus could do no good there because of their lack of faith, except that he laid hands on a few of the sick and healed them.

Luke:

Jesus was given the scroll of Isaiah and said: "The spirit of the Lord is upon me because he has anointed me; he has sent me to announce good news to the poor, to proclaim release for prisoners and recovery of sight for the blind; to let the broken victims go free, and to proclaim the year of the Lord's favour." He handed back the roll, sat down and then said, "Today this text has come true in your very hearing."
Jesus continued, "I expect you will quote to me the proverb, 'Physician, heal yourself' and expect me to do the same as you have heard I did in Capernaum. I tell you this: 'No prophet is accepted in his own village or in his own family; no physician can heal those who know him.[1] There were many widows in Israel in Elijah's time when there was drought for three and a half years and famine throughout the country. Yet Elijah went to none of them; he was sent to a widow of Zarephath (Sarepta) in Sidon. And in the time of Elisha, there were many lepers in Israel, but none was healed. It was Naaman the Syrian who was cured."
The congregation was infuriated; he was a stumbling block for them. They were so angry they drove

him out of the town, meaning to throw him over the edge
of the cliff, but he walked through them all and went
away.

The introductory quotation in Luke's version is a composite of several passages: 'The Spirit of the Lord God is upon me because he has anointed me to bring good tidings to the afflicted, he has sent me to bind up the broken-hearted, to proclaim liberty to the captives and the opening of the prison to those who are bound, to proclaim the year of the Lord's favour' (Is. 61:1-2); 'To let the broken and oppressed go free' (Is. 58:6); 'Behold my servant whom I uphold, my chosen, in whom my soul delights; I have put my spirit upon him ... Thus says the Lord ... I have given you as a covenant to the people, a light to the nations to open the eyes of the blind, to bring out the prisoners from the dungeon, and those who sit in darkness from the prison' (Is 42:1,5-7).

There are aspects of the passage from Luke which are of great interest. It would have been impossible to read these passages at one place in a scroll and the quotations suggest that Luke was writing in or about 76-77 CE, when the Jubilee year was due to take place. This was after the destruction of the Temple, there was no High Priest to make a decision for all the Jews, and probably the date of the celebration that year was unusual. The evangelist presents Jesus as proclaiming that the New Era has begun, with himself as the prophet of the coming kingdom. It is interesting that the quotation from Isaiah 61 stops short in the middle of a verse and omits the words: 'and the day of vengeance of our God'.

In this passage, too, there are indications that part of its purpose was to remind the audience of the early history of the Israelites. The initial message of Jesus was welcome, that it was the year of God's special blessing, and that he had chosen it to show God's love for his people. It was therefore the time for the release of the oppressed, sight for the blind, etc., so all were happy to hear his exposition of the verses of Isaiah. For his listeners, the message was a fulfilment of the covenant bringing peace to the faithful and retribution for enemies.

Jesus then went on to say something which was less acceptable. He pointed out that the covenant also meant forgiveness and mercy for all, especially as the new era was beginning, and that, although there had been down-trodden, poor widows and lepers in Israel, it was the Gentiles with faith (for example, the widow of Zarephath) that the prophets helped and the new kingdom is open to all. Israel suffered from drought and other calamities because of God's disapproval of her lack of faith and obedience. So it was now too: those listening would suffer the same distress unless they repented. Such an insult!

The people were bound by the Law to eradicate a false prophet saying such things: 'The prophet who presumes to speak a word in my name which I have not commanded him to speak ... that prophet shall die' (Dt. 18:20). The Israelites in the wilderness, had had no faith in God's promises and had rejected the true leaders of their own day, Moses, Aaron, Joshua and Caleb. Now they were rejecting a prophet sent to save them from their own complacency and Jesus' walking straight through the mob corresponds with Moses' escape from the Israelites: 'So Moses cried to the Lord, "What shall I do with this people? They are almost ready to stone me." And the Lord said to Moses, "Pass on before the people, taking with you some of the elders of Israel, and take in your hand the rod with which you struck the Nile, and go'" (Ex. 17:4-5).

The consequences would be similar. 'The Lord said to Moses, "How long will this people despise me? How long will they not believe in me, in spite of all the signs which I have wrought among them? I will strike them with pestilence and disinherit them and I will make of you a nation greater and mightier than they'" (Num. 14:11-12).

'Today' at the end of the Luke's first paragraph probably meant in the life-time of Jesus, rather than on that particular sabbath. The word usually translated 'carpenter' could mean 'artificer' or 'hand-worker', and it is a word which had been used as a name for one specially favoured of God: 'There was a wise man, a great artificer, and the Lord conceived love for him, and received him that he should see ... the realm of God' (II En. prologue.).

In one of the Dead Sea Scrolls (11Q Melch), from the first century BCE, the same teaching is found, although relating to Melchizedek. In rabbinical writings: 'God clothes the naked, visits the sick, comforts mourners and buries the dead' (b.Sot.14a). In another passage it is said, 'A feast to the Lord is to be kept three times a year'; those who are not eligible to attend are listed: 'women, strangers, intersexes, hermaphrodites, blind, deaf, slaves, the sick, sinners, the defiled, the insane and the aged' (Mek. Kas. 3).

[1] The last part of this sentence is from the Gospel of Thomas.

* * *

Two of John's disciples came to Jesus and said,
"John (the baptiser) has sent us. He has heard of your
activities and he is anxious to know whether you are
the one to come, or are we to expect another?" Jesus
answered, "Go: tell John what you see and hear: the
blind recover their sight, the lame walk, the lepers are
cleansed, the deaf hear, the dead are raised to life and
the poor receive the gospel. Happy is the man who does
not find me a cause of stumbling!"

After John's messengers had left, Jesus said
to those present, "What was it you went out into the
wilderness to see? Was it to watch the reed-grass
swaying in the wind, or a courtier dressed in the
luxurious silks and satins of a king's palace? No? 'To
see a prophet', you say. Yes, indeed, and more than
a prophet. It is of him scripture says, 'Here is my
herald, whom I send on ahead of you, and he will prepare
your way ahead of you." It is the certain truth that
I tell you: no one who has yet appeared on earth is
greater than John, and yet the least in the kingdom of
God is greater than he."

The phrase, 'It is the certain truth' is intended to indicate the strength of the word, 'Amen.' This does not simply indicate agreement and is stronger than 'Verily', or 'Truly' and applies in other contexts, too.

John the Baptiser had been informed of the works of Jesus which were, according to the prophets, those of the Messiah, and he made his enquiry by sending his disciples, being himself imprisoned. Jesus answered John's question by citing a mixture of O.T. verses, by which he indicated that he was not come to be a conquering general but to bring the people back to God: 'In that day the deaf shall hear the words of the book ... the eyes of the blind shall see and the poor shall rejoice because of the Lord, and they that had no hope among men shall be filled with joy' (Is. 29:18-19, LXX); 'Then the eyes of the blind shall be opened and the ears of the deaf unstopped, then shall the lame man leap like a hart, and the tongue of the dumb sing for joy' (Is. 35:5-6); 'The Spirit of the Lord is upon me, because he has anointed me to bring good tidings to the afflicted, he has sent me to bind up the broken-hearted, to proclaim liberty to the captives ... to proclaim the year of the Lord's favour' (Is. 61:1-2); Also in I.T. literature: 'Those who have hungered shall rejoice; moreover they shall behold marvels every day' (II Bar. 29:6); 'Blessed is the one who does not fill his heart with spitefulness, helps the offender, lifts up the broken and shows compassion to the needy' (II En. 44:4). The rabbis thought that on Mount Sinai none of the Israelites was blind, or deaf, or lame, or mad. (Mek.Bah. 9), and that 'When one welcomes his fellow man it is ... as if he had welcomed the Divine Presence' (Mek.Ama. 3).

These were the signs of the beginning of the kingdom of God amongst them. Jesus goes on to remind his listeners of other prophecies: 'Behold I send my messenger to survey the way before me and the Lord ... will come suddenly into his temple, even the angel of the covenant whom you take pleasure in. Behold he is coming, says the Lord Almighty. But who can endure the day of his coming ...?' (Mal. 3:1-2 LXX); 'Behold, I send my angel before your face, that he may keep you in the way.' (Ex. 22:20 LXX). Like other prophets, Jesus would be rejected because his message was that God's love was open to all, and those who stumble, that is are thrown off balance, by Jesus' words, will be in dire straits. Those who accept them will enter the kingdom. Unfortunately, Israel, and especially the religious leaders, had remained obdurate, and had refused to accept John's call to repentance. They had stifled the understanding of the people. The evangelists portray Jesus showing the way to God's realm on earth, here and now. He will not lead people astray.

Reed-grass swaying in the wind could be a simile for a 'yes-man', who would never resist evil, but in rabbinical writings reeds are a metaphor for the endurance of Israel. All the winds cannot uproot them, but the unyielding massive cedar tree is blown down in a storm. (ARN 41) This is true even though in the O.T. they were God's trees: 'The trees of the Lord are watered abundantly, the cedars of Lebanon which he planted' (Ps. 104:16). Those dressed in silks and satins, were thought to be flatterers and sycophants in the king's service, - a great contrast to John and his garments.

Jesus continued: "Ever since the coming of John, the kingdom of God has been subjected to violence and violent men are seizing it. All the prophets and the Law prophesied until John appeared. Since then the kingdom of God is being preached and everyone is pressing, and John is the destined Elijah if you will but accept it."

This passage is difficult to understand and some think a better translation of the latter half of the passage is: 'The Law and the prophets were in effect until John the Baptiser; now the reign of God is being announced and every person should belong to it. John is stated to be Elijah, who would come before the day of Judgement: 'Behold, I will send you Elijah the prophet before the great and terrible day of the Lord comes' (Mal. 4:5), when there would be chaos in society, with violence and warring factions within families: 'The son treats the father with contempt, the daughter rises up against her mother, the daughter-in-law against her mother-in-law, and a man's enemies are the men of his own house' (Mic. 7:6).

It was thought that Elijah would go first to make a way for them: 'One who makes a breach has gone up before them; they enlarge it to a gate and leave by it. Their king is passed on before them and the Lord at the head of them' (Mic. 2:13). Three days before the Messiah comes, Elijah will stand upon the mountains of Israel (P.R. 35); he would reconcile those who were fighting, and turn their hearts to God: 'And he will turn the hearts of fathers to their children and the hearts of children to their fathers, lest I come and smite the land with a curse' (Mal. 4:6).

Elijah is not mentioned in the Torah (the first five books of the O.T.) yet when the passage says 'all the Prophets and the Law', and that John is Elijah, it seems he ought to be. However, many thought Elijah was Phineas come back to life on earth. He was revered because he had turned God's anger from Israel at a critical moment:

'And the Lord said to Moses, "Phineas ... has turned back my wrath from the people of Israel ... Therefore I say, Behold, I give to him my covenant of peace"' (Num. 25:10-12).

Elijah in the figure of John, had not been listened to. People should stop their strife and hate, and show love to one another, as God had commanded, that God's anger be deflected. Elijah, in the Law as Phineas, in the Prophets as Elijah and coming now as John: this was a certain sign that God was about to visit his people. Only a remnant would be left; repent now or face the consequences!

This passage may reflect Matthew's view that the early church was assailed by many enemies. On the other hand, some other beliefs in Judaism may help to throw some light on it. For example, in the O.T.: 'They all come for violence' (Hab. 1:9), which the prophet says will be revenged by the Lord on the day of Judgement. Rabbinical thought was that, 'Men of good works wax feeble and men of violence and men of loud tongue prevail. There is none that expounds (the Law) to Israel, none that seeks compassion for them and none shall utter reproof ... Children shall shame the elders and the elders shall rise up against the children ...' (m.Sot. 9:15).

It was popularly believed that Elijah was a divine agent who would solve all points of dispute when he came to herald the advent of the Messiah and the resurrection of the dead (m.Sot. 9:15).

* * *

A 6. The death of John - Mt. 14:1-12. Mk. 6:14-29. Lk. 3:19-20.

John was beheaded by order of Herod, but the prison in which prisoners were held was many miles from Herod's palace, where the party is said to have taken place. This story is full of such peculiarities.

Herod had married his brother Philip's wife Herodias, and John had told him that it was not permitted to do so. Herodias nursed a hatred of John because of his words, and wanted to get rid of him, but Herod was rather afraid of him, knowing him to be a righteous man. Maybe Herod protected him from Herodias by keeping him in custody, and Herod enjoyed conversing with him, though he sometimes was perplexed by John's remarks.

One day, Herod gave a birthday party and invited all the chief officers of state, military captains and important Galileans. His step-daughter danced for the company, to the delight of Herod and his friends. Herod said to her, "Ask me for what you will, and I will give it to you - up to half my kingdom."

The girl went to her mother and asked her what she should request. Herodias answered, "Ask for the head of John the baptiser."

"I wish for the head of John the baptiser on a plate," said the girl to Herod. He was stricken with grief but out of regard for his oath and because he did not wish to disappoint his guests or the girl, he gave the order. A soldier of the guard went out and later returned with John's head and the girl gave it to her mother.

When John's disciples heard this they came and took away the cadaver and buried it in a monument.

Now when King Herod heard about Jesus' fame and his miraculous powers, he, like many others, thought, "This is John, whom I beheaded, who has been raised to life."

But many others did not agree; they said it was Elijah returned from heaven. Still others maintained he was like one of the prophets of old.

There are many problems with this passage. Herod was not a king but a tetrarch, and Herodias was probably not the (ex)-wife of Philip but of another brother. Nor was Herod's oath binding. Jews were always swearing oaths and then disclaiming them and one of this character was one which Herod could have avoided either by paying a penance, or because he was a ruler. It was against God's commandments and the law to put someone to death without a trial and the testimony of two witnesses, even for a king. No doubt John was troublesome but it was Herod's birthday, and his actions should promote joy, by releasing prisoners, rescinding taxes on the poor, etc. The whole incident appears to be as far from the expected as possible. Why then did Herod keep his oath?

It would seem it was the presence of the very important persons which made the situation difficult. An oath sworn in God's name was to be kept if it was good, and paid for if it was not; God would punish a 'king' who had been so foolish and only the High Priest could absolve him from his oath. Herod was in a dilemma. He could perjure himself and refuse to fulfil his oath; he could eat humble pie and ask the High Priest for absolution paying the required penance; or he could fulfil his oath and risk divine disapproval for an unlawful killing.

To perjure himself would mean losing face and authority before his nobles, including those present; to approach the High Priest was to allow the latter to have the ultimate authority, something which Herod could not permit. Suppose the High Priest refused, for example!

Herod's councillors, as well as Herodias, had probably been telling him for months or years that John was fomenting trouble and the country would be better without him. Here was Herod's chance! Admittedly it was a rash oath and the killing was unlawful, but the end justified using the occasion. Herod gave the order.

There are other interesting aspects to this passage. It suggests that some at least, saw John as equivalent to Balaam rather than as Elijah. It was tradition that Balak had a daughter who led the dance which drew the Israelites into sin, so that correspondences include Herod, a half-Jewish king comparable in his sinfulness to Balak; a daughter who dances and leads men into evil; Balaam, a prophet like John; and that the sword was the chosen means of execution for them both: 'They also slew Balaam the son of Beor with the sword.' (Num. 31:8). Balaam acted as God's mouthpiece proclaiming Israel to be blessed and prophesied that, 'A sceptre shall arise out of Israel ... By Jacob shall dominion be exercised and the survivors of cities be destroyed' (Num. 24:17,19), which was taken to be a prophecy of the coming of the Messiah.

Like Moses, whom God did not allow to enter the promised land, John did not live long enough to see Jesus' campaign to the New Promised Land; but like his namesake Joshua, Jesus took over the leadership from John by his baptism and set out on his ministry.

* * *

A. Summary and comment.

These passages tell of the beginnings of Jesus' ministry and give some information about John, the baptiser. It is difficult to conclude much from this limited material, but it is clear that the passages reflect O.T. events and imagery. Jesus is portrayed as another Abraham or as another Moses, while John has affinities with Elijah and Balaam.

Repentance was required and a baptism of water and fire was called for. It has been denied that baptism was associated with repentance or the forgiving of sins in Judaism, although it is said to have been used as a rite of 'purification' when a convert was admitted to Judaism. It is possible therefore that the passages relating to baptism arose as a result of the practice of the early church.

Some scholars think that Jesus had been one of John's disciples but had separated from him to start his own ministry with his own disciples, and both seem to have some affinities with the Essenes.

That there is only one God is fundamental to the O.T., N.T. and Judaism; but, although God was the only object of worship, God was not thought to be the only divine being. God was looked upon more as a heavenly king presiding over a court of powerful beings, one of whom was more prominent than the others. It is to this special being that Israel particularly related, and this being is known by various titles such as Wisdom, God's Son, and the heavenly Messiah bringing salvation on the day of Judgement

B. The kingdom of God is nigh.

B 1. Prepared for the day of Judgement - Mt. 24:42-5; 25:13. Mk. 13:33-37. Lk.12:35-48; 21:34-36.

A discussion among the disciples and followers of Jesus turned on when the day of Judgement would come, and the feeling of insecurity they felt. How would they fare on that day? The prophets had spoken of it, of course, but that was a long time ago. What was Jesus' opinion?

His answer was a 'lecture' on the implications of what his followers had noticed, using many texts from the O.T. to illustrate his meaning. Without adequate care a person could end up being rejected on that day. It was as necessary to remain on guard against evil, as a door-keeper, awaiting his lord, must remain awake.

If a householder knew when a thief was coming, he would keep awake and not let the wall of his house be dug through. The day of Judgement is like a thief - you have no idea when it will come, but you must be prepared for it nevertheless. Be like slaves, alert and ready for action, belts on, lamps lit, ready to welcome home the lord of the house when he returns. Happy are those slaves whom the lord finds alert when he arrives. I tell you this: he will buckle his belt, seat them at table and wait on them himself! The slaves must do their work while the lord is away and the door-keeper must be ready to open the door for him, evening or midnight, cock-crow or early dawn.

Peter said to Jesus, 'Are you saying this specially to us, or does it apply to everyone?' Jesus replied, "What I say to you, I say to all: keep awake, keep watch! The trusted slaves, authorised with power by the lord of the house to manage the household are happy if they are found at their tasks when the lord returns unexpectedly. It is certainly true that such slaves will be put in charge of all the lord's property. But if some of them are bad slaves who think to themselves, 'My master is away on the journey and will not be back for a long time yet', and begin to bully the other slaves and act as if they were the master themselves, then they will get a rude awakening when the master turns up without warning. Such bad slaves will be separated from the others, put away with the ungodly, and their lot will be to be with the unbelievers.

Keep a watch on your selves; do not dull your wits with dissipation, like drunkenness or gluttony, nor let your minds be full of life's anxieties. The great day could close on you suddenly like a trap and that day

will surprise all men throughout the whole world.
Be alert, praying at all times for strength to pass safely through all these imminent problems, and to stand in the presence of the son of man.

The house is three things: (i) a real house, (ii) Israel, who had so often ignored God's rule, proper obedience to his covenant and so on; and (iii) a person who is subject to attacks by demons (as in D 12) and who must be on guard against them.

(i) Wealthy people had large houses with several servants or slaves, and a door-keeper, whose duties included opening the door to let in his lord whenever he came home, since normally the outer gate would be kept locked.

Thieves would enter a house by digging through the mud wall. That this is not fanciful is shown by the complaint of a householder in 98 CE: "Certain men, having dug through the wall of the yard ... entered and drove off eight of my sheep." (P.Oxy.3467). No one could know when a thief would attack the house, and a householder cannot limit his precautions to particular times or places; hence his servants must remain alert at all times.

It was normal practice for slaves to wait for their master to return and take his meal before they ate. In this story the master was so happy to find his servants dutiful and obedient, he did something almost unprecedented: he sat them down and waited on them himself!

(ii) The householder, Israel, had been warned many times: "Teachers of lies have smoothed your people with words and false prophets have led them astray." (DSS, H7); but Israel remained so blind that evils such as the perversions of Temple worship which Ezekiel spoke out against, were continuing. 'Son of man, dig through the wall. I did so and there was a door: "Go in and see the vile abominations that they (the Israelites) are practising there"' (Ezk. 8:8-9). He was told to show the Israelites that they would be abandoned by God: 'Son of man ... prepare what you need for a journey into exile ... Before their eyes, dig a hole through the wall and carry your belongings out through it. You must go forth yourself at evening in their sight as men do who must go into exile; in their sight you shall lift the baggage on your shoulder and carry it out in the dark. ... For I have made you a sign to the Israelites' (Ezk. 12:1-6). The religious leaders were acting as though having shut the door, not only had they shut out evil, but God as well, and therefore they could arrange things to suit themselves. Their abominations were as wicked as those of their forefathers.

The prophecy is severe. Israel may face destruction similar to exile. They had ignored the prophecy of Isaiah: 'There is an inheritance to them that serve the Lord and you shall be righteous before me, says the Lord' (Is. 54:17), and the plea of Psalms: 'Who will rise up for me against the transgressors?' (Ps. 93:16 LXX). They were worse than grape-pickers who at least leave some for gleaners. 'If thieves or plunderers come to you by night, though you may lose much, would they not steal only enough for themselves? If grape-pickers come to you, will they not leave gleanings?' (Ob. 5). Israel can expect nothing to remain: 'Beware, the Lord will lay waste the earth and make it desolate ... The earth shall be utterly despoiled ... The earth mourns and withers and grows sick ...' (Is. 24:1-4). Only those who try to correct the evils can expect to be welcome in the kingdom because their treasure is in heaven.

There were four watches of the night, but, according to the O.T., on the day of Judgement there would be continuous daylight: 'On that day it shall be all one day, ... without distinction of day or night and at evening time there shall be light' (Zch. 14:7). In I.T. books similarly: 'For thus shall the day of Judgement be: a day with neither sun nor moon, nor stars; neither cloud, nor thunder, nor lightning; neither wind nor rain-storm, nor cloud-rack, neither darkness, nor evening, nor morning...' (IV Ezr. 7:39-40).

Wakefulness is required: Israel had to wait for salvation, but God was good to those who kept themselves in good shape (spiritually and otherwise), so they could do his will until he arrived: 'The Lord is good to those who wait for him, to the soul that seeks him. It is good that one should wait quietly for the salvation of the Lord' (Lam. 3:25-26). There was a belief that the Messiah would come at night, as the angel of destruction had visited Egypt and killed all the first-born infants, but those who kept watch would be rewarded with a banquet where God's generosity would be so great he would wait on his slaves while they ate. Those who ignored God's will, who were unrighteous, would be cut to pieces: 'You sinner, even now the Lord is standing with a drawn sword ... that he may cut you in pieces' (Sus. 59).

(iii) Throughout Judaism's history, a person could be likened to a house in which there were several servants. Each servant represents one of our senses, like taste, smell, sight and so on, within the house or person. If evil broke into the house the door-keeper had not been alert enough to prevent it, and the other servants could be seduced by the evil. In this picture, the door-keeper is thought of as the 'heart', a mixture of intellect and conscience, who keeps the servants in order and properly employed. His heart will always remain awake, if he is a good door-keeper: 'I sleep, but my heart is awake' (S.S. 5:2); 'My soul waits for the Lord more eagerly than watchmen for the morning' (Ps. 141:3-4); 'Mortal, I have made you a sentinel [against transgression] (Ezk. 3:17); 'Let us then arm ourselves with divine reason's mastery of the passions' (IV Mac. 13:16).

It was obvious too, that if the door-keeper himself invites evil demons into the house, it goes to ruin. The allegory could be applied to small groups forming the early church, the warning against worldly temptations and the encouragement to prayer applying in their situation, as in others'.

It is perhaps significant that Jesus, after the beginning of his ministry, is not shown as being always welcome in the synagogues. Much of his work took place apparently in houses instead, and those house 'synagogues' would probably have formed the basis of the early community's religious life. The delay in the day of Judgement meant that there was danger that many would become indifferent ('go to sleep') and the leaders at the time would have been anxious to prevent this. The kingdom had begun, but no one could know when God would come on the day of Judgement. He will come without warning, like a trap catching a bird when it least expects it. Nevertheless, the message of the passage is not directed only towards the day of Judgement, but can be applied to all at all times.

Luke adds:

The servant who knows his master's wishes yet makes no attempt to carry them out will be flogged severely. But one who did not know them and earned a

beating will be flogged less severely. Where a man has been given much, much will be expected of him: and the more a man has had entrusted to him the more he will be required to repay.

Among the Jews of the time, some believed that a sin committed in ignorance would not be condoned or overlooked by God, any more than by human masters. For example, God smote Uzziah when he accidentally stumbled and touched the ark (II Sam. 6:6-7) and: 'As long as the Shekinah (the Divine Presence) is on the mountain, whoever touches it will surely be put to death' (Mek.Bah.3). Saul would put Jonathan to death when he disobeyed his father's instructions even though he had no knowledge of them. 'Saul laid an oath on the people ... so no one tasted food ... But Jonathan had not heard his father charge the people ... so he dipped the tip of his staff in the honeycomb and put his hand to his mouth ... And Saul said, "You shall surely die"' (I Sam. 14:24,27,44).

Some accepted that ignorance should mitigate the punishment to be suffered, but it could not remove its necessity, since God had made clear his wishes in the Law and prophets: 'Abimelech said to God, "In the integrity of my heart and the innocence of my hands have I done this." Then God said to him, "Yes, I know ... Now restore the man's wife to him and he will pray for you, and you shall live"' (Gen. 20:4-7). In rabbinical books: 'If a man intended to eat pork but was served mutton, he is as guilty as if it was pork that he had eaten' (b.Kid. 81b) but some rabbis claimed that one was punished only if one was aware that the action was expressly forbidden by God.

Some Jews thought that conduct and its consequences were collective in Judaism and the sins of fathers could require punishment of their children. In any case, punishment was a sign of God's love in both O.T. and I.T. books: "Know then in your heart that, as a man disciplines his son, the Lord your God disciplines you." (Dt. 8:5); "Oh, for Wisdom's lash to curb my thoughts and discipline my mind, without overlooking my mistakes or condoning my sins" (Sir. 23:2); "The chastening of the righteous for sins done in ignorance, is not like the overthrow of the sinner. The righteous is chastened sparingly ... for God corrects the righteous as a beloved son"(P. S. 13:6-9); "Happy is the man whom the Lord remembers with reproving and whom he restrains from the way of evil with strokes of the whip, that he may be cleansed for sin ... He that makes his back ready for the whip will be cleansed, for the Lord is good to them that endure chastening. For he makes straight the ways of the righteous and does not pervert them by his discipline" (P.S. 10:1-3). On the other hand there were those who disagreed that the fathers' sins could be visited upon their children. As rabbinical writing has it: "In Israel a destroyer is not a son of a destroyer (unless the son follows the evil of the father). There is no hereditary wickedness in Israel" (b.Sanh. 27b).

Those leaders full of pride in their own interpretations of God's will, would be severely punished, those who were misled by them would suffer less severely.

The last section of the passage indicates the same thing as the parables about the use of resources (B 2, E 7, F 4, etc.). God's gifts are not to be buried and left unused; they are to be used for his purposes, to bring God benefit.

The word translated 'watch' or 'be alert' from biblical Hebrew came to mean in later Jewish books 'be industrious'.

One of the concepts found throughout the synoptic gospels is the Jewish one of 'yetser'. This is 'inclination', but not in just a passive sense. On the contrary, the inclinations were very active and wilful, and there were two of them, one good and one bad. Jesus repeatedly extols the cultivation of the good and the eradication of the bad, exactly as other Jews did. The faculty of rational intellect, combined with compassion was the best means to accomplish this end. This could keep the emotions and passions in their proper, very limited, places. One of the I.T. books puts it like this: 'Therefore all things are by twos; there are the two ways of good and evil, and with those are the two inclinations (yetsers) in our breasts discriminating them. Therefore if the soul take pleasure in the good yetser, all its actions are righteousness ... But if it incline to the evil yetser, all its actions are wickedness ... even though it work what is good. It is perverted to evil ... a person then may with words help the good for the sake of the evil, yet the issue of the action leads to mischief' (T.Ash. 1:3-2:1); 'The nature of all children of men is ruled by these two spirits and ... all ... men have a portion of their divisions and walk in both their ways. The whole reward for their deeds shall be ... according to whether each man's portion in their two divisions is greater or smaller. For God has established the spirits in equal measure ... Truth abhors works of injustice and injustice hates all the ways of truth' (DSS, C.D. 4:15-19).

This teaching would have been understood at the time as an exhortation to live a life in accordance with God's will requiring constant care not to allow evil desires and habits to gain a hold in one's heart. It is not right to suggest it means we should keep awake all night in case God or Jesus suddenly appears to us.

For the Jews, the Torah was a treasure from God: 'The evil inclination has no power over him who has Torah in his heart' (Midr.Ps. 119:7).

* * *

B 2. The narrow gate and the closed door - Mt. 7:13-14, 21-23; 8:11-12. Lk. 6:46;13:22-30.

A man approached Jesus one day and asked him, "Sir, are only a few to be saved on the last day?"

We can imagine that he was not the only one to have wondered. There could well have been a discussion among the disciples on that very topic, when one of them had pointed out that some refused to use the good way even when shown it: 'Thus says the Lord: "Stand by the roads and look and ask for the ancient paths where the good way is and walk in it and find rest for your souls. But they said, "We will not walk in it"' (Jer. 6:16). He could have quoted some other opinions: 'The road of sinners is smoothly paved, and it leads straight to the pit of hell' (Sir. 21:10); and: '... the entrance (to the city) is narrow and steep, with fire to the right and deep water to the left. There is only one path ... wide enough for one man at a time. If this city be given to a man for inheritance, how shall the heir receive it, unless he pass through the dangers before him?' (IV Ezr. 7:6-8).

There are other texts in which the prophets tell us the pathway of the faithful is smooth, levelled and straight: 'Go through the gates, prepare a way for the people: build up the highway, clear it of stones ...' (Is 62:10); 'The way of the righteous is level; make smooth the path of the righteous' (Is. 26:7); 'The way of a sluggard is overgrown with thorns, but the path of the upright is a level highway' (Pvb. 15:19).

The main city gates are shown as entrances for the Lord and his sons: 'We have a strong city whose walls and ramparts are our deliverance. Open the gates to let a righteous nation in, a nation that keeps faith' (Is. 26:1-2); 'Lift up your heads you gates, lift yourselves up, you everlasting doors, that the king of glory may come in' (Ps. 24:7); 'Prepare a road for the Lord ... Every valley shall be lifted up, every mountain and hill brought down; rugged places shall be made smooth and mountain-ranges become a plain' (Is. 40:3-4). Perhaps Jesus answered the man's question and the disciples' discussion by saying:

The gateway is wide which leads to perdition; there is plenty of room on that road and many go that way. The gate that leads to life is very small and the road is narrow. Strive to find and get through that gate. Many do not find it, and others try to enter but cannot do so.

It is quite possible that this story arose because often there would be one main entrance to a walled town, and there the traveller would be subject to the attentions of toll-collectors. They would demand toll on the man himself, his entourage and his merchandise. These charges could be ruinous and local inhabitants would utilise 'holes' in the walls, narrow gates and passages, to slip in and out, avoiding the toll-gatherers.

To go through the narrow gate meant, however, giving up all encumbrances and taking the difficult way. A merchant or rich man burdened with many possessions could not go through, let alone a camel! Jesus' teaching is that the way into the kingdom of God is through a gate before which all this world's superfluity must be discarded.

On another occasion, their thoughts returned to this teaching of Jesus. It was all very well to be free from superfluity, but how would they be assessed? Who would be admitted to God's house? As Israelites, they would be, wouldn't they? After all, they were the chosen people: 'I brought the Israelites to the foot of Mt. Sinai and I bowed the heavens and came down ... and interrupted the storm of the heavenly hosts so as not to break my covenant. All things were set in motion when I came down and everything was brought to life when I arrived. I will take your souls and store them in peace until the time allotted to the world is complete' (P.P. 23:10). Israel had been depicted as the only nation which would pass through the needle's eye into the kingdom. Even the unrighteous Jews would be admitted, because they did nonetheless acknowledge there is a divine Law and its maker.

But what about other nations? Isaiah and Micah both say they will come to Zion to confess and learn from Israel: 'And all the nations ... shall come and say: "Come let us go up to the mountain of the Lord, to the house of the God of Israel, that he may teach us his ways, and we may walk in his paths. For out of Zion shall go forth the Law and the Word of the Lord from Jerusalem"' (Is. 2:3 and Mic. 4:2).

The Qumran community thought the same: 'O, Jerusalem ... keep your gates ever open that the hosts of the nations may be brought in! Their kings shall serve you all, your oppressors shall bow down before you, they shall lick the dust of your feet ... Sovereignty shall be to the Lord, and everlasting dominion to Israel' (DSS, WR 12); 'They brought their offerings to your great Name, silver and gold and precious stones, together with all the treasures of their lands, that they might glorify your people and Zion your holy city and house of your majesty' (DSS, LF 4). The teaching Jesus gave the questioner in reply must have been a great surprise!

Jesus said, "After the master of the house has locked the door, you may stand outside the house and knock and cry, 'Sir, let us in'. He will answer, 'Not everyone who calls me 'Lord, Lord', will enter God's house, but only those who do his will.' When the last day comes the latter will be justified, but many will say, 'Lord, did we not prophesy, cast out demons and perform many miracles in your name? We shared meals with you and you taught in our streets.' They will be told, 'I never knew you and I do not know where you come from. Depart from me all of you, you and your lawless, wicked ways. Many will be there in the kingdom of God from north and south, east and west, with Abraham, Isaac and Jacob and all the prophets, reclining at table, but those born to be sons of the kingdom will be driven away into the place of darkness.'

A son belongs to his father's house, born of his wife and is the father's legitimate heir. Among the 'sons of the kingdom', those who were like their (heavenly) father were accepted; the others were to be cast away.

What then was the criterion for admittance? It wasn't to cry 'Lord, Lord;' false prophets did that (see D 2). It wasn't to do miracles exploiting the faith of the crowd; that was like the mockery the religious leaders were guilty of. It wasn't even to prophesy claiming to be appointed by Jesus himself, or prophesying in his name. It was simply to concentrate on following God's rule; that was the only requirement to enter into the kingdom. That those born to be sons of the kingdom, presumably the Israelites of the whole world, were among those the Master actively got up to exclude, must have been beyond comprehension and totally insulting to most of the Jews. They were sure they would be eligible to join the fathers at the messianic feast in God's kingdom: 'O, give thanks to the Lord, for he is good; for his steadfast love endures for ever! Let the redeemed from the power of the enemy, and those gathered in from every land, from east and west, from north and south, tell of it' (Ps. 107:1-3). They were less clear that they could be told: 'Depart from me all you workers of evil ... for the Lord has heard the sound of my weeping; he has hearkened to my supplication and accepted my prayer. My enemies shall be put to shame and sorely troubled' (P.S. 6:8-10). Not all Israel would be excluded - not all were enemies of God, but Jesus speaks against false followers even including his disciples. Faith is not always to be found in Israel (among Jews); it can equally well occur among Gentiles.

'Lord, Lord' was thought to be the correct mode of address to the Judge of the world on the day of Judgement (God), and it is connected with: 'You shall keep my ordinances ... I am the Lord your God' (Lev. 18:4), and 'Do not turn to mediums or wizards; do not seek them to be defiled by them. I am the Lord your God' (Lev. 19:31). It may also be connected with the Jewish suspicion that those seeking conversion when the Messiah comes are not really honourable and acceptable.

The phrase, 'I never knew you', was one used by a rabbi to exclude one of his followers from his circle.

It would seem that the emphasis was on the situation of the day of Judgement, but in fact the teaching could equally well have applied to becoming one of the sons of the kingdom there and then. It was necessary to change over to a righteous inner attitude or inclination, but theory was not enough; it must produce the fruit of deeds of loving-kindness. Otherwise hell, the place of darkness would be the destination of unbelievers and unpractitioners: 'The inheritance of sinners is destruction and darkness and their iniquities shall pursue them to Sheol' (P.S. 15:11).

Jesus teaches that nationality, or ethnic background is irrelevant, but the message is not only sweetness and light; it is also clear and sharp. Those who do not listen to Jesus' warnings and do not repent, can risk being excluded, not by accident, but because God will not accept them. Any form or taint of ulterior mixed motives disqualified; even those prophesying or those performing miracles in God's name, those fully occupied with all manner of pious talk, will be unwelcome. Even those claiming to have been appointed by Jesus himself can be condemned on the day of Judgement if their intentions were impure. The message is: be good, then the fruits will necessarily follow. Change now, before you find yourself on the wrong side of the door to the kingdom.

This message is found in rabbinical writings also: 'After God has waited for the wicked to repent and they do not, then if finally they desire to repent, God removes from them the power to do so. Even if they wish to turn back to the Lord ... they cannot, for he shuts the door on them' (Ex.R. 11:1) The picture of a fork-junction in the road is found also: 'It is like one who sat by a fork in the road and before him were two paths, one of which was smooth to start with and ended in thorns; the other was thorny to start with, but became smooth. So Moses said to Israel, "The wicked whom you see prosperous, have prosperity but for the brief space in this world, but their end is to fall. And you see the righteous who suffer torments in this world; it is but for a short time that they suffer; their end is rejoicing' (Sif.Dt. 11:26). The teaching is that the whole-heartedly righteous will be punished in this world for their few bad deeds, while the whole-heartedly unrighteous will be rewarded in this world for their few good deeds.

* * *

B 3. Ten maidens meeting the bridegroom - Mt. 25:1-12.

This is a strange story which has given rise to many interpretations. There is a bridegroom, but no bride is mentioned directly. The bridegroom arrives in the middle of the night or, at midnight. Those with oil will not share it with those without; and so on. It has many links with texts from the O.T. and the understanding of them in the Judaism of the day.

Jesus said, "Here is a story to show how it will be with the kingdom of God when the day of Judgement comes.

There were ten maidens who set out with lamps to meet a bridegroom. Five of them were foolish and took no extra oil with them; the other five were sensible and had small jugs of oil ready to use. The bridegroom was so late that they dozed off, until a cry at midnight woke them: 'Here is the bridegroom. Come out and meet him!'

The girls got up and trimmed their lamps and the prudent ones replenished theirs with oil, so that they burned brightly. Those of the foolish girls were going out and they had no more oil. They said to the prudent girls, 'Give us some of your oil.' 'No, we cannot do that; there will not be enough for us then. Go to those selling oil, and buy some for yourselves.'

But while they were gone, the bridegroom arrived and the girls who had their lamps alight went into the (wedding) feast, and the door was shut.

When the foolish ones came back they asked to come in but it was too late: 'I do not know you,' they were told.

At one level, this parable shows the importance of being prepared. When the bridegroom comes after a long wait, those who go to welcome him with their lamps and cries of joy, are invited in to the banquet. They had served him and were welcome to his feast. Jewish thinking was that any service or gift must be reciprocated. Here the reciprocation is not in proportion to the service - it is as the wages paid to the workers in the vineyard (B 7). Those who did not bother to prepare properly, were rejected. They had offered no service, because when they had the opportunity, they couldn't be bothered to prepare themselves for the future, that is be righteous.

Almost every parable or passage has implicit in it a much greater richness of meanings which, though obscure to us today, would have been clear to the Jews of Jesus' day. In this story of the ten maidens, there are numerous references which Jesus' listeners would have recognised. The word 'lamp' for example, would at once bring to mind God's word, the Torah, whose light showed the way to go, and to light a lamp was to obey a commandment. As in the O.T.: 'Your word is a lamp to my feet and a light to my path' (Ps. 119:105). Those bearing lighted lamps symbolise those who studied the Torah, the scholars: 'David slept till midnight and then arose to study the Torah', and the psalmist says: 'At midnight I will arise to give thanks...' (Ps. 119:62). In Judaism, night time was the time to study the Torah (Lev.R. 19:1-2) which was the lamp of God. To light this lamp one must obey the commandments (Ex.R. 36:3) and it needed filling with 'oil' that is, good deeds (Num.R. 13:15-16). Trimming the lamp (to make it burnt brighter) meant speaking righteously (Cant.R. 4:41).

The story, and that of B4, have connections with that of the Song of Solomon. When the bridegroom (God) comes to his garden, he finds his bride asleep, although her understanding remains awake: 'I slept, but my heart was awake' (S.S. 5:2); she heard the cry at midnight at which she arose, but too late. She had not opened the door in time and her beloved had departed: 'I opened to my beloved, but he had turned and gone. My heart failed me when he spoke. I sought him but found him not, I called him but he gave no answer' (S.S. 5:6). The imagery from the Song of Solomon was used on more than one occasion to depict the relationship between God and his people, the Israelites.

Oil in the bible is often a symbol for good deeds or merit, but half of those hoping to enter with the bridegroom, had no more oil: they speak well but lack merit. 'You may listen to what they say, but not do as they do.' Once again the religious leaders are upbraided for their lack of righteousness and they are told, 'I do not know you.' This was the reply of a master to one whom he does not wish to have as a disciple.

It could also be taken to mean that God has not taken them into his nuptial chamber, as his bride. This was the image used when Israel was espoused to God at Sinai: Israel became God's bride; when she promised to accept the covenant and obey God's rule. Like those who were impatient and worshipped the golden calf, these 'maidens' without enough oil were unfit to enter the king's chamber and become espoused to him.

They had not worried too much about righteousness and were sinners not because they were particularly actively wicked but because they did not concern themselves to live according to God's rules. They had acquired so little merit they could not meet the bridegroom worthily and had to go off to get some more 'merit'! By then, of course, it was too late.

One of the things that exercised the minds and hearts of the Jews of the time was whether someone with much merit could transfer some of it to someone else on the day of Judgement. Could a man give some to his wife? Could a father give some to his son? This question had been answered negatively in the O.T., in rabbinical literature and in several I.T. books: 'Even as no man shares in the reward of his fellow in this world, so he does not share in the reward of his fellow in the world to come' (ARN 12). This parable suggests Jesus agreed.

It is not possible to acquire merit from another's efforts, vicariously. The evil and the good one has done are no one else's responsibility: 'Therefore I will judge you, Israel, everyone according to this deeds' (Ps. 62:12); 'Do not say: "Our father is standing before God, and is praying for our sins," for there is no helper of any man who has sinned' (II En. 53:1); 'On the day of Judgement, will the just be able to win pardon for the wicked, or pray for them to the Most High? Can fathers do so for sons, or sons for their parents? Can brothers pray for brothers, relatives and friends for their nearest and dearest?' "I (the angel) will tell you," he said. 'The day of Judgement is decisive ... A father cannot send his son in his place, nor a son his father ... When that day comes every individual will be held responsible for his own wickedness or goodness'" (IV Ezr. 7:102-105).

In rabbinical literature a similar opinion is found as a comment on Psalm 49:7-8: 'No man can by any means redeem his brother, or give to God the price of his life; no one can pay for atonement and no brother can save his brothers' (Midr.Ps. on 49:7-9); 'If men give all the world's wealth they cannot ransom another's soul; for the soul with which a man sins, no indemnity can ever be paid by another' (Sif.Dt. on 32:39). There can be no transfer of piety or merit derived from piety.

On the other hand there was in Judaism the idea that ancestral merit in some way was responsible for the treatment of the good and the bad (b.Ber.7a), while others said: 'The afflictions of the righteous and the prosperity of the unrighteous is not for humans to understand' (m.Avot 4:15).

Superficially, the refusal of the five wise girls to share what oil they had, might be thought to show lack of charity, but this ignores the deeper significance of Jesus' teaching, that service brings merit but that this cannot be transferred to others. The first group represents those with the merit of good deeds sufficient to be accepted into the kingdom of God and to meet the bridegroom of Israel on the day of Judgement. It is these who have the merit of righteousness. The other group are those who have fine words but few good deeds. They are not 'acceptable to the Lord'.

* * *

B 4. Separation of the sheep and the goats - Mt. 25:31-46.

The setting of this parable is the day of Judgement, when the good and evil ones are separated, and its meaning is similar to passages in other Jewish literature. The passage also points to the connection between behaviour in this life, and its consequences in the future, but it is very rich in allusions to many other ideas. Some experts think that in Jesus' time the disciples were Jews simply preaching one variety of Judaism, of which there were certainly several, existing side by side. There is no reason to suppose that they were persecuted and perhaps the passage has been elaborated later, in order to encourage those active as missionaries, when Jewish opposition to the new sect was fiercer.

"On the day of Judgement," said Jesus, "the son of man will come in his glory (and all the angels with him) and he will sit in state on his throne. All the nations will be assembled before him and he will separate them in two groups, like a shepherd separates the sheep from the goats.
Then the king will say to the sheep on his right: 'Come into the kingdom which has been awaiting you from before the creation of the world, blessed of my Father. When I was hungry you gave me food and when I was thirsty you gave me water; when I was in a strange land you took me into your home; when I was naked you clothed me, when I was in prison or when I was sick and had no one to care for me, you visited me'
But the righteous ones will be puzzled and say, 'Lord, when did we see you hungry and feed you, or thirsty and give you something to drink? When did we see you naked, and give you clothes? When did we meet you as a stranger or sick or imprisoned and take you into our homes or visit you?'
The king will reply, 'I'll tell you when! You did these things to me whenever you did it for the least of my brothers here, however humble.'
Then to those on his left the king will turn and say, 'Depart from me. The curse is upon you and you must go to eternal fire where the devil and his angels await you. When I was hungry you gave me nothing, nor when I was thirsty. You cared nothing for me when I was a stranger; you were indifferent to me when I was naked, ill or in prison.'
'But, your majesty,' they will say, 'when did we see you hungry, or thirsty, or a stranger, or needing clothes, or ill, or in trouble, and did not minister to you?'
The king will reply, 'I tell you this: whatever

you did not do for one of these least important people, however humble, you did not do it for me.'

Then they will go to eternal punishment; but the righteous will go to eternal life."

The story depicts a king separating sheep from goats, and echoes O.T. passages: 'They shall be mine, says the Lord of Hosts ... on the day that I appoint, and I will spare them as a man spares the son who serves him. Then you shall again distinguish between the righteous and the wicked, between one who serves God and one who does not serve him' (Mal. 3:17-18). Ezekiel uses a similar idea but separates different kinds of sheep: 'Thus says the Lord God to them: "Behold, I judge between sheep and sheep, rams and he-goats. I will separate the strong fat sheep and weak lean sheep: ... I will save my flock and they shall no longer be a prey and I will judge between sheep and sheep"' (Ezk. 34:17,20,22). The principle is that by serving one's fellowman with love, one assists God's purposes.

Some think that the prophet is thinking primarily of good and bad Israelites, not Israelites versus Gentiles but it is also said: 'On the day of Judgement the Gentile nations will be overthrown and tried' (Is. 3:13; Dan. 7:14). Those who had refused help to those needing it, will be separated from those who had shown kindness and been helpful to others and had thereby followed God's rule. Similar teaching is found throughout Jewish writing; for example: whenever you feed the poor, it is the same as if you feed me; and for some it applied to non-Israelites too: 'God does not leave unrewarded the heathen who does good deeds' (j.Peah 1:1).

Lists of deeds of mercy and love are to be found in O.T. and I.T. books: 'I (the Lord) require of you ... to loosen the fetters of injustice, untie the thongs of the yoke, let the oppressed go free ... to share your bread with the hungry, and bring the homeless into your home, to clothe the naked ... and never evade a duty to your kinsfolk' (Is. 58:6-7); 'If your enemy is overthrown do not exult; if he stumbles (sins) let not your heart rejoice' (Pvb. 24:17); 'I was sold into slavery and the Lord of all set me free. I was taken captive and the Lord succoured me. I was sick and the Lord visited me. I was in prison and God showed me favour: in bonds and he released me, falsely accused and he testified on my behalf' (T.Jos. 1:5-7); 'This place is prepared for the righteous ... who give bread to the hungry, cover the naked with clothing, raise up the fallen...' (II En. 9:1); 'You have exacted pledges of your brothers for nothing and stripped the naked of their garments. You have given the weary no water to drink, nor bread to the hungry ... You have sent widows away empty ...' (Job 22:6-9).

Missionaries necessarily went out to those ignorant of their message. They were in contact with pagans and Gentiles. Would these be acceptable too, if they were kind to their visitors? Matthew shows Jesus approving those who, though pagans, did works of loving-kindness to his brothers, because in doing so they were obeying God's rule. Even the minimum kindness - a cup of water - would not go unmarked.

The setting of the parable, the day of Judgement, coming of the Messiah and its aftermath, is typical for this kind of literature, in which there are many names given to the son of man figure: the Elect One, Messiah, the Pure from sin, Being of perfect righteousness, Lamb, Warrior, King, etc. In the book of Enoch a vivid picture is painted of the Messiah on his throne of glory which is similar to the vision given in the N.T.: 'The Lord of Spirits seated the Elect One on his throne of glory and the spirit of righteousness was poured out upon him. The word of his mouth slays all the sinners and all the unrighteous are destroyed. ... In that day all the kings and the mighty shall stand up and they shall ... recognise how he sits on the throne of his glory ... Then shall pain come upon them ... and one part of them shall look on the other and they shall be terrified ... when they see the son of man sitting on the throne of his glory. All the kings and the exalted ... shall fall down before him on their faces ... and petition him ... for mercy at his hands ... Nevertheless ... he will deliver them to the angels of punishment ... and they shall be a spectacle for the righteous. ... They shall rejoice over them. The righteous and the elect shall ... cease to be downcast and they shall be clothed in garments of glory, and these shall be the garments of life from the Lord of Spirits. Your garments shall not grow old nor your glory pass away' (I En. 62:15-16); and 'In those days the unrighteous shall be led off to the abyss of fire, condemned and destroyed ...' (I En. 10:13).

The use of 'king' to refer to the Messiah, is also I.T. teaching: 'Behold O Lord, and raise up to them their king the son of David ... that he may reign over Israel your servant. Gird him with strength that he may shatter unrighteous rulers and purge Jerusalem from Gentiles that trample her down to destruction ... He shall thrust out sinners from the inheritance ... with a rod of iron he shall break in pieces all their substance, he shall destroy the godless nations with the word of his mouth' (P.S. 17:23-27); 'Then from heaven God shall send a king who shall give every land relief from war; some he shall slay and on others he shall impose vows of loyalty' (SO. 3:652).

The concept of the final Judgement belongs to Judaism, beginning with the idea that nations would be assessed and assigned their proper portions, good or bad: 'Open to me the gates of righteousness, that I may enter therein and give thanks to the Lord. This is the gate of the Lord and the righteous shall enter through it.' (Ps. 118:19-20); 'The Most High shall be revealed upon the throne of Judgement ... Judgement alone shall remain, truth shall stand and faithfulness triumph, recompense shall follow and reward be made manifest. Deeds of righteousness shall awake and deeds of wickedness shall not sleep. Then shall the ... furnace of Gehenna appear and opposite to it the Paradise of delight. Then shall the Most High say to the nations that have returned from the dead: "Look now and consider whom you have despised!"' (IV Ezr. 7:33-37).

Later the idea developed that evil would be destroyed and each would be released from sin and the grip of Satan: '...the host of the armies which are ordained to work vengeance on the spirits of deceit and Satan on the day of Judgement' (T.Lev. 3:3); 'Then his kingdom shall appear throughout all his creation and Satan shall be no more ... Then the hand of the angel shall be filled ... and he shall forthwith avenge them of their enemies. The Heavenly One shall arise from his royal throne and go forth ... with indignation and wrath on account of his sons and the earth shall tremble' (A.M. 10:1-3).

There has been an association of the right-hand side with good, and the left-side with evil, from very early times. In Judaism, study of the Torah, honourable good inclinations and alms-giving, were on the right, while their opposites pertained to the left: 'For years of life are in her (Wisdom's) right hand, and in her left are wealth and glory. Out of her mouth proceeds righteousness and she carries law and mercy on her tongue' (Pvb. 3:16); 'A wise man's understanding is at his right hand; a fool's is at his left' (Ecc. 10:2).

(I Kgs. 22:19 is not relevant here. It depicts God with his angels to his right and to his left. This is because those on the right were those who would be for an acquittal, while those on the left would lean towards the conviction of the accused.)

* * *

B 5. The barren fig tree - Lk. 13:6-9.

A fig tree and a vineyard were very well-known metaphors from the O.T. The picture of Israel as a vineyard of the Lord with the righteous as fruitful trees and the wicked as barren trees, was associated with calls to the wicked to repent, and promises of God's mercy on those who do so: 'Even now, says the Lord, turn back to me with your whole heart, fast and weep and beat your breasts ... for I am gracious and compassionate ...' (Jl. 2:12-13); 'Like grapes in the wilderness I found Israel. Like the first fruit on the fig tree in its first season, I saw your forefathers. But ... they consecrated themselves to Ba'al, and became detestable ... Woe to them when I depart from them' (Hos. 9:10,12).

The inference is that repentance cannot be postponed endlessly. A little while yet will God be merciful, but if there was no improvement in the behaviour of the Israelites, he would destroy the vineyard and its barren trees as the prophets had said: 'Vine-dressers, lament! ... The vintage is perished and the fig tree has failed' (Jl. 1:11-12); 'My beloved had a vineyard ... He looked for it to yield grapes, but it yielded wild grapes ...What more could have been done for my vineyard that I did not do in it?... Why ... did it yield wild grapes? I will break down the walls ... and I will leave it derelict ... The vineyard of the Lord of Hosts is the house of Israel, and the men of Judah are the plant he cherished. He looked for justice, but behold, bloodshed; for righteousness, but behold, shrieks!' (Is. 5:1-7).

When things got to this state, the New Adam would take over the Lord's vineyard and in the resulting messianic age, all the righteous trees would bear fruit in abundance: 'Blessed is the man who trusts in the Lord. He is like a tree planted beside streams of water ... and does not fear when the heat comes, for its leaves remain green ... for it does not cease to bear fruit' (Jer. 17:8); 'Blessed is the man who walks not in the counsel of the wicked, nor stands in the way of sinners ... He is like a tree planted by streams of water, that yields its fruit in its season and its leaf does not wither' (Ps. 1:1,3); 'Be not afraid ... for the trees shall bear fruit, the fig and the vine yield their harvests. O people of Zion, rejoice and be glad in the Lord your God who gives good food ... and sends rain as of old' (Jl. 2:22-24).

Jesus said, "A man had a fig tree growing in his vineyard and he came to see if there was any fruit on it, but there was none. So he said to the vine-dresser, 'Look here. For the last three years I have come to look for fruit on this tree but there never is any. You know that these trees take a lot of nourishment from the soil. You must cut it down.'

But the vine-dresser said, 'Leave it, lord, one year more. I will dig round it and manure it and if it gives fruit in the future all is well, but if not, then you shall have it cut down.'

After three years of proper pruning and manuring, a tree with no sign of fruitfulness could be condemned as barren and cut down, but it is only in the fourth year that vines begin to produce usable grapes. It is then that the produce is first tithed or devoted to God. For men, too, there was a 'fourth year', when it was required of them to show by their behaviour some profit for God. If not, it was clear they did not belong under God's rule in his kingdom.

Similar stories are common in the literatures of many countries. In I.T. literature the following story occurs: 'My son you have been like a palm-tree growing beside a stream, but casting all its fruit into the water. The owner decided to cut it down, but the tree said to him, "Let me abide this year. I will bear fruit for you next year." But the owner replied, "You have been no use to me so far, and you will not be useful to me in the future either"' (Ahk. 8:25).

In rabbinical literature, the messianic age is pictured as one in which the productivity of trees and plants would be very great: 'One grape bush will yield 30 measures of wine. Fruits will ripen in four weeks and grains in two weeks. Garments will be of the finest quality' [and so forth] (b.Keth. 111b); 'Ruins will be restored and Jerusalem with be decked with jewels' (Midr.Cant. 4:4).

The picture in the O.T. is similar: 'The moon will shine as bright as the sun and the sun will be seven times as bright as now and all diseases will be healed' (Is. 30:26); 'Fresh water will spring out (in Jerusalem)' (Ezk. 47:9); 'Weeping and wailing will cease' (Is. 65:19); 'Death will be abolished' (Is. 25:7).

* * *

B. Summary.

Each of the passages has an obvious message and another which is for us more obscure but which the hearers of the time would have found quite apparent.

The first passage is a simple 'keep watch' message, much elaborated by Matthew followed by Luke, in expectation of the day of Judgement. The deeper message is that each one must make sure his or her 'heart' is vigilant. The basis of this idea is that of the Jewish concept of "Yetser", inclinations, which could be good or bad. Yetser is the faculty underlying loving-kindness, determined by one's reason or mind, since the heart was thought of as the seat of the mind at that time.

Jewish teaching about punishment attempted to explain adverse experiences as God's discipline. This idea is more fully exposed in other passages. In parts of the O.T., the broad highway was taken to be that which leads to perdition and the underlying message of this passage is that no one should continue to possess anything in excess of his or her own needs.

There were many who said and did all the 'correct' things, but they would be excluded from the kingdom in spite of being of the chosen people. Those who do not produce good fruit in the form of service of their fellowmen, however humble, cannot expect any return from God, while God's reward for those following his rule far exceeds any service they might accomplish. The important underlying message is that there is no possibility for merit to be transferred, and those lacking it must suffer the consequences. Some had tried to dodge the unpleasant fact by supposing that a father or a son, a sister or a mother could take the place of the one being judged on the last day. This was definitely not possible.

Israel had been discovered by God in the idealised past and valued as the first fruit of the first season of ripe fruit, but she had turned away from God's realm and reign. She was rotten fruit, and would be destroyed. It was no use hoping to repent when the signs showed the day of Judgement was approaching; it would come totally unexpectedly. There would be no warning! It was therefore necessary to repent immediately.

C. God's plan and responses to the kingdom of God.

C 1. The treasure, the pearl and the big fish - Mt. 13:44-46.

Treasure trove and pearls symbolize great value. These two short parables teach that God's faithful servants are 'on loan' in this world and are treasured by God, as the labourer and the merchant valued the treasure they found. On the day of Judgement they will receive God's special care and cherishing, and they need not be dismayed by their lack of appreciation in the present world.

Jesus said, "The kingdom of God is like treasure buried in a field which a man found and covered up again. In his joy he went and sold all he possessed and bought that field.
Here is another picture of the kingdom of God: a merchant on the look-out for fine pearls, saw an especially beautiful one, and sold all he had in order to obtain it."

The behaviour of the labourer who found the treasure has given rise to consternation. Some have thought that such a deed could only be condemned, but this is not the case. The man can be imagined ploughing in an unused place for the first time; it was not in a settled area but on the outskirts where no one had ploughed before. The owner of the field did not know of the treasure, and could not have been its owner. It had been left buried perhaps years before, when to bury valuables was the best mode of safe-keeping commonly used in Palestine, scene of frequent upheavals, riots and conquests. The law was that by not lifting it out of its hiding-place, the man was not guilty of stealing: 'If a man found an object in a heap of stones it belongs to him' (m.B.M. 2:1-2). It was sensible to do what he did: say nothing and buy the land first. He was not being immoral. No one had any right to the treasure, until the one who owned the land discovered it.

There was a difference in Judaism between finding something by searching for it, like the merchant who found his pearl by looking out for it, and finding something by accident, like the labourer who found the treasure. The former is like someone who sifts and searches until the treasure remains and dross is removed, while the latter is like someone receiving God's wisdom without turmoil, unexpectedly, as when a person suddenly comes to be aware of God's Spirit. A rabbinical story shows this well: 'A martyr was thrown into a furnace because he would not worship false gods. When this happened a voice was heard saying that he was destined for eternal life in the world-to-come: "One wins eternal life after a struggle of years; another finds it in one hour"' [that is, in his last hour] (b.A.Z. 17b-18a).

There are connections between these parables and the O.T.: 'A record was written before the Lord of those who feared him and kept his name in mind. "They shall be mine," says the Lord of Hosts, "my own possession against the day that I appoint, and I will spare them as a man spares the son who serves him. You will again tell good men from bad, the servant of God from the man who does not serve him"' (Mal. 3:17-18); 'Now, therefore, if you will obey my voice, and keep my covenant you shall be a special treasure to me from among all peoples; for all the earth is mine' (Ex. 19:5). Similarly in rabbinical writings: 'All deeds are written in the heavenly book' (m.Avot. 2:1).

The obvious meaning is that when you have found the kingdom of God, nothing else is of importance, and you will devote all your wealth and all your personal resources in order to gain one thing alone - God's kingdom.

Some have suggested Matthew had another purpose for this parable. He wished to show that Jesus limited his activity to Israel, the chosen people: 'The Lord has chosen Jacob to be his own and Israel as his special treasure' (Ps. 135:4), and that the Gentiles should receive his message later from his disciples. Others dispute this.

Similar stories are found in rabbinical writings. In one of them a man inherited a piece of land which he sold for a trifle. The buyer found a large treasure there, and the seller was very cross about it. (Mek.Besh. 2). The rabbis, however, use these stories to point out that the Egyptians were like the sellers. They sent the Israelites out of their land, but did not realize until too late what a treasure they had missed.

In later Jewish writing a common motif was things in fours. For example, four kinds of men: 'One says, "What is mine is mine and what is yours is yours." This is the commonest type. Another says, "What is mine is yours the what is yours is mine." He is ignorant. A third says, "What is mine is yours and what is yours is yours". A saintly man. The fourth says, "What is your is mine and what is mine is mine". He's a wicked man.' Similar passages relate to four kinds of character, of disciple, of almsgiver and of those who study the Torah (m.Avot.5:11).

One of the nice stories is about those who sit with the Sages: 'The "sponge" soaks up everything; the "funnel" takes in but loses it at once; the 'strainer' lets the wine run away and collects the dregs; and the "sifter" collects the fine flour and discards the coarse parts' (m.Avot.5:10).

In the gospel of Thomas, there is a parable on very similar lines to those of the treasure and the beautiful pearl: *"There was once a fisherman who cast his net into the sea and found in his catch a really magnificent fish. It really was the 'big one'. He didn't even bother with the rest of his catch, but was completely delighted with that one fish he had caught."*

* * *

C 2. The sower - Mt. 13:4-9,18-23. Mk. 4:3-9,13-20. Lk. 8:4-8,11-15.

This famous parable shows the differing responses of people to the gospel message: some are indifferent, some are shallow and rootless, some are too busy with everything else, and yet others respond positively and produce great yields. It also shows that proclaiming God's word involves much of it being wasted.

"Listen", said Jesus one day. "A farmer went out to sow and as he sowed, seed fell on the path and the birds came and ate it. Some fell on rocky ground where there was little soil. It soon sprouted but it had no root, so that in the sun it was scorched and died. Another seed fell where there were thistles and thorns which grew more quickly and choked the corn, so it yielded no grain. Yet other seed fell on to good deep soil, grew and produced ears with much fruit, some thirtyfold, some sixtyfold and some one hundredfold."

Jesus was later questioned by his disciples about this parable. He said to them, "Don't you understand? The sower sows the Word of God. The Word sown on the road is that sown in people who make no response to it, because Satan comes and snatches it away from them.

The Word sown on rocky ground is the seed which is immediately accepted with enthusiasm but it develops no roots and soon withers away. At the first sign of testing or persecution on account of the Word, they back out, and desert their commitment. Others receive the Word with joy, but the cares and anxieties of this world, or love of pleasures and wealth, like the thistles and thorns, choke it and it withers in them.

The Word sown in good soil, that is in people who welcome and nurture it, hold fast to it and persevere, yields great harvests."

There are many interpretations and opinions about this passage. Some think the explanation given in the second part of the passage was originally a separate story, but was added to the first part because both were concerned with seeds, sowing and harvesting. Others think the explanation was added by the early church.

The obvious meaning is that God's word is like seed sown in various more or less favourable conditions. Some take root, flourish and produce a large harvest: 'For as the rain and snow come down from heaven and ... water the earth, making it sprout and bear fruit, giving seed for sowing and bread to eat, so shall the word which goes forth from my mouth prevail ... It shall accomplish that which I purpose and prosper in the task I gave it' (Is. 55:10-11). In the wilderness, God sent his word, manna, on which the Israelites survived, and Jesus points out that God's word is still being sown broadcast among his people. But those who refuse to accept the word will die of hunger: 'Their hunger will not be satisfied nor their bellies filled...' (Ezk. 7:19).

Another interesting view of this passage is that it illustrates the Shema'of Jewish daily prayer. This includes the passage from Deuteronomy in which the ones faithful to the covenant are those who love God and his rule with all their 'heart', with all their soul and with all their strength. The seeds which fall on the path and which are snatched up by Satan symbolize those falling on persons whose 'heart' is hard; that is, their understanding is lacking. Those which fall on rocky ground are sown in those who do not love God with their whole lives or souls; when suffering is imminent they save their lives, whereas, to remain within the covenant with God, the righteous have to love God even though he takes away their lives. In I.T. literature, seed which sprouts in rocky ground was likened to sinners: 'The children of the ungodly shall not bring forth many branches, but are as roots of sinners upon a hard rock' (Sir. 40:15); and: 'The many progeny of the wicked shall not thrive, nor take deep roots ... nor gain any firm foundation. Their branches may flourish for a while, yet ... they shall be shaken and uprooted by the winds' (W.S. 4:3-4).

Seeds sown among thorns are those sown in people whose love of material well-being and wealth chokes their love of God. Their love of material well-being and wealth means that they do not devote all their strength (taken in Judaism to mean status and prestige as well as riches) to God's purposes.

Seeds taking root in good soil bring a great yield. They are sown in those who are loyal to the covenant against all temptations. Some think the yields given in this passage are exaggeratedly high, but others maintain that the normal yield of an ear, measured by the number of grains produced by one plant, is similar to the figures given. In one of the I.T. books it is said one seed shall bear one thousand new seeds (I En. 10:19), which is like O.T. teaching that miraculously large yields will be normal in the messianic age: 'Isaac sowed seed in that land, and that year he reaped a hundredfold, and the Lord blessed him' (Gen. 26:12); 'I will call to the corn and make it plentiful; I will bring no more famine upon you. I will make the trees bear abundant fruit and the ground yield heavy crops, so you will never again have to suffer the reproach of famine among the nations' (Ezk. 36:29-30).

It is a curious fact that in Mark's gospel, the order of the numbers is 100, 60 and 30, the opposite to the expected sequence as in Matthew's version. This has given rise to considerable speculation. One explanation is that the numbers are derived from the initial letters of the Hebrew words for shoot, ear and corn respectively, which it would be natural to think of when telling a parable about sowing and reaping. They also occur in the parable in Mark's gospel immediately after the present passage (see C 3).

There are many similar ideas in I.T. and O.T. books. For example: 'Prince Mastema (Satan) sent ravens and birds to devour the seed which was sown on the land; ... before they could plough in the seed, the ravens picked it from the ground' (Jub. 11:11); 'For just as the husbandman sows much seed upon the ground and plants a multitude of plants, yet not all which were sown shall be saved in due season, nor shall all that were planted take root, so also, not all they that are sown in the world shall be saved' (IV Ezr. 8:41); 'Thus says the Lord to the men of Judah and to the inhabitants of Jerusalem: "Break up your fallow ground and sow not among thorns"' (Jer. 4:3); 'They have sown wheat and have reaped thorns' (Jer. 12:13); 'I have harnessed Ephraim to the yoke, Judah must plough and Jacob must harrow his land. Sow for yourselves righteousness, reap the fruits of steadfast love. Break up your fallow land. It is time to seek the Lord that he may come and rain salvation upon you. You have ploughed wickedness and the crop is injustice; you have eaten the fruit of lies' (Hos. 10:11-1-3).

In Judaism, there were good plants and trees, which belonged to the fruitful land of Palestine and bad ones, like thorns and thistles, which belonged to the desert where demons held sway: 'Cursed is the man ... whose heart turns from the Lord. He is like a tamarisk shrub in the desert and shall not see any good come. He shall dwell in the parched places of the wilderness' (Jer. 17:5-6).

* * *

C 3. The patient, but confident, farmer - Mk. 4:26-29.

At one level, this little story seems to have a vital message. So little seemed to be happening! True, there was a handful of disciples with Jesus, but where was the kingdom of God he kept referring to? There did not seem to be much sign of it! Onlookers and sceptics may well have mocked Jesus and his little group. They seemed quite ordinary, even a bit rough and ready; they didn't suppose they were the beginning of the New Era, did they?

> Jesus said, "The kingdom of God is as if a man scattered seed on the earth. Afterwards he followed his usual routine, got up in the morning, and went to bed at the end of the day. Meanwhile the seed germinated; first the shoots came up then the ears formed and then the full fruit in the ears. How it grew he had no idea, the earth produced fruit by itself. Then when the ears had formed and the corn was ripe, he worked with the sickle, because harvest-time had come."

Like manna in the desert which appeared and disappeared like dew, no one knew how, growth of the Word is as silent and certain as the growth of seeds sown in the ground. Once the seed has been sown, you must await the fulfilment at the time of the harvest. In the meantime you must be patient; God's creativity continues and no man can hasten the growth which will give the triumphant end.

This understanding is not likely to have been that of Jesus' listeners. Careful examination of the language used and comparing the passage with the O.T. and other Jewish writings suggests a more subtle message.

When the corn is fully grown and ready for harvesting, the ears are not solely grain or fruit, but contain chaff as well. Harvesting is a metaphor not only for the time of obtaining the good grain from full ears, but also the time when the chaff and stubble are discarded. It was thought of as the time when merit is assessed, as well as when the wicked were separated from the righteous: 'Ply the sickle, for the harvest is ripe. Go in, tread, for the wine press is full. The vats overflow for their wickedness is great' (Jl. 3:13).

Plants which produce good grain also produced waste like chaff and stubble. Similarly, most deeds have both bad and good consequences, and no one could expect to produce only good, perfect fruit and nothing else. Everyone producing good fruit will produce some useless rubbish too. As the rabbis put it: 'Everything in the world is useful: death, hell, evil and good desires, sleep and suffering' (Gen.R. 9:5-9).

Not all seed was good seed either: the good could be mixed with seed giving plants which appeared to be good, but which gave no fruit; they were weeds in the field. Our aim must be to produce good fruit by sowing whatever good seed we can find. The earth will take the seed and make ears of full grain; that is, God will make the good seeds produce abundant grain: 'Just as you do not know how the breath comes to the bones in the mother's womb, so you do not know the work of God who makes everything' (Ecc. 11:5). It was not a question of balancing sins against righteous actions. God will sift out the dross and throw it away at harvest time. The good grain was interest or profit on the capital of the seeds of good deeds, and God was interested in the profit from the investments of his servants.

It was not necessary to try to do oneself what the earth and God would do: 'As the earth brings forth its shoots and ... causes what is sown to spring up, so the Lord God will cause righteousness and praise to spring up before all nations' (Is. 61:11). If one does the good deeds, the rest will be taken care of, even if it was not possible for someone to know how much profit would come from any particular good deed: 'If you follow my statutes and keep my commandments ... I will give you your rains in their season and the earth shall yield its produce ...' (Lev. 26:3-4). Each one must trust that some profit would arise and even though there would be chaff too, God would add to one's credit at once. It was not necessary to wait for the day of Judgement before the results of investment become clear; as the Kingdom of God begins to be manifest, they will be obvious much sooner: 'I will lie down in peace and sleep; for you, Lord, have caused me to dwell securely' (Ps. 4:8 LXX).

Those who did not bother with good deeds, or did them in order to get God's approval, found their seed (capital) gave no fruit or profit and they ended up worse off than before: 'Sow good things in your souls, that you may find them in your life. If you sow evil things, you shall reap every trouble and affliction' (T.Lev. 13:6).

There were all sorts of hazards and problems which the growing plants of good deeds have to contend with. It is not possible for a person to foresee all the results of an action before doing a good deed, but there was no record of demerit in heaven. Mistakes and failures were dismissed in the kingdom of God like the chaff and stubble.

There is another interesting point in the language used. The passage says that the plants (or God) permit the crop to 'hand itself over' to the harvest. This idea is found in other contexts in the gospels and suggests that it is not a question of the harvest destroying the plants but that they freely offer up their produce.

There is similar teaching elsewhere in the gospels, for example in the parables of the wheat and tares (C 9), talents (E 7), and the slave's reward (E 8).

* * *

C 4. The mustard seed and the leaven - Mt. 13:31-33. Mk. 4:30-32. Lk. 13:18-21.

Were there any signs of the kingdom yet? Were people responding to Jesus' message? There did not appear to be much change in the attitude of most people! These two parables may have been told at the beginning of Jesus' ministry to encourage his disciples and followers.

Jesus said, "How shall we think of the kingdom of God? It is the case with the kingdom as with the smallest of seeds, that of the mustard plant. When it is sown, this tiny seed grows to be a tree which forms branches in which the birds can find shelter. Or it is as if a little yeast had been hidden in three measures of flour until all was leavened."

The ideas of the passage are very like the visions found in several I.T. books, in which a marvellous tree, growing at the centre of the earth, or on the top of the highest mountain, is the tree of life, where God rests: 'As for this fragrant tree ... it shall be given to the righteous and holy. Its fruit shall be for food for the elect' (I En. 25:4-5). It is this which will grow up and provide God's food and shelter for those who follow Jesus and become his disciples.

Similarly in the O.T.: Ezekiel says God will plant a cedar tree (Israel) which will grow to be a safe haven for all the birds and beasts: 'These are the words of the Lord God: "I, too, will take a slip from the lofty crown of the cedar and set it in the soil; I will pluck a tender shoot from the topmost branch and plant it. I will plant it high on a lofty mountain, the highest mountain of Israel. It will put out branches, bear its fruit, and become a noble cedar. Winged birds of every kind will roost under it, they will roost in the shelter of its sweeping boughs"' (Ezk. 17:22-23).

Ezekiel also compares proud Assyria to a magnificent cedar tree (which God destroyed when it became proud and haughty): 'Behold Assyria, a cedar in Lebanon with fair branches and forest shade ... it towered high above all the trees of the forest; its boughs grew large and its branches long, from abundant water in its shoots. All the birds of the air made their nests in its boughs; under its branches all the beasts of the field brought forth their young; and under its shadow dwelt all great nations' (Ezk. 31:3,5-6). He continues: 'Because it towered high ... and its heart was proud of its height ... I cast it out. Foreigners ... will cut it down ... and upon its ruin will dwell all the birds of the air and upon its branches will be all the beasts of the field ... I will make the nations quake at the sound of its fall, when I cast it down to hell ...' (Ezk. 31:10-13,16).

Nebuchadnezzar had similar visions: 'As I was looking, I saw a tree of great height at the centre of the earth; the tree grew and became strong, its top reaching the heavens and it was visible to the ends of the earth. Its foliage was lovely, its fruit abundant and it yielded food for all. Beneath it the wild beasts found shelter, the birds lodged in the branches, and from it all living creatures fed' (Dan. 4:10-12).

To live under the protection of a tree or bush was a common metaphor of people living under the protection of a powerful king: 'Under his shadow we shall live among the nations.' (Lam. 4:20); '... the birds of the air have their habitation and sing among the branches' (Ps. 104:12); 'Under God's wings you shall find refuge' (Ps. 91:4). This is another facet of the passage.

Beginning as a tiny seed or as a pinch of yeast, God's creative power ends up producing a great sheltering bush, or loaves without number. Likewise, the word Jesus proclaims will bring messianic crops sufficient for all who will partake. The kingdom of God may not be obvious to most people, since it is at work under the surface like the germinating seed, or like leaven hidden in a large mass of dough, but it is working there, developing and will show itself at the proper time. That this will be on the day of Judgement is hinted at by reference to three measures or an 'ephah' of meal. This relates to the O.T. stories of Abraham, Gideon and others: 'The Lord appeared to Abraham ... and three men stood before him ... Abraham said to Sarah, "Make ready three measures of fine meal ..."' (Gen. 18:1-2,6); 'So Gideon ... prepared a kid and unleavened cakes from an ephah of flour' (Jdg. 6:19).

It has been argued that the mustard plant may form a bush when it is full-grown, but could never be a tree. In Jewish legend, however, it could become a tree large enough to cover a potter's hut.

It is more usual that in Judaism leaven represented poisonous evil (b. Ber. 17a), but it can also mean the kingdom of God. It is not unknown for one word to have contrary meanings: wheat for example can mean Torah or sin; and thorns can be for protection or entanglement.

* * *

C 5. Fig tree and faith - Mt. 17:20-21; 21:18-22. Mk. 11:12-14, 20-24. Lk. 17:5-6.

According to Jewish teaching, when God's reign is fully present on earth, that is among men, much will be different. All the trees and crops will bear in abundance, not just in season but all the time, whenever their fruit is wanted: 'On both banks of the river will grow all kinds of trees. Their leaves shall not wither nor their fruit fail, but they will bear fresh fruit every month. Their fruit will be for food and their leaves for healing' (Ezk. 47:12); 'When the Messiah begins to be revealed ... the earth will yield its fruit a thousand fold and on each vine shall be a thousand branches, and each branch will produce a thousand clusters and each cluster a thousand grapes and each grape a cor of wine' (II Bar. 29:3,5-6); 'There is no tree without fruit there (in Paradise) and every tree will be blessed' (II En. 8:7).

The trees will provide shade for travellers, all the rough places along the way will be made smooth, mountains and valleys leading to Zion will become level ground, and so on: 'Stand on the height, O Jerusalem, and behold your children from the east and west, gathered together by the Lord ... High mountains has he made a plain for them, the hills fled at their coming and every sweet-smelling plant ... sprang up for them.' (P.S. 11:3,5-7).

The next day, Jesus and his disciples were on their way to Jerusalem and, feeling hungry, Jesus examined a fig tree to see if it had any fruit on it. There were only leaves to be seen for it was not the season for figs and Jesus said, "May you produce no more fruit, nor any eat your fruit, until the (New) Era".

The next day, they saw the same tree withered from the roots up, and Peter pointed this out to Jesus: "Master, look, the fig tree you 'cursed' has withered."

Jesus said, "Have (the) faith of God. This I tell you: if anyone has faith without doubts, he will do more than that. He will say to this mountain, 'Be hurled into the sea,' and it will be done. Whatever you pray for in faith, you will receive."

On another occasion Jesus said to his disciples, "I tell you this truth: if you have faith no bigger even than a mustard seed, you will say to this mountain, or this tree, 'Go from here into the sea,' and it will happen."

This passage is difficult to accept at it stands, and numerous attempts have been made to soften it or explain it, but they have only served to distort its message. It would be much simpler were it not for the words, "for the season of fruit had not yet come." If that was the case, why was Jesus looking for what he would have known could not have been there? It is very unlikely the evangelists recorded this incident to show that Jesus was an optimist, and the problem is to understand the passage in a way which includes this crucial remark.

It was generally believed that if the New Era had begun, the fig tree should

46

have been able to produce fruit for Jesus, the righteous one who was hungry and needed it. But it did not. What then was wrong? Had the kingdom of God not started, or was the tree one of Satan's, recalcitrant and fruitless? There were similar useless vines and trees in the O.T. too: 'Ephraim is stricken, their root dried up, they yield not fruit' (Hos 9:16); 'There are no grapes; when I would gather them, says the Lord, there are no grapes on the vine nor figs on the fig trees; even the leaves are withered' (Jer. 8:13).

There are numerous references to fig trees in the O.T., and in the rabbinical commentaries. The fig tree was thought of as like the Torah; the more one sought, the more one found (b.Erub. 54b). It was also one of the symbols of the tree of life or wisdom, that is, the Torah, giving eternal life, which Adam, by his disobedience to God's command, had to forego. He was the first fruit from God, who by his fall spoiled the perfection of God's creation and until the Messiah comes on the day of Judgement, perfection would not be restored.

Several scholars believe that the passage is concerned to show Jesus as the new Adam, who would not disobey and would be entitled to eat of the tree of life or wisdom. Jesus is said to put the unfruitful tree under a ban and says if it will not bear the fruit expected of it in the messianic age now beginning, it will not bear any in its normal season either!

The tree symbolizes the Israelites and just as God's gift of eternal life was withdrawn from Adam and Eve, so Jesus condemns Israel, as previous prophets had done from time to time: 'All their host shall wither away, like a leaf withering on a vine or fruit withering on a fig tree' (Is. 34:4). Just as God's gifts were withdrawn from Adam and Eve, so Jesus implies that the Israelites will no longer be able to enjoy God's gifts. The passage symbolizes the inadequacy of Israel, especially the Temple worship and its rituals, searching for figs being a well-known O.T. metaphor for searching for righteousness in Israel. 'Like grapes in the wilderness I found Israel; I looked on their forefathers like the first figs' (Hos. 9:10); but as Jesus had discovered: 'There is no cluster (of grapes) to eat, no first-ripe fig, which my soul desires. The godly man has perished from the earth, and there is none upright among men' (Mic. 7:1-2). By his ban, Jesus proclaimed Israel unworthy, the old epoch at an end, and the New Era, God's kingdom was about to begin.

For the rabbis, souls were thought to be stored in the seventh heaven and the Messiah will come down from God when the storehouse of souls is empty (b.Yeb.62a).

The stories of Adam and Israel were parallel. Both had disobeyed and Jesus is seen in this passage proclaiming that the old epoch was at an end. He wished to make clear that by steadfast faith, his followers could help to bring to full fruition God's reign on earth. Then things would be such that by their prayers, all sorts of remarkable events would be possible. As the prophets had said, the mount of Olives would divide: 'On that day the Lord shall stand on the Mount of Olives ... and it shall be split in two from east to west by a very wide valley; so that one half shall withdraw northward, and the other southward' (Zch. 14:4).

Such faithful followers of God totally desire the kingdom to be manifest on earth in this life, though it may betoken upheavals and changes enough to frighten all out of their wits. (See J3). They would be under God's protection and their faith in this would be sufficient to keep them safe: 'God is our refuge and strength ... Therefore we will not fear though the earth should change, though the mountains shake in the heart of the sea, though its waters roar and foam, though the mountains tremble with its tumult' (Ps. 46:1-3). In the same way that the trees will bear abundant fruit, so will the righteous bear God's good fruit, although there were bad trees in Israel producing bad fruit (see F 7).

Thus faith in God's protection in such times is another element in this passage, and God will not go back on his promises: 'I will sing of your steadfast love, O Lord; for ever with my mouth I will proclaim your faithfulness to all generations. For your steadfast love was established for ever, your faithfulness is as firm as the heavens' (Ps. 89:1); 'Though the fig trees and the vines do not blossom ... the produce of the olive fail, and the fields produce no food ... yet I will rejoice in the Lord, in the God of my salvation' (Hab. 3:17-18). Faith is not a short cut to obtaining God's gifts just for the asking. A prayer cannot be a demand on God; it can only be a recognition of one's own obedience to God, and having faith will make one behave so that his reign will be brought nearer. God's reign is within and cannot come about because some are watching for it, but only through the fruits of changes within one's self.

There are connections between this passage and the experience of Jonah. He eventually obeyed God, went to Nineveh and proclaimed God's message, and was angry when the Ninevites repented of their ungodly ways. He was sure that they could not be better than the Israelites and repent before the latter did! God sent a climbing plant to give him shelter but the following day he sent a worm which caused it to wither: 'The Lord God ... made a plant come up over Jonah that it might be a shade over his head ... But then the next day came; God appointed a worm which attacked the plant and it withered' (Jon. 4:6-7), and Jonah was even more angry! He, a son of Abraham, treated in this way. The passage suggests clearly that Gentiles were as acceptable as Jews to Jesus.

To move a mountain or a tree was a common expression for the more or less impossible, and is found in rabbinical writing: 'May this carob tree be moved, and it was' (b.B.M. 59b).

* * *

C 6. Plaintiff and defendant - Mt. 5:25-26. Lk. 12:57-59.

There were several kinds of courts in Palestine in Jesus' time, including Jewish ones which used the Torah and tradition as the basis of their decisions. Relatively minor crimes were dealt with in the local synagogue; more serious ones were transferred to regional courts or, for the most serious crimes, to the Sanhedrin in Jerusalem, while ultimately the divine court would give the final judgement.

There were also the civil or administrative courts of the Roman civil power (see D 10). Very often Jewish courts took a long time to reach a decision and sometimes they would even refuse to give a judgement, arguing that these cases must be left to God's jurisdiction.

Jesus said, "Why cannot you judge for yourselves what is the right course to take? When you go to the court with your accuser, try to find a way to be reconciled with him: lest before you know what has happened, he takes you before another judge, who will hand you over to the constable, and have you put away. And there you will stay until you have repaid your last cent; of that you can be quite certain."

Jewish teaching was that transgressions against God are forgiven on the Day of Atonement, but those committed against a neighbour or fellowman are expiated only when he tries to be reconciled with his neighbour and admits his own fault: 'I will act as a relentless accuser against those who have no fear of me' (Mal. 3:5); 'Forgive your neighbour the wrong he has done, then your sins will be forgiven when you pray' (Pvb. 28:2).

Confrontation or reproach was also accepted in Judaism: 'Confront your friend ... lest he does something, or if he has done it, he continues to do it. Confront a neighbour lest he says something, or if he has already said it, lest he repeats it. Confront a friend, for often it is false slander, and do not believe every word ... Confront your neighbour before you threaten him and let the Law of the Most High take its course' (Sir. 19:13-15,17). This was the path of wisdom: 'How much better it is to complain than to nurse a grudge, and confession saves a man from disgrace' (Sir. 20:2); 'The Lord reproves him whom he loves' (Pvb. 3:12).

The accuser takes you to court because he thinks you have done him a wrong; he considers himself to be the injured party. By refusing to be reconciled with him, you thereby show yourself to be equally a transgressor. By acting in this way you become liable to much greater punishment in the world to come. There you will find the tables turned on you. Then the accuser will bring the case before God in the highest court and point out how implacably hard-hearted you were. God will dispatch you to jail, hell, where you will remain until the impossible happens! 'Those who wish me dead, defame me, those who mean to injure me spread cruel gossip and mutter slanders all day long. But ... I am like a man who cannot hear and whose tongue offers no defence. On you, O Lord, I fix my hope; you will answer, O Lord my God' (Ps. 38:12-15) but 'Those who spread slander and those who listen to them, those who give false witness, deserve to be thrown to the dogs' (b.Pes. 118a).

The judicial system tried not to convict. For any case which could incur the death penalty, there had to be a majority of two to convict; if there was a majority of only one, the judge was not allowed to add his vote for conviction, but he could do so for acquittal. There are many warnings against false witness. It was wrong to try to procure a witness in your own favour or persuade someone to witness untruthfully for you and, as this was not an unknown occurrence, one is advised to be very careful about signing any document (Mek.Kas. 2).

Such an unforgiving man would be advised to stop and think before things have gone too far. Come to terms: be reconciled while you still can. Better to suffer loss in this world than end up for ever in hell. As the rabbis said about Lev. 16:30, 'From all your sins you shall be clean before the Lord', it was necessary to be reconciled with an opponent before atonement is possible (b.Yom. 85b); and 'When a man owes money to another he is apt to say, "Let us go and try our case before a judge;" who at times succeeds in making peace between them and at times does not. In any event, both are not likely to come away satisfied' (PRK 18:6).

It was Roman, not Jewish, law that a debtor could be imprisoned, as was the use of a single judge. See also D 10.

* * *

C 7. The tower builder and the king facing the threat of battle - Lk. 14:28-32.

Jesus had spoken before about what appeared to be a lack of progress in bringing in God's kingdom (see C 3), but the topic came up more than once. The disciples were not at all convinced. Satan and his forces seemed to be everywhere and powerful too; there was plenty of wickedness about and by no means all who came to hear Jesus were persuaded to join him. How then could Jesus be so sure it would all work out in the end?

Luke has two short parables which show what could have been Jesus' answers to this question.

Jesus said to them, "Would any of you start to build a tower without first sitting down and calculating the cost and whether you have the resources to complete it? Otherwise you could finish the foundations, but no more, and you would be a laughing-stock: 'That's the fellow who started to build but could not finish', they would say.

Or again, what king will march to battle against another king without first sitting down to consider whether with ten thousand men he can face an enemy coming to meet him with twenty thousand? If he cannot, then long before the enemy approaches , he will send envoys and ask for terms."

A common misunderstanding of these two parables is that one should count the cost before one begins to follow Jesus. It is supposed that its message is like that of the Greek philosopher Epictetus: 'In every affair consider what precedes and what follows and then undertake it. Otherwise you will begin with spirit but not having thought of the consequences, when some of them appear, you will shamefully desist.'

This is a good example of an interpretation which is not in accordance with the rest of the gospels. It is necessary to trace the connections between these parables and the O.T. and the I.T. literature in order to understand them correctly.

The tower has many connections: the tower of Babel, a watchtower, a stronghold for the weak, a storehouse, the Temple, Jerusalem, etc. As a refuge, it represents God, who will succour the faithful in time of war: 'But I shall be as one who enters a fortified city, as one who seeks refuge behind a high wall until deliverance comes ... For you will set the foundations on rock ... to build a mighty wall which will not sway ... For no enemy shall invade it ... and its bars shall be firm and no man shall break them' (DSS, H 10). In the messianic new kingdom, everyone will use a language that all understand: 'At that time, I will change the speech of the peoples to a pure speech that all of them may call on the name of the Lord and serve him with one accord' (Zph. 3:9).

God with Wisdom has designed and planned his tower or house. He laid the foundations of the world; he knows the opposition on the way: 'By your Wisdom all things exist from eternity and before creating them you knew their works for eternity'

(DSS, H 1).

God planned and costed the whole building, and he was not one to begin a project without being able to finish it: 'By Wisdom a house is constructed, by understanding it is founded; by knowledge its storerooms (towers) are filled with all wealth that is precious and pleasant ... A mighty hero is wise in his strength and a man of knowledge summons up power. For by wise counsel you may conduct war successfully and victory or salvation lies in the greatness of a rich mind which gives counsel' (Pvb. 24:3-6); 'Unless the Lord builds the house, those who build it labour in vain' (Ps. 127:1).

There is another link between the two parables. The word for 'tower' can also mean a column of troops in battle array. A king, who may be numerically inferior, could be militarily superior if his army fights for and with God: 'When you go forth to war against your enemies and see horses, chariots and an army larger than your own, you shall not be afraid of them, for the Lord your God is with you...' (Dt. 20:1); 'If I whet my glittering sword and my hand takes hold of judgement, I will take vengeance on my adversaries and requite those who hate me' (Dt. 32:41-42); 'One man puts to flight a thousand, since it is the Lord your God who fights for you ...' (Jos. 23:10).

Thus another king would be wise to think twice before attacking. He may appear to have a stronger force, but that is an illusion. When he receives an offer of terms, he would do well to accept it. Asa, with an army of half a million men defeated the Ethiopians with one million because he called on the Lord: 'O Lord, you are God; let not man prevail against you' (II Chr. 14:11); 'A king is not saved by his great army' (Ps. 33:16).

God would never put himself into the position of having to ask for peace terms. God's army need have no fears about the outcome. If they have faith in God's word all will go well, but they can not retain links with their former worldly lives. They must, as disciples, apostles and followers of Jesus, commit themselves fully. Only such were fit to be the elite front-line troops (see E 4). Even if there were only a few of the faithful, victory was assured.

Jesus called those with faith, not those who calculated the pros and cons, the odds for or against success. Nor does Jesus suggest one must have all the necessary powers in one's hand before one helps to fight evil. With God's support, a man can do anything; without God's help, man can do nothing.

The emphasis is not on Jewish nationalist conquest or prestige, but on the war against sin, in order to bring about the kingdom of God on earth.

* * *

C 8. Signs of the coming of the kingdom - Mt. 12:38-42;16:1-4. Mk. 8: 11-13. Lk. 11:16, 29-32; 12:54-57; 17: 20-21.

There are several occasions recorded in the gospels when Jesus was asked when the day of Judgement would happen, the Messiah come and the kingdom of God be fully established. Each time Jesus refused to consider the question a proper one, partly perhaps because he knew that those who put the question would not accept the answer anyway.

The Pharisees questioned Jesus about when the kingdom of God would come, and Jesus answered, "You will not be able to tell if the kingdom of God has come by observation. There will be no question of 'Here it is' or 'There it is', because it is within you."

The passage relates to an O.T. text in which Israel is first promised God's blessings if she obeys God's commandments, and then continues: 'For this commandment which I lay on you this day is not too hard for you, neither is it too remote. It is not in heaven ... nor is it beyond the sea ... But the word is very near you; it is in your mouth and in your heart, and in your hands to do it.' (Dt. 30:11-14). The prophets also say that God's commandments will be within the Israelites when he writes the new covenant upon their hearts: 'This is the covenant I will make with the house of Israel after those days, says the Lord: I will put my Law within them, and I will write it upon their hearts ...' (Jer. 31:33); 'A new heart I will give you, and a new spirit I will put within you; I will take out your heart of stone and give you a heart of flesh. I will put my spirit within you and cause you to walk in my statutes and be careful to observe my ordinances' (Ezk. 36:26-27).

In many places in the gospels, the message was that God's reign was observable to any with faith, who were open to see the signs of its presence, but in rabbinical literature there was the belief that one would never find the messiah, treasure or scorpions if you lie in wait for them. The messiah will come when one's attention is on something else, when you are not expecting it (b.San.97a).

There has been much argument whether the last clause means 'it is within you' or 'it is amongst you'. In classical Greek, and in the writings of the Church Fathers, the word is not used elsewhere to mean 'amongst', and the meaning of the passage seems to be that anyone is capable of discerning the signs of the Kingdom, so that searching for outward signs of it shows the person lacks the faith to see it.

Again the Pharisees came to test him. "Show us a sign from heaven," they said. Jesus groaned inwardly, and replied, "Why do you people ask for a sign? It is a wicked generation that asks for a sign; the only one to be given is that of Jonah; he was a sign to the Ninevites; likewise I and my gospel shall be to this unbelieving generation. Even the Ninevites listened to Jonah and repented, and the Queen of the South came from the ends of the earth to hear the wisdom of Solomon.

They will both witness against this generation on the day of Judgement when the men of this generation are on trial. Their condemnation is ensured. What is here is far greater than either Jonah or Solomon."

Jonah went to the heathen town of Nineveh to tell them God's word and their repentance and acceptance of God's covenant saved them from the destruction which had been planned for them: 'So Jonah arose and went to Nineveh according to the word of the Lord ... When God saw what they did, how they turned from their evil ways, God repented and did not bring on them the evil he had threatened' (Jon. 3:3,10). The people and the king of Nineveh heard the word of God from Jonah; 'they proclaimed a fast and everyone ... put on sackcloth' (Jon.3:5) and were converted by Jonah's message.

The Queen of the South or Sheba, a Gentile, came to learn the true way from Solomon: 'The Queen of Sheba came to test him with hard questions ... and Solomon answered all her questions; none of them was too difficult for him to answer' (II Chr. 9:1-2).

It was the mission of Jesus which was the sign of Jonah, the only relevant sign for his contemporaries. He brought the word of God but it seemed that pagans would respond before the Jews. The latter were hard-hearted and unwilling to repent and change, opposite to the men of Nineveh. On the day of Judgement these, with the Queen, would witness against those who listened but would not understand, the people of Israel (see J 2).

Jesus continued, "When it is late in the day and the sky is red and blushing, you say it will be fine; or if it is red and angry early on, you say it will be stormy. When you see cloud rising up in the west you say rain is coming and when the wind is from the south you tell us it will be scorching hot!" You hypocrites can discern the face of the heavens. Why do you not know how to discern the face of heaven at this fateful time?

This passage has in it a pun on 'the face of heaven'. By this is meant the face of God and the point is that the people were clever at reading the meteorological signs in the sky, the face of the heavens, but they were totally unable to read God's face showing divine favour or divine wrath. Many O.T. passages testify to this concept: 'May God be gracious to us and bless us and make his face shine upon us, that his ways may be known on earth ...' (Ps. 67:1-2); 'You have said, "Seek my face", and my heart says, "Your face Lord, do I seek"; hide not your face from me' (Ps. 27:8). Also in I.T. books: 'Now we follow you with all our heart, we fear you and seek your face' (P.Az. 18).

The picture of clouds bringing rain is similar to the story about Elijah: 'At the seventh time, the servant said, "Behold a little cloud like a man's hand is rising out of the sea." Elijah said, "Go up, say to Ahab, Prepare your chariot and go down lest the rain stop you." And in a little while, the heavens grew black with clouds and wind and there was great rain.' (I Kgs. 18:44-45).

There was plenty of evidence to see, since it was accepted in Judaism that healing of lepers and raising of the dead were very clear signs of the kingdom of God. To ask for any further sign or to ask when the kingdom would come demonstrated that the questioners were unwilling to follow their own teaching. They were blind and unwise: 'The heavens are telling the glory of God and the vault of heaven reveals his handwork' (Ps. 19:1); 'The instruction of the Lord is certain, making wise the simple' (Ps. 19:7); 'The mind of a wise man will know the time and way, for every matter has its time and way ...' (Ecc. 8:5-6).

In many places the gospels make it plain that the words and deeds of Jesus were a clear sign of the kingdom of God on earth, yet in these passages the religious leaders are refused a sign with groaning distress and anger. The language used, especially by Mark, shows that the sign wanted was one direct from God and not like other manifestations of Jesus' work. They were wanting to know whether the final salvation was come and what was going to happen in accordance with O.T. teaching: '...the Lord has given me signs and portents in Israel...' (Is. 8:18); and '...for I have made you a sign for Israel' (Ezk. 12:6).

The sign was also 'for this generation', that is for those who expected Jesus to become a great king of Israel, expelling the oppressor and restoring Israel to its rightful place in the world. That the sign was given means that it belonged to the category of those given by false messiahs who claimed to be sent by God but who were false leaders.

Rabbinical literature gives an idea of the way in which the religious leaders responded. Their scepticism was boundless and they were not impressed by so-called "miracles", as the following story shows:

'Two rabbis disputed together. The first, R. Eliezer, tried to impress his opponents, R. Joshua and his friends. Eliezer said, "If I am right, may this tree move a hundred yards from its present place." It did so, but the others said, 'You cannot get proof from trees'. So Eliezer ordered the stream to prove he was right, and the water began to flow backwards. But, again, the opponents said that no more than trees could water prove anything.

Eliezer then told the walls of the house to prove it, and they bent inwards until the house was about to fall down. Joshua rebuked the walls and they reduced their bending, so Eliezer then said, "Let the heavens prove it." Then a voice was heard from heaven saying, "What have you all against Eliezer? His view is right." Then said Joshua, "We pay no attention to a heavenly voice. The Law was given to us on Sinai and then we were told, 'by a majority you shall decide'" (b. B.M. 59b).

There is much in these passages that suggests that they have been written or modified by later editors.

* * *

C 9. The weeds among the wheat - Mt. 13:24-30, 36-43.

It was a prevalent Jewish dream at the time that all sinners would be eradicated when the Messiah came and the kingdom of God was inaugurated:: 'The furnace of Gehenna shall appear and opposite, the paradise of delight. Then shall the Most High say to the nations "Behold, here delight and refreshment, there fire and torments"' (IV Ezr. 7:36-38); 'Into darkness ... and a burning flame ... shall your (sinners') spirits enter' (I En. 103:8); 'There shall be no escape for the guilty of heart ... they shall be utterly trampled down without any remnant' (DSS, H 10); 'A little while and the wicked shall be no more; look well, and you will find their place empty' (Ps. 37:10). In a rabbinical passage we find that: 'If all Israel repented one day, the Messiah would come immediately' (b.Keth.111b, a comment on Dt. 23:14).

How could Jesus hope to see God's kingdom here on earth unless evils like the Roman occupation were removed? And evil-doers: they must be totally eliminated. Why not make a start straight away? There was enough to be going on with, yet Jesus didn't seem to be anxious to exterminate those who were quite uninterested in the kingdom or in changing their ways. Surely Jesus wanted to purify Israel, and create a community of Holy Saints? Then all nations would come to Jerusalem to acknowledge the primacy of Israel and learn God's rule there: 'All nations you have made shall come and bow down before you, O Lord, and glorify your name' (Ps. 86:9); 'Then every nation that attacked Jerusalem shall come up year after year to worship the King, the Lord of Hosts, and keep the pilgrim feast of Tabernacles' (Zch. 14:16); and in I.T. books: "There will be one aeon and all the righteous ... will live eternally and then there will be neither labour, nor sickness, nor humiliation, nor anxiety, nor need, nor violence, nor night, nor darkness, but great light' (II En. 65:8-9).

"The kingdom of God has (already) become like this," said Jesus. "There was once a farmer who sowed his field with good seed, but while all were asleep his enemy came and sowed darnel among the wheat.

When the corn sprouted and the ears began to fill out, the darnel could be seen among the wheat. The farm-workers went to their master and said, 'Sir, was it not good seed you sowed in your field? Where then has the darnel come from?'

'This is an enemy's doing,' the farmer replied.

'Shall we go and pull out the weeds?', they asked.

'No,' he answered, 'lest in pulling them up you might uproot the wheat too. Let them both grow until the harvest. Then I will tell the reapers to gather the darnel first and tie it in bundles for burning. The wheat they can collect afterwards and put it into my barn.'

Jesus then dismissed the people and explained the parable to his disciples. 'The sower of the good seed is the son of man who sows it in the world. The good seed stands for the sons of the kingdom while the darnel represents the sons of Satan. At the harvest, on the day

of Judgement, the son of man will send out his angels
who will gather up from the kingdom all causes of sin,
and all whose deeds are evil. They will be thrown into
the furnace, the place of wailing and grinding of teeth.
Then the righteous will shine brightly as the sun in the
kingdom of their Father. If you have ears, hear."

Darnel (perhaps a kind of rye-grass) is a weed which is identical in appearance to wheat plants until the ears begin to form on the wheat, but not on the weed. Perhaps it is intended to mean that it is similarly nearly impossible to distinguish between true people of God and false believers, until one can see what kind of fruit they produce. Eventually, when the time is ripe, the harvest will occur, and the good will be separated from the bad, on the day of Judgement: 'Behold the day comes, says the Lord of Hosts ... when all the arrogant and wicked will be stubble and the day comes that shall set them ablaze, leaving them neither root nor branch' (Mal. 4:1).

It is not for men to try to separate them before then. God's plan decides when the time of harvesting is ripe and on the day of Judgement the wheat and the weeds will be separated. Compare this story with those of the separation of the sheep and goats (B 4), and the good and bad fish. (C 10).

It has been suggested that this parable is Matthew's equivalent to the story of the seed growing automatically (C 3) which occurs only in Mark. There are grounds for thinking that Matthew himself, if not created, at least elaborated this passage.

* * *

C 10. The seine net - Mt. 13:47-50.

This story depicts what appears to be Jesus' viewpoint about one of the topics which caused much controversy, namely, the place of non-Jews in the world to come. There was more than one opinion. Some thought all Jews would enter Paradise: 'Then he (the Lord) will raise a signal to the nations and gather together those driven out of Israel; he will assemble Judah's scattered people from the four corners of the earth' (Is. 11:12); 'I will gather them from amongst the Gentiles ...' (Jub. 1:15); 'As heaven is purer in the Lord's sight than the earth, so are you, the lights of Israel purer than all the Gentiles' (T.Lev. 14:3-4). All non-Jews would be destroyed: 'Behold, I am against you, Pharaoh, the great dragon that lies in the midst of his streams, that says, "My Nile is my own; it was I who made it." I the Lord God will put hooks on your jaws and make the fish of your streams cling to your sides; and I will draw you up out of the midst of your streams ... You shall fall upon the open field and not be gathered and buried. To the beasts of the earth and to the birds of the air I have given you as food' (Ezk. 29:3-5).

Others thought it was God's will that the gospel should be brought to the non-Jews and that God would bring in the day of Judgement only when all Gentiles had had an opportunity to accept or reject his redemption: 'He (the son of man) shall be the light of the Gentiles and hope of those who are troubled of heart' (I En. 48:4); 'There shall be given to you a blessing and to all your seed, until the Lord visits the Gentiles in his tender mercies for ever' (T.Lev. 4:4); '... the Gentiles shall be multiplied in knowledge of the earth and enlightened by the grace of the Lord' (T.Lev. 18:9); 'The Lord shall bring back all the Gentiles into zeal for him' (T.Zeb. 9:8); 'All kings shall worship him and all Gentiles shall serve him' (Ps. 72:11 LXX); 'Keep the commandments of God, until the Lord shall reveal his salvation to all Gentiles' (T.Ben. 10:5). In rabbinical writing it is expressed even more strongly: "I call heaven and earth to witness that whether it be Gentile or Israelite, man or woman, slave or handmaid, according to the deeds which he does, so will the Holy Spirit rest upon him." (T.d.E 48)

"Here's another illustration," said Jesus. "The kingdom of the heavens is like a net let down in the sea. All kinds of things were caught in it. When it was full, they pulled the net on to the shore, and sitting down, collected the good into containers, but cast out the rotten. That is how it will be at the end of time; the angels will separate the evil men from the midst of the righteous, and cast them into the blazing furnace, with wailing and gnashing of teeth."

It is uncertain if and how much this passage has been edited later. Some say that the last sentence was added by the evangelist or the early church; others deny this. It is not a simple matter to decide just what it was intended to teach, but it is known that it has strong connections with Ezekiel: 'The Lord God said to me, "This water flows out to the region lying east, and down to the Arabah; at last it will reach that sea whose water are foul, and they will be sweetened. When any one of the living creatures that swarm upon the earth comes where the torrent flows, everything shall live. From En-gledi as far as En-eglaim fishermen shall stand on its shores, for nets shall be spread there. Every kind of fish shall be there in shoals, like the fish of the Great Sea; but its swamps and pools shall not have their waters sweetened but shall be left as salt-pans. Beside the torrent on either bank all trees good for food shall spring up. Their leaves shall not wither, their fruit shall not cease; they shall bear early every month. For their water comes from the sanctuary; their fruit is for food and their foliage for enjoyment"' (Ezk. 47:8-12).

In this passage, the fresh water of the spring represents the 'water of life' from the sanctuary, which gives life to everything that swims in it. The foul water is the salt water of the Dead sea in which fish die and rot. They have not received the water of life. It also underlines the fruitfulness of the messianic age and the kingdom of God on earth: all the trees will give foliage and fruit all the time (See also C 5).

Zechariah has similar teaching: 'On that day living water shall issue from Jerusalem to the eastern and to the western seas, in summer and winter alike. Then the Lord shall become king over all the earth.' (Zch. 14:8-9).

There seem to be two main lessons to be drawn from the story: first that the gospel must be broadcast, that is proclaimed to all, Jew and Gentile, neighbour and foreigner, and not limited to those who accept it. There is every reason to mix with all sorts of people in the world. Second, it was intended to suggest that in the new community of believers there will be both good and bad, and it is only on the day of Judgement that they will be separated by God himself. (See also C 9.)

* * *

C 11. Places at a wedding feast - Lk. 14:7-10.

It was expected that in the messianic age the righteous would be invited to a great feast, and the following parable shows that it is for God to assign his guests to their places, and no one else should presume to decide this.

When Jesus noticed how guests were trying to secure the places of honour, he told them a parable.
   "When you are invited to the wedding festivities do not recline in the best place. Perhaps someone more distinguished is invited and then the host will come and ask you to give your place to the newcomer. Then you will feel shame and begin to take the lowest place. No, when you receive an invitation, go to the lowest place, so that when the host comes in he will say, 'Friend, go up higher'. Then you shall have glory in the presence of those who eat with you."

This is not a homily on decent manners at a party. Nor is it simply an exhortation that the humble shall be exalted while the exalted shall be abased, a common enough adage at the time, both in the O.T. and rabbinical literature: 'Do not put yourself forward in the king's presence or stand in the place of the great, for it is better to be told: "Come up here" than to be put lower, in the presence of the prince' (Pvb. 25:6-7 and b.M.K. 28b); 'Go two or three seats lower and take your place until you are told, "Come up", rather than go up and they say to you, "Go down"' (Lev.R. 1:5). That it is a wedding banquet, and that the guest who is invited to go to a higher place is glorified, points directly to the messianic feast in the world to come after the day of Judgement. The highest place will be filled by God and it was not to be taken by anyone else. The message is like that given in response to the request of James and John when they asked for the two best places at the 'top table' (E 2).

There are parallels with the story of the anointing of Saul by Samuel. Saul and his servant seek for the prophet or seer, who will tell them about their journey, and they are told they should hurry because he has just arrived and is on his way to the high place to bless the sacrifice or feast: '... for the people will not eat till he comes since he must bless the sacrifice' (I Sam. 9:13). Now Samuel has been warned by God that the one who shall seek him is to be anointed a prince over Israel. Saul exclaims, 'Am I not a Benjaminite, from the least of the tribes of Israel? Is not my family the humblest of all the families of our tribe...?' Then Samuel took Saul and his servant and brought them into the hall and gave them places at the head of those who had been invited' (I Sam. 9:21-22).

The parable pictures the time when those who have fought for God's kingdom against the forces of evil are invited to the victory banquet, and God would show them to their rightful places at the table.

There was a recognized custom in those days as to the placing of guests at a feast: 'When there are two couches, the more important guest reclines first, and the other above him; when there are three the chief guest takes the middle one, the next important the one above him and the third, the one below him' (b.Ber. 46b). The reason for this was that when lying on couches the heads of the first and second guests would be together, while the head of the third guest would be by the feet of the first.

* * *

C 12. An undivided kingdom - Mt. 9:34; 10:25; 12:22-28. Mk. 3:22-26. Lk. 11:14-15,17-20.

At least some of the religious leaders supported the Jewish dream that there was no possibility for God's realm to become manifest until Israel was triumphant. Jesus should be supporting the pious, righteous ones against the corrupt ones, until God's chosen people were purged and perfected. Satan could not be defeated by casting out demons; they would simply find another home somewhere else. It was obvious: Jesus was a miracle-working impostor and probably himself possessed by Satan to divert attention from the primary task - getting rid of foreign domination.

Jesus cured a man of his dumbness and the bystanders had been amazed, but the doctors of the Law, who had come down from Jerusalem, said, "It is by Beelzebub, the prince of demons, that he casts out demons."

Jesus guessed their thoughts, and pointed out that any kingdom or household divided against itself goes to ruin. "If it is Satan that casts out his own demons," said Jesus, "Satan is divided against himself; how then can Satan's kingdom remain intact? Again, if I cast out demons by Beelzebub, by whom do your sons cast them out? They shall be your judges.

But if it is by the Spirit of God that I drive out the unclean spirits, then you must acknowledge that God's kingdom came upon you."

In I.T. books, demons were pictured as being fallen angels, causing all the sin in the world, and it will not be until the day of Judgement that they will finally be removed or destroyed: '... the name of the first, Jeqon, who led astray the sons of God ... The second, Asbeel, gave the sons of God evil counsel ... The third, Gadreel, showed the children of men all the blows ... and all the weapons of death ... The fourth, Penemue, taught men the bitter and the sweet and the secrets of wisdom. He instructed mankind in writing ... and thereby many sinned ...' (I En. 69:4-11); '... the unclean demons began to lead astray the sons of Noah and to make them err, and to destroy them.' (Jub. 10:1).

Satan and his demons were thought of as a kind of counter-kingdom of sin, opposed to God and his kingdom, so it would be strange for Satan to reduce his own population and kingdom. On the contrary, Jesus had driven out the demons by God's Spirit, the only means to accomplish this.

In the O.T., Satan was the accuser or God's adversary: 'Then he showed me Joshua the High Priest standing before the angel of the Lord, and Satan standing at his right hand to accuse him' (Zch. 3:1); 'Set a sinner against him and let the devil stand at his right hand (to accuse him)' (Ps. 109:6); see also the first two chapters of Job and C6.

Luke uses the phrase, 'the finger of God' instead of 'the Spirit of God'. This recalls Moses receiving the two tablets of the Law: 'And the Lord gave me two tables of stone written with the finger of God' (Dt. 9:10), and Luke may wish to imply that God was again intervening directly through Jesus. He was casting out the adversary's demons, and thus showing that the kingdom of God was present among them. Just as God had given his words to Moses, so had God given his message to this new Moses-like prophet who had been awaited so long.

A house divided against itself goes to ruin. This was something important for the disciples and Jesus' followers to remember. In unity, they were strong, but separated they would become easy prey for their opponents.

It is well documented that much exorcism was practised in the ancient world and it is still practised on the basis that the exorcist, becoming possessed by the chief of the sufferer's demon, can order the demon to leave the sufferer. In Christian circles, it is the Holy Spirit which is the stronger and which could cast out demons. The idea is also found in I.T. literature: 'Beliar (Satan) shall be bound by him (Messiah) and he shall give power to his children to tread upon evil spirits' (T.Lev. 18:12).

* * *

C 13. Satan must be bound first - Mt. 12:29. Mk. 3:27. Lk. 11:21-22.

"No one can break into a strong man's house and steal his goods unless someone stronger has first bound him fast. Then the stronger carries off his weapons and defences and ransacks the house."

God was overcoming Satan's defences and rescuing those imprisoned in Satan's house. When the Holy Spirit expelled demons through Jesus, Satan's kingdom was pillaged, thus enhancing the kingdom of God, the two kingdoms being opposed to one another (see C 12): 'Can his prey be taken from the strong man or the captive rescued from a tyrant? The Lord answers, "Even the captives of the mighty shall be taken ... I will contend with all who contend against you and save your children from them"' (Is. 49:24-25); 'There shall arise from the tribe of Levi the salvation of the Lord to you, and he shall war against Satan, execute an everlasting vengeance on our enemies ... and turn disobedient hearts to the Lord' (T.Dan. 5:10-11); 'No man can take spoil from a mighty man' (P.S. 5:4).

* * *

C 14. A prayer - Mt. 11:25-27. Lk. 10:21-22.

Was it possible for ordinary people to understand what God's message was, or did one have to have special training to do so? Was it like the Judaism of the time, where a very long apprenticeship was necessary? Jesus did not think so. Matthew and Luke relate the following prayer of Jesus after the missionaries returned from their journeys.

Jesus said, "I thank you Father, Lord of heaven and earth, for hiding these things from the learned and wise, and revealing them to the unlearned. Yes, Father, such was your good pleasure. Everything is entrusted to me by my Father and no one attains to an understanding of who is the Son except the Father, and no one fully knows who is the Father except the Son, and those to whom the Son chooses to reveal him."

The phrase, 'such was your good pleasure' is understood in rabbinical books as meaning, 'may it be well pleasing in your sight' (j.Ber. 7d).

Some think the passage does not mean that the stupid and uneducated are the only ones who can grasp Jesus' message, though of course it is sometimes true that convictions are much more effectively defended by intellectuals. The point is that the message is so obvious that simple, humble people, those with ears, eyes and hearts to hear, see and respond, can readily accept the message. It is not necessary to have had higher education to detect if a man is righteous or not, and God's fellowship is not to be found in the precise findings of the doctors of the Law.

On the other hand there are connections with earlier teaching. It is only those who belong to the kingdom of God who can know Wisdom. In the O.T. this idea is common: 'Wisdom ... is hidden from the eyes of all living ... God understands the way to it and he knows its place' (Job 28:20,23). In some places Wisdom is pictured sitting at the door of her house and inviting in passers by: 'You that are simple, turn in here!' (Pvb. 9:4).

Other passages proclaim that all who will can know God's word: 'The testimony of the Lord is sure, making wise the simple' (Ps. 19:7); 'Your word is revealed and all is light; it gives understanding even to the untaught' (Ps. 119:130); 'Therefore behold, I will proceed to remove this people ... I will destroy the wisdom of the wise, and hide the understanding of the prudent' (Is. 29:14 LXX).

In I.T. writings: 'Humble yourself in all greatness and you will find grace in the sight of God. Many are exalted and esteemed, but the mysteries of God are revealed to the lowly ... To the humble he reveals his secret (or: by the humble he is glorified)' (Sir. 3:18-20). The Qumran Thanksgiving Hymns begin with a very similar prayer: 'By your wisdom all things exist from eternity, and before creating them you knew their works for ever and ever. Nothing is done without you and nothing is known unless you desire it' (DSS, H:1).

Jesus was delighted that his disciples had met with a positive response among the people of the countryside even if the religious leaders were unwilling to recognize the value of Jesus' teaching. One of the basic assumptions of his message was that all are potentially God's priests and servants.

The authenticity of the last sentence has been a cause of doubt and rejection for many, not least because of the use of the phrase 'the Son'. Some suppose it is possible that Jesus spoke of himself in this way, but there are good reasons for thinking that in this passage the word 'Son' means 'Wisdom'. Wisdom was believed to have existed before the creation and was God himself, or a being like his son, or sometimes his wife or queen: 'When God established the heavens, I (Wisdom) was there; ... when he made firm the skies above ... when he assigned limits to the sea ... when he marked out the foundations of the earth, then I was beside him like a master workman ...' (Pvb. 8:27-30); 'When I (God) had finished all, I told my Wisdom to create me man' (II En. 30:8); 'Before all was Wisdom created ...' (Sir. 1:4); 'It is given to Wisdom to live with God, and the Sovereign Lord of all loved her' (W.S. 8:3); 'She, though but one, has power to do all things' (W.S. 7:27); 'Give me Wisdom, her that sits beside you on your throne' (W.S. 9:4).

Alternatively, some thought the Father was God and the Son was Israel: 'The honour due to the Father (God) as well as the honour due to the Son (Israel) ...' (Mek. Pis. 1).

There is an interesting similarity between this part of the passage and the O.T. story of Moses who said to the Lord, '... if I have found favour in your sight, show me your ways that I may know you ...' (Ex. 33:13); 'Thus the Lord used to speak to Moses face-to-face as a man speaks to his friend' (Ex. 33:11). Thus it may be that the evangelists show Jesus as a new Moses, (see also the next passage), or it could also be the title 'Son' was given to Jesus when the early church was in the process of differentiating from Judaism.

* * *

C 15. The light yoke - Mt. 11:28-30.

Passages in the O.T., and in I.T. and rabbinical books, condemn Israel for not submitting to God's yoke, the yoke of the Torah, or encourage her to take it up again: 'Every one who receives upon him the yoke of Torah, they remove from him the yoke of government and the yoke of worldly occupation. And every one who breaks off from himself the yoke of Torah, they lay upon him the yoke of government and the yoke of worldly occupation'. The Qumran community had the same idea but expressed it differently: 'God has created man to govern the world and has appointed two spirits in which to walk until the time of his visitation: the spirits of truth and injustice. Those born of truth spring from a fountain of light but those born of injustice spring from a source of darkness' (DSS, CR. 3:17-18).

The Law was not a burden to Jews: 'How I love the Law! It is my meditation all the day!' (Ps. 119:97); 'Great peace have those who love your Law; nothing can make them stumble' (Ps. 119:165). Taking the yoke of God was, for the Jew, a joyful and voluntary surrender to the entire will of God as he understood it. God's yoke breaks the burden of sin: 'I (God) have broken the bars of your yoke and made you walk erect' (Lev. 26:13), it gives respite from constant labour, and under it all the humble and lowly in Israel would be gathered together.

Jesus said, "Come to me all you labouring and burdened and I will give you rest. Take my easy yoke and my light burden and learn from me. I am meek and lowly in heart, and with me you will find repose for your souls."

The passage has connections with O.T. and I.T. books: 'With a yoke on our necks we are driven hard, we are weary, we are given no rest' (Lam. 5:5). The people had rebelled and had to suffer the consequences: 'Long ago you broke your yoke and burst your bonds and said, "I will not serve"' (Jer. 2:20); 'Because you did not serve the Lord with joyfulness... therefore you shall serve your enemies ... and he will put a yoke of iron upon your neck ...' (Dt. 28:47-48); 'They have rejected my commandments and my yoke ...' (II En. 34:1); 'I see many of your people who have withdrawn from your covenant and cast from them the yoke of your Law' (II Bar. 41:3). Here, the infidelity of Israel is pointed out, but in other places the faithful are encouraged to seek the true path: 'Thus says the Lord ... ask for the ancient paths where the good way is and walk in it and find rest for your souls' (Jer. 6:16); 'The Lord will come at once and break loose the yoke ... as it is said, " I have broken the bars of your yoke"' (Midr.Ps. 129; 1,3,4).

The passage has often been associated with the I.T. book of Ben Sira, in which he speaks of the yoke of Wisdom: "Acquire Wisdom for yourselves, without money; bend your necks under her yoke and let your soul bear her burden."' (Sir. 51:23,25-26); 'Bring your feet into her (Wisdom's) fetters and put her chain round your neck. Bow down, put your shoulder under her to carry her and do not chafe under her bonds.' (Sir. 6:24-25); 'Come to me who desire me, and eat your fill of my fruits' (Sir. 24:19); 'Her yoke is a golden ornament ... you will wear her like a splendid crown [of gladness]' (Sir. 6:30-31).

However, it seems more correct to think that for Matthew, Jesus in this passage was not Wisdom incarnate, but the shepherd who gathers Israel, breaks the yoke of sinfulness, and brings rest. As God had promised: 'I will leave in your midst a people humble and lowly ... the remnant of Israel. They shall do no wrong and utter no lies ... they will feed and lie down and none shall terrify them' (Zph. 3:12-13). The passage is also one in which Jesus is likened to a new Moses: 'Moses was very meek, more than all men that were on the face of the earth' (Num. 12:3).

* * *

C. Summary.

No society has all good or all bad members and Jesus would not encourage hopes of political or military changes by divine or other agency. Those who wanted to begin to cultivate a new plot of land, sow it and produce fruit from it, must have trust that God will look after it, and although enemies will come to spoil their work, God will give his servants shelter, food, healing and security and will reward them generously.

The faithful ones helped to bring the day of harvest, the day of Judgement, nearer when God would separate the righteous and the wicked, who would depart to their respective fates. That day was known to God alone, and then the righteous ones would sit down to the messianic feast.

Satan and the demons of his kingdom belonged to the desert but they would be overthrown on the day of Judgement. Then the world would revert to its sinless state as it had been in the Garden of Eden, with plants and trees which would fruit continuously and plentifully. At present, according to one passage, there were no righteous people in Israel, no ripe figs at all, while the words of Jesus are given as being very like those God spoke to Moses. The intention is to show Jesus making a new beginning bringing in the New Era of perfection, God's reign in his own kingdom.

Some might think nothing was happening, but underneath changes were occurring. The process was already at work: the signs were there and the kingdom of God was within and amongst people. It shows in conduct promoting forgiveness and reconciliation. It shows in a refusal to bear a grudge or nurse anger and hatred, and it requires faith based on commitment not on calculation.

The kingdom of God was not only for Jews. All who followed God's will were welcome into his realm.

One quotation suggests that the Messiah would be of the tribe of Levi, and it is not correct to say that all were agreed he would be of David's line.

D. The characteristics of God and his kingdom.

D 1. Good and bad foundations - Mt. 7:24-27. Lk. 6:46-49.

Jesus again (see B 2) protests about those who use the double name 'Lord, Lord'. They were talking as though they understood that the day of Judgement was near and God would come to earth, but their actions did not match their words. Like some of their forefathers against whom Jeremiah had warned: 'Do not trust in these deceptive words - this is the temple of the Lord, the temple of the Lord, the temple of the Lord' (Jer. 7:4), they proclaimed a great deal but made no attempt to behave according to God's Law.

"Why do you keep calling me 'Lord, Lord'?, said Jesus. "You hear what I say, but you do not act upon my words. Those who come to me, listen to my message and act upon it - what will they be like? They will be like a prudent man who built his house on foundations dug deep into the solid rock. The winds blew, storms smote the house, the river flooded over, but it was strong and secure. Those who hear, but ignore what I say - they will be like a man who built his house on the ground without foundations. As soon as the rains came, or the river flooded, the whole house collapsed to total ruin."

To Jews, to build a house, also meant to study the Torah, so that without such a firm foundation of God's word no building or understanding could survive: 'You will set the foundations of rock and the framework by the measuring cord of justice ... to build a mighty wall which shall not sway. O Lord, you have made me like a strong tower and have established my edifice upon rock' (DSS, H 10,11).

Similar ideas are to be found in the O.T., where the storm is a sign of divine punishment: 'Therefore thus says the Lord God, "In my rage I will unleash a stormy wind; rain will come in torrents in my anger, hailstones hard as rock in my fury, until all is destroyed ... I will demolish the building ... so that its foundations are laid bare. It shall fall and you shall be destroyed within it"' (Ezk. 13:13-14); 'Hail will sweep away the refuge of liars and water will overwhelm their shelter' (Is. 28:17).

Those, on the other hand who try to follow God's rules, can expect to be blessed: 'If you truly amend your ways and your doings, if you truly act justly one with another, if you do not oppress the alien, the orphan, and the widow, or shed innocent blood in this place and do not go after other gods, ... then I will dwell with you in this place, in the land that I gave of old to your ancestors forever and ever' (Jer. 7:5-7).

The passage suggests that those who ignore Jesus' teaching will never enter the kingdom of God: 'Those who build unrighteousness and oppression and lay deceit as a foundation ... shall suddenly be overthrown' (I En. 94:6); but those who heed his words will build a house which will last: 'They shall build up the ancient ruins ... repair the ruined cities, the devastations of many generations' (Is. 61:4).

In rabbinical writings too, the same meaning is expressed, though wrapped in a little story: 'Whoever has knowledge of the Law greater than his deeds, to what is he like? He is like a tree with many branches and few roots, and the wind comes and uproots it ... But whoever shows by his actions that they are greater than his knowledge of the Law, to what is he like? He is like a tree with few branches and many roots, which, even if all the winds of world blow on it, they cannot disturb it' (m.Avot. 3:22).

* * *

D 2. The grateful forgiven sinner - Lk. 7:36-50.

This passage is about forgiveness of sins, and, as is so often the case, it has several layers of meaning. The Jewish attitude on which this passage builds, was that sin, like merit, could be graded quantitatively. The greater the number of sins forgiven, the greater was the obligation of the forgiven to repay his forgiving creditor, namely God. Those who felt they had few sins, thought they needed little forgiveness and therefore had few obligations to God. Although Israel was unlikely to acknowledge it, God had had to forgive her multiple sins, since she was at least as wicked as other nations, if not worse.

The parable also points to forgiveness amongst the Israelites - the creditor forgives the debts of both his debtors (see below). The central message is twofold. Firstly, that those who have repented are forgiven their sins by God. Second, that those who acknowledge Jesus as bringing God's message and proclaiming God's will, are accepted by God; those who are ashamed of him and his words, will find no help on the day of Judgement.

One day a Pharisee invited Jesus to dinner, and a young woman of the city, a sinner, heard Jesus was there and came to the Pharisee's house. She had brought with her an alabaster box of scented ointment and she came and stood behind Jesus, weeping. Her tears wet his feet, and she untied the hair of her head in order to clean Jesus' feet. She kissed his feet fervently and anointed them with the unguent.

When the host saw this, he thought to himself, 'If this Jesus were truly a prophet he would know what sort of woman this is who is touching him, because she is a sinner.' Jesus answered, "Simon, I have something to say to you." "Yes, teacher, tell me", said Simon.

"There were two men, both in debt to the same money-lender," said Jesus. "One owed him five hundred pieces of silver, the other fifty. Neither could pay, but the money-lender forgave them both. Which of the two would love him more, do you think?"

"The one who was let off the bigger amount, I should think," replied the Pharisee. "Right," said Jesus, and pointed to the woman at his feet. "When I arrived, you poured no water for me to wash my feet but she has wet them with her tears and wiped them with her hair. You gave me no welcoming kiss, but she has not stopped kissing my feet. You did not anoint my head with oil, but she has used her perfume on my feet. Therefore I tell you, because she loved much her many sins have been forgiven, but to whom little is forgiven, little he loves." Jesus turned to the woman and said, "Your sins are forgiven."

> The others present began to mutter, "Who is this
> who even forgives sins?", but Jesus continued, "Enter
> into peace. Your faith has saved you."

To anoint one's head with oil symbolised well-being and happiness: 'Let not oil be lacking on your head' (Ecc. 9:8). To anoint another was a mark of great respect, and to wash and anoint the feet was a mark of even greater respect. It is possible to see in the woman's action an attestation that she took Jesus as God's prophet: 'The Lord hears my supplication ... What shall I return to the Lord? ... I will pay my vows to the Lord in the presence of all the people' (Ps. 116:12,14). She followed the O.T. precept: 'Serve the Lord with fear, with trembling kiss his feet' (Ps. 2:11); and since the word for 'foot' could also mean 'way' she showed she wanted to follow his way, to be his follower: 'My steps have held fast to your paths, my feet have not stopped' (Ps. 17:5). In rabbinical work it is said: 'Wherever you find the mark of man's feet, there God is before you' (Mek.Vay.7).

Jesus interpreted the woman's actions as showing her repentance for her misdeeds and her forgiveness by God; hence his comment, 'Your sins are forgiven', that is, 'I can see from your actions that you have repented of your previous sins and therefore God has forgiven you.'

The Pharisee's welcome was real but limited. He was interested enough to invite Jesus for a meal, but he did not wish to appear to be a relative of Jesus. A kiss of welcome would be given only to family, near relatives or persons of high rank entitled to respect. Had he recognised Jesus as God's prophet, the welcome would have been more ostentatious than that accorded to a king or high priest. He showed none of the woman's responses, which drove her to such an exhibition of full obeisance.

The woman is said to have been a sinner, and she might have been either the wife of a man with a dishonourable job, or she may have been a prostitute. Luke describes the events as though the woman may not consciously have seen Jesus as a messenger sent by God, but her actions are a prophecy that he was. He was one whose feet were to be washed (Gen. 18 and 19), and who was to be anointed: 'How beautiful upon the mountains are the feet of him who brings good tidings, who publishes peace, who brings tidings of good, who publishes salvation.' (Is. 52:7). In rabbinical writing, too, the coming of the Messiah would be known from his footprints (b.Sot 49b).

She acknowledged Jesus before all present and was not ashamed to do so. (See also F 11): 'O my God, in you I trust, do not put me to shame; let not my enemies exult over me. No man who hopes in you is put to shame, but shame comes to all who are wantonly treacherous' (Ps. 25:2-3); 'Let those who persecute me be put to shame, but let not me be put to shame; let them be fearful, but let me not be dismayed' (Jer. 17:18). Jewish doctrine was: 'If a man was a repentant sinner one must not say to him, "Remember your former deeds." If he was a son of proselytes one must not taunt him, "Remember the deeds of your ancestors;" you shall neither wrong a stranger nor repress him' (b.B.M. 58b).

Luke has created other echoes in this story by the language he chose. It suggests a connection with the bride of the Lord in the Song of Solomon, and she was the equivalent of the daughter of Jerusalem: 'Sing aloud O daughter of Zion; shout, O Israel! Rejoice and exult with all your heart, O daughter of Jerusalem. The Lord has taken away the judgement against you, he has cast out your enemies. I will save her that stumbles and gather up her that was driven away' (Zph. 3:14-15,19). This repentant sinner represents those who have accepted God's reign in their lives and live in God's kingdom.

* * *

D 3. Help for sinners - Mt. 9:9-13. Mk. 2:13-17. Lk. 5:27-32.

To eat with a group signified a close association and for the Pharisees it usually meant learned discussions and prayers. The religious leaders could see only that Jesus would be polluted by proximity to sinners: 'My son, it is not becoming to eat with an unrighteous man' (Ahk. 1:16). They had not realised that sinners could be cleansed by contact with Jesus.

As he went by, Jesus saw Levi, son of Alphaeus, sitting in his office. Jesus said to him, "Follow me." Levi, who was a tax-gatherer, followed Jesus to his house, where they reclined at a meal, together with many others and Jesus' disciples.

Some religious leaders saw this, and exclaimed, "Look at that! Why does he extend his table fellowship to tax-collectors and other sinners?"

Jesus, hearing this, rebuked them. "It is not the strong and healthy who need a doctor, but the weak and ill. I am not here to invite the righteous ones but sinners. You ought to find out what the text means which says, 'I require mercy not sacrifice.'"

Jesus tells Levi to follow him, which is what a teacher would say to his student, and Levi's father's name is given as 'Alphaeus', that is an apprentice or learner.

It was significant that Jesus called a tax-collector to be a disciple. The social standing of these men was not acceptable to the pious, even if Levi had been a levite. They had led the Israelites out of Egypt towards the promised land, and Jesus likewise tells the 'new' Israelites to follow him to the kingdom of God though there is no suggestion that adherence to his person was an indispensable condition of righteousness for Jesus.

One may perhaps take Jesus' remark about not inviting righteous people to eat with him as sincere. There were righteous people among the Jews and no doubt none was more pleased about that than Jesus. Others were sure they were real servants of God, having a strict morality, and living in obedience and fear of the Lord, but they were wrong to ignore the needs of those who had fallen away, become lost or 'dead'. God intended that these should be rescued: 'I will seek the lost, and I will bring back the strayed, I will bind up the cripples and I will strengthen the weak ...' (Ezk. 34:16). Others had forgotten the essential of steadfast love towards their fellowmen as well as to God.

It was this lack of understanding rather than any lack of devotion which Jesus pointed out to them by his quotation from Hosea (Hos. 6:6). That God was concerned with true virtue instead of sacrifices follows from much O.T. teaching: 'Do I eat the flesh of bulls or drink the blood of goats? Offer to God a sacrifice of thanksgiving and pay your vows to the Most High' (Ps. 50:13-14); 'Though you offer me your burnt offerings and cereal offerings, I will not accept them, and the peace offerings of your fatted beasts I will not look upon ... But let justice roll down like water, and righteousness like an ever-flowing stream' (Am. 5:22,24); 'The Lord lifts up the poor .... causing them to inherit the throne of glory, granting his petition to him that prays' (I Sam. 2:8, LXX).

Similar sentiments are found in I.T. and rabbinical books: 'Blessed are you, O Lord, for you have not abandoned the fatherless or despised the poor ... You have done marvels among the humble in the mire underfoot' (DSS, H 9); 'God ... does not want from men sacrifices nor burnt offerings but pure and contrite hearts' (I En. 44:5); and 'More beloved by God are justice and righteous than sacrifices'.

Note on 'sinners'. They were those who were unconcerned about their transgressions of the Law. They included a wide range of people, from those who did not try to keep to the exact prescriptions of the Pharisees, to those whose work involved transgressing the Law, such as usurers. Others whom Jesus tried to win over were the poor and the oppressed, those at the bottom of society. Tax-collectors could be violent people, and the phrase 'publicans and sinners' is similar to the rabbinical 'publicans and robbers'.

* * *

D 4. Zacchaeus - Lk. 19:1-10.

It was a firm opinion in Judaism that penance as well as repentance was necessary before it was possible for God to forgive a sinner. The following story shows Jesus' opinion was rather different.

Zacchaeus was a rich superintendent of tax-gatherers in Jericho and when he heard that Jesus was coming to the town, he ran forward and climbed up a tree to wait for Jesus to pass by. Otherwise, being small in stature, he had no chance of seeing anything going on.

Jesus looked up and saw him when he came to the place. "Zacchaeus," he said, "be quick and come down. I shall come and stay with you today." All who saw murmured, saying, "Look, he will be at the house of that sinful man."

Zacchaeus, he hurried down and welcomed Jesus at his house. "Here and now, Lord, I give half my wealth to the destitute, and if I have cheated anyone, I am ready to repay him fourfold."

Jesus said, "Salvation has come to this house today! This man too is a son of Abraham, and I have come to find and rescue all who are lost."

That Jesus called him down and wished to stay with him, must have surprised Zacchaeus as much as it disturbed the rest of the people there. Zacchaeus' response showed that he valued Jesus' wish, and subsequent events showed clearly that he had become a new Zacchaeus. Like the woman who, being forgiven, could not help her extravagant gestures to show her happiness (D 2), so Zacchaeus shows his repentance by his actions. He promises to pay back four times what he had gained unlawfully, a spontaneous gesture, the fruit of his happiness, believing himself forgiven. It is true that under Jewish law extortion required more than simple restitution but quadrupled repayment would not be demanded except in the case of theft: 'If a man steals an ox or a sheep, and kills it or sells it, he shall pay five oxen for an ox and four sheep for a sheep' (Ex. 22:1), 'since an ox can work the fields whereas a sheep cannot do work' (b.B.K. 79b); in more general terms, 'Wrong behaviour when repented requires restoration plus one fifth of its value' (Lev. 5:24). In the case of theft from a dwelling, the compensation was set at twice the value of the stolen goods.

The evangelist, Luke, seems to imply that it was enough for Jesus that Zacchaeus made his declaration. What counted was his intention. The practical matter of repaying the unlawful excess taxes to their owners was left until that could be arranged. Jesus' acceptance of Zacchaeus' hospitality is taken to indicate that Zacchaeus and God were reconciled. He had repented: regretted his earlier wrong-doing and returned to living under God's laws. He was a true son of Abraham, a true Jew.

There are similarities between this story and that of the previous passage (D 3), both involving table-fellowship with Jesus, while there are also echoes of the stories of the visitors to Abraham (Gen. 18) and of Rahab who helped the Israelites to capture Jericho.

It could be irony that the man was named 'Zacchaeus' (originally Zakkai), meaning 'the innocent one', but a rich man of this name is known from other sources to have lived in Jericho at the time. Any chief tax-gatherer who reformed and sought to see Jesus must have been one of the wonders of the world to the people of the time, and he would have been talked about everywhere. It is not surprising Jesus is depicted as knowing who he was.

Although this is the usually accepted understanding of this story, some have asserted that the language allows a different translation. According to these scholars, Zaccheus was saying that he already gave half his wealth to the poor and should he accidentally defraud anyone, he recompensed them fourfold. This would suggest that Zaccheus was defending himself against any accusation of wrong-doing rather than announcing he had repented and turned over a new leaf.

* * *

D 5. The anointing - Mt. 26:6-13. Mk. 14:3-9.

This story may be related to the death of Jesus. He is shown anointed like the High Priests had been in earlier times, and as one who atones for Israel's sins with the perfumed incense used in the ceremonies on the Day of Atonement. Did Jesus foresee his coming atoning death, beginning not in the pomp, splendour and extravagance of the Temple, but in the house of an outcast, anointed by a woman with a doubtful past, among narrow-minded quarrelsome friends? The story may have been intended to indicate that Jesus was prepared for the worst in Jerusalem, but it certainly shows how he assessed an action, which could have been very improper, and found the merit and the good inclination behind it.

Jesus was at Bethany staying with Simon, a leper. Jesus was reclining at table, when a woman came in with an alabaster phial of very expensive perfumed oil. Breaking open the container she poured the contents on to Jesus' head.

Some were angered by this action. They said the perfume could have been sold for three hundred denarii and the money given to the poor. "Why this waste?", they said. "Pouring it on Jesus' head like that!", and they upbraided the woman heavily.

"That's enough," said Jesus. "Let her alone. It is a beautiful thing she has done for me. The destitute are always there and you can help them at any time, but I shall not be here always. She has done what was within her power, anticipating anointing my body with myrrh for burial. Certain it is that whenever the gospel is proclaimed in the whole world, her action will be her memorial."

It was not unknown to anoint a guest while reclining at table, but the woman's action must have caused a gasp of amazement among the company present. It was a very bold action for a woman to pour expensive perfume over a man's head, and it could have been interpreted by some of those present as enticement with an aphrodisiac. There are hints too, in the language used, which indicate that the woman may have been a reformed prostitute. If this were so, the situation was even more precarious. The perfumed oil might have been bought by her earnings and would have been 'unclean'. Thus she took a considerable risk. Had Jesus been an ordinary Jew, he and his followers could have been very angry and offended, as indeed some of them were. The woman either knew or guessed that Jesus' reaction would be different, and she took the risk, because the perfume was the most valuable thing she possessed with which she wished to honour him.

The others present complained that the perfume could have been put to better use; it could have been sold and the money used to benefit the poor, especially as it was near Passover time, when greater alms-giving than usual was expected: 'Blessed is he who considers the poor' (Ps. 41:1). Jesus rebuts this argument by saying, 'The poor will never cease out of the land' (Dt. 15:11), with an implication perhaps that he was thinking of the Jubilee year which would inaugurate the new kingdom.

It is necessary to realise that for Jews at that time giving alms and being righteous were the same thing. Their attitude was that having given alms, they had put some merit into their heavenly 'bank account'. Thus to 'squander' precious nard on Jesus prevented the disciples from adding to their stock of merit, and it was this which worried them so much. It was a piece of self-centred special pleading and certainly had in it more love for themselves than love for the poor.

Jesus disallows criticism of the woman, and accepting the perfuming as an act of worship and love, turns it into an action which the woman herself almost certainly had not thought of, namely, anointing him in anticipation of his death. To anoint a corpse was a work of the greatest merit, and it could legitimately be performed before death under special circumstances.

Jesus looked below the surface, and showing his love for the repentant sinner, accepts the woman's action on her own level, but utilises it on another level appropriate to his disciples.

Note. It would not have been possible for a leper to live at home, and presumably the passage should say that Simon had been a leper, but later had been pronounced cured by the priests. Some scholars think this passage and that of D 2 are two versions of the same event.

* * *

D 6. The two sons, or promise and performance - Mt. 21:28-32.

In some rabbinical teaching it is explained that to intend to do a good deed gives merit or treasure in heaven but in others: 'If a man intended to eat pork but was given mutton, he is as guilty as if it was pork that he had eaten' (b.Kid. 81b).

By both intending and doing a good deed, one could acquire double merit! Gradually, to 'intend' came to be accepted as the same as to 'do'. On the other hand, to intend to do a bad deed was not punished; only doing it required punishment. Jesus had no time for such dishonest thinking.

"What do you think about this? There was once a farmer with two sons. He went to the first and asked him to go to work in the vineyard. 'Yes, certainly, lord', he said; but he did not.

The father went to the second son and asked him to work in the vineyard, too. 'No', he said, 'I won't.' But after a while he changed his mind, he repented, and went to the vineyard.

Which of these two sons did as his father wished, do you think?"

"The second", replied the priests. "Right", said Jesus, "and I tell you this for sure: repentant tax-gatherers and prostitutes will be received into the kingdom of God before you. John came and showed you the right way to live, but you did not believe him, but tax-gatherers and prostitutes did. Although you saw this, you still did not repent yourselves."

The story tells of a typical situation in which the privileged elder son is polite and apparently obedient to this father, but in fact does what he himself chooses. The younger son is rebellious, and wishes to assert his independence, but comes to wiser thoughts, repents of his impetuousness, and goes to the vineyard to do the necessary work there. He obeys his father in deed though not in his answer. Ideally he should have done both presumably: 'My son, honour your father by word and deed that you may receive his blessing' (Sir. 3:8), but the passage shows that it is honest intention resulting in good actions which count.

Jesus says that the religious leaders are just like the elder son, and because they have prestige in the society, they suppose they are favoured and approved of by God: 'My people hear what you tell them but they will not do it; for with their lips they show much love, but their heart is set on their gain' (Ezk. 33:31). The sinners repenting of their behaviour, changed; they accepted the challenge of John, although it may have cost them their livelihoods and they were surely laughed at by the worldly foolish. They would enter the kingdom while the others would be admitted either later, or, it could mean, not at all. They made fine promises but lacked performance: 'A wise son hears his father's instructions, but a scoffer does not listen to rebuke' (Pvb. 13:1); 'These are the scoffers in Jerusalem who have despised the Law of the Lord and scorned the word of the Holy One of Israel' (DSS C.Is.ii).

D 7. The Pharisee and the tax-collector - Lk. 18:9-14.

Many looked upon their religious duty as an exact and careful performance of the Law: 'See that you observe everything I command you; you must not add anything to it, nor take anything away from it' (Dt. 12:32); 'I (Moses) have taught you statutes and laws as the Lord my God commanded me ... You must observe them carefully' (Dt. 4:5-6). In rabbinical writings too: 'Be pleased, O God, to purify Israel, wherefore increase to them the Torah and precepts as it is said: "It pleased the Lord for his righteousness sake, to magnify the Torah and make it honourable"' (Is. 42:21; ARN 41).

The Torah had been given by God to Moses, on behalf of Israel, so it was necessary to be punctilious about following God's commandments. This story illustrates that Jesus was more concerned with repentance and what he is reported to have quoted from Hosea on other occasions: 'I require steadfast love not sacrifice, the knowledge of God, rather than burnt offerings' (Hos. 6:6).

"Two men went up to the Temple to pray, one a Pharisee and the other a tax-collector. The Pharisee stood and prayed: 'I thank you, Lord, that I am not like other men, greedy, dishonest, adulterous, not like that tax-collector over there. I fast twice a week, and I pay tithes on all I get.'

The tax-collector stood away in the corner and did not dare to raise his eyes to heaven; he beat his breast in deepest contrition, and said, 'My God, have mercy on me, sinner that I am.'

I tell you this truth: it was this man who went home justified as a righteous man, and not the Pharisee, because everyone exalting himself will be humbled and the one humbling himself will be exalted."

The Pharisee stood apart in a prominent place, perhaps in order to set a good example to others, and began to recite the required prayer which is full of thanksgiving, asking for nothing. The Pharisee did more than the Law required in his desire to fulfil God's demands as he saw them. To fast twice a week was more than normal practice and he paid tithes on goods whether they had already been tithed or not. His devotion to his view of God was total. In Jewish eyes this Pharisee was blessed more than most men, because he had a foretaste, in his obedience to the Law, of the World to Come. Rabbinical teaching was: 'When you pray, know before whom you stand;' or: 'Know what is above you: a seeing eye, a hearing ear and all your deeds written in a book' (m.Avot. 2:1).

The tax-collector, on the other hand, echoed the prayer found in an I.T. book: 'Because my sins exceed the number of the sands of the sea ... I have no strength to lift up my eyes. I do not deserve to lift up my eyes and look to see the height of heaven ... I have sinned, O Lord ... and I certainly know my sins. Forgive me, O Lord, forgive me, I beseech you! In me you will manifest your grace and although I am not worthy, you will save me according to your manifold mercies' (P.M. 9-14). He might have thought, too, of: 'I am counted among those who go down into the Pit, I am like those who have no help.' (Ps. 88:4) He would need to: tax collectors were wicked thieves, supporting the occupying Romans, and guilty of idolatry by helping the emperor who claimed to be God.

He could not see how he could be forgiven, since he had no chance of paying back those whom he had cheated, and even less of paying the extra twenty per cent the Law demanded; but: 'Whoever commits a transgression and is filled with shame, all his sins are forgiven' (b.Ber 12b); 'Let the wicked abandon their ways and evil men their thoughts: let them return to the Lord, who will have pity on them; return to our God, for he will freely forgive' (Is. 55:7). He was justified; he was accepted by God: 'The Lord is merciful and ... good to all; to him belong compassion and forgiveness' (Mek.Shir.1); and there was a saying, 'Give God an opening of repentance no bigger than the eye of needle and I will widen it into openings through which wagons and carriages can pass' (Cant.R. 5:2).

The contrast is between those who considered themselves righteous and those whom God considered righteous. God's compassion for the repentant tax-gatherer was greater than God's satisfaction with the Pharisee, in spite of his holiness and piety. He did not direct his heart to God but to himself, and used observance of the details of the Law as a measure of his righteousness, instead of love of God and love of his fellowman. It was not only that he believed he had a special relationship with God, but he thought those who were not pious as he was, would be unacceptable to God, repentant or not. No doubt he thought that: 'The crown of a good name or reputation excels the crowns of Torah, priesthood and royalty' (m.Avot. 4:13). The story shows also the danger of being good leading to despising others.

The portrayal of the Pharisee in this story should not be taken as typical of them. While undoubtedly some were wicked, there were many who fought to make practice imitate teaching. Pharisees were often very critical of other Pharisees. In rabbinical writings we find a picture very like that which Jesus advocates and an even greater understanding of the practical difficulties repentance can bring: 'Let not a man say after he has sinned, "There is no restoration for me", but let him trust in the word and repent, and God will receive him. Let him not say, "If I confess, I shall lose my office", but let him hate office and humble himself and return in repentance.'

Some Pharisees undoubtedly had a good conceit of themselves exemplified in the prayer: 'I thank you, O Lord, my God, that you have given me my lot with those who sit in the House of Learning, and not with those who sit at the street-corners; for I am early to work on the words of the Torah, and they are early to work on things of no moment. I weary myself and profit thereby, while they weary themselves to no profit. I labour and receive a reward, whereas they labour and receive no reward. I hasten towards the life of the Age to Come, and they hasten towards the pit of destruction' (b.Ber.28b).

Others were not so arrogant or deluded, as the following prayer shows: 'I am a creature of God and my neighbour is also his creature; my work is in the city and his in the field; I rise early to my work and he rises early to his. As he cannot excel in my work, so I cannot excel in his work. But perhaps you say, I do great things and he does small things. We have learnt that it matters not whether a man does much or little, if only he directs his heart to heaven.' (b.Ber. 17a). Other rabbinical teaching warned against a serious sin: 'He who puts the crown of the Torah to profane use is uprooted from the world. Do good deeds for the sake of their Maker and speak of them, the words of the Torah, for their own sake. Make them not a crown to magnify yourself' (b.Ned. 62a). Repentance and forgiveness by God is also open to Gentiles: 'God bids the peoples of the world repent so that he may bring them near beneath his wings' (Ps. 36:7).

The part played by the Temple in Jewish religious life cannot be overestimated: 'Not one Israelite was in distress as long as the Temple stood, for when a man entered there laden with sin and offered a sacrifice, he was forgiven' (Ex.R. 36:1).

* * *

D 8. The lost sheep and the lost coin - Mt. 18:12-14. Lk. 15:1-10.

There must have been times when the disciples discussed what would happen to those who did not bother about God's rule. A lot of them seemed to do quite well in spite of being sinners. Of course, the psalmist says God does try to bring them back into his kingdom: 'I have strayed like a lost sheep; come search for your servant, for I have not forgotten your commandments' (Ps. 119:176); but the psalmist speaks of one who wanted to return to God's kingdom. What about those who are blind to their danger, who couldn't care less, and what would happen to those appointed to tend the sheep of Israel?

Ezekiel had spoken about that: 'I, the Lord, hate the shepherds of Israel who care only for themselves. Should they not care for the sheep? They have not encouraged the weary, tended the sick, bandaged the hurt, recovered the straggler or searched for the lost ... I myself will go in search of my sheep and rescue them no matter where they are scattered ... I will bring them out of every nation, gather them in from other lands and lead them home ... to the mountains of Israel' (Ezk. 34:2-4,11-13).

Jesus said, "Suppose a shepherd, in charge of a hundred sheep, loses one of them, would he not leave the ninety-nine in order to search for the one missing? Certainly, he would rejoice more over the one which went astray if he finds it, than over the ninety-nine which had not wandered off. He would take it on his shoulders and, coming to his house again, he would call his neighbours and friends together. 'Rejoice with me,' he would say, 'I have found the sheep which was lost.' Similarly there will be more joy in heaven over one sinner who repents than over ninety-nine righteous ones who do not need to repent.

Leaving the sheep out on the mountain might be risky, but there were other shepherds who would be willing to keep an eye on them. It might be one of theirs next time! When he returns he calls out to his neighbours and friends that the missing lamb was found again. This is a relief, since then none could be suspected of theft. The Law said that animals which have strayed must be adequately cared for if found, and to find and keep any animal, without attempting to return it to its owner was theft, and punished accordingly.

In rabbinical teaching, all articles, such as loaves, coins, fruit, fish, etc., lacking a mark to show who the owner was, are the property of the finder. Things such as a purse, a heap of coins, and similar valuables had to be advertised until his neighbours all knew about it (m.B.M. 2:1,6); Finding the sheep completed the flock, and enhanced the shepherd's reputation as a good shepherd.

"Or again," continued Jesus, "if a woman has ten silver coins and loses one of them, would she not light the lamp, sweep out the house and look in every corner

84

till she has found it? When she has found it, would she
not call her friends and neighbours together to tell
them the missing coin is found? 'Rejoice with me', she
would say: 'I have found that which I had lost.'

So it is in heaven: there is joy among the angels
of God over one sinner who repents."

The woman was anxious to find the coin, to complete the ten, and to save her friends and neighbours from the embarrassing suspicion that one of them had found it and kept it.

Some think that completing the hundred and the ten was significant as the Jews reckoned in hundreds and tens. Ninety-nine was no good; a full house was necessary, and according to Jewish teaching, ten was the necessary number to make a quorum before God would accept public prayers.

The word for 'coin' was a pun, since it could also mean 'those who have gone away'. The lost sheep and missing coin had gone astray, but were still within the house of Israel. It was necessary to search for those who were lost, and if that was true of a sheep or a coin, how much more true of one of Israel's sons! As a shepherd seeks for the lost sheep, or a housewife searches for a lost coin, God seeks for lost people; the religious leaders ought to be helping, not grumbling about it!

Rabbinical teaching is similar. In a commentary on 'The priest shall make atonement for all the congregation of Israel' (Num. 15:25), it is said: 'When one of Israel falls, it is to God as if all had fallen. If one of them is taken away, it is to God as though the whole of creation is lost' (Sif.Num. 15:25). In another comment, on 'Before his elders he will manifest his glory' (Is. 24:23), it is said, 'God has more sorrow over one elder who has gone astray than over the whole of Israel.' Another comment gives the same message: 'The people of Israel are compared to a lamb ... If it is hurt in one limb all its limbs feel the pain. If one of Israel sins, all suffer the punishment' (Mek. Bah.2).

There is a legend that Moses lost one of his sheep and when he found it, he carried it back to the fold over his shoulder and Jesus uses this story in his own teaching. In rabbinical writings, the proverb, 'If you seek her (Wisdom) out like silver ...' (Pvb. 2:4), receives the following comment: 'If you seek after the words of the Law as for hidden treasures, God will not withhold your reward. If a man loses even a small coin in his house, how many lamps and wicks does he not light till he finds it! ... How much more should you search ... after the words of the Law which give life in this world and in the one to come' (Cant.R. I; 1,9).

There are indications of the feast of the Passover in this passage. The sheep carried on the shepherd's shoulders, lighting a lamp and sweeping the house out thoroughly, in order to make sure there was no trace of leaven still in the house, were all preparations for this celebration, when all Israel remembered God's care of them at the time of the Exodus from Egypt.

A rabbinical story pictures God's happiness when someone becomes a proselyte, a new member of Israel: 'God may then be compared to a king who had a flock of sheep and goats which went out to the field each day to graze. One day a stag came in with the flock ... and when they went out he went with them.

The king felt special affection for him and he gave orders that the stag should have good pasture. No one should beat him and he had to be treated carefully.

The king's servants came and said, "Lord, you have many he-goats, lambs and kids, yet you never warn us about them, while you give us special instructions about this stag!" The king said, "The flock have no choice ... The stag, however, belongs in the wilderness and it is not its nature to come into places inhabited by man. Shall we not count it as merit to this one who has come to stay in our courtyard?"

Likewise, ought we not to be grateful to the proselyte who has left behind him his family, and his father's house, even his own people ... and has chosen to come to us? Accordingly, God has provided him with special protection: "Love therefore the alien, for you were aliens in the land of Egypt'" (Num.R. 8:2 on Dt. 10:19).

These parables acknowledge that some in Israel were righteous. They were honestly trying to be true servants of God, while others had become sinners. It is the latter who must be sought out and brought back into the flock.

* * *

D 9. Help from a friend - Lk. 11:5-8.

How could Jesus talk as if God were a human friend? It stands to reason that it would be impertinent even for a servant to ask his lord for favours as though he were a friend. For a person to ask God, creator of the world, and Lord of lords for help, as one would ask one's friend, seemed strange but it was what this Jesus seemed to be advocating!

Jesus used the very Jewish concept of the obligation to care for a traveller. This was a specially strong form of charity: Abraham's house was always open to wayfarers (Gen.R. 48:9). To reciprocate a service was thought to be another important duty and these two ideas throw light on this passage: 'Refuse no man any favour that you owe him when it lies in your power to pay it. Do not say to your friend, "Go now, and come back later; you can have it tomorrow", when you have it with you.' (Pvb. 3:27-28). Judaism's rule was that any poor traveller must be given not less than a loaf of bread. (b.Shab. 118a).

"Supposing one of you has an unexpected visitor who turns up in the middle of the night," said Jesus. "You go to your friend and say, 'Lend me three loaves, for a visitor has come to my house and I have nothing to offer him.'

Can you imagine your friend will call to you from within, 'Do not bother me! The door beam is in place for the night, the children are asleep in bed with me. I cannot get up to give you what you want'? Such a refusal would be unthinkable - you know it is imperative to give hospitality to a visitor. No, your friend will get up and give you what you need because of your lack of shame."

For the Asian today, as in Jesus' time, reciprocal co-operation with relatives and friends is a necessary part of survival. Friendship involves honour, the most important factor of life, so that to refuse a request from a friend is unthinkable, especially when the one asking has not been guilty of negligence. In any case, O.T. and I.T. teaching required a Jew to lend to others less fortunate without grumbling: 'Lend to your neighbour in his time of need; repay your neighbour when a loan falls due [for repayment]' (Sir. 29:2).

When the host of the unexpected visitor came to ask his friend for food, the friend would never reply, 'Go away ... etc.' This would be even more true towards one who, without any diffidence or shame, asked for food for his visitor. Because he asked boldly, he showed the close friendship he had with his neighbour and the imperative of the mutual obligation between them. Such shameless asking is not to be confused with immodest, impertinent cheek. The former stems from the trust and confidence of mutual helpfulness, the latter is to be condemned: 'There is shame that brings sin; and there is a shame that is glory and grace' (Pvb. 26:11,LXX); 'There is a modesty which leads to sin as well as a modesty that brings honour and favour' (Sir. 4:21).

The shamelessness shown by the righteous in their approach to God must be the confidence of probity, not impertinence or cheekiness. There is no need to pester God; repeated knocking is not necessary. The host knocked on his friend's door but once.

There are indications in the original language that the passage may have symbolism relating to the day of Judgement, when sleepers will be called by God to come out from their graves and enter the kingdom. The bread is the symbol of God's word and that bread gives eternal life. The visitor arrived unexpectedly and his host goes to his friend and causes him to awaken (using the same words as those used to tell of God wakening the dead), and asks for bread, eternal life, for his visitor: 'The dead shall live, their bodies shall rise ... and the earth will bring those long dead to birth again. Come ... enter your rooms ... hide yourselves for a little while ... for behold the Lord is coming ... to punish the iniquities of the inhabitants ...' (Is. 26:19-21). This is emphasised by the use of a word for 'room' or 'inner chamber' which could also mean 'grave'. Those who have used their inner room for prayer during their life-time need have no fear either in life or in their tombs. They can ask boldly in full confidence of eternal life when the day of Judgement comes. They will be called out to share in the messianic banquet, and receive all they need.

This is one of several passages in which similar approaches are seen. The man brought by his friends (I5), the woman gate-crashing the Pharisee's party (D2), the Caananite woman (I 11), the blind man at Jericho (I 12) and the woman with a haemorrhage (I 8) all show those in real trouble risk an approach to an authority, even with an element of impudence: "Impudence wields great power and lacks only a crown" (b.Sanh. 105a). This is quite typical of Judaism: it was common for the rabbis to argue with God. Choni prayed to God demanding rain, but not too much! (m.Ta'an. 3:8).

* * *

D 10. Justice for a widow - Lk. 18:1-8

Jesus said that God cares for ordinary people, the poor, the rejected, the despised. Yet ordinary people knew only too well that there's a difference if one of them goes to court and if one of the leaders asks for justice. The judges say they follow God's law in the Torah, so maybe God will be like them on the day of Judgement. That was not much to look forward to! Jesus tried to allay their anxiety.

Jesus spoke to them in a parable to show that they should pray at all times and never lose heart: "There was once a judge who did not fear God and cared nothing for what people said about him. A widow repeatedly came before him asking for vindication against her adversary.

Although at first he refused, at last he took up her case: 'I shall have to vindicate her or she will blacken my reputation and disgrace me by her continual returning.'

If an unrighteous (secular) judge will vindicate those who come before him, will not God vindicate the elect who cry to him by day and night? Would he put their long-suffering to the test, or delay long over them? Never! He will see to it that they will receive justice and that quickly.

The question is, 'When the son of man comes, will he find faith on earth?'"

The story derives from the contemporary situation, and it will be helpful if certain points are made clear first. There were three Jewish courts of justice: those trying less serious crimes with three judges, those trying more serious offences, with twenty-three judges, and the supreme court in Jerusalem with seventy-one members, trying the most serious crimes, such as idolatry, false prophecy or a wicked High Priest. In addition there were non-Jewish courts, in some of which the judge could use the law of the Torah rather than secular law if he chose and others were administrative courts with simple procedures.

The procedures of the Jewish courts were very cumbersome and time-consuming, and although Jews were expected to use them, it is not surprising many would turn to the non-religious courts. The administrative courts, though occasionally arbitrary, at least had proceedings which were quick. In many ways, God was pictured by Jews as behaving like 'civil' judges: independent, sometimes ignoring precedents, acting as both advocate and judge at the same time.

The phrase 'To cry for help' had a technical meaning at the time, indicating that the widow was out to avenge some wrong she believed had been done to her, perhaps over repayment of a loan.

In the passage, the widow goes to the civil court. She needs an advocate, since she cannot put her case without one. The judge himself agrees to help her, becoming both judge and advocate, something not unusual at the time and also mentioned in the

O.T.: 'They have a powerful advocate whose name is the Lord of Hosts' (Jer. 50:34); 'Therefore the Lord says, "I will plead your cause, I will avenge you"' (Jer. 51:36); and in I.T.: 'The Lord will not delay ... till he pleads the cause of his people and rejoices with them in his salvation' (Sir. 35:18-19).

According to this explanation, the judge is indifferent to men's attempts to manipulate him; that is, he is impartial and anxious only to follow the law he was appointed to uphold. His reputation for impartiality was extremely important to him. That the widow kept coming could suggest that he could not take her case because he was in league with her adversary, or he was being unfair to her. Thus he was in danger that she would 'blacken his face', his reputation, that is 'wear him out;' he could lose his honour, his most valued asset and he took upon himself the double duty of judge and advocate to put a stop to possible gossip.

O.T. teaching was: "Consider what you are doing, for you judge not on behalf of human beings but on the Lord's behalf. Let the fear of the Lord be upon you; take care what you do ..." (II Chr. 19:6-7). Rabbinical sayings have similar lessons: 'One who puts another to shame (publicly) has no part in the world to come' (b.B.M. 59a); 'Whoever gives a true judgement is ... as if he had been a co-worker of God ... in the work of creation' (Mek. Ama. 4); 'You shall not pervert justice in favour of the poor, the rich or the pious ones even if they are opposed by the wicked one' (Mek. Kas.3). What do people in Palestine carefully avoid? Putting others to shame: literally "making faces white" [with hate or fear] (b.B.M. 58b).

Jesus used the story to illustrate a religious truth. Like the earthly judge of the story, God also has a reputation to maintain: 'I prayed to the Lord: O Lord God, do not destroy your people ... remember your servants ... and overlook the wickedness and sins of your people. Otherwise the people in the land out of which you led us, will say it is because the Lord was not able to bring them into the land which he promised them' (Dt. 9:26-28); 'Remember, O Lord, the taunts of the enemy, the scorn a savage nation pours on your name. Rise up, O God, plead your cause. Remember how the impious scoff at you all day long' (Ps. 74:18,22); 'I had concern for my holy name, which the house of Israel caused to be profaned among the nations to which they came' (Ezk. 36:21); 'Yahweh, I have heard of your reputation; I have been awe-struck by your work ...' (Hab. 3:2).

God is even imagined as repenting of his intention: 'Why should the Egyptians say, "With evil intent he brought them forth, to slay them in the mountains and to consume them from the face of the earth? ... Remember Abraham, Isaac and Israel ... to whom you said you will multiply your descendants as the stars of the heaven, and all this land that I have promised I will give to your descendants ..." And the Lord repented of the evil which he thought to do to his people' (Ex. 32:12-14).

Other rabbinical teaching was: 'Judges should not think they sit alone. The Holy One, praised be he, says, "Know that I sit beside you, for I love justice and if you submit to righteousness so I submit to you; and, as it is written, I am near you in judgement"' (Midr.Ps.82:1); 'If a case comes before you several times, you may not say, "I have tried this case carefully several times; you must remain always thoughtful and considerate"' (Sif.Dt. on 1:17) and 'The Shekinah (God's spirit) is present with judges and those giving false decisions will be sent to hell' (b.San. 7a).

It is not possible to know exactly what is meant by the verse: '... will not God vindicate the elect who cry to him by day and night? Would he test their long-suffering, or delay long over them?' Some think this sentence means, 'Will he ignore the pleas of the faithful', at least for a time? Others suggest, 'Will he try their patience?' is better; that is will he test their faith by making them wait? Neither fits the original language well, and other experts have proposed instead: 'Will not God vindicate his elect who cry to him day and night, and to whom he shows mercy?' The next verse answers this question: 'He will vindicate them speedily. Indeed, the Lord will not delay ... until he repays mortals according to their deeds' (Sir. 35:24).

God could not be seen to be in league with the opponent or adversary (Satan) and therefore his judgements would be correct, impartial, righteous and they would follow without delay: 'At the destined hour (the appointed time for God's judgement) it will come in breathless haste, it will not fail. If it delays, wait for it, for when it comes there will be no time to linger' (Hab. 2:3); 'The Lord listens to the poor man's appeal and his verdict follows without delay' (Sir. 21:5); 'Do not offer the Lord a bribe; he will not take it ... The Lord is a judge who knows no partiality. He has no favourites at the poor man's expense, but listens to his prayer when he is wronged. He does not ignore the cry of the orphan, nor the widow, when she pours out her complaint.' (Sir. 35:12-17).

The last sentence of the passage is almost certainly a version of the thought: 'Many a man protests his own loyalty, but where can one find one who is faithful?' (Pvb. 20:6). It emphasises that the true hero was the one who remained faithful to, and relied on, God and his word, and who left to God judgements, punishments and rewards. The question is very relevant to the central meaning of the passage, that God will give full and complete justice and vindicate the righteous. Jesus is also concerned to promote the characteristics of the kingdom of God - peace, reconciliation and forgiveness, in place of the quarrelsome, litigious attitude that so many showed then, as now.

The idea that only by persistent nagging will God respond to the cry of those who pray to him is contrary to so much else in the gospels, that the initial sentence may have been a misunderstanding, either of the evangelist or of a later editor. In Judaism earnest prayer was efficacious: 'But Moses implored the Lord ... Turn from your fierce wrath; change your mind and do not bring disaster on your people ... And the Lord changed his mind about the disaster he had planned to bring on his people.' Moses' prayer was because God had allowed the Israelites too much gold and they therefore could make the golden Calf. Moses blamed God and dared to speak to God without reserve (b.Ber. 32a). There is the contrary idea too: 'A king had a single pearl. His son came and said to him, "Give the pearl to me". The king replied, "It is not yours". But when the son wearied him with begging the king gave him the pearl' (Midr.Ps. 28:6).

The day of Judgement will come suddenly, and the faithful elect will receive the favour they deserve. It is those under God's rule who trust in his ultimate justice and who hold fast, or have held fast, in faith whom the Messiah will find and save when he comes. It is not that their prayers will cause God to change his planned day of Judgement and shorten the time of waiting, but that by prayer they will receive grace to keep faith and be prepared for the last day when it comes.

This parable is one of two 'crisis' parables in which action is taken which fulfils the Law by someone not expecting to have to do so. The other is the parable of the (un)scrupulous steward (G 3).

* * *

D 11. The workers in the vineyard - Mt. 20:1-15.

This parable shows clearly that it can be understood at two levels. The meaning which today is thought to be obvious, is not the one which might have struck those listening to it originally. They would probably have thought of the O.T. teaching that God's mercy and generosity are incalculable: 'For as the heavens are high above the earth, so great is his steadfast love toward those who fear him' (Ps. 103:11). What today seems to be a difficult passage relates to a problem of the greatest importance to the Jews of Jesus' day.

We can imagine the disciples wondering whether the kingdom Jesus was proclaiming and teaching about was acceptable to God. Did it not sound as though Jesus had a new covenant to offer them? Could they be sure that God would reward those who followed this new covenant? Perhaps he would favour only those who had followed the old covenant.

In any case those who had laboured throughout their lives according to the old one would surely get a greater reward from God than those who had only laboured a short time in the new one! How would God deal with the problem of those who died young? If the rewards were in proportion to the amount of work one had put into righteous living on earth, those who had lived longest would be far better off than those who had died in their youth. Could that be true?

Another problem was that there had been more than one covenant in the course of the history of Israel. The first had been made with Moses on Mt. Sinai: 'The Lord our God made a covenant with us at Horeb' (Dt. 5:2). That covenant had been renewed with Noah: 'God said to Noah and his sons with him, "I now make my covenant with you and your descendants after you ..."' (Gen. 9:8-9). Then God had made promises to Abram: 'The Lord made a covenant with Abram and said, "To your descendants I give this land"' (Gen. 12:7) and again, 'And God appeared to Abraham and said to him ... "I will establish my covenant between you and me ..."' (Gen. 17:1-2 LXX). This covenant was renewed with Isaac and Jacob. Later Jeremiah said that God would write a true covenant on the hearts of his people: 'The time is coming, says the Lord, when I will make a new covenant with Israel and Judah. It will not be like the covenant I made with their forefathers when I ... led them out of Egypt' (Jer. 31:31-32). As a rabbinical commentary (on S.S. 1:14) puts it: 'Abraham said, "Lord of the universe, you made a covenant with Noah that you would not destroy his seed from off the earth and I arose and gathered a stock of good deeds ... and you removed his covenant to make way for mine. Shall perhaps another arise and perform ... good deeds surpassing mine, so that my covenant shall be removed to make way for his?"' (Cant.R. I, 14:3).

"There was once a farmer who went out before dawn to hire men to work in his vineyard at the usual rate of pay. Three hours later (about 9 a.m.) he went to the square again and found some men hanging about waiting for work. 'Why aren't you working?', asked the farmer. 'No one hired us', they replied. The farmer said to them, 'Go to the vineyard and work there, and I will pay you a just wage for the day. At noon, and about 3 p.m., he did the same. Finally, about an hour before sunset he returned to the market place and found still others who had not been hired. He said to them, 'Go to the vineyard and join the others.'

When it was nearing sunset, the owner instructed his servant to pay the workers, beginning with those who were engaged last. They were paid one denarius, the rate for the day.

Those who had worked all day were cross: 'What's all this then?' they said. 'We have worked longer and through the heat of the day. We ought to get more than these others.'

The owner, hearing the noise, came out and spoke to the labourers: 'My friends, I have done you no wrong – did you not agree with me for a denarius? In any case, is it not good for me to be generous? Take your pay and go home! With my own assets I do as I choose. Is your eye evil, because I am good?[1]

It was essential to get the grapes in at just the right time: 'The day is short [or, The harvest is due], the work great, the labourers lazy, the reward much and the master of the house urgent' (m.Avot. 2:15).

It became even more urgent if rain or a storm threatened, or if it was Friday when any grapes left would have to remain untouched for thirty-six hours. Payment had to be made in time for the workmen to get home before nightfall, especially if it were a Friday. Since other farmers were probably after extra help also as the day wore on, the rate of pay demanded by those hired later could have been higher than for those hired earlier. In this story they were all paid the same, showing that the labourers hired later had not tried, or had not been able, to exploit the owner selfishly.

The law about engaging labourers was that they could be asked to begin early and/or finish late but the owner could not compel them to do so. If they are offered more money, they may rightly reply, 'The greater pay is only for better work, not longer hours' (b.B.M. 83a). Moreover, while the work went on, the labourers (and their families who would come to help), could eat as many grapes as they wished. 'When you go into another man's vineyard, you may eat as many grapes as you wish to satisfy your hunger, but you may not put any into your basket' (Dt. 23:24). This was a loss to the farmer and the longer the term of hire, the greater his loss. Also if he said he would provide food during the day he had to do that too.

There was also teaching that there was a minimum wage, which had to be paid to those who waited to be engaged for a job. They could not be blamed for having had to stand idle and were entitled to a day's pay for even an hour's work. This applied with greater force where the agreement was to pay 'a just wage'. Thus the story does not tell of a quixotic owner but of one who played fairly with the labourers. He was a business man, concerned that his vineyard should pay its way, but equally concerned that those who worked in it should receive a proper reward. He sees his workers as fellow Jews; he treats them as brothers. He paid each one a labourer's wage, not a wage for their labour. It was considered that one penny was both the minimum and maximum.

Jesus uses a situation familiar to his hearers to point out a religious truth. He shows by this parable that God does not want to be thought of as a mean employer, or to get a bad name among his workers. God first hired Adam as his gardener, but he sinned; Noah was hired next, but his sons were unrighteous; then the covenant was renewed with Abraham, but his son Jacob had descendants who worshipped the Golden Calf, and Moses had to hire other labourers to renew the covenant. These labourers also were unsatisfactory. They were not concerned to work to maintain God's covenant with Israel, to work in his vineyard: 'Wicked men remove landmarks, they seize flocks, drive away the ass of orphans, take the widow's ox for a pledge. They snatch the fatherless infant from the breast and take in pledge the child of the poor ...' (Job 24:2-3,9). Both Jeremiah and Ezekiel said that there would come a new covenant, written on the hearts of God's workers, and now Jesus was asserting that the time had come for the prophecy of Leviticus to be fulfilled: 'I will confirm my covenant with you. Your old harvest shall last until you must clear out the old to make way for the new' (Lev. 26:9). The understanding among the rabbis about covenants was complex. Some thought David accepted another covenant and in a rabbinical book it says: 'The covenant with Jonadab ... was greater than the one made with David. The former was unconditional, the latter dependent on the Israelites keeping the commandments' (Mek.Ama. 4).

Jesus was inviting mankind to a new covenant with God or perhaps rather to renew the original covenant which the first Adam had so disastrously broken. As it is written in one of the I.T. books: 'I will give a light to the world ... and establish my covenant with the sons of men and glorify my people above all nations' (P.P. 11:1). The parable ends with sunset and payment of the workers, a reference to the end of this world, the coming of the Messiah and the day of Judgement.

It was Judaic belief that those who had faithfully laboured in God's vineyard would be rewarded, whether they had laboured throughout a long life or had had only a few years to do so. Those who died young did so because God willed it, so that they could not be blamed for not having been able to continue working for him longer. Similarly those who began to work for God at different times, under any of the covenants from the time of Adam to Jesus' own day, were equally valid workers and would receive the same reward.

This story show Jesus confirming and extending one of Judaism's important beliefs and the parable answers the anxiety of his followers - that God might not accept them. Even if they began to work at the eleventh hour, just before the day of Judgement, God would accept them and invite them to the messianic feast where their reward would be the honour of God's approval. The correspondences are clear. Throughout history, God's agents had hired the people of Israel to work in his vineyard; even at the latest hour, a new set of labourers had been recruited, had accepted Jesus as God's agent and his gospel as God's will and they would be treated by God with loving kindness, receiving a full day's pay even though they had only been at work an hour or so.

There are many connections with O.T. and I.T. texts. There are those which tell us how to treat others: 'You shall not keep back the wages of a man who is poor and needy, whether Jew or alien living in your country in one of your settlements. Pay him his wages on the same day before sunset, for he is poor and his heart is set on them; he may appeal to the Lord against you and you will be guilty of sin' (Dt. 24:14-15). Conditions of work are dealt with: 'Give the labourer his pay, and do not afflict the poor. Give it him at once and do not tell him to come tomorrow' (P.Ph. 19,22); 'If you have a servant, treat him as an equal - you are related in blood; treat him like a brother - you will need him as much as you need yourself' (Sir. 33:30).

Other texts show that God will reward those who act righteously: 'Do your duty in good time and in his own time the Lord will reward you' (Sir. 51:30); 'The Holy One ... will be a swift witness against ... those that defraud the hireling in his wages, the widow and the fatherless and that turn aside the stranger from his right and fear not me' (Midr.Ps. 82:1); 'I (the Lord of Hosts) will draw near to you for judgement; I will be a swift witness against the sorcerers, the adulterers, those who swear falsely, those who oppress the hired workers in their wages, the widow and the orphan, and against those who thrust aside the alien and do not fear me' (Mal. 3:5); '... those who bring in the corn shall eat and praise the Lord, and those who gather the grapes, shall drink in his holy courts.' (Is. 62:9).

Similar stories are found in the rabbinical literature, though with different conclusions. On the death of Rabbi Abun ben R. Hiyya at the age of 28 in the fourth century C.E., his friend spoke at his funeral on a verse in Ecclesiastes: 'Sweet is the sleep of the labourer, whether he has eaten much or little' (Ecc. 5:12). (This quotation lies behind Jesus parable also. It was understood as meaning that if one died young, one would be fully rewarded by God, since it had been God's wish that the life had been cut short.) He said, 'To what can R. Abun be likened? To a king who possessed a vineyard and hired many labourers to tend it. One of them greatly exceeded the others in his work. The king took him by the hand and walked with him the length and breadth of the vineyard.

At the end of the day, the labourers came to be paid and the good worker was paid in full. The others were aggrieved and said, "We have toiled all day and he worked only two hours; yet he is paid in full!" The king replied, "Why are you disgruntled? By his diligence this man has done more in two hours than you in the whole day." Just so did R.Abun achieve in his short life more than many in a whole life-time' (S.S. R. 6:2,6).

Another rabbinical story, based on the passage in Leviticus:"I will confirm my covenant with you. Your old harvest shall last you until you must clear out the old to make way for the new", is: 'A king had many labourers and among them was one who had worked for him for many days. When they came to receive their wages, the king said to this worker, "I will have respect for you and deal with you at my leisure. These others have done little work for me and I give them small wages; but you shall have a great wage."

Even so did Israel claim their reward from God, the other nations likewise wished to get their pay. God said to Israel, "I shall respect you and deal with you at my leisure. The other nations did little work for me and they will receive small rewards, but you will receive great reward"' (Sif.Lev. on 26:9-10). Another example: 'One who hires workers who work well, and pays them fairly, merits no praise. When they are lazy and he pays them fully - then he deserves praise' (Midr.Ps. 26:3).

[1] Or: 'Do you begrudge that I am generous because I am a good Israelite?'

* * *

D 12. Home for spirits or the Spirit? - Mt. 12:43-45. Lk. 11:24-26.

There was a popular belief at the time, that demoniacs 'contained' a demon. Demons were supposed to be descended from the offspring of heavenly beings, the sons of God, or 'Watchers', and human women, in the days before Noah. 'When mankind began to increase and to spread over the earth and daughters were born to them, the sons of the gods[1] saw the daughters of men were beautiful; so they took for themselves such women as they chose' (Gen. 6:1-2); 'In the days of Jared, the angels of the Lord descended on earth, those who are named the Watchers, that they should instruct the children of men, and they should give judgement and do righteousness on the earth' (Jub. 4:15); 'And it came to pass when the children of men began to multiply on the face of the earth and daughters were born to them, that the angels of God saw them ... and they were beautiful to look upon; and they took themselves wives of all whom they chose' (Jub. 5:1-2).

Demons were supposed to be spiritual beings but unable to go far from the earth. They destroy, cast men on to the ground, give them fits, make them mad, and so on: 'And now those who are produced from the spirits and flesh shall be called evil spirits on the earth and on the earth shall be their dwelling' (I En. 15:8); the only place where they will remain is in a human being or a pig, but otherwise they roam the dry wilderness: 'The smell of the fish baffled the demon and he ran away to the upper part of Egypt' (i.e. the desert area)' (Tob. 8:3). There they waylay and seduce unwary travellers: '... the unclean demons began to lead astray the children of the sons of Noah ...' (Jub. 10:1).

On the day of Judgement, they will be destroyed: 'Here shall stand the angels who have connected themselves with women, and their spirits, which assuming many different forms, are defiling mankind and leading them astray ... until the day of great Judgement in which they shall be judged and made an end of' (I En. 19:1).

Jesus said, "When an unclean spirit comes out of a man, it wanders over the dry desert seeking a resting-place. Finding none, it says, 'I will return to my house from which I came.' So it returns and finds the house unoccupied, swept clean and put in order. It goes off to find seven other spirits more wicked than itself, and they all take up residence in the house. Thus in the end the man's condition is worse than ever. That is how it will be with this wicked generation."

The seven demons return to plague the person; this may refer to those listed in the Testament of Reuben: 'Seven spirits appointed against man ... First, the spirit of fornication is seated in the nature and in the senses; second the spirit of insatiableness, in the belly; the third, the spirit of fighting in the liver and gall. The fourth is the spirit of flattery and trickery, that through officious effort one may be at the height of one's powers. The fifth is the spirit of pride, that one may be boastful and arrogant. The sixth is the spirit of lying to practise deceit and secretiveness from kindred and friends; the seventh is the spirit of injustice with which are thefts and acts of rapacity, that a man may fulfil the desire of his heart' (T.Reu. 2:2, 3:3-6).

In Judaism, it was thought that spiritual influences work through the 'inclination' of one's heart, which in turn governs the behaviour of a person, so that to leave the heart empty, was an open invitation for Satan's demons to take the opportunity to enter into the person and govern him or her. If that happened then all the senses would have free reign and the person would behave as though he or she was possessed by several demons. One should make sure one's self was occupied by an inclination under God's direction: 'The inclination of the good man is not in the power of Satan, for the angel of peace guides his soul (or life)' (T.Ben. 6:1). Was Jesus perhaps thinking of the Pharisees, who appeared externally to be clean and in good order, but within were empty with no virtues of love, compassion and so on?

The passage is found in the section of Luke which is thought by some to be modelled on Deuteronomy, and the seven spirits more wicked than the first, may represent the seven nations larger and stronger than Israel, which Israel must eradicate with God's help: '... seven nations greater and mightier than yourselves and when the Lord gives them over to you, you must utterly destroy them ...' (Dt. 7:1-2).

[1] Or: 'the sons of God'.

* * *

D. Summary.

Jesus had come to proclaim God's message of forgiveness for those who repent. He had come to assure the most sinful that even they could be saved from the strength of their bad inclinations, so that they could begin to live in God's realm instead of Satan's. It did not matter how long they had accepted God's reign working on his behalf; even those whose service was short would be honoured at the messianic banquet after the day of Judgement.

The first sign of one who is entering God's realm is repentance, that is turning from evil ways to God's way. Forgiveness follows, and there was no question of retribution before God would forgive someone turning to him. Especially at Passover, all should repent and return to God's kingdom and live under his rule. Good inclinations then take charge in one's life, showing themselves in steadfast love. Giving alms, for example, was not in itself meritorious in God's eyes, unless it was the unselfish fruit of good inclination, of righteousness.

Many promise allegiance to God's will, but they do not fulfil their promise. They build their houses on no foundations. Their prayers were from a conceited heart, not from one which was contrite and humble, and they would not be justified. They were full of fine words but it was deeds that mattered.

Those who build on a secure foundation, by acting as God asks, find God will not let them down. He has a 'reputation' to maintain, he will not take Satan's part and he will bestow on his faithful followers all they need in this life, and eternal life at the end of the era.

E. Jesus' message - mainly to his disciples.

E 1. God is Father, Teacher, Master - Mt. 23:8-11.

In the O.T. the fatherhood of God was a fundamental tenet of the relation between God and his chosen people, Israel: 'You, O Lord, are our Father; from of old, "our redeemer" is your name' (Is. 63:16). In a rabbinical commentary this opinion is more emphatically expressed: 'Beloved are Israel, for they were called children of God; still greater was the love by which they came to know this, as it is written: "You are the children of the Lord your God" [with reference to Dt. 14:1]' (m.Avot. 3:15). Some prophets had warned that God had withdrawn from the relationship and Israel had 'orphaned' itself: 'We have become orphans, fatherless ...' (Lam. 5:3), though longing to enter the kingdom again: 'Restore us to you, O Lord, that we may be restored!' (Lam. 5:21). The word 'Father' also often refers to the patriarchs, especially Abraham, Isaac and Jacob.

"You are not to be called 'Master'," said Jesus. "You have one master or instructor and you are all learners[1] and brothers. You are to call no man on earth 'father', because you have only one Father, and he is in heaven. You are not to be called leader either, because you have a leader, the Anointed."

The original could have been:
'Call no one on earth "My master", for One is your Teacher (or Rabbi).
Call no one instructor, for One is your instructor.
Call no one on earth Father, for One is your Father.
Remember, you are all brothers and learners together.'

In the new covenant of the kingdom, God's law will be written on the hearts of its citizens: 'This is the covenant I will make with the house of Israel after those days,' says the Lord. 'I will put my Law within them and I will write it on their hearts ... They all shall know me from the least to the greatest,' says the Lord, 'for I will forgive their iniquity and I will remember no more their sin' (Jer. 31:33-34); 'I will give them a different heart and put a new spirit in them. I will take away their hearts of stone and give them hearts of flesh, that they may conform to my statutes, and obey' (Ezk. 11:19). God will teach them himself, and each one will know God's wishes: 'All your sons shall be taught by the Lord, and their prosperity will be great' (Is. 54:13); 'Make your ways known to me, O Lord, and teach me your paths; lead me in your truth and teach me' (Ps. 25:4-5).

The passage may be a warning to the early community that those who passed on the gospel had to be particularly careful. They were not to set themselves up as intermediaries between God and mankind. Even Jesus does not claim to be an intermediary though he explains God's will in his gospel to those who will listen. He is God's apostle, giving out God's word. 'A person's life must be centred on God's rule', is the message here.

---

[1] The word 'learners' is not found in all versions of the gospel.

E 2. The greatest in the kingdom of God - Mt. 20:20-28. Mk. 10:35-45. Lk. 22:24-27.

In the O.T. to 'drink the cup' was to meet hardship and persecution or God's wrath: 'You, Jerusalem, have drunk the cup of wrath, at the hand of the Lord ... you have drunk to the dregs the bowl of drunkenness; of all the sons you have borne there is none to guide you, of all you have reared, there is not one to take you by the hand' (Is. 51:17-18). Baptism or immersion was often connected with thoughts of frightful, dangerous straits which could lead to death: 'Save me, O Lord, for the waters have risen up to my neck. I sink in the mire and have no foothold. I have come into deep waters and the flood carries me away' (Ps. 69:1-2).

One day, James Zebedee and his brother John, came to Jesus and said, "Master, we want you to do whatever we ask you to do for us." "And what is that?", asked Jesus. "Grant us the right to sit with you in glory, one on your right hand and one on your left."

Jesus was taken aback. "You do not know what you are asking", he said. "Can you drink the cup that I am to drink, or be baptized with the immersion I am to be baptized with?"

"We can", they replied.

"Very well", said Jesus, "you shall share the cup I am to drink, and my immersion shall be yours, but I cannot offer you the places on my right side and on my left. They are for those for whom my Father has prepared them."

When the other ten disciples heard about this, they were incensed with James and John, and a rivalry broke out amongst them as to who would rank the highest in the kingdom.

Jesus called them to him and said, "In this world kings and great men rule over their subjects, and are called benefactors. For you, it is not like that: among you, whoever wishes to attain greatness must be your slave; whoever wants to be first must be your servant, like one waiting at table. For who is the greater: the one reclining at table or the one who waits on him? Surely the one at table; yet here I am, a servant among you. The son of man did not come to be served, but to serve and to give his life in the stead of many."

The request of James and John showed how they transposed the scale of values of their own experience to the world to come. They thought they could become legates of God, sharing in Jesus' glory. They supposed they could share any fate that lay in store for Jesus, even the direst fate of martyrdom, and by that means have the most desirable places in recognition of their sacrifice. Jesus tells them that those who are counted as the greatest in the kingdom of God are those who become the servants of others. Martyrdom in itself was not necessarily a service to others, and there could be no hierarchy nor preferences in God's kingdom. Even if rulers were beneficial that was not enough because they still treated others as inferiors.

The teaching of Judaism never includes direct information about the situation after the day of Judgement, and God's disposition of the places at the messianic feast was not something Jesus could give any assurance about. Nevertheless there was a common belief that the Elect would assist, at least, in the Day of Judgement (see F4), and there were other speculations in Judaism. In a discussion about the throne of God in heaven and a second throne beside God's, rabbis had different ideas. One said, 'One throne was [placed] for God and one for David [the Messiah];' another said, 'One throne is for justice and the other for mercy' (b.Sanh. 38b).

The concept of vicarious suffering for the sins of fathers, as a means of redeeming the present generation and the theory that an innocent man's death could atone for the sins of the nation is clearly pre-Christian and well known in the O.T.: 'Our fathers sinned, and are no more, and we bear the burden of their guilt.' (Lam. 5:7). In I.T. writings the same idea is found. The last words of the Maccobean martyr Eleazar show this: 'He lifted up his eyes to God and said, "You know, O God, that though I could save myself, I am dying by the torments of the fire for your Law. Be merciful to your people ... and make my blood their purification, and take my soul to ransom their souls"' (IV Mac. 6:27-29); and: '(Jacob said to Joseph), "In you will be fulfilled the prophecy of heaven, that a blameless one shall be delivered up for lawless men and a sinless one shall die for ungodly men"' (T.Ben. 3:8). In rabbinical writing too, there are passages which agree with this: 'As the day of Atonement atones, so the death of the righteous atones' (Lev.R. 20:12).

The greater the innocence the more efficacious the sacrifice was thought to be: 'These men having sanctified themselves for God's sake ... through them the enemy had no more power over our people ... and our country was purified, they having, as it were, become a ransom for our nation's sin. Through the blood of these righteous men and the propitiation for their death, divine Providence delivered Israel ...' (IV Mac. 17:20-22). The idea is even found in descriptions of heaven: 'The holy ones who dwell in the heavens shall unite with one voice and supplicate and pray ... on behalf of the blood of the righteous which may have been shed ...' (I En. 47:2). Only God can effect such a ransom: 'Have no fear; for I (the Lord) have paid your ransom. I have called you by name and you are my own. When you pass through the waters, I will be with you; when you pass through the rivers, you will not be swept away; when you walk through fire ... the flames shall not consume you' (Is.43:1-2). No one else could do this: 'No man can ever ransom himself nor pay God the price of that release; his ransom would cost too much, for ever beyond his power to pay ...' (Ps. 49:7-8).

It is Isaiah who portrays the suffering servant most prominently: 'It was the will of the Lord to bruise him; he has put him to grief ... by his knowledge shall the righteous one, my servant, make many to be accounted righteous and he shall bear their iniquities. I shall divide him as a spoil, because he poured out his soul to death, and was numbered with the transgressors; yet he bore the sins of many, and made intercession for the transgressors' (Is. 53:10-12). The Aramaic version of these verses is different: 'It was the Lord's good pleasure to refine and purify the remnant of his people, to cleanse their soul from sin; they shall look upon the kingdom of the

Messiah ... By his Wisdom he shall justify the just, in order to subject many to the Law.'

The last sentence of the passage needs clarification; the reconstructed Aramaic original was probably: 'It is the purpose of the son of man (namely, Jesus himself and those who follow his example) to serve and to devote his life, taking no heed of the risks or even death, as a ransom for the sins of others (Israel).'

In Matthew's gospel, it is the mother of James and John who makes the request to Jesus on behalf of her sons.

* * *

E 3. The blessing of the children - Mt. 5:29-30; 18:1-10; 19:13-15. Mk. 9:33-37, 42-48; 10:13-16. Lk. 9:46-48; 17:1-3; 18:15-17.

Jesus is shown in this passage actively blessing children, demonstrating that his teaching is the means whereby they and others of a similarly lowly status in contemporary society, can enter the kingdom. A child is enthusiastic about anything he enjoys. There is in them the potential for divine fellowship and this must not be endangered in any way. The idea is not that children should be humble. They should be innocent; in rabbinical writings, there is no belief in original sin but 'One should give back one's soul at death as pure as when being born' (j.Ber.4d); 'Young children are pure ...' (PK 6:3), so that one thought to be wholly righteous might be described as a child one day old. It is also that those who enter the kingdom are those who embrace it with the enthusiasm of children without let or hindrance. A passage relating to children is rare in Judaism although in the O.T. there is, 'Out of the mouths of babes and sucklings you have perfected praise' (Ps. 8:2 LXX); and in I.T. books 'For a father's blessing strengthens the houses of the children' (Sir. 3:9).

One day, the disciples were arguing about who was the greatest and Jesus, realizing this, said to them, "If anyone wants to be first he must make himself last of all and servant of all. It is the least among you who is the greatest."

He took a child into his arms and said to them, "The kingdom of God belongs to such as this child. Quite certainly, unless you take to the kingdom of God as this child, you will never enter it.

Whoever receives such a child in my name receives me, and whoever receives me, receives not me but God who sent me. As for anyone who leads astray one of these little ones who have faith in God, anyone who lays traps for them, it would be better for him to be drowned in the depths of the sea with a millstone around his neck."

Jesus embraced the children and thoroughly blessed them, laying his hands on them, and said, "If your eye is a stumbling block which leads you astray, tear it out and fling it from you. If your hand or foot is the cause of your undoing, cut it off and throw it away. Better to enter maimed into life in the kingdom of God than to end up whole in Gehenna, where the worm never dies and where every one shall be burnt up in the everlasting fire. Causes of stumbling and snares must exist in the world, but woe betide the ones through whom others are misled. Everyone will be burnt with fire. I tell you this, these little ones have their angels in heaven who look continually on the face of my heavenly Father."

It is not always clear to whom the 'little ones' refers. The Greek word used here for 'little ones' is not the same as that used for 'children', and it might also refer, as in Judaism, to a humble believer, rather than a child of tender years. It was a very old idea that such could have direct contact with God (see God's face): 'I shall see your face and be blessed with a vision of you when I awake' (Ps. 17:15).

The passage is reminiscent of the treatment God promised to the children of the Israelites in the wilderness. During their wanderings in the wilderness after escaping from Egypt, the Israelites did not keep to the covenant with God. 'They rebelled against me and would not listen to me: not every man cast away the detestable things their eyes feasted on, nor did they forsake the idols of Egypt' (Ezk. 20:8). As a result, all those over twenty years of age were not allowed to enter the promised land, and their children had to serve forty years punishment in the wilderness for the idolatry and wickedness of their forefathers, before the Israelites could conquer Canaan: 'Here in this wilderness your bones shall lie, every man ... from twenty years old and upwards ... your sons shall be shepherds and wanderers in the wilderness forty years, paying the penalty for your wanton disloyalty, until the last man of you lies there' (Num. 14:29-33).

It is the 'children', faithful to Joshua and Caleb, who will attain the land promised the them: 'Your little ones, your dependents (slaves and servants) whom you said would become prey, and your children, who have as yet no knowledge of good or evil, who shall go into the land to possess it' (Dt 1:39).

Jesus emphasized the seriousness of the sin of those who seduce and mislead others. The same assertion is found in rabbinical writings: 'He who causes another to stumble is punished in equal measure to him who stumbles, and he who turns another to righteousness will be rewarded like the doer of righteousness himself' (Sif.Num. 5:21); 'Causing someone to sin is worse than killing. Being killed leaves the victim the enjoyment of the world to come, while sin prevents enjoyment of both this world and the one to come' (Sif.Dt. 252) and 'One who causes many to sin is not given the opportunity to repent' (m.Avot. 5:18).

It is also connected with the strong prohibition against misleading others into worshipping false gods: 'Any ... who gives any of his children to Moloch shall be put to death; the people of the land shall stone him with stones. I myself will set my face against that man and will cut him off from his people' (Lev. 20:2-3); 'If (anyone) entices you secretly saying, "Let us go and serve other gods" ... you shall not yield to him ... nor shall you spare him ... You shall stone him to death with stones ...' (Dt. 13:6-10).

The punishment advocated in the passage, drowning was even worse than first appears, because to be drowned in this way precluded burial. The land of Israel was thereby not polluted by the corpses of such sinners, but also the souls of the dead could never hope to take part in the 'Promised Land', after the day of Judgement.

In rabbinical writings, the argument put forward is that things were created in six days, which did not leave time to perfect them, so that the imperfections must be cut away. (An example of this is the rite of circumcision.) Eyes, feet and hands were traditionally associated with crimes of various kinds. The hand and the foot were connected in rabbinical thought with sexual sins and the language suggests sexual abuse of minors is what is condemned. The eye was also the source of lustful glances: 'One who sins with his eye is also condemned.' (Lev.R. 23:12).

In other writings, the hands and feet were associated with fraud and robbery respectively. The part of the body removed was thought to be appropriate to the type of crime committed. In I.T. literature is found: '... the hand that is not industrious shall be cut off from its shoulder and the eye which gives me no light shall be plucked out by the ravens' (Ahk. 8:14,20). In rabbinical terms, it is like a tree with boughs which overhang an unclean place. By cutting off these branches, the tree becomes clean and although it is not very nice to lose them in this world, it means happiness in the next world (b.Kid. 40b).

Before you commit a sin, weigh up the prospects! In the first place, unlike a crime, no sin can escape God's knowledge. Therefore root out the bad inclinations which lead to sin, and especially those which may lead astray others. Some thought 'sins committed unwittingly cannot be atoned for by the priests with a sin-offering but R. Eliezer said this was not so: 'It concerns all Israel and therefore sins intentional or not have to be atoned for by a sin offering' (Sif. Num. on 15:22-31).

By cauterizing the 'self' (see F 11) one avoids ending up rotten (breeding worms), suffering the fires of hell: 'They shall go forth and look on the carcasses of those who have rebelled against me (the Lord); for their spirits shall not die, nor their fire be quenched, and the wicked shall be judged in Gehenna' (Tg.Is. 66:24); 'The Lord ... will take vengeance on all nations which rise up against Israel ... put fire and worms in their flesh and they shall weep and feel pain for ever' (Jud. 16:17); 'The punishment of the ungodly is fire and worms' (Sir. 7:17).

The last but one sentence of the passage is usually given as: 'Everyone will be salted with fire'. This is meaningless and probably due to a misunderstanding of the underlying Semitic language.

* * *

E 4. The great feast - Mt. 22:1-10. Lk. 14:15-24.

We can imagine that the disciples must have wondered whether one could ever be excused from active support of God's will because of other legitimate duties. Had there not to be a balance between work for God and the jobs everyone had to do to stay alive? And what about good deeds which were done by someone through force of circumstances: did they earn merit too? They got their answer here.

At the house of a Pharisee when they were reclining at table, one of the company said to Jesus, "Happy is he who shall partake of the messianic feast in the kingdom of God!"

Jesus commented: "There was once a rich man who arranged a large party and sent out many invitations to various important people. As is usual, when the time came he sent his servant to those he had invited with the message:'Please come, everything is ready.' But each had an excuse and could not come. One had just bought some land and had to go to see it; another had to do some ploughing on his farm with some oxen he had just bought; and a third had just got married and would not leave his new wife.

When the servant returned, the master was very cross. 'Well, if those well-standing people I have invited will not come, we shall invite those who will. I won't have the food wasted. Go out into the city and invite in any poor, any maimed, any lame and any blind you find.' Even after this, there was still room, so the servants were next sent outside the town to find all they could - good and bad alike. 'Insist that they come in; I want my house to be full', the master said, 'and not one of those who were invited first shall taste my banquet.'

The kingdom of God is like that. Those who have not accepted the invitation to the feast, cannot partake of it, but those who respond to the call, enjoy God's banquet. The others will be astonished that it is the poor, the weak and sinners who sit at table, while the rich important personages are locked out from my Father's house."

The O.T. gave four reasons which excuse a man from joining the army in a war: 'What man is there that has built a new house and has not dedicated it? Let him go back to his house, lest he die in the battle and another man dedicate it. And what man has planted a vineyard and has not enjoyed its fruit? Let him go back to his house, lest ... another man enjoy its fruit. And what man is there that has betrothed a wife and has not taken her? Let him go back to his house, lest ... another man take her. And ... what man is there that is fearful and fainthearted? Let him to back to his house, lest the heart of his fellows melt as his heart' (Dt. 20:5-9).

Three of these four exceptions are paralleled in the gospel passage. Thus the reasons the original guests gave for their refusal of the invitation were all perfectly legitimate according to Jewish law and the customs recognized by the community. One who had bought some land had to visit it in order to confirm the purchase. This was a legal requirement. It was a religious duty, too, to farm land responsibly according to the Torah and a good farmer ploughs when the time is right: 'A land which the Lord your God tends and cares for, the eye of the Lord is upon it, from the beginning to the end of the year' (Dt. 11:12). Similarly, the newly-wed was required to be at home for the first year of his marriage. All those originally invited had proper, legal and religious reasons for doing what they did. The same things are mentioned in I.T. passages: 'Do not resent manual labour or farm work for it was ordained by God ... Have you cattle? Take care of them yourself. Have you a wife, do not forsake her' (Sir. 7:15,22,26); 'They ... shall make all the fearful of heart withdraw ...' (DSS, W 10:5-6).

The initial remark was an expression of comforting pride and conceit: 'We, who are so punctilious in our religious observances, we can look forward to blessedness in Paradise.' They had obeyed the principles demanded of them by their concept of the Law, but by their refusals these law-abiders had ignored God's call to the colours. They had been invited, but other matters had come first and they could not complain if others took their places. If God calls and we do not respond, we can not play 'dog in the manger' and stop 'less religious' folk taking our places. Only those who come when God sends for them to bring the message further are righteous and will partake of the messianic banquet in the New Era.

It is usually supposed that the city represents Israel, so that those who came in from the alleys and by-ways are the sinners and Gentiles. The parable is typical Jewish teaching and is related to O.T. texts: 'The Lord has prepared a feast and has consecrated the guests he has sent for' (Zph. 1:7-8); 'Wisdom has slaughtered her beasts; she has mixed her wine and set her table. She has sent out her servants to call from the highest places in the town. Whoever is simple or foolish, come ... eat of my bread, drink of my wine' (Pvb. 9:2-5). The invited guests were those who thought they were the chosen sons of Israel on whom God relied, but who were replaced by others who obeyed his summons. In rabbinical literature there are sayings of great understanding and tolerance: 'God said, "Both Gentiles and Israelites are my handiwork; why should I let the former perish because of the latter?"' (b.San. 98b).

Judaism had become distorted by a very specific and exact system of reciprocal entertaining and present-giving. This was so artificial that it is believed one person could formally complain that his friend had returned less than the amount or value the first had given him! The rich man could not expect any reciprocation from his new guests, and by giving them the feast he did a good deed. Even though he did so only because the intended original guests did not come, his action was a good one, because he used the chance to follow his good inclination.

Nevertheless, this explanation may not be the whole story. If the reasons for not responding to God's call were indeed invalid, as the parable indicates, some believe their significance is that they were the sort of excuses Jesus' listeners knew only too well. They would appreciate the needs of the farm, ownership of an estate, 'the wife wouldn't let me' and so forth. These were perhaps little jokes, used by Jesus not only to point his message, but also to catch the interest of his listeners.

The basic story line is known from earlier sources. For example in I.T. literature: 'On the feast of Pentecost ... a good dinner was prepared for me ... I said to Tobias my son, 'Go, and bring to me any poor man of our brethren ... and he shall eat with me ...'' (Tob. 2:2, and PR 9:11). The story of Bar Ma'jam, a rich tax-collector from rabbinical literature, is another example: 'One day, Bar Ma'jam arranged a large banquet for the town dignitaries but none of them came when the banquet was held. Bar Ma'jam was so annoyed he sent his servants out to find anyone to take the empty places, so the food should not be wasted. The servants came back with many poor people who enjoyed the feast. This was the one good deed of his life, and immediately afterwards, he died. His reward for this good deed was a splendid funeral, attended by all the dignitaries.

A poor scholar, who was kind and responsible for many good deeds, also died about this time, but he received no special attention at all, nor a fine funeral' (j.San. 6:23c). The story continues with Bar Ma'jam being tormented in hell while the poor scholar resides in Paradise, and is given with the story of the rich man and Lazarus (see G 4).

Matthew's version tells of a king, not a rich man, whose servants were seized, maltreated and even murdered by the prospective guests, and he adds:

The king was furious; he sent troops to kill those murderers and set their town on fire.

There have been several attempts to account for this addition. It could be an allegory of how the apostles of God, the prophets, had been maltreated by the religious leaders of Israel, God's chosen nation. It may be connected to the story of Esther, in which King Ahasuerus later destroys those led by Haman who were intending to kill all the Jews. (He could be represented by the figure of the man without wedding clothes in the next passage, E 5). A third idea is that it is related to the first chapter of Zephaniah in which it is said that God will destroy all those who worship idols and are unrighteous.

Another suggestion is that the refusals were taken to be a political insult. A king would suppose it was an act of rebellion if all the notables of the kingdom ignored his invitation to dinner and especially by an apparently concerted action. Those insulting a king would be punished and how much greater than a king was God! He would avenge his prophets, who invite men to the banquet of his realm, but who refuse to come to it.

Another rabbinical story illustrates the theme: 'It is like a king who made a banquet and brought in guests and seated them at the entrance to his palace. The guests saw the dogs as they left with pheasants in their mouths and the heads of fatted calves. They said, "If this is what the dogs get to eat, how much richer will our banquet be!"' and in the O.T. similarly: 'The wicked of Israel are likened to dogs. The dogs are the greedy ones' (Is. 56:11) and they prosper in the world. All the more so will the righteous of Israel prosper in the world-to-come, as its says, 'you will put joy into my heart' (Midr.Ps. 4:11).

The sentiments of the passage in Luke are much nearer to subsequent rabbinical tradition than those in Matthew.

* * *

E 5. The guest without the correct clothes - Mt. 22:11-14.

Some maintain this is an integral part of the previous parable about the great feast (E4), but others say it has that association because it is so associated by Matthew. Luke omits it, and there is much to be said for the view that E 4 is a story without a proper ending, and this passage is a story without a proper beginning! One might surmise that both began: 'The kingdom of God is like this. There was once a king (or, a rich man) who prepared a feast for his son's wedding (or, his guests).'

This parable is concerned with the need to assume the correct dress before entering the king's palace and partaking of his banquet. A wedding garment, a clean, newly washed, white garment is expected because that is the symbol of a repentant sinner, one of the redeemed community. To attend in a dirty garment was a serious insult to the host; it was a symbol of mourning or idolatry.

"You remember the story of the king who invited people to a banquet?", said Jesus. "When the king came in to see that his guests were enjoying themselves and had all they wished, he noticed one man who had not put on a wedding garment. 'Well, well, my friend! How do you come to be here without your wedding clothes?', he asked. The man made no reply. 'Bind him hand and foot and throw him out into the place of darkness', said the king to his servants. 'For many are called but few are chosen.'"

It was normal that the host did not eat with his guests at a formal banquet, but he would come to see that they had all they needed during the meal.

Those whom the king rejected were dispatched to the place of darkness which is where the wicked await their fate on, or until, the day of Judgement. This imagery was widely used: 'Here their spirits shall be set apart in great pain until the day of Judgement, with punishment and torture of the accursed, and retribution for their spirits. There he shall bind them to the end of the age' (I En. 22:11); 'After that, their faces shall be filled with shame and the son of man will deliver them to the angels for punishment, to execute vengeance on them' (I En. 62:10-11); 'The sinner falls and rises no more, the destruction of the sinner is for ever' (P.S. 3:13). More specifically, it was how rebellious Azazel was treated when Raphael was told by God to cast him out of heaven: 'Bind Azazel hand and foot and cast him into the darkness ... and on the day of the great judgement he shall be cast into the fire' (I En. 10:4-6). The Israelites who refused to recognize Jesus' message, who rejected God's call, would be thrown out of the kingdom if they dared to show themselves there.

The last sentence seems to be an adage used in many circumstances but the underlying Aramaic may mean, 'The more numerous are called, the less numerous are chosen or elected, that is saved. Not all in Israel were the elect and no one could take for granted that he or she belonged to God's chosen. In Jewish teaching, God is envisaged sometimes as an army commander, preparing to battle with the forces of evil. He will call for recruits and no doubt many will turn up believing themselves suitable for such a battle, but God can use only the truly righteous. He will reject many who are spiritually unfit: 'Many have been created, but few shall be saved!' (IV Ezr. 8:3); 'There are more who perish than shall be saved' (IV Ezr. 9:15). He will accept help from those who are handicapped in other ways. They may lack knowledge or deep understanding and they will not necessarily find a place in the front-line with the elite soldiers but their support behind the lines is just as valuable.

As so often, detailed study shows that the language of Jesus' story is made more memorable by puns and little jokes. Here he uses a word for 'to fight' which is very like that which means 'to feast' or 'to eat bread', making a link between the battle and the banquet or feast which always followed a successful battle. (Note, too, the exclamation at the beginning of the previous passage: 'How fortunate to be able to eat bread in the kingdom of God!') The Pharisees were complaining that Jesus wanted to open the door of heaven to all sorts of ungodly people, even Gentiles, while Jesus fought against the pharisaic attitude that heaven's gate had to be protected from the riff-raff by these 'pious' Pharisees (see G 10). In this little story, Jesus makes a crack at them, indicating that God invited all but he would not take them just as they were. Heaven's gate was open to everyone, but first they had to repent, and put on the garment of redemption.

There is a story told in rabbinical literature to illustrate the verse: 'Behold my servants shall eat, but you shall be hungry' (Is. 65:13): 'A king invited some guests to a feast, but did not specify the time for it. The astute ones thought to themselves, "There is nothing the palace lacks; the feast can begin at any moment!" They changed their clothes and dressed suitably for the occasion.

There were others who thought, "Well, it always takes time to prepare a feast, we can relax and wait a while. There will be time enough to get changed later." They carried on with their ordinary work until suddenly the king sent for all the guests. He was pleased to see those in their clean clothes, but annoyed by those who were still in their working clothes. "Let those who have clean garments sit down and eat; the others must stand back and look on", said the king. "They can have the punishment of being hungry and unable to take part"' (b.Shab.153a).

Another Jewish story is similar to Jesus' parable: 'There was a certain king who made a feast and invited to it all the wayfarers and strangers in his dominions; but he made a decree that every one should bring with him something to sit on. Some brought beautiful and comfortable cushions, and some brought handsome but hard seats, and some ... brought logs of wood, and some stones or boulders. The king provided everything for the nourishment and entertainment of all comers, and to adorn the court of the palace but ordered that each man should sit, at the feast, on the couch or seat that he had brought for himself.

Then they who were sitting on logs and stones ... grumbled at the king and said, "Is it to the honour of the king that we should be sitting here is such discomfort, on stones and bits of wood?"

When the king heard their complaints he said to them, "It is not enough for you that you disgrace my palace with stones and logs, my palace that I have built and beautified at so much cost; but will you also insult me and fasten an accusation upon me? Your honour and splendour are such as you make for yourselves."

Thus in the world to come the wicked are adjudged to Gehenna and they complain in loud anger against the Holy One, and say, "Behold we were hoping for the salvation of God and this is what has come to us!"

And the Holy One says to them: "In the world in which you were, were you not quarrelling and fighting against each other, and doing all evil things; and were you not contentious and acting with violence? ... Perhaps you will say that you have this at my hands. It is not so; but you yourselves have made all this for yourselves and therefore, 'You shall lie down in sorrow' (Is. 50:11) and: '... it is at your own hands that you suffer all this' (Mal. 1:9); "The condition of one's soul in the life to come, in the banquet of eternal splendour that God has provided, will be such as one prepares for one's self'" (Ecc.R. 3:9,1).

Many aspects of this and the previous passage remain difficult, compounded by the differences between the passages in Matthew and Luke. In I.T. books the separation of the sinners from the righteous is portrayed in various ways: 'And he [the Son of Man] sat on the throne of his glory and the whole of judgement was given to him; he caused the sinners to pass away and be destroyed off the face of the earth' (I En. 69:27).

The word used for 'servants' in this passage refers to servants of God, indicating that it is concerned with the messianic feast in the kingdom of God.

* * *

E 6. Forgiveness and the unforgiving servant - Mt. 6:14-15; 18:21-35. Mk. 11:25. Lk. 17:3-4.

Some of the religious leaders of Jesus' day may have taught what is recorded of a rabbi in about 180 C.E.: 'If a man commits a transgression once, One (i.e. God) forgives him; if a second time, One forgives him; if a third time, One forgives him; if a fourth time, One does not forgive him. For transgressions between man and God, the Day of Atonement effects atonement. For transgressions between a man and his fellow, the Day of Atonement effects atonement only if he has appeased his fellow' (m.Yom. 8:9). Peter asked his question to find out Jesus' view on this point, perhaps. He was being generous by proposing to forgive seven times, and Jesus' answer no doubt astonished him!

Peter came to Jesus and asked him, "Lord, how often am I to forgive my brother if he goes on wronging me? As many as seven times?"

Jesus replied, "Seven times? No, I say seventy times seven! If your brother wrongs you rebuke him; if he repents forgive him. Even if he wrongs you seven times during the day and returns to you seven times, saying, "I repent", you shall forgive him. And, when you pray, forgive anyone against whom you have a grievance, so that your Father in heaven may forgive you the wrongs you are guilty of. If you forgive others the wrongs they have done to you, your heavenly Father will also forgive you, but if you do not forgive others, then the wrongs you have done will not be forgiven by your Father."

The background for this passage is the strong Jewish legal opposition to blood-feuds. They could destroy societies, because it was often the case that the revenge was greater than the initial crime. As Lamech boasted, his vengeance would be seventy times seven as much: 'Vengeance has been exacted seven times on Cain's behalf, and on Lamech's it shall be seventy times seven' (Gen. 4:24 LXX). In early O.T. writings the doctrine of talion (an eye for an eye, rather than two eyes for one, for example) was advocated to stop the increasing scale of revenge, but this assumed that one eye was exactly the same as another, which was clearly not the case. It was soon abandoned for financial penalties which were remarkably lenient.

Later the idea developed that vengeance belonged to God and that forgiveness was better than any other remedy: 'The vengeful man will face the vengeance of the Lord, who keeps a strict account of the sinner's transgressions. Forgive the wrong your neighbour does to you, so that when you pray, your sins will be forgiven. If a man harbours a grudge against another, can he expect healing from the Lord? If he has no mercy on his fellowman, can he ask for forgiveness for his own sins?' (Sir. 28:1-4); 'Do not be so confident of pardon that you add sin to sin. Do not say his mercies are great, he will pardon my sins, however great' (Sir. 5:5-6). The same idea is found in rabbinical writings: 'You shall not take vengeance nor bear a grudge' (b. Yoma 23a on Lev. 19:18); 'So long as we are merciful to others, God is merciful to us, but if we are not merciful to others, God is not merciful to us' (b.R.Sh. 17a); 'A man shall bestow loving kindness even on one who does evil to him; a man shall not be vengeful nor bear a grudge. This is the way of Israel' (P.B. Le'olam 7).

Jesus tells Peter he must forgive with no limit those who repent of their wrong-doing and perhaps the phrase 'seventy times seven' was used in stark contrast to its purpose in the story of Lamech, in order to emphasize the difference between such teaching and that of Jesus.

On another occasion, Jesus drew attention to the consequences if one refused to forgive others: "The kingdom of God has become like the following situation. There was once a powerful king who required his servants to go through their accounts and settle up with him financially. One of them was found to owe him ten thousand talents. The man had no means of paying such a sum and he was sentenced by the king: 'All you have is to be sold', said the king. 'Your house and lands, and your wife and children.'

The servant fell prostrate at his feet. 'Defer your anger with me a little while', he said, 'and I will repay in full what I owe.' The king was moved by his plea, and, filled with compassion, decided to remit the debt.

No sooner had the servant gone out than he met one of his fellow servants who owed him a hundred dinars. He took him by the throat and said, 'Pay me the money you owe me.' The fellow fell at the servant's feet. 'Please be patient with me a little while yet', he begged. 'I will pay it all back to you.' 'No', said the servant, 'you go to prison until the debt is paid.'

When the others in the king's service heard of this, they were distressed and told the king, who sent for the servant. 'You are indeed a wicked scoundrel', said the lord. 'I freed you from the whole of your debt, when you appealed to me. Were you not bound to show the same mercy to your fellow servant?' The king was so angry he delivered the man to the tormentors until he had paid the debt in full.

That's how it is with my heavenly Father. He will deal with you likewise unless you forgive one another from your hearts."

Some scholars think the legal system of the time underlies the parable. The servant may be thought of as a governor or satrap of a province of a powerful king. The system was that tax-collection was farmed out to the highest bidder, who in turn arranged under-collectors to collect sufficient taxes to cover the amount demanded by the king, with normally a good deal of profit for both the under-collectors and the satrap himself. Revenues collected by the governor were due to be paid when the king called for them, but if people were unable to pay because of wars, famines, epidemics, and so on, the satrap would be unable to produce the amount he had contracted to provide for the king. Thus the difficulty is the short-fall which he offers to pay, since it is part of the agreement that he makes up any short-fall and pockets any excess. Alternatively, he could ask for the debt to be carried over into the following year in the hope of better times.

It was not unknown for a righteous Jew to forgive a debt, or give more time for it to be repaid: 'If there is among you anyone in need ... do not be hard-hearted or tight-fisted towards your needy neighbour. You should rather ... lend willingly ... Be careful that you do not entertain a mean thought, thinking, "The year of remission is near" and therefore view your needy neighbour with hostility' (Dt.15:7-9); 'If a man is righteous ... he does not oppress anyone but restores to the debtor his pledge' (Ezk. 18:5-7). It was not acceptable to extract oaths from debtors nor to harass them. In this story the king perhaps decided the amount he had originally demanded was too great and he remitted the debt in the interests of his subjects in that province. The king behaved generously and wisely.

The satrap goes out and notices one of his under-officers and demands that he pay what he owes the satrap. Probably he thought the king would be pleased to see that he was even more active in extracting the king's taxes! He was quite blind to the example of the king who showed wise concern for his subjects. He did not realize that it was an example he himself should follow in his dealings with his own band of tax-collectors. He showed no sign that he had just benefited from financial generosity on a grand scale, and the blessing he had received had made no impression on him. As it says in the O.T.: 'The wicked borrows and does not repay, but the righteous is generous and gives. Truly those whom the Lord has blessed shall possess the land but those whom he curses shall be destroyed' (Ps. 37:21-22); and in I.T. literature: 'You taught the people ... that the righteous must be a lover of men; and you made your sons to be of good hope because you gave repentance when men have sinned' (W.S. 12:19).

The satrap did not behave as if he had been forgiven because the process had been entirely one-sided. For forgiveness to be effective it requires both one to forgive and one to accept it and be changed by it. The parable was not to suggest there is a kind of barter: 'You be nice to others in order that God will be nice to you.' For Jesus, the point was that only someone with a forgiving spirit in himself towards others was in a state whereby he could receive God's forgiveness. There could be no forgiveness without repentance for one's own wrong-doing. The one who receives forgiveness, values it and makes it active in his life becomes automatically a person who forgives others: 'The Lord redeems the life of his servants and none of those who take refuge in him will be condemned' (Ps. 34:22). The true disciple is happy only when every barrier between himself and his brother has been removed. Or as Jerome said, 'Never be joyful except when you look on your fellowman with love.'

The point is not to show one who forgives innumerable times compared with one who does not. It shows one who was forgiven ten thousand talents, a sum so large that it was an almost impossible debt to repay, compared with one who refused to forgive a trivial debt. It was not necessarily told to illustrate Jesus' answer to Peter's question, which is found only in Matthew's gospel. It was Jewish teaching about the relationship between one person forgiving another and God forgiving a person: to forgive a debt was a good 'investment' - it meant acquiring credit with God. The story suggests that Jesus was concerned to reduce or cancel the debts of all who repented (see also the story of G 3).

Since Matthew begins by referring to a king in the first part of this passage, but then changes it to a lord, some think the original form of the passage has been modified. Similarly, it is argued that ten thousand dinars may have been changed to ten thousand talents in order to impress his readers, although this conflicts with other points of the parable. No servant could possibly amass a debt of ten thousand talents and the sale of his family and goods would cover only a small fraction of the debt. No relatives or friends could hope to redeem the man from prison on condition the full amount was paid. These considerations have led other scholars to suggest that the story is about a lord and his chief servant.

It should be pointed out that the chief servant's demand for repayment by the second servant was the expected behaviour of the time. Not only was it in contrast with the forgiving mercy of the king or lord, showing that the harshness, hard-heartedness of normal life was totally opposed to the kind of behaviour advocated in the O.T. and found in God's realm. His behaviour was also against the Roman law, which is the background to this passage, since only under Roman law could a wife and children be sold to redeem a debt, or a debtor forcibly seized and taken to court or prison. Since the chief servant had not repaid his debt to the king, any money he obtained from others belonged to the king and he was dishonest to try to keep it for himself. In doing what he did, the chief servant forfeited his forgiveness and all his goods could be seized and sold. He would be tortured to make him disclose all his assets.

Some have reacted against the king's harshness in revoking his word and sending the servant to prison especially when the king is taken to represent God, but it is not uncommon for the gospels to portray God as severe against unrepentant sinners. In Judaism, it is accepted that a wrong done to one person by another, can be forgiven only by the victim.

* * *

E 7. The use of resources - Mt. 13:12; 25:14-30. Mk. 4:25. Lk. 8:18; 19:12-27.

This parable is open to more than one interpretation. Some think that Jesus uses the very Jewish idea of God and men as business partners, responsible for increasing the world's riches by lending out capital: 'For the Lord your God will bless you, and you shall lend to many nations but you shall not borrow ...' (Dt. 15:6). Profit was to be gained legitimately by judicious investment: 'Do not be ashamed ... of settling accounts with a partner ... or of business dealings large or small and making a profit out of trade' (Sir. 42:1-5). So also in rabbinical literature: 'He who lends is greater than he who gives alms; and he who provides capital for a useful enterprise is greatest of all', and 'Merit has a capital and bears interest (fruit)' (b.Kid. 40a).

The whole parable shows the need of God's followers to be good agents, using the capital they have received to maximize their return to God (his profit). 'Do not say: "What use am I? What greater good can the future hold for me?"' (Sir. 11:23). The capital from God for the Jew comprised his soul, the Torah, and worldly wealth. They were not for selfish pleasure, but for God's benefit, the result being God's approval and happiness, and even greater confidence in the worth, loyalty and faithfulness of his servants. Not all may be endowed with the same abilities and advantages but that cannot excuse lack of faithfulness to God's rule.

There is a sense of testing in this passage. Given God's capital, it was not enough to keep it safe. Those whom God will accept are those who have done the best they could with it so that God profits from their labours.

Jesus said, "The kingdom of God is like a man going abroad who called his servants to him and gave them some capital which they were to use for business so that there would be a good profit when the master came back. The first received five bags of money, the second two and the third one.

When, after a long time, the master returned, he called his servants to him and asked them how they had acquitted themselves in his absence. The first showed him ten bags of money - he had doubled his original sum and the second had done the same - he could give his master four bags.

The master was very pleased: 'You two are my good and trusty bondsmen. You have proved yourselves trustworthy in a small matter, now you shall be entrusted with even greater responsibilities. Come and share your master's feast.

But what about you my third servant? How have you got on? 'Sir,' said the third servant, 'you are a strict master. You reap where you have not sown, and gather where you have not winnowed. I have kept your money buried for safety, for I was afraid of you. Here is your own money back.'

'You have been indifferent and useless. You say

116

you know what I am like, so you ought to have deposited my money in the bank, so I could at least have had some interest from it. Take his bag and give it to him who has ten.'

Take heed how you hear; for the man who has, will be given more and he will have an abundance; but the man who has not, will forfeit even what he has."

The relation between servant and master was not as we think of it today. The servant was not a slave, but a quasi-son or relative. The rich master gave him capital to use, to make money with. It was not simply a commercial relationship; the master had to trust the servant not to embezzle or squander the capital selfishly, and the servant that the master would share both possible profit and loss in an equitable manner. We can suppose that the amounts entrusted to the servants differed in accordance with the master's assessment of the business acumen of each servant. The first two doubled the money entrusted to them, the profit expected in those days. It was not deemed to be usury because no specific rate of profit was demanded!

The third servant in this parable was given a paltry sum to invest, indicating that the master had little confidence in him. The servant was offended, and would not bother even to lend the money to a bank, since if anything went wrong, he would have to repay half the loss, whoever was at fault. On the other hand, were there to be some profit, it would be very small and not worth his trouble. He did nothing with his share, merely keeping it for the master on his return. This was a nice insult to the master, which was reinforced by his comments on the nature of his master, one who reaps what others have sown. He is contemptuous of his master, and adds injury to his insult of not having placed the capital where it could at least have acquired some interest.

To be like the third servant was to ask for trouble. He was removed from this post; Matthew assigns him, in his favourite style, to 'the dark, the place of wailing and gnashing of teeth.' The moral is drawn that those who make good use of their capital (in all its forms) will receive even more; those who refuse to make use of that which they have been given, will lose that too, and thereby any chance to profit from it.

This parable shows how to be a good master and a wise and careful servant (compare with C 3). Even though a servant might think God was taking all the profit from the servant's good deeds, that was no excuse for not doing good deeds. It was necessary to do them, trusting God to bring them to such fruition as God alone thought proper (see E 8).

In a partnership, each must be able to rely on the probity and responsibility of the other. One who can be trusted in small affairs, can be trusted in greater; he who is dishonest or useless in little matters cannot be trusted in greater. You cannot expect to be trusted with greater capital if you prove to be unconcerned with wealth you have been given to use. Those who have been given God's word in this life and do not follow and obey it, cannot expect to enjoy even greater riches in God's fellowship. God is strict: half-hearted commitment, trying to have it both ways, serving God and mammon, will not do.

In rabbinical writings the following is found: 'God's method is not like men's. With men, a full vessel receives no more; an empty vessel gets filled. With God the full is filled and the empty remains empty. If you have heard, you will continue to hear; if you have not heard, you will not hear in the future. If you have heard the old, you will hear the new; if you have turned away, you will hear no more' (b.Ber.40a); 'If someone listens to God's word a little, he ends by hearing much' (Sif.Dt. 96).

A rabbinical parable gives a human dimension to similar thinking: 'A king appointed two administrators, one of whom was made superintendent over the treasury of straw and the other over that of silver and gold. When accusations were brought against the former he complained that he had not been made superintendent of the treasury of silver and gold. The other, who had that post, chided him; "Your administration has been unfaithful in respect of the straw - how much more would this be the case with silver and gold!"' (Mek. Bah. 5)

Even from a very early stage this parable has been understood in a quite different manner. The picture in this explanation is of an oppressive thieving master, whose greed for money meant that an excessive rate on interest was demanded. The third servant neither cheated not profited at others' expense and the condemnation was of the first servant who had wasted his share with harlots, etc. This seems to be at least a plausible idea.

In Luke, a similar parable is found although there, each of ten servants is given the same amount to trade with, but only three are interviewed by the lord of the house when he returns. The parable is also mixed up with verses telling of a noble who went to be made king, opposed by a delegation of his subjects who hated him, and the passage ends with the new king demanding that his opponents be slaughtered in his presence.

As for these enemies of mine, who did not want me for their king, bring them here and slaughter them in my presence.

Such sentiments are hardly in tune with the rest of what we know of Jesus' teaching and have been a problem a long time.

There are good grounds for thinking that this last verse is connected with the story of Achan and the five kings in the book of Joshua, chapters 7 to 10. Achan in that story also buried property in the ground and only when Achan and his family were eliminated did things go well again for the Israelites. They captured five kings and kept them trapped in a cave. Afterwards they were slain, they were crucified by hanging on trees, and the corpses were again sealed up in the cave. The stories can be understood allegorically, the five kings being the five senses, which are fine while they remain bottled up and not allowed to run out of control, but if they get free, they have to be suppressed to enable one to follow God's rule.

Thus in this interpretation, the third servant is an evil man like Achan, who buried the treasure for his own use, so his master (God) should not profit from it. The five kings represent the evil inclinations in men, which could contaminate the kingdom of God and which must therefore be removed.

Others have argued the passage in Luke refers to the event when Archelaus journeyed to Rome in order to have his inheritance of half of the Kingdom of Herod the Great confirmed by Caesar. An embassy of Jews also went to Rome to try to prevent this, and presumably were treated mercilessly on their return. There is no reason for Luke to include this story and it does not seem likely that this explanation is true.

* * *

E 8. A slave's reward - Lk. 17:7-10.

It was all very well to follow God's way, obeying him in daily life, but it seemed as if the faithful ones spent their time serving others with no acknowledgement or recompense. Surely God could show some sign of approval, at least! Perhaps Jesus told the following to answer this dilemma:

"Well, John," said Jesus, "let me tell you a story. Suppose you had a slave who was out ploughing or tending the sheep. When he came back to the house, will you at once say to him, 'Come, please sit down'? Will you not rather say to him, 'Gird yourself ready for work. Prepare my supper, and wait at table until I have finished. Then you can eat your meal'? Would you give the slave thanks because he obeyed your orders?

It is the same with you. When you have done all things commanded you, you should say to yourselves, 'We are slaves, unprofitable, we have simply done what we were told to do."

Both master and slave benefit when the slave's labour is profitable. A bankrupt master could not keep his slaves, and the alternative to being a slave was usually much worse.

Moral credit arose if one did someone else a good turn, but a slave cannot acquire moral credit by this means because he has no option but to do the work set for him. He can acquire some merit by doing his work willingly, cheerfully, anticipating his master's needs, showing love to his master, as in a rabbinical saying: 'Do not be like slaves who serve their master with a view to receiving a present, but be like slaves who serve their master with no view to receiving a present, and let the fear of God be upon you' (m.Avot.1:3).

It was hopeless for a slave of God to try to show a large profit on his work; for what could possibly be compared with the innumerable blessings from God?: 'Can a man be profitable to God? ... Is it any pleasure to the Almighty that you are righteous, or is it any gain to him, if you are blameless?' (Job 22:2-3). A man's only hope was to make a profit by the quality of his service and to show by his devotion that he loved his master, God: 'What does the Lord require of you but to do justice, to love steadfastly, and to walk humbly with your God?' (Mic. 6:8). And in rabbinical writings: '... it is all one whether a man offers much or little, if only he directs his mind towards heaven' (m.Men. 13:11). To do a good deed to someone which was not reciprocated, did not make one a creditor to that person, nor make him your debtor. Your debtor was God and it was certain that God would reciprocate those to whom he was indebted.

The previous passage (E 7) teaches that those who are active in God's service, and create profit from the capital gifts they have received, are meritorious. Here the emphasis is that productivity is all well and good, but it is up to the master to assess that, as in these I.T. and rabbinical sayings: 'If you have studied the Torah a great deal, do not claim merit for that; for this you were created' (m.Avot. 2:8); 'Blessed is the man who does not direct his heart with malice against any man, helps the injured, raises the broken down and shows charity to the needy ...' (II En. 44:5). Devoted service could still be considered as meritorious even if the slave's activities turned out to be less profitable than could have been hoped for.

The picture of waiting at table is one used by Jesus on more than one occasion to show humble obedient service.

* * *

E 9. The widow's mites - Mk. 12:41-44. Lk. 21:1-4.

It was a requirement of Judaism to bring offerings of various kinds to the Temple: 'We have brought the Lord's offerings ... to make atonement for ourselves before the Lord' (Num. 31:50); 'From every man whose heart makes him willing, you shall receive the offering for me' (Ex. 25:2). The religious leaders enjoyed the benefits, became rich and full of pride. The people began to bow down to them and needless to say, these leaders did not prohibit them from continuing to bring their offerings. Then the leaders allowed money to be given instead of the offerings prescribed, which saved a lot of bother and filled the treasury.

The glory and prestige the religious leaders gained for themselves as leaders of the nation by the support of poor people, was immoral. If they had been servants of God, they would have given the widow their support, rather than accepting hers. 'The poor will never cease out of the land: therefore ... you shall open wide your hand to your brother, to the needy and the poor, in the land' (Dt. 15:11).

Sitting by the treasure-chest of the Temple one day, Jesus began to notice how the crowd put their gifts of copper money into the treasury. Many rich men threw in much money, and then a destitute widow came and put in two lepta, the smallest of coins.

Calling his disciples to him Jesus said to them: "Truly I tell you, that poor widow put more than any of the others into the treasury. They put in money from their abundances but this woman put in the little she had, her whole means of existence."

The passage can be seen as a strong denunciation of the social system which beggared the poor to provide extravagance for the religious leaders, and it has connections with the O.T.: 'Man, say to Israel: your princes are like lions, growling as they tear their prey, devouring men and seizing all their treasure and wealth. They have made many widows in Israel. Her priests have done violence to my Law, and have profaned my holy things' (Ezk. 22:25-26); 'In arrogance, the wicked hunts down the poor ... boasts of the desires of his heart ... and all his thoughts are that there is no God ... He thinks ... "I shall not be shaken; I shall never meet adversity." His mouth is full of lies and violence ... he says to himself, "God has forgotten; he has hidden his face and sees nothing"' (Ps. 10:2-4,6-7,11).

In I.T. literature, too: 'Give alms of your substance, turn not away from any poor man, and God will not turn away from you. Give alms according to your wealth. If you have much, give much; if you have only a little, give that ... for you lay up a good treasure for yourself against the day of necessity. Alms deliver from death and save from the darkness' (Tob. 4:7-10).

In Judaism, it was considered of greater merit to put money into the charity box than to give money directly to a poor person, since in the former case neither the giver nor the recipient knows the identity of the other. It was also said: 'God prefers the handful of a poor man's free-will offering to the heap of incense offered by the High Priest' (Ecc.R. 4:6); and, 'He who sustains God's creatures is as though he had created them' (Tanh.B. 16a).

Charity was good: 'Greater is the one who performs charity than he who offers all the sacrifices. It is not the greatest good: practice of kindness is greater than charity because charity can be done only with money but kindness can be practiced with both money and one's loving kindness. Also charity can be given only to the living; kindness can be practised for both the living and the dead (by attending a funeral and burial)' (b.Suk. 49b-50a).

The word "charity" also could mean righteousness so that giving alms was a sign of repentance. Giving alms is a duty, not an act of grace and favour. All a man's possessions are from God (on loan) and giving alms helps towards a more equitable distribution: 'Even the beggar who is maintained by charity must practise charity himself' (b.Git. 7b).

* * *

E 10. Reversals - Mt. 18:4; 19:30; 20:16, 26; 22:14; 23:11-12. Mk. 9:35; 10:31. Lk. 6:31; 9:48; 14:11; 13:30; 18:14; 22:26.

Several sayings have the same intention and meaning, here arranged in two groups.

(i)

```
Many who are first shall be last, and the last,
first. If anyone wants to be first, he must make himself
last of all and servant of all.
```

```
For the least among you is the greatest.
```

```
Whoever wants to be great among you must be your
servant.
```

```
...the highest among you must bear himself like
the youngest, the chief of you like a servant.
```

Similar sayings occur in I.T. literature. 'He said to them: "I will liken my judgement to a ring (or, round dance): just as there is no retardation of them that are last, there is no hastening of those that are first"' (IV Ezr. 5:42); 'For the first (who have become angels) will receive the last, whom they were expecting; and the last will join those whom they heard had passed away' (II Bar. 51:13); 'Then all who have fallen asleep in hope (of God) shall rise again ... and the first shall rejoice and the last shall not be disappointed' (II Bar. 30:2).

(ii)

```
For whoever exalts himself will be humbled; and
whoever humbles himself will be exalted.
```

```
Let a man humble himself till he is like this
child, and he will be the greatest in the kingdom of
God.
```

Similarly, in O.T. and I.T. books: 'The Lord gives new heart to the humble and brings evil doers down to the dust' (Ps. 147:6); 'The greater you are, the humbler you must be' (Sir. 3:18), and in rabbinical commentaries: 'He who humbles himself, God will exalt; he who exalts himself, God will humble', and as a comment on Is. 66:2: 'I will look to the humble and contrite in spirit who trembles at my word' (b.Erub. 13b).

* * *

Jesus said, "Nobody lights a lamp and puts it under the bed or in a secret place, or covers it with the meal-tub. It is put on the lamp stand so that its light shines for all outside and all who enter the house. It cannot be hidden any more than a city[1] on a hill.

It may well be that it is not the normal domestic lamp which is referred to here, but the lamp used once a year during the feast of dedication, Hanukkah. It is held during December and lasts eight days. The lamp was placed high up in a prominent position and kept burning during this time when the people gathered at the Temple to celebrate God's blessings on Israel throughout history and the restoration of the Temple at the time of the Maccabees, some two hundred years earlier than Jesus' day. It was both a religious and political celebration and subject to special regulations. For example it was not permitted to use its light to count coins or to prepare food.

The lamp of the body is the eye. When the eye is single, your whole body will be shining, but if your eye is not single, your whole body is dark. See to it then that the 'light' which is in you is not darkness. If your whole body is luminous with no part dark, it will be fully luminous, as when the lamp illuminates you with a flash like lightning."

The second part of the passage appears to be obscure. At that time vision was thought to be due to light from the eye shining on the objects seen. When the eye or soul or heart was single, it was generous and not guilty of meanness: its light was pure: 'I never slandered anyone, nor did I censure the life of any man, walking as I did in singleness of eye ... I bestowed the good things of the earth in the singleness of my heart' (T.Iss. 3:4,8).

Some Jews also thought that man was endowed with both 'light' and 'darkness': 'The evil man's spirit consists of eight parts in the House of Darkness and one part in the House of Light. The good man's spirit consists of eight parts in the House of Light ... and one part in the House of Darkness (DSS, Hor. 4Q186); 'God has appointed for man two spirits in which to walk until the time of his visitation - the spirits of truth and falsehood' (DSS, CR 3).

The perfect man would be all light with no element of darkness. When the body is wholly light, the person has attained perfection and this is a clear reference to the person's state after the day of Judgement: 'The wise leaders and those who turn many to righteousness, shall shine like the brightness of the heavens, like the stars for ever' (Dan. 12:3). Only those with a single eye (that is with singleness of righteous purpose) will find a favourable outcome on the day of Judgement. They will stand in heaven's light, be made fully bright and illuminate God's realm on earth.

The light from the feast of Dedication (Hanukkah) lamp reminded the family of God's covenant with Israel: 'The commandment of the Lord shines clear and gives light to the eyes' (Ps. 19:8); 'For a command is a lamp and teaching a light' (Pvb. 6:23). A sound 'eye' was generous and its owner's goodness shone brightly, while one who was mean or miserly had a dim eye and was concerned with mammon rather than God. The lamp should call forth conduct which was 'light' (good) rather than 'dark' (evil): 'For the good man has not a dark eye, for he shows mercy to all, even sinners' (T.Ben. 4:2); '... while you are in darkness you cannot do the works of light' (T.Nap. 2:10).

In rabbinical writings, too, the eye has a special significance: 'ninety-nine die from the evil eye as against one from natural causes' (b.B.M. 107b); based on: 'Truly, one who touches you (Israel) touches the apple of my eye' (Zch. 2:8), there is the comment: 'No member of the body is as precious as the eye and God compares Israel with it' (Sif.Num. 15:17-20).

[1] It is very likely that this word should read 'fire'.

* * *

E 12. Discipleship - Mt. 6:1-13, 16-18; 7:7-12; 16:19; 18:15-20. Mk. 12:38-40. Lk.11:1-4, 9-13.

E12 a. On being a disciple.

It was inevitable that sometimes quarrels and arguments would arise amongst Jesus' followers and it was important to know how to tackle them. Such situations arose in the early churches and this passage suggests ways of dealing with them.

"If your brother commits a sin, go and reprove him, strictly between yourselves," said Jesus, "and if he listens to you, you have gained your brother. If he will not listen, take others with you, so that all the facts may be duly established on the evidence of two or three witnesses. If he refuses to listen to them, report the matter to the church; and if he still will not listen, even to the church, you must then treat him as you would a pagan or tax-collector.
This is certainly true: whatever you bind on earth, will have been bound in heaven, and whatever you loose on earth, will have been loosed in heaven. For where two or three have been assembled in my name there I am with them."

The first part of this passage concerns the love of members of the early church or community for one another. It was necessary to remember that human beings were created in God's image and therefore must treat one another with kindliness. 'You must not say: "I am despised, let my fellowman be despised as well. I am cursed, let him be cursed too. If you act so, know whom it is you despise or curse ..."' (Gen.R. 24:7).

Some think that the word 'church' may not indicate the developed Christian church, since the word was also in use among the Jews at the time. Adopting the tenets of Judaism, it was desirable to go to a brother who may have sinned and point it out to him and reprove him for it: 'You shall surely rebuke, or reason with, your brother' (Lev. 19:17). Should this not prevail, it would be necessary to take the matter up with the group and for this two or three witnesses were necessary: 'A single witness may not give evidence, or prevail, against a man in the matter of any crime or sin he commits. A charge must be established on the evidence of two or three witnesses' (Dt. 19:15).

The erring member must repent and change, but there is no sign that any punishment was to be inflicted except for expulsion of the fully intransigent: 'I will bear no rancour against them that turn from transgression but I will have no pity on all who depart from the way' (DSS, CR10).

The second part of the passage concerns the situation if two members disagree or quarrel about some matter. This was unseemly and not as God would have it. In Judaism, the decisions of the elders of a synagogue were reckoned as approved by God because it was thought that when three sit and judge, God's Spirit is in their midst and thus a righteous person's decision to 'bind' or 'loose' was considered to have the authority of heaven: 'God has taken his place in the divine council' (Ps. 82:1); 'They that feared the Lord spoke one with another, the Lord hearkened ... and a book of remembrance was written before him ...' (Mal. 3:16). Some thought that: 'Consideration for the honour of one's fellowman is so important that on account of it, a prohibition of the Law can be ignored' (b.Ber. 19b).

In rabbinical writing: 'Whenever ten are assembled in a synagogue, then God's Spirit is with them, with a court of three people, where there are two and with even one' (Mek.Bah. 11); 'In every place where I cause my name to be remembered, I will come and bless you' (Ex. 20:24); Some thought that: 'The Lord is good to those who wait for him, to the soul that seeks him. It is good that one should wait quietly for the salvation of the Lord; it is good for a man to bear the yoke in his youth. Let him sit alone in silence when he has laid it on him' (Lam. 3:25-28).

The Hebrew term for God's spirit is *Shekinah* which is not God but an abstraction, a way of thinking of God without turning God into a material being. A little story illustrates the point: 'You say the Shekinah rests on every group of Jews. How many Shekinahs are there?' asked the Emperor. Rabbi Gamaliel called the Emperor's servant and asked him, 'Why does the sun enter the Emperor's house?' 'But the sun shines over the whole world,' replied the servant. 'If the sun, a servant of God shines on all, so much more does the Shekinah also,' said the rabbi.

In rabbinical teaching it was even thought that sometimes God gives way to a righteous person: 'I [God] rule over men; who rules over me? The pious, for I enact and he annuls' (b.MK 16b); 'Even if I [God] say thus, and you say otherwise, then your word is valid and mine invalid' (j.Ta'an 67a).

In order to solve disputes, the disciples are recommended to follow the Jewish system, namely that each side should nominate a respected senior person, and ask these two arbitrators to help with the problem. If they could not produce an agreement, a third person would be brought in and the matter would be settled by a majority verdict, binding on both parties.

The process demanded peacemakers and reconciliation in compromise. This was what God approved. When the members of the group have solved their quarrel and come to amity again, God will be happy to approve their accord. God is present with the leaders who are convened in his name to find the answer to the litigants' difficulty. He will ratify their common decisions in heaven; that which the group decides to prohibit or that it decides can be permitted, will receive God's approval: 'Any assembly ... that is for the sake of heaven shall ... be established; and any assembly ... that is not for the sake of heaven shall not be established' (m.Avot. 4:11).

It should not be thought that God's discipline was always resented: 'Who will set ... the discipline of wisdom over my mind so as not to spare me in my errors?' (Sir. 23:2); 'Despise not the chastising of the Lord, for the Lord loves whom he corrects' (Pvb. 3:11-12).

Not all scholars agree with this understanding of the last sentence of the passage. Some think it is concerned with the disciples' practice of exorcism in which a person may be loosened from the bonds or fetters of Satan. They are freed from sin and death and can enter the kingdom, while those who remain bound cannot.

* * *

E12 b. No ostentation.

There can be little doubt that some religious leaders were guilty of more concern for this world's opinion than for God's. They followed and advocated traditions which were not part of the Law. They were the poor advertisements for Judaism and Jesus points out the importance of following God's rule, rather than seeking men's approval.

"Do not make a show of your righteousness before others," said Jesus. "There is no reward for that in your Father's house in heaven. So when you do some act of charity, do not bring out the trumpets to draw attention to it! That's what the ungodly ones do in the synagogues and streets, to win glory with men. I tell you this: they have had their requital. No, charitable deeds must be in secret; do not even let your left hand know what your right is doing! Your Father in heaven will see, and will reward you.

When you fast, do not look glum and miserable like the hypocrites, who distort and disfigure their faces, so that people will see that they are fasting. Quite certainly, they have had their reward. No, when you fast, wash your face and anoint your head with oil, so that no one could guess you are fasting, except your Father who sees all that is done in secret and will reward you."

The passage advocates that alms should be given secretly, while God's reward would be given openly. The reverse was also taken to be true as in this rabbinical saying: 'Whosoever profanes God's name in secret, receives vengeance openly' (m.Avot. 4:4). There was no merit (capital) in heaven from good deeds and therefore no fruit (interest), unless they were done solely from love of God. It was not to win over enemies in order to make them friends, nor to find favour with God, that one sought the way of peace. Giving alms was righteousness, and Jesus is not reported denying that alms redeem sins, which was a Jewish belief of the time: 'Almsgiving delivers from death and purges away all sin' (Tob. 12:8); 'Almsgiving atones for sin' (Sir. 3:30).

For those who impress men and make sure of getting glory in men's eyes, that is their reward. That is the pay they get for that. Those who thought they could cheat God, the hypocrites or 'actors', had been condemned in the O.T. too: 'Declare to my people their transgressions, to the house of Jacob their sins; although they ask counsel of me by day and say they delight in knowing my ways [yet they say], "Why fast, if God does not observe it? Why mortify ourselves, if God pays no heed?" ... Behold, you fast only to quarrel and fight, hitting viciously with the fist ... Is it such a fast that will carry your cry to heaven? Is it such a fast I require? ... Is this what you call a fast, a day acceptable to the Lord? Is it not this that I require of you as a fast: that you loosen the bonds of injustice, break the thongs of the yoke, let the oppressed go free? Is it not sharing your food with the hungry, bringing the destitute into your homes, clothing the naked when you meet them? Then shall your light shine forth ...' (Is. 58:1-8).

To anoint one's head with oil and to have a newly washed face could be taken as signs of being committed to God, and of happiness, which is thought to have connections with the prohibitions in Leviticus: 'You shall not round off the hair on your temples nor mar the edges of your beard. You shall not gash yourselves in mourning ...; you shall not tattoo yourselves' (Lev. 19:27-28). To fast enabled someone to devote himself to study of the Torah, so this also was not to be looked on as a penance, but here those who are not bothered about what men think, but try to obey God and love others, are sure of a heavenly reward: God will 'pay his debt' to them.

Similar ideas are found in rabbinical writings: 'Seek not greatness for yourselves, nor covet honour ... Faithful is your taskmaster who will pay you the reward for your labour' (m.Avot. 6:5); 'You are not to make the Torah a crown to signify yourself' (m.Avot. 4:5); 'Whoever is boastful, if he is a Sage, his wisdom departs from him; if he is a prophet, his prophecy leaves him' (b.Pes. 66b); 'Every man in whom is haughtiness of spirit is as though he worshipped idols. He will not partake in the resurrection' (b.Sot. 4b).

It should be remembered, however, that to appear with a clean face and oiled hair on the day of Atonement, when the Law demanded the opposite, would not have been tolerated. (See also G 2.)

In rabbinical writings an optimist exclaims: "I have kept a fast and my blood and fat has diminished. 'May it be your will to account this as if I had offered them before you on the altar.' (b.Ber. 17a).

* * *

E 12 c. Prayer.

It was a common practice for a prophet or teacher to frame a prayer for his disciples. It was given as a pattern to be followed - short, succinct and significant. It was not meant to be recited simply for its own sake.

"When you pray, do not be like the actors, who love to stand and pray in the synagogues and at the corners of the squares, so that everyone can notice them. I tell you this: they have already had their reward. No, go into a room by yourself and shut the door and pray to your Father who is there in the secret place. He sees what is secret and will reward you. And don't go babbling vain repetitions like the heathen. They think the more they say, the more likely they are to be heard. Do not imitate them; your Father knows your needs before you open your mouths! This is how you should pray:

Our Father in the heavens, your name be revered.
Let your kingdom come.
Your will be done on earth as in heaven.
Give us each day our daily bread.
Forgive us our debts;
We have forgiven all indebted to us.
Do not put us to the test and rescue us from evil.

Ask and you will receive; seek and you will find; knock and the door will be opened. For one who asks receives, he who seeks finds, and the door will be opened to him who knocks. Is there any father among you who would offer his son a stone when he wants bread, a snake when he asks for fish, or a scorpion instead of an egg? If you know what to give your children in spite of being unrighteous, how much more does your heavenly Father give good things and the Holy Spirit to those who ask him. Always treat others as you would like them to treat you: that is the Law and the Prophets."

In public prayers, the one leading, the precentor, would take a prominent place in order to be seen. Jesus is more concerned with private prayer, and recommends an inner room. This would normally be without windows and the door could be locked. For Jesus, the important thing was private prayer, which did not need a special place for God to hear it: 'Go my people into your rooms and shut the door behind you' (Is. 26:20); 'Elisha ... went into the room, shut the door ... and prayed to the Lord' (II Kgs.

4:33); and in rabbinical teaching 'Whoever performs the will of God and directs his heart to him in prayer is heard' (b.Ber. 31a; Ex.R. 21:3); 'When you pray, know before whom you stand' (b.Ber. 32b); 'Pious old men used to wait an hour in silence before they prayed in order to direct their hearts of God' (m.Ber.5:1).

Some O.T. teaching is concerned with the making of sacrifices in order to speak to God and to receive his blessing: 'To be accepted, you shall offer a male without blemish of the bulls or the sheep or the goats. You shall not offer anything that has a blemish for it will not be acceptable ... To be accepted it must be perfect' (Lev. 22:20-21). This is not advocated by the teaching of Jesus.

The inner chamber or room could function as the bridal chamber: 'Bring me to your chamber, O king; ... let us praise love more than wine, and your caresses more than any song' (S.S. 1:4); or as the tomb or grave: 'Her house is the entrance to Sheol (hell), leading down to the chambers of death' (Pvb. 7:27). Those who had become used to using their inner room for prayer need not fear the tomb. They will awake when the call comes on the day of Judgement.

All those who call on God, need not fear that he will not know about it: 'The Lord hears the prayer of every one that fears him and every request of the soul that hopes for him, the Lord accomplishes' (P.S. 6:8); 'You will hear the prayer of your servant according to your good favour towards your people' (Sir. 36:17); 'If you seek the Lord your God, if you search with all your heart and soul, you will find him' (Pvb. 8:17); 'If you call upon me and pray to me, I will listen to you. You will seek me and find me; when you search for me with all your heart, you will find me, says the Lord' (Jer. 29:12). Those who ask, will receive, those who seek will find, and one must knock only once for the door to be opened. God responds to a repentant sinner who turns to him and prays to be accepted as one of his sons.

A lot of babbling and vain repetitions are also condemned as worse than useless in the O.T and in I.T. books: 'You shall call and the Lord will answer' (Is. 58:9); 'Do not rush into speech, let there be no hasty utterance in God's presence. God is in heaven and you are on earth, so let your words be few; ... the fool talks and it is so much chatter' (Ecc. 5:2-3); 'Never repeat yourself when you pray' (Sir. 7:14); and in rabbinical comments: 'We have learnt that it matters not whether one does much or little so long as one directs one's heart to heaven' (b.Ber.5b); 'Prolonged prayers are folly if the idea is to elicit an answer [from God] (b.Ber. 32b.); 'He that makes his prayer a fixed task, his prayer is no supplication' (m.Ber. 4:14); 'The value of prayers depends on the intention behind them' (b.Meg. 20a); God was not to be besieged with supplications, but there was not to be a spirit of resignation either. The point was to have faith to become a true sibling of Jesus, a son of God.

A rabbinical comment on Num.12:10 is similar: 'The righteous has to say only one word and it is accepted by God and therefore it is not necessary to pray long' (Sif.Num. 105); and, 'Even before a thought is born in a man's heart, it is already revealed to God ... Before even my tongue gives expression, God fully knows about it' (Gen.R. 9:3). In other books a different opinion is given: 'Why is the prayer of the righteous compared to a hind? Because just as a hind grows antlers which form more branches every year, so with the righteous: the longer they abide in prayer, the more will their prayer be heard' (b.Yoma 29a).

The use of 'Father' to refer to God, was common in Judaism.: 'Father of the fatherless, the widow's champion, God in his holy dwelling' (Ps. 68:5); 'But now,

O Lord, you are our Father' (Is. 64:8); 'My Father, you are the friend of my youth' (Jer. 3:4); 'David will say to me, "You are my Father, my God, my rock and my safe refuge"' (Ps. 89:26); 'The Lord's decree: "You are my son", he said, "this day I become your Father"' (Ps. 2 :7); 'Have we not one Father?' (Mal. 2:10); 'I cried, "Lord, you are my Father, do not desert me in time of trouble"' (Sir. 51:10). Jesus used a different word, which everyone used for their own fathers and it may indicate that Jesus wanted to make the poor and rejected realise they too could speak to God as though to an earthly father .

The next line of the Lord's prayer is to be found in I.T. literature: 'As his will in heaven may be, so shall God do' (I Mac. 3:60) and is echoed in rabbinical teaching. For example, 'Do your will in the heavens above, grant tranquillity of spirit to those who fear you on earth and do what is good in your sight' (b.Ber. 29b).

The bread referred to may be that which we eat as food, in which case it is likely that the meaning is, 'give us the food we need for today' as in the O.T.: 'Feed me with food that is needful for me' (Pvb. 30:8). It was not to be hoarded, because God would provide enough for each day: 'He whose hope is set on God will have no lack of gifts' (P.S. 5:17); 'No good thing does the Lord withhold from those that walk uprightly' (Ps. 84:11); 'Those who seek the Lord lack no good thing' (Ps. 34:10). 'Bread' can also refer to God's word, the manna received in the wilderness, which turned the hearts of the Israelites to the Lord.

The prayer shows that forgiveness of those who have sinned against us was a prerequisite of being forgiven by God and this echoes O.T. teaching: 'Let the wicked abandon their ways and evil men their thoughts ... let them return to our God, for he will freely forgive ... (Is. 55:7); 'Who is a God like you, pardoning iniquity and passing over the transgression ... He does not retain his anger forever, because he delights in showing clemency' (Mic. 7:18). This was true in I.T. and rabbinical writings too: 'Even as a man does to his neighbour so also will the Lord do to him' (T.Zeb. 5:3); 'God is merciful to those who show mercy (to others); and is not merciful to those who show no mercy to others' (j.B.K. 6c); and: 'He who ignores occasions for retaliation has all his transgressions ignored' (b.Meg. 28a); 'Repent today, lest you die tomorrow' (b.Shab. 153a).

But this is not the whole story. Every seventh year in Judaism, all debts were to be cancelled, and poor people could never get a loan in the sixth year since the lender could lose his money in the following year. O.T. teaching demands that those capable of lending should do so in all years, and the righteous man will forgive his debtors their debts, and Jesus supports this viewpoint. The forgiving of debts is the same as not hoping for, expecting or demanding any return for services rendered. Thus Matthew says, 'Forgive us our debts, for we have forgiven those indebted to us.' The two versions are compatible because sins were often referred to as debts. Some have concluded that the whole prayer relates to a Jubilee year.

The prayer 'Lead us not into temptation' has been interpreted in two main ways. The first sees it as asking God not to put temptations to sin before us; the second as asking God not to test us by treating us badly. Neither accords with Jesus' teaching, and various unsatisfactory additions have been made to alleviate the difficulties. It seems more likely that the semitic word behind the word 'temptation' refers to being tried, as in a court of law. In the O.T. this sense is used when the Queen of Sheba questioned Solomon: 'Now when the Queen of Sheba heard of the fame of Solomon

... she came to test him with hard questions.' (I Kgs. 10:1) and in I.T. books: 'As the furnace proves the potter's vessels, discussion tries a man ... Do not praise a man before he has discoursed for that is the test.' (Sir. 17:5,7).

The prayer is for God to be merciful and not to test us in the sense of judging us as we deserve. We already know what the result of that would be! It is as the psalmist says: 'O Lord ... enter not into judgement with your servant for no man living shall be justified' (Ps. 143:1-2).

The prayer to be saved from the evil one has also been understood in two ways. Some think it was originally a prayer that Satan should not enter into us and take over our 'inclinations'. Some early versions, for example, include also: 'Your Holy Spirit come upon us and cleanse us'. Others suggest that it meant God's punishment, and that if he does not remove it from us, he has not yet forgiven us. 'May it be your will to deliver us from their hands [the evil impulse and foreign domination]' (b.Ber. 17a).

The prayer is like the fixed prayers used by the Essenes and it was probably intended as a model rather than sufficient in itself. It may look forward to the coming of the New Era, when all nations will revere God, hallowing his name and all will obey his rule. The bread of life will be given to those who set their lives right before the day of Judgement, forgiving and forgiven, and they ask to be spared from the fiery test, the expected trials and tribulations of the Evil One.

The principle of treating others as one would wish to be treated oneself, is not particularly sensible, since it assumes each would wish for the same thing. Fortunately, this saw is far from being the Law and the Prophets nor does it accord with much of the teaching of the gospels. It is found in both I.T. and rabbinical books, either in the positive form as here, or in the negative form: 'What you do not wish to be done to you, do not do to another.' (Tob. 4:15; b.Shab.3a) and 'Judge your neighbour's feelings by your own.' (Sir. 31:15).

* * *

E13 a. The beatitudes.

The beatitudes have been intensively studied by numerous scholars and opinions about them are equally numerous. They were probably addressed to the disciples, those who could be missionaries and martyrs, the elect.

Recent disclosures from the Dead Sea Scrolls show that there were probably eight beatitudes originally and that the passage beginning: 'Happy is the person who meditates on Wisdom and reasons intelligently, who reflects in his heart on her ways and ponders her secrets ...' (Sir. 14:20-27), may have been the basis of Matthew's version.

Jesus went with his disciples up into the hills and began to teach:

How blessed are you poor - the kingdom of God shall be yours.

How blessed are you who mourn - you shall find consolation.

How blessed are those humble in spirit - the earth will be given them.

How blessed are you who hunger and thirst for righteousness - you shall be satisfied.

How blessed are those who are compassionate - they shall be shown God's compassion.

How blessed are the pure in heart - they shall see God.

How blessed are the peacemakers - God shall call them his sons.

How blessed are those persecuted on account of righteousness - the kingdom of God shall be theirs.

How blessed are you, when you are hated, reviled and persecuted, and when evil is uttered against you falsely[1] because of me. On that day be glad and dance for joy, for you have a rich reward in heaven.

The prophets were persecuted in just the same way. Alas for you rich - your happiness is over. Alas for you who always have enough to eat - you shall go hungry. Alas for you who laugh now - you shall mourn and weep. Alas for those of you whom men praise - just so did their fathers acclaim false prophets.

Some think that the poor, or 'the poor in spirit', in the first beatitude, meant those who followed God without deviation, but others think they were those who had no illusions of self-righteousness. They had renounced status-seeking and prestige, and did not envy another's prosperity: 'If a man prospers more than you, do not be aggrieved, but pray for him that he may have perfect prosperity ... For the poor man, if free from envy pleases the Lord in all things, and is blessed beyond all men, because he has not the temptations of vain men' (T.Gad. 7:1,6); 'Be not envious of the good fortune of your enemy and do not rejoice at his misfortune ... If your enemy meet you with evil, meet him with good' (Ahk. 1:18,22). In any case, 'He who does righteousness lays up life for himself with the Lord' (P.S. 9:9).

Others think that the poor were those who had lost all hope so that the coming Kingdom of God will bring them renewed hope even for these the rejected ones. The Qumran documents show that some Jews, at least, understood this beatitude to refer to those who observed God's law, in the hope of the salvation promised by God's personified heavenly Messiah or heavenly partner, Wisdom.

The second may concern those who grieve over their own sins and those of Israel. They will be comforted by God: '... to comfort all who mourn, that there should be given to them ... glory instead of ashes' (Is. 61:2-3); 'As one whom his mother comforts, so I will comfort you' (Is. 66:13). Another view is that the mourners were those who could find no reason for joy, but that when the new Kingdom is established they will find much joy: 'They who long for the years of the consolations [i.e. the end of the era], I shall lead back to Zion' (Jer. 31:9).

The third beatitude, which is not always placed third in different manuscripts, is about those who are the dispossessed, slaves or captives. In the coming Kingdom they will receive their fair share of the promised land. This beatitude echoes the O.T. and I.T. books: 'But the meek shall inherit the earth; and shall themselves have an abundance of peace. ... The righteous shall possess the land and dwell upon it for ever' (Ps. 37:11,29); 'He who makes me his refuge shall possess the earth' (Is. 57:13); 'This is the man to whom I will look,' says the Lord, 'he that is humble and contrite in spirit and trembles at my word' (Is. 66:2); 'But the meek, the afflicted, the miserable shall inherit the earth and delight in abundant peace. They will accept the season of affliction but will be saved from the snares of Belial and thereafter all who inherit the earth will delight and luxuriate in all the delights of the flesh' (DSS, 4QPs., ii 9-10) [a commentary on Ps. 37:11]; 'Theirs is the earth in the new era which is promised' (II Bar 44:13).

The fourth beatitude concerns those who are starved for justice. They yearn for God to right wrongs and for the justice which is a necessary part of God's creation. The concept here is greater than that of the psalmist's: 'He satisfies him who is thirsty and the hungry he fills with good things' (Ps. 107:9). Compare O.T. and I.T. sayings: 'Come to me, all you who desire me (Wisdom) and be filled with my good fruits, for my instruction is sweeter than honey ... They that eat shall still hunger for me and they that drink me shall still thirst for me' (Sir. 24:19-21); 'Come, all you who are thirsty, come and fetch water; come, you who have no food, buy corn and eat' (Is. 55:1); 'I will ... open the windows of heaven for you and pour down on you an overflowing blessing' (Mal. 3:10); 'Therefore these are the words of the Lord God: my servants shall eat but you shall starve, they shall drink but you shall go thirsty: they shall rejoice but you shall be put to shame; they shall shout in triumph in the gladness of their hearts but you shall cry from sorrow and wail from anguish of spirit' (Is. 65:13-14).

These first four beatitudes tell of the reversal of fortune which the coming Kingdom will bring about for those who suffer disadvantages in their current life. There is an implication of the new world to come, whether on earth or in heaven.

The next four beatitudes are more concerned with rewards for those who are virtuous. The merciful are those who care that others are fed, healed, and their debts cancelled. They are those who give alms and show deeds of loving kindness. As they have shown mercy in this life, they will receive it on the day of Judgement. This fifth beatitude reminds one of: 'Have therefore compassion towards every man with mercy, that the Lord also may have compassion and mercy for you' (T.Zeb. 8:1); 'Blessed are the merciful and meek in their words' (II En. 42:13). Compassion, steadfast love, a characteristic of God, does not insist on the letter of the Law, but on its spirit: 'The righteous is ever giving liberally and lending' (Ps. 37:26); 'Your steadfast love, O Lord, extends to the heavens' (Ps. 36:5), and 'endures for ever' (Ps. 100:5). The Hebrew underlying this beatitude may mean that those who are excluded, the excommunicated and outcasts, will receive mercy in the new kingdom.

The word 'heart' in the sixth, refers to intention, inclination, motivation, but also to other aspects of personality. It means the innermost attitudes only to be acknowledged by those of honest integrity. These are those who are prepared for persecution to see that right prevails. They show the world a vision of godliness. It was thought that the follower who attains the highest degree of sanctity would be admitted to God's presence, as Moses and a few others had been: 'The Lord loves the righteous ... the upright shall see his face' (Ps. 11:7); 'The pure in heart shall see God' (Ps. 24:3-4).

The seventh is concerned with those who love their enemies and work for unity and reconciliation. The language here indicates that it is not only peace as an abstract idea which is intended, but also that there should be economic welfare and justice for all. The word means also 'to make whole'. They imitate God who will have peace, but peace in the O.T. did not simply mean tranquillity and order but full justice for all: 'Behold, I give Phineas my covenant of peace' (Num. 25:12); 'Seek peace and pursue it' (Ps. 34:14); 'When a man's ways please the Lord, he makes even his enemies to be at peace with him' (Pvb. 16:7).

It is similar to a saying in the I.T. literature: 'Blessed is he who cultivates love of peace' (II En. 52:11). God will accept the righteous as his sons: 'They will fulfil my commandments and I will be their Father and they shall be my children' (Jub. 1:24), and in rabbinical literature, 'One who brings peace on earth, it is as though he had done it in heaven.' (ARN 24); 'Great is peace - it is the greatest channel of blessing' (Sif.Num.on 6:26); 'Great is peace, for all benedictions and prayers conclude with peace' (Lev.R. 9:9).

It was Judaic belief that all prophets were persecuted in their own generation, but that those who were persecuted because of their obedience to God (the eighth), would be at peace in God's realm. They had merited God's reward, their 'treasure' in heaven. As in the O.T., the rejection of the rich, the extravagant and the worldly, meant that they could not partake of the kingdom: 'He gives new heart to the humble and brings evil-doers down to the dust' (Ps. 147:6); 'This was the iniquity of ... Sodom: she ... had pride of wealth and food in plenty, comfort and ease; yet she never helped the poor and wretched' (Ezk. 16:49); 'You ... in whose heart is Law, fear not the reproach of men, nor be dismayed at their revilings. For the moth will eat them up ... but my deliverance will be for ever' (Is. 51: 7-8). In I.T. books the same attitude is found: 'But for the elect there shall be light and joy and peace, and they shall inherit the earth' (I En. 5:7).

Those who show mercy, who work to establish God's peace, and those committed to righteousness and justice, and who are pure in heart, they will stand persecution and not be the seed falling on shallow soil that withers as soon as things get difficult. They are God's agents in establishing the Kingdom to come.

The next paragraph uses 'you' rather than 'they'. The disciples are being warned that they, too, will be reviled and rejected because of their devotion to righteousness and justice, but not only the disciples: it will happen to all who follow the teaching of Jesus: 'They who were poor for the Lord's sake shall be made rich, and they who are put to death for the Lord's sake shall awake to life. The harts of Jacob shall run in joy and the eagles of Israel shall fly in gladness' (T. Jud. 25:4-5).

In rabbinical literature similar commandments are given: 'You shall walk after the attributes of God. As he clothes the naked: 'The Lord God clothed Adam and for his wife coats of skin and clothed them' (Gen. 3:21); God visited the sick, comforted mourners: 'It came to pass after the death of Abraham God blessed Isaac his son' (Gen 25:11); and God buried the dead: 'God buried him in the valley' (Dt. 34:6).

At Qumran there are some similar prayers: 'To [have appointed] me in your truth a messenger [of the peace] of your goodness, to proclaim to the meek the multitude of your mercies, and to let them that are of a contrite spirit he[ar salvation] from [everlasting] source, and to them that mourn everlasting joy' (DSS, H 18:14-15). The Jewish prayer of the Day of Atonement is likewise: 'Your people and your heritage, who hunger for your goodness, who thirst for your grace and who long for your salvation, will recognise and know that to the Lord, our God, belong mercy and forgiveness.'

The four antitheses in the last paragraph are from Luke and are reminiscent of O.T. and I.T. books: 'A time to weep and time to laugh; a time to mourn and time to dance' (Ecc. 3:4); 'Do you not know ... that the exulting of the wicked is short and the glee of the godless lasts but for a moment?' (Job. 20:4-5); 'Woe to you sinners, for your riches make you appear righteous, but your hearts convict you of being sinners ... Woe to you who work unrighteousness ... Woe to you, you mighty, for the day of your destruction is coming' (I En. 96:4,7-8).

Similar lists of blessings are found in I.T. books, sometimes with corresponding list of anathemas or curses:

Blessed is he who fears God and serves him; learn to bring gifts to the Lord, that you may enjoy life.

Blessed is he who delivers a judgement justly to the widow and orphan and helps all who are wronged, clothes the naked with garments and gives the hungry bread.

Blessed is he who turns back from the changeable path and walks along the straight path.

Blessed is he who sows the seeds of righteousness for he shall reap sevenfold.

Blessed is he in whose mouth is mercy and gentleness.

Blessed is he who understands the Lord's works and glorifies the Lord God. (II En. 42:6-14).

Blessed is he who opens his lips blessing and praising God.

Cursed is he before the Lord all the days of his life, who opens his lips to curse and abuse.

Blessed is he who blesses all the Lord's works.

Cursed is he who brings the Lord's creation into contempt.

Blessed is he who looks down and raises the fallen.

Cursed is he who looks to, and is eager for, the destruction of what is not his.

Blessed is he who keeps the foundations of his fathers, made firm from the
   beginning.

Cursed is he who perverts the decrees of his forefathers.

Blessed is he who cultivates love of peace.

Cursed is he who disturbs those that love their neighbours.

Blessed is he who speaks with humble tongue and heart to all.

Cursed is he who speaks peace with his tongue while in his heart there is not peace
   but a sword. (II En. 52:3-14).

[1.] Some versions omit 'falsely' here.

* * *

E 13b. Anger and hatred.

As today, there was in Jesus' day discussion about the commandment not to murder, since some pointed out that the removal of the wicked was a desirable activity. Some even supposed this was necessary in order for the New Era to begin. Others tended to approve of killing the wicked although they recognised that there were two sides to it: 'Many in killing the wicked do works of good and evil, but the whole is good because that which was evil has been uprooted and destroyed' (T.Ash. 4:2).

The phrase, 'You have heard ...' or 'You have been told ...' refers to the oral traditions of the elders and was a very common expression.

You have heard that our forefathers were told: 'Do not commit murder; anyone who does so must be brought to judgement.' But I say to you, he who is angered by his brother without cause, must be brought to judgement. If he abuses his brother, he must answer for it to the council, and whoever says 'You fool' shall be liable to go to the fire of Gehenna."

Jesus said, "So, if you suddenly remember that your brother has a grievance against you, when you are bringing your Temple offering, leave it before the altar and make peace with your brother first. Then you can return and offer your gift on the altar.

Why cannot you judge for yourselves what is the right course to take?"

It seems likely that Jesus was here referring to the heavenly council: 'God has taken his place in the divine council; in the midst of the gods he holds judgement' (Ps. 82:1); 'For who among them has stood in the council of the Lord ...?' (Jer. 23:18). It is here that a murderer was supposed to answer for his wrong-doing, but Jesus extends this to include anger, thoughts of hatred against another. Anger blinded and prevented the right attitude: 'For anger is blindness and though he or she be a father or a mother, he (that is angry) treats them as enemies; though he be a brother, he does not know him; though he be a prophet of the Lord, he disobeys him; though a righteous man, he regards him not' (T.Dan 3:2-3).

It was clearly understood in Judaism that the prohibition of killing included associated emotions. Hatred, causing shame, anger are all steps towards violence: 'He who is angry with his brother without cause shall be liable to be tried; and Eliezer says anger is equivalent to killing' (DER 11; Sif.Dt. 187, b.B.M. 58b).

The words "without cause" are not found in all gospel versions, so there has been much disagreement over the full implications of this passage. Where they are omitted the passage means that all anger is reprehensible. Their inclusion alters this sense of the passage to one in agreement with the much of the rest of the gospels and most of the behaviour of Jesus himself.

The original language means that one should never be provoked to anger or hatred by the conduct of one's brother or fellowman. As in the O.T., the sin is

139

allowing oneself to respond with anger or hatred: 'You shall not curse the deaf or put a stumbling block before the blind, but you shall fear your God ... You shall not go up and down as a slanderer among your people, and you shall not stand forth against the life of your neighbour ... You shall not hate your brother in your heart, but you shall reason with your neighbour, lest you bear sin because of him. You shall not take vengeance or bear any grudge against the sons of your own people, but you shall love your neighbour as yourself. I am the Lord' (Lev. 19:14,15-17).

In I.T. books: 'Beware of hatred for it works lawlessness even against the Lord himself. For if a brother stumble, hatred delights at once to proclaim ... that it is urgent that he should be judged and punished and put to death' (T.Gad. 4:1). One should try to persuade one's neighbour to amend his ways if he sins, without seeking vengeance, which is in accordance with the teaching of E 12a and this is similar to a rabbinical prayer: 'If any design evil against me, speedily make their counsel of no effect and frustrate their designs' (b.Ber 17a).

But there was a righteous anger as well as an unrighteous anger. God was recognised as being angry with wrong-doing: 'The Lord is slow to anger and ... will by no means clear the guilty ... Who can stand before his indignation? Who can endure the heat of his anger?' (Nah. 1:3,6). Jesus, too, is sometimes stated to have been angry with the wickedness of the religious leaders and to have called the rich man a fool. It is anger and hatred arising in defence of oneself which was sinful.

The teaching here is common to many other religions; in Indian writings, for example, the ascetic must bear hard words, he must never insult even when insulted, he must never show anger and must bless when he is cursed. In Judaism, all human beings are considered to be from one ancestor and therefore they should show love to one another as members of the same family. The conduct expected is: 'Let the honour of your neighbours be as dear to you as your own' (ARN. 15); 'Love all and hate only the heretics, the apostates and the informers' (ARN. 16); 'They who suffer insults but do not inflict them; who hear themselves reviled and do not answer back; who perform religious precepts from love and rejoice in chastisement, ...' (b.Git. 36b); and 'Any man who remains silent when he hears himself reviled, even though he has the means to strike back, becomes a partner of the Holy One, who remains silent as He hears the nations revile Him to His face. Such a man is merciful.'

* * *

E 13c. Love for all.

The morality the disciples and followers are expected to live up to is contrasted with that of 'sinners', i.e. wicked people, and especially in the financial sphere is the difference marked. Accepting adversities and sufferings cheerfully, brings merit and exonerates others. The chance to acquire merit was far more important than monetary loss. There is no pharisaic self-afflicting piety for one's own benefit in this passage.

"You have been told, 'an eye for an eye, a tooth for a tooth', but I tell you this: when a man hits you on the cheek, offer him the other cheek too. If someone sues you for your shirt, give him your cloak also. If a man in authority makes you go with him one mile, go willingly a second.

You have been told that you shall love your fellow-countryman (but that you need not love your enemy): but I tell you, you must love your enemies, and pray for those who abuse you, and do good to those who hate you. You must not resist afflictions and you must pray for those who curse you and treat you maliciously.

If you love only those who love you, or do good only to those who do good to you, what merit is that to you? Even sinners are capable of that! Give when you are asked to give, and do not turn away from a man who wants to borrow. If a man takes what is yours, do not demand it back. If you lend only where you expect to be repaid in full, capital and interest, what credit is that to you? Even sinners will lend on those terms.

You must love your persecutors and lend without expecting interest. Only so can you become the children of your heavenly Father who is himself kind to the ungrateful and wicked. You must be as compassionate, generous and good as your heavenly Father, who makes the sun to shine on the wicked and good, and the rain to fall on the just and unjust alike. Then you will have a rich reward of much grace. You must therefore be perfect, just as your heavenly Father is perfect."

The law of talion is that the punishment is to be the same as the crime: '... it shall be done to him as he has done, fracture for fracture, eye for eye, tooth for tooth; the injury and disfiguration that he has inflicted upon another shall in turn be inflicted upon him' (Lev. 24:19-20); 'If any harm follows (from strife), you shall give life for life, eye for eye, tooth for tooth, hand for hand, foot for foot, burn for burn, wound for wound, stripe for stripe' (Ex. 21:23-25).

This doctrine had arisen early in the history of the Israelites in order to stop the development of blood feuds. It was only too easy for one tribe to do twice as much damage to another in retaliation for an injury to one of its members. Thus talion was a curb on worse excesses, but it soon came to be superseded by much more lenient and civilised laws in Judaism which were far in advance of those of neighbouring societies. Monetary compensation was used more than physical punishment.

Jesus' teaching follows other O.T. texts: 'You shall not take vengeance or bear any grudge against the sons of your own people but you shall love your neighbour as yourself: I am the Lord' (Lev. 19:17); 'You shall be holy for me, for I the Lord your God am holy, and have separated you from the peoples, that you should be mine' (Lev. 19:26). Jesus will take this to its ultimate conclusion. He will avoid punishment altogether - all were brothers under one Father - and good must repay evil.

It was taken as a serious insult by the religious leaders to be struck on the face or cheek, since it was argued that man had been created in the likeness of God: 'He that brings into contempt the face of man, brings the Lord's face into contempt' (II En. 44:1). It was an intolerable attack on a man's dignity, demanding retribution. Jesus on the other hand is here seen advocating conduct which follows the advice of other prophets: 'Let him give his cheek to the smiter and be filled with insults' (Lam. 3:30); 'I offered my back to the lash, and let my beard be plucked from my chin' (Is. 50:6). Jesus argues that one must not let one's pride demand reciprocation, but be humble and behave generously. One should give up not only one's shirt but also one's cloak if someone is so mercenary as to sue for the former.

Roman officials could impress ordinary people to carry baggage for them for one mile: that a superior impressed you was God's way of discipline and must be welcomed. Jesus says that they must go twice as far, because afterwards God will lift his yoke and accept his obedient servant into his kingdom: 'Every grievous and cruel yoke that comes upon you, bear for the sake of the Lord, and you will receive your reward on the day of Judgement' (II En. 51:3); 'If in fury the Lord strikes me, he himself will heal me and if he chastises me with his whips, he himself will look again on me in his mercy; and if he is furious at me in my sins, he will again be reconciled with me and forgive my every sin' (J.A. 11:18).

It was contrary to Jewish teaching to demand a poor man's garment nor could he be deprived of his house or the tools of his trade: 'If he is a poor man, you shall not sleep in the cloak he has pledged. Give it back to him at sunset so that he may sleep in it and bless you; then it will be counted to your credit in the sight of the Lord your God' (Dt. 24:12-13). In rabbinical teaching, too: 'You must restore to him early in the morning things needed during the day (e.g. a spade, an axe) and at night things he needs during the night (for example, a blanket)' (Sif.Dt. on Dt. 24:13; m.Peah 8:8).

To give loans to those who had no likelihood of repaying them was to imitate God who opened the treasury of his heavens to send rain to the land and make it fruitful: 'May the Lord open the heavens for you, his rich treasure house, to give rain upon your land at the proper time and bless everything to which you turn your hand' (Dt. 28:12); 'He who is generous to the poor lends to the Lord, who will pay him in full measure' (Pvb. 19:17). In rabbinical literature similarly: 'Those who suffer insults but do not inflict them, who hear themselves reviled and do not answer back, who perform religious precepts from love and rejoice in chastisement - they are like the sun when it goes forth in its might' (b.Git. 36b); 'He who lends money is greater than he who performs acts of charity and he who forms a partnership is greatest of all' (b.Shab. 63a).

Getting interest on money lent was not condoned. 'Do not lend with interest.

This applies to the lender, the borrower, the scribe, the witnesses, a guarantor and even the notary. If a man owed another 100 shekels and had a cloak worth 200, the lender cannot tell the borrower to sell his cloak, so that he may pay the lender his 100 shekels and buy a cheaper cloak for the other 100.' It was also rabbinical advice that 'One should lend to the poor man before the rich one; give preference to your own poor rather than the poor of the city and the poor of your city in preference to the poor of another city.' Avoiding interest was required by the rule that 'You may lend money on condition the borrower repays money, not produce, since the price of produce might have increased during the term of the loan and the lender would get greater benefit' (Mek.Kas. 1).

The wicked receive God's rain (his word) and sun (his favour) and this will continue until the New Era is completely established, when all will be righteous. God could determine where the rain fell: 'It was I who withheld the showers from you while there were still three months to harvest. I would send rain on one city and no rains on another; rain would fall on one field, and another would be parched for lack of it' (Am. 4:7). God made the sun to shine, even to the extent of giving some protection to a burglar from the reaction of the house owner: 'If a burglar breaks in after sunrise and is fatally injured, then it is murder' (Ex. 22:2-3).

This is not to say that all except Jesus and his followers were unrighteous. Some were good and some were evil but just as Moses had offered the blessings of God to a pagan (Hobab): 'If you will go with us, then all the good fortune with which the Lord favours us we will share with you' (Num. 10:32); so too, in this passage, the gospel was not to be confined to Israel. Making converts required inclusiveness not exclusiveness.

The clause in brackets in the passage is found only in Matthew, and is nowhere in the O.T. although there are some passages in which God is said to take vengeance on his enemies: 'God takes vengeance on his adversaries and bears a grudge against his enemies' (Zad. 10:3).

In all Jewish literature one can find passages which glory in the destruction of Israel's enemies and in revenge on one's own personal adversaries, usually praising God for his help or his direct intervention of behalf of the Jews. In the bible, for example: 'In the cities which the Lord your God gives you as an inheritance, you shall save alive nothing that breathes but you shall utterly destroy them' (Dt. 20:16-17); 'Wait for the Lord and keep his way, and he will exalt you to possess the land: you will look on the destruction of the wicked' (Ps. 37:34); 'O daughter of Babylon, you devastator! Happy shall he be who requites you with what you have done to us! Happy shall be he who takes your little ones and dashes them against the rock' (Ps. 137:8-9).

In I.T. literature more extreme measures are desired: 'Let his portion, O Lord, be dishonoured before you; let him go forth groaning, and come home cursed. Let his life be spent in anguish and penury and want, O Lord; let his sleep be beset with pains and his awakening with perplexities. Let sleep be withdrawn from his eyelids at night, let him fail dishonourably in every work of his hands. Let him come empty-handed to his house, and his house be void of everything to satisfy his soul ... Let God destroy them that insolently work all unrighteousness, for a great and mighty judge is the Lord our God' (P.S. 4:16-23,28); 'The sinners shall see the reward provided for those who have believed the covenant of the Most High, and they shall see the tortures to which they themselves will come in the last days. Those who have kept the ways of the Most

High ... shall see the gyrations of the souls of the wicked and the punishment which awaits them. They know the rest which now, being gathered in their chambers, they enjoy in profound peace, guarded by angels; and the glory that awaits them in the last days' (IV Ezr. 7:83-84,91-95).

Yet Jesus' teaching is found in the great majority of passages dealing with righteous behaviour towards, and treatment of, one's enemies, national or personal. Firstly in the O.T.: 'If your enemy is hungry give him bread to eat; if he is thirsty, give him water to drink ... and the Lord will reward you' (Pvb. 25:21-22); 'If I have withheld anything that the poor desired, or caused the eyes of the widow to fail, or have eaten my morsel alone and the fatherless have not eaten of it ... If I have raised my hand against the fatherless because I saw help in the gate, then let my shoulder blade fall from my shoulder and let my arm be broken from its socket' (Job 31:16-22); 'When one of your fellow-country men ... becomes poor, do not be hard-hearted or close-fisted with him but open your hand to him and lend him sufficient for his need' (Dt. 15:7-8).

Secondly, in I.T. books: 'Love each one his brother ... in deed and word, and in the inclination of the soul. Love one another from the heart; and if a man sin against you, speak peaceably to him, and in your heart hold no venom of hatred; if he confess and repent, forgive him. But if he deny it, do not get into a passion with him, lest catching the poison from you, he take to swearing, and so you sin twice over. Though he deny it, yet shows a sense of shame when reproved, stop reproving him ... But if he be shameless and persist in his wrong-doing, even so forgive him in your heart and leave the avenging to God' (T.Gad. 6:1-7); 'In patience and meekness spend your days, that you may inherit endless life. Endure for the sake of God every wound, every injury, every evil word and attack. If others requite you with evil, do not return it to them, neither to neighbour nor enemy, because the Lord will ... be your avenger on the day of Great Judgement' (II En. 50:2-4); 'Love one another my sons, your brothers as a man loves his own soul, and let each seek how he can benefit his brother, and act together on earth and let them love others as themselves' (Jub. 36:4); 'Be patient with the penniless and do not keep him waiting for your charity; for the commandments' sake help the poor and in his need do not send him away empty-handed. Be ready to lose money for a brother or a friend; do not leave it to rust under a stone' (Sir. 29:8-12); '... do truth each one to his neighbour and love each one his brother' (T.Reu. 6:9); 'Cast away all wrath and all lying; love truth and long-suffering' (T.Dan. 6:8).

In the O.T. the message was: 'Rejoice not when your enemy falls, let not your heart be glad when he stumbles' (Pvb. 24:17) Rabbinical teaching was: 'A man should always give the soft answer that turns away wrath, increasing peace with his brethren and relatives and all men' (b.Ber 17a); 'Receive all men with cheerfulness' (m.Avot. 3:13).

In later rabbinical literature, the practice of loving-kindness was without any limitations, was understood as more than charity, and included service to all men of all classes: 'He who waives his right to retribution is forgiven all his sins.' (b.Meg. 28a); 'He who does not visit the sick is like one who sheds blood; he who does, will be delivered in the day of evil.' (b. Ned. 40a). Other aspects are: 'Acts of loving kindness are greater than acts of fear, for the latter give merit which lasts a thousand generations, while the former give merit lasts for two thousand generations' (b.Sot. 31a); and [in the Torah]: 'You are not to do as the heathen does - praise God when

144

things are going well. Israel must praise God in both good and bad times' (Dt. 6:5-9).

The teaching of Jesus was that sufferings and persecution must be accepted without retribution, although it was not to be denied that those who sin by their hostility, should be rebuked by the righteous. The full disciple will act positively towards all his fellowmen and not wait to react to whatever they have done. God bestows his benefits on evil ones and the righteous alike; so shall his slaves. 'The spirit of hatred works with Satan through human frailty to the death of men; but the spirit of love works with God's law through forbearance to the salvation of men' (T.Gad. 4:7).

The last sentence of the passage has given rise to misunderstanding. The idea of perfection is not that one is totally free from sin, but that one is totally committed to God's will. It is similar to the Jewish principle: 'Just as God is, so should you strive to be', and is the N.T. equivalent of the O.T.: 'You shall be holy, for the Lord your God is holy' (Lev. 19:2), since 'holy' and 'perfect' come from the same Hebrew word.

* * *

E 13d. Oaths and vows.

The passage is an extension of the ninth commandment: not only must one not commit perjury in court by bearing false witness, one must not swear falsely under any circumstances.

> **You have also learned that they were told, 'Do not break your oath', and 'Oaths sworn to the Lord must be kept', but I tell you this: do not swear an oath at all – not by heaven, that is God's throne, nor by earth, for it is his footstool; nor by Jerusalem, that is the city of the great king; and not by the life of your own head because you cannot turn one hair of it white or black. Let your 'Yes' be yes, your 'No' be no. Anything else is evil.**

The swearing of oaths was prevalent among the Jews, but an oath was not binding if sworn by Jerusalem, or the Temple, or the altar. Oaths sworn on one's own head were thought to be binding by some, but not by others, while those evoking God's name (suitably disguised) were considered binding by all. One such disguise is to swear 'by heaven' and then the oath became binding. Another example is the oath of Korban (see G 8). Swearing an oath was not totally forbidden by the Qumran community: 'He shall not swear by the Name, nor by Aleph and Lamed, nor by Aleph and Daleth but by a binding oath on the curses of the covenant' (DSS, DR15). Aleph and Lamed and Aleph and Daleth are Hebrew letters indicating the two names of God, Elohim and Adonai respectively.

In other I.T. and rabbinical books, swearing was forbidden: 'The Lord said, "I swear to you my children but not by any oath, neither by heaven nor by earth, nor by any creature which God created ... There is no oath in me nor injustice but truth. If there is no truth in men, let them swear by the words, 'Yes, yes' or 'No, no'" (II En. 49:1); 'Do not accustom your mouth to oaths nor make a habit of naming the Holy One' (Sir. 23:9).

Jesus' teaching is based on O.T. ideas: 'You shall not steal, nor deal falsely, nor lie to one another. You shall not swear by my name falsely, and so profane the name of your God: I am the Lord' (Lev. 19:11-12); 'If you choose not to make a vow, you will not be guilty of sin; but if you do make a vow to the Lord your God ... do what you have promised' (Dt.23: 22- 23). Rabbinical teaching was even more strict; the 'yes' of the righteous is yes, and their 'no' is no: 'God said to Israel, "Be careful in making vows and do not become addicted to doing so, for whoever is so addicted will in the end sin by breaking his oath: and he who breaks his oath denies me without hope of pardon"' (Tanh.79a). This was the teaching of the Essenes in Jesus' day.

Those who think it is necessary to swear an oath so that their word be believed, act as if they sometimes tell lies. Otherwise their simple 'yes' or 'no' would be enough. Those who do not lie, do not need an oath to bolster their plain words. Similarly in rabbinical books: 'The verse Lev.19:36 means your 'yes' should be just and your 'no' should be just' (b.B.M. 49a). By a play on the Hebrew words it also means a verbal agreement must not be violated: 'A false oath destroys what fire cannot

- even if it is sworn carelessly or not known to be false. Therefore one should not swear oaths at all' (j.Shebu.6:5); 'If one who falsifies the words of his companion is liable to death, so certainly is he who falsifies the words of God' (Sif.Dt. on 13:6).

Jesus nevertheless goes beyond this position. To swear an oath implied God would support or punish if the oath were or were not kept, but in the New Era, men would be as angels and could not think of pledging God's reaction. One who followed Jesus would rather suffer than go back on his word.

The great king of the passage is thought to be Herod Agrippa I who persecuted the early community which suggests that this phrase was added by them in hatred of him.

* * *

E 13e. Fornication, or promiscuity.

You have learned that they were told, 'Do not
commit fornication.' But what I tell you is this: if
a man looks at a woman with desire and longing, he has
already committed fornication with her in his heart.

The word translated 'fornication' did not mean then what it means today. The point was that sexual intercourse in which one of the pair could not marry the other, or had no intention of doing so even if they could, was wrong. The extreme case was that of incest. The translation 'adultery' is too narrow. It probably refers also to one who deliberately arouses sexual desire in another not his or her spouse, no doubt as prevalent an activity in Jesus' time as in ours. It seems probable that the way in which the teaching is recorded reflects the place of men in that society in which it was supposed they had responsibility for what women did. It is difficult to think that Jesus thought women were any less immoral to arouse men other than their husbands than men were to arouse women other than their wives.

Jesus' teaching here was not very different from that found in the literature of Judaism. In a rabbinical commentary on the verse of : 'The eye of the adulterer waits for twilight, saying, "No one will see me" (Job 24:15) it is said, 'Not only he who sins with his body is an adulterer; he who sins with his eye is also an adulterer' (Lev.R. 23:12); and, 'A man who counts out money for a woman from her hand into his or from his on to hers, in order to look at her, will not be free from judgement' (b.Erub.18b, Pes.113b); 'Unchaste imagination is more injurious than the sin itself' (b.Yoma 29a); 'I gave my eyes strict instructions not to gaze on a maiden' (Job 31:1).

The O.T. takes a similar standpoint: 'If my heart has been enticed to a woman and I have lain in wait at my neighbour's door ... that would be a sin to be punished by the judges' (Job 31:9,11); 'If my heart has been secretly enticed ... this would be an iniquity to be punished ... for I should have been false to God above' (Job 31:27-28). There are also many warnings against the temptations of harlots, but few against women in general; a virtuous woman is very highly valued: 'Who can find a virtuous woman, for such a one is more valuable than precious stones?' (Pvb. 31:10); 'A virtuous wife is a crown to her husband' (Pvb. 12:4).

Jesus once again follows O.T. teaching: 'None of you shall approach any one near of kin to him to uncover nakedness ... You shall not lie carnally with your neighbour's wife ... Do not defile yourselves by any of these things ... for whoever shall do any of these abominations ... shall be cut off from among their people (Lev. 18:6,20,24). To indulge in illicit sexual activity was to defile not only oneself but also the whole of Israel. Jesus' teaching is an extension of the commandment not to commit 'adultery': one is not to even consider it.

In I.T. literature, women are often seen as sources of trouble, evil and as a constant temptation to men to stray from God's way: 'He that has a pure mind in love, does not look after a woman with a view to fornication, for he has no defilement in his heart, because the Spirit of God rests upon him' (T.Ben. 8:2); 'I was never promiscuous by lustful glance' (T.Iss. 7:2); 'Beware therefore of promiscuity, and if you wish to be pure in mind, guard your senses from every woman' (T.Reu. 6:1); 'Rule me, O God, keeping me back from wicked sin and from every wicked woman that causes the simple to stumble, and let not the beauty of a lawless woman beguile me' (P.S. 16:7-8).

* * *

E 14. Why parables? - Mt. 13:10-11, 13-17, 34-35. Mk. 4:10-12. Lk. 8:9-10; 10:23-24.

The gospels often record that the disciples were puzzled by the parables which Jesus related, even those which appear to us to be very straightforward. Sometimes, he seemed to say that only some of his listeners could understand them, and that the majority, who could not do so, would not be able to belong to the kingdom of God.

It was not uncommon in Jewish writings that something was explained in ways that those who had been accepted into the group would grasp the significance of, while those outside could not. The word "mystery" in English gives a false impression. It did not originally signify something secret or concealed, but something which only those "in the know" would understand. In the context of Jewish life at the time of Jesus, such mysteries were things which would be understood by those to whom God had granted the necessary knowledge. Such understanding should have marked the members of the disciples and it must have been a real disappointment to Jesus that they needed further help.

Jesus' disciples were somewhat mystified by some of the parables and riddles Jesus used. "Why do you speak to the people in parables?", they asked. Jesus replied, "It has been granted to you to know the mystery of the kingdom of God, but to outsiders everything is parables: 'They may look and look but never see, they may hear and hear but understand nothing, for this people has grown gross at heart; their ears are dull and their eyes are closed. Lest they turn back and are forgiven by God.' But blessed are your eyes because you see, and your ears, because you hear! There is one thing for sure: many prophets and righteous ones longed to see and hear what you see and hear, yet neither saw nor heard it.

The passage appears difficult to accept and has caused much speculation. Some think it is legitimate to translate part of it: 'He spoke to the extent they could understand', that is, not very much at all, but the idea of the passage is from the O.T. Here God asks whom he can send to warn Israel of their situation. They were stubborn and not keeping to God's ways; they would not see and understand. Isaiah volunteers and God's message is given to the Israelites: 'Go and say to this people, "You shall hear indeed, but you shall not understand; and you shall see indeed, but you shall not perceive. For the hearts of this people have become gross, their ears are dull of hearing, and their eyes they have closed; lest they should see and understand with their heart, and be converted and I should heal them"' (Is. 6:8-10 LXX). Isaiah then asks how long this situation will continue and the reply is: 'Until the cities lie waste without inhabitants, and houses without men and the land is utterly desolate' (Is. 6:11-13). The Aramaic version reads: 'Make the heart of this people fat and make their ears dull and stop up their eyes, lest they see with their eyes, hear with their ears and understand with their hearts and turn again and it be forgiven them' (Tg.Is. 6:10). The last verse of this passage in Isaiah continues: 'Though a tenth remain in it, it will be burned again like a terebinth or an oak whose stump remains standing when it is felled. The holy seed is its stump' (Is. 6:13). In the Greek version of the O.T. it reads: 'And yet there shall be a tenth upon it, and again it shall be for a spoil, as a turpentine tree and as an acorn when it falls out of its husk' (Is. 6:13,LXX), while in the Aramaic version of Isaiah's book it is given as: 'And a tenth shall be left in it, and they shall be burned up again: like a terebinth and like an oak, which appear to be dried up when their leaves fall, though they still retain their moisture to preserve a seed from them: so the exiles of Israel shall be gathered together, and shall return to their land, for a holy seed is their plant' (Tg.Is. 6:13). The idea is repeated in: 'Cut down the tree and destroy it, but leave its stump and roots in the ground ...' (Dan. 4:23).

The implication of this O.T. passage is that God has given up most of Israel as obdurate and blind. Only from a small minority will a shoot arise which will be true to God's rule. These few, which was naturally interpreted at the time as including the disciples, will hear and understand, will see and perceive and will be granted insight into the mysteries and secrets of God. They are the 'holy seed' which God reserves to bear fruit abundantly in the New Era and they can look forward to the kingdom of God, which they are already experiencing, unfolding in their lifetime. They will pass on the true message to succeeding generations, 'so that they set their hope in God and not forget his words' (Ps. 78:7). This was Jewish teaching also: 'And I [God] ... saved one grape of a cluster and one plant out of a great forest' (IV Ezr. 9:21).

On this understanding, Jesus' parables are clear to those willing to see the dawn of the New Era, but those who are unwilling to commit themselves, who have no faith in God, respond neither to Jesus' teaching, nor to his actions. A hard-hearted person will always reject God's kingdom. Those who long for its coming are the righteous ones even if they are imperfect in some ways.

There are several other passages in the O.T. which could well have been in the mind of Jesus: 'Moses said to Israel: "You have seen all the Lord did before your eyes in Egypt ... the great trials your eyes saw, the signs, the great wonders, but the Lord has not given you a mind to understand or eyes to see or ears to hear"' (Dt. 29:2-4); 'Proclaim it in Judah: Hear this, O foolish and senseless people, who have eyes but see not, who have ears but hear not' (Jer.5:20-21); 'Son of man, you live in the midst of a rebellious people, who have eyes to see but see not, who have ears to hear but hear not, for they are a rebellious house. Therefore prepare yourself an exile's baggage ...' (Ezk. 12:2-3). (See also B 1.)

It is found, too, in I.T. books: 'But as for the peoples, seeing and not understanding ... for they will see the wise man's end and not understand what the Lord intended for him' (W.S. 4:15,17); 'Their wickedness blinded them and they did not know the secret purpose of God' (W.S. 2:22). It was evidently a widespread idea since it is also found in the writings from Qumran: 'He shall conceal the teaching of the Law from men of injustice but shall impart true knowledge and righteous judgement to those who have chosen the way' (DSS, CD. 9:18).

In rabbinical books there are several similar passages. A commentary on: 'The secret things belong to the Lord our God, but the revealed things belong to us and to our children forever...' suggests that 'When all Israel obeys the Law, God will reveal the hidden mysteries and the New Era will begin' (Sif. Num. on Dt.29:28). Another piece of rabbinical teaching was based on: 'O, mortal, propound a riddle and speak a parable to the house of Israel' (Ezk. 17:2). God did not speak to Moses in riddles and parables as he did to other prophets: 'With Moses I speak face to face - clearly and not in riddles [or parables]' (Num. 12:8).

The Aramaic version of Isaiah has other passages in the same vein: 'Has that which has been revealed to you been revealed to any people? ... I have announced to you new things from this time, even hidden things which you have not known' (Tg. Is. 48:6); and: 'I brought forth the people out of Egypt, who were as the blind though they had eyes and as the deaf though they had ears' (Tg.Is. 43:8).

Some think that the passage in the gospels gives a slightly different message, namely, not to treat Israel as special, but to be inclusive of all people who follow God's will, Jews or Gentiles. Not for the only time, Jesus perhaps was irritated by the dullness of the disciples. They were insiders to whom the mysteries are revealed yet even so the disciples understood very little!

Matthew adds another quotation:

`I will open my mouth in parables; I will utter things kept secret since the foundation of the world.`

This is from Psalms: 'I will open my mouth in parables: I will utter riddles from the foundation of the world' (Ps. 78:2,LXX). The word for riddles is also used in this sense in the O.T.: 'And Samson said to them, I propound you a riddle ...' (Jdg. 14:12). The Syriac version of this text gives: 'I will utter things hidden before the foundations of the world' indicating belief in the pre-existence of Jesus.

There may be a connection with the very old idea that parables were in some way magical and brought about what they prophesied. 'After that ... Enoch gave me the teaching of all the secrets in the parables which had been given to him ... Michael said, 'The power of the spirit ... makes me tremble because of the severity of judgement of the secrets, the judgement of the angels: who can endure the severe judgement which has been executed?' (I En. 68:1-2).

Some scholars think that the passage reflects the situation at the time when the gospels were being assembled and written down. There was conflict between those of the Jerusalem church and those who did not keep the practices of Judaism, which led to serious disagreement. Those who take this point of view see the passage as a piece of polemical writing saying that the leaders of the Jerusalem church were apostates and were not following the precepts Jesus had taught. They were those who would not see, would not hear and would not understand. (See also F 1).

This passage occurs in the gospels in the middle of the parable of the sower (C 2), but many scholars think it did not originally belong there.

* * *

The missionaries were sent out in pairs, which may have been because, according to Jewish legal tradition, two was the minimum to give valid testimony. They gave witness of the nearness of God's kingdom: 'What great nation has gods close at hand, as the Lord our God is close at hand?' (Dt. 4:7); 'The Lord is near to all who call on him in truth' (Ps. 145:18); 'Surely his salvation is at hand for those who fear him' (Ps. 85:9).

They were given power to heal and to exorcise evil spirits, or free sufferers from demons. These would be rendered so harmless they could be trodden underfoot: 'Satan shall be bound by him and he shall give power to his children to tread upon evil spirits' (T.Lev. 18:12); 'Then shall all the spirits of error be trodden underfoot and men shall rule over wicked spirits' (T.Sim. 6:6).

The sight of the people so moved Jesus that his bowels were churned with compassion; the people were like sheep without a shepherd, harassed and helpless and he called his disciples to him and said, "The crop is heavy but labourers are scarce. Pray therefore the Lord of the harvest to send out workers into the fields."

He sent them out in pairs on a mission, giving them authority over spirits of uncleanness and to cure diseases. "Heal the sick and call the people to repentance, but do not stop to greet people on the way. Tell them the good news that the kingdom of God is close at hand. You received without payment, now give freely.

You are to take nothing for the journey, no bread, no pack, no money, no second coat, just a staff and sandals on your feet. When you come to a place, find some good person and make his home yours for your stay. Give the house a blessing of peace so that if it is worthy, your peace will enter it; if not, it will return to you. At any place where they will not receive you, shake the dirt from under your feet as a warning and testimony to them. It is certain that it will be worse for them on the day of Judgement than for Sodom.
To receive you is to receive me, and to receive me is to receive the One who sent me: To reject you is to reject me, and to reject me is to reject the One who sent me. Whoever receives a prophet because he is a prophet (God's messenger), will be given a prophet's reward; and whoever receives a good man because he is righteous (one who shows God's way), will be given a righteous man's reward. Certain it is that if anyone gives a cup of water to one of these little ones because he is a follower of my gospel, that man will not go unrewarded."

153

So they went off and proclaimed the gospel of
repentance, cast out many demons and healed many sick
people.

The beginning of the passage reminds one of several similar passages in the O.T., some of which Jesus or the evangelists may have had in mind: 'My bowels writhe within me' (Lam. 1:20); 'Ply the sickle for the harvest is ripe; tread the grapes for the press is full; make the vats overflow for great is the wickedness of the nations ...' The day of the Lord is at hand in the valley of Judgement' (Jl. 3:13); 'The Lord has trodden the virgin daughters of Judah as in a wine press' (Lam. 1:15). In rabbinical books: 'The harvest is due, the work great, the labourers slow, the reward much and the master of the house urgent' (m.Avot. 2:15).

It is not only an encouragement to missionary work, but a warning that the sickle will harvest the wicked as well as the righteous: 'Our end drew nigh, our days were numbered, for our end had come' (Lam. 4:18). In other words, the metaphor of harvest has both positive and negative connotations (see C 9) and it is likely that the workers to be sent out are the disciples themselves. They are to offer blessings to the harassed and helpless.

The image of the shepherd and his sheep as a picture of God's agent and his people is from the O.T.: '... that the congregation of the Lord may not be as sheep which have no shepherd' (Num. 27:17); 'And Macaiah said, "I saw all Israel scattered upon the mountains as sheep that have no shepherd"' (I Kgs. 22:17); 'Strike the shepherd that the sheep may be scattered' (Zch. 13:7), and also in Ezekiel chapter 34. In I.T. books sheep (or lambs) can represent the faithful who were persecuted in their day: 'I saw in the vision how the ravens flew upon those lambs and took one of them ... Eagles, vultures, ravens and kites kept tearing at the sheep ... and devouring them ...' (I En. 90:8,11); 'My God, in whom you trust; he will deliver you from the snares of the fowler ...; under his wings you will find refuge' (Ps. 91:1-3).

The disciples were told to teach others without demanding a fee, just as they themselves had been taught by Jesus. Compare the rabbinical saying : 'God said to Moses, "Just as you received the Torah without payment, so teach it without payment"' (D.E.Z. 4:2); and in I.T. literature: 'I learned to know Wisdom without guile and I impart without grudging' (W.S. 7:13).

There were laws in Judaism against those who proclaimed false doctrines and also against those who abused preachers of true doctrines. Two or more preachers, staying in a place for more than a month, were liable for their own activities, unless they spoke in the name of someone else. Then that person, their leader, was responsible for his followers' actions. In addition, anyone with one of the preachers as a guest in his house was also liable to penalties if the preacher turned out to be unreliable. The disciples will not compromise their hosts and leave at once if they are unwelcome, albeit with the sign of God's displeasure.

The disciples were not to waste time on trivialities on the way. It was believed that those sent out on a mission took with them the charisma of the leader, and to greet others on the way, to come into conversation with them, was to waste the charisma, so that enough might not remain for its real purpose of converting unbelievers. This instruction repeats that given to Gehazi by Elisha: 'Gird up your loins, take my staff in your hand and go. If you meet anyone do not salute him; and if anyone salutes you, do not reply ...' (II Kgs. 4:29).

The disciples were to demonstrate their dependence on their hosts, not because they wished to appear ascetic or parasitic, but because in the kingdom interdependence was the norm. Those worthy of God's kingdom would be confident enough to give hospitality to his messengers, even angels from heaven as Lot had done: 'Two angels came to Sodom ...When Lot saw them he rose to meet them and bowed ... and said, "My lords, turn aside I pray you, to your servant's house and spend the night ..."' (Gen. 19:1-2). The disciples brought a vital message, and were to be provided for. This was Jewish practice: 'Every true prophet ... is worthy of his food' (Did. 13:1), and it was a general practice for pious Jews when entering a place unknown to them to find out who paid tithes and was faithful. In such houses they could lodge safely.

The disciples gave a greeting of peace to the house or family and if it were accepted, they remained there. If it were rejected, or ignored and not reciprocated, their peace would return to them: 'When my prayer returned unanswered, I walked with head bowed in grief ...' (Ps. 35:13). Those who refused the disciples, refused the message too. They became as the inhabitants of Sodom, the city destroyed by God because of its wickedness. The places where the disciples were dismissed could be destroyed likewise, and even the dirt of such a place was polluting: 'The wicked are like the restless sea ... its waters toss up mire and filth. There is no peace for the wicked, says the Lord' (Is. 57:20-21). The disciples must get rid of the dirt on their feet in a manner which acts as a warning to those living there.

There are differences among the three gospel accounts of the instructions given to the missionaries. Matthew's version is one of the examples found in his gospel showing he identified himself and his readers with the Jewish community but he also approved of Gentiles joining the new (Jewish) movement, although he says the disciples are to avoid Gentile and Samaritan areas (see also E 14). There are differing opinions in the O.T. and rabbinical books about whether Gentiles could be admitted to Judaism. Some are positive: 'Open the gates so that the righteous nation that keeps faith may enter in' (Is. 26:2); 'The Lord looks down from heaven ... he who fashions the hearts of them all' (Ps. 33:13,15); 'One who brings a heathen near to God (i.e. as a proselyte) and converts him, is as though he had created him' (Gen.R. 39:14). Others are negative: 'God's Spirit does not rest on other nations so Israel is distinguished' (b.Ber. 7a); 'Moses charged us with the Torah as a possession for the assembly of Jacob' (Dt. 33:4); '...we shall be distinct, I and your people, from every people on the face of the earth' (Ex. 33:16).

According to Mark, the missionaries were told to travel without bread, wallet and money, but, having been shod with sandals, they were to take a staff. Matthew says that neither staff nor sandals were permitted and Luke agrees about the sandals. Rabbinical teaching was: 'A man must not enter on to the Temple mount with his staff, nor with his sandals, nor his wallet, nor with dust on his feet' (b.Ber. 54a).

If Matthew's account were correct, it has been suggested that this was because Jesus and his disciples were about to begin their campaign of proclaiming the onset of the kingdom, which would supersede the Temple and its rituals. If on the other hand, Mark's account were correct, because the New Era had begun or was expected at any time, they were like the Israelites in the wilderness depending on God to provide for them. They had received manna from heaven, and their clothes had shown no signs of wear. Likewise, an extra shirt or coat was unnecessary in the new kingdom when

155

circumstances will be as they had been, just before the children of Israel went into the promised land: 'The elect shall be clothed with garments of glory ... garments of life from the Lord of Spirits. Your garments shall not grow old, nor your glory pass away ...' (I En. 62:15). The staff, which was necessary, was a wand, or staff, like Moses' staff, with all its remarkable properties, and the evangelists emphasise the correlation between Jesus' campaign and the first Passover feast: 'In this manner you shall eat it: your loins girded, your sandals on your feet and your staff in your hand; and you shall eat in haste' (Ex. 12:11).

The teaching of the last section of the passage reflects the traditional relationship between principal and agent, between teacher and pupil, scholar and student. It is those who receive a prophet or sage, a wise man or good man, for his own sake, with no ulterior motive, who will receive an appropriate reward. Even the students or disciples, the little ones, represent their master, and kindness done to them, is a kindness done to their teacher.

Matthew gives Jesus' instruction to the missionaries as:

"Do not take the road to Gentile areas nor to Samaritan places, but go to the lost sheep of Israel."

Luke says that the disciples, and Jesus, were not accepted in a Samaritan village:

Jesus sent messengers ahead and they went into a Samaritan village but they were rejected and were sent away because Jesus was going to Jerusalem. James and John suggested calling down fire from heaven to destroy such a place, but Jesus rebuked them and they went on to another village.

These two passages are of interest. Matthew's statement suggests Jesus was not concerned about the non-Jewish population receiving his message. Luke shows the antipathy of the Samaritans for the Jews, but clearly Jesus and his disciples had been going through a Samaritan area. In John's gospel likewise, Jesus passes into the Samaritan place and meets the woman at the well (Jn. 4:3-10). In rabbinical teaching, non-Jewish areas were unclean and no Jew should enter them (b.Git 7b). It would seem that in spite of this, Jesus did want his message to be heard by non-Jews, even Samaritans. It is an example of Jesus defying the teaching of the religious leaders in favour of bringing his good news to all.

A similar story, found only in Luke, is about seventy-two missionaries being sent out. Whether this was a separate event, or whether the stories are two versions of the same event is not known. Some claim that the number seventy-two symbolised completeness or comprehensiveness.

* * *

156

E 16. Prospects for disciples - Mt. 7:15; 10:16-31, 34-36; 24:9-14. Mk. 4:22-23; 13:9-13. Lk. 6:40; 8:17; 12:1-7, 11-12, 49-53; 21:12-19.

Many in Judaism thought that before the day of Judgement and the arrival of the Messiah, there would be a period of terrors and miseries, at least for the wicked: 'On the day of their anguish and affliction ... I will give them over into the hands of my Elect. As straw in the fire shall they burn before the face of the holy' (I En. 48:8-9); 'There shall come forth a shoot from the stump of Jesse ... and the Spirit of the Lord shall rest upon him ... With righteousness he shall judge the poor and decide with equity for the meek. ... He shall smite the earth with the rod of his mouth, and with the breath of his lips, he shall slay the 'wicked' (Is. 11:1-2,4).

Conflict in families had also been prophesied in both O.T. and I.T. books: 'For the son treats the father with contempt, the daughter rises up against her mother, the daughter-in-law against her mother-in-law, a man's enemies are the men of his own house' (Mic. 7:6); 'In those days the fathers with their sons shall be smitten and brothers one with another shall fall in death, till the streams flow with their blood. A man shall not withhold his hand from slaying his sons and his grandsons ... nor from his honoured brother; from dawn to sunset will they slay one another' (I En. 100:1-2); 'They shall strive with one another, the young with the old and the old with the young; the poor with the rich, the lowly with the great and the beggar with the prince on account of the law and covenant' (Jub. 23:19).

The message seems to be that those who hold out and remain faithful in righteousness will win eternal life: 'But as for me, I will look to the Lord, I will wait for the God of my salvation; my God will hear me' (Mic. 7:7); 'He who walks in integrity will be delivered.' (Pvb. 28:18). Jesus, like other martyrs, dies according to God's plan, just as no sparrow dies without God's will and help.

Nothing is hidden except that it may be manifested, nor become covered but that it may come into the open, and there is no secret which cannot be made known by some means. What you said in the darkness will be heard in the light, and what you whispered in your private rooms will be proclaimed from the roofs.

A disciple does not rank above his teacher, nor a servant above his master. The pupil should be content to share the teacher's fate and the servant his master's. When the disciple's training has been perfected he will become as his teacher.

Beware of the 'leaven' of the hypocritical Pharisees, and be on your guard - many false prophets will arise and mislead many; they are men who come to you dressed as sheep but underneath they are rapacious wolves. Be as wise as serpents, and as pure and simple as doves.

You will be brought before kings and governors for my sake to testify before them. Beware of princes, for they will hand you over to the councils for punishment and execution and you will be scourged in the synagogues. When you are arrested, do not worry about what you are to say: this is your chance to testify, for, before the end, the gospel must be proclaimed to all nations throughout the whole world. So do not prepare your defence beforehand, because when the time comes the words needed will be given to you. It is not you who will speak, but the Spirit of your Father speaking in you.

To you who are my friends, I say this: do not fear those who kill the body but can do no more than that. Fear rather him who had also authority to cast into Gehenna. He is the one to fear. Are not sparrows two a penny? Yet not one falls to the ground without your Father's leave, or is forgotten before God. The hairs of your head are all counted, and you are of greater worth than many sparrows.

When you are persecuted in one town take refuge in another; I tell you this: before you have gone through all the towns of Israel the son of man will have come.

Would that the fire that I came to cast on the earth were already alight. I am so hard pressed until the baptism I have to be baptised with is completed!

Do you suppose I came to give peace to the earth? No, I tell you, rather the opposite. From now on, a family of five will be divided, three against two and two against three. There will be dissension between a father and his son, a daughter and her mother, and a young wife and her mother-in-law. A brother will deliver his brother to death, and friends in your household will hand you over to be put to death. Many will lose their faith and many false prophets will arise and will mislead many. As lawlessness spreads, the love of many for one another will grow cold. All will hate you on account of my name, but those enduring to the end will win true life."

This passage has several points worth noticing. No matter how carefully one covers up what one does or thinks, God knows about it. It is the good 'inclination' within us, in the Jewish understanding of this word, which watches over our thoughts and deeds. The righteous would meet face to face with those who insult, accuse and condemn, but the best preparation for such crises is to have developed a faithful life, true to God's guidance of one's inclination: 'For he that is just and humble is ashamed to do what is unjust, being reproved, not by another but by his own heart, because the Lord sees his inclination' (T.Gad. 5:3). The fruit of this will become obvious in the hour of trial: 'Now therefore go, and I, the Lord, will be your mouth and teach you what to speak' (Ex. 4:12); 'I will speak of your decrees before kings and shall not be put to shame' (Ps. 119:46); 'And the Lord said to Jacob: "I will bring all things to your remembrance"' (Jub. 32:25). Not only the master or teacher must be prepared to accept what can happen to him; the servants or apprentices can expect no better treatment.

The problem of how to detect false prophets, preachers and religious 'charismatics' has always been difficult: 'When a prophet speaks in the name of the Lord, and the word does not come true, it is not a word spoken in the name of the Lord. The prophet has spoken it presumptuously ...' (Dt. 18:22). Thus one solution was to wait to see if the prophecy came true or not:'The prophets prophesy falsely and the priests rule at their direction; my people love to have it so, but what will you do when the end comes?' (Jer. 5:31). The solution here is to be found on the day of Judgement.

In the O.T. other suggestions are made: 'The Lord said, "The prophets are prophesying lies in my name. I did not send them nor did I command or speak to them. They are prophesying a false vision, worthless divination and the deceit of their own minds!"' (Jer. 14:14); 'Thus says the Lord of Hosts: "Do not listen to the words of the prophets who prophesy to you, filling you with vain hopes; they speak visions of their own minds not from the mouth of the Lord. They say continually to those who despise the word of the Lord, 'It shall be well with you;' and to every one who stubbornly follows his own heart, they say, 'No evil shall come upon you"' (Jer. 23:16-17).

The solution suggested here seems to be to question and evaluate the content of the prophet's words. Much the same was applied a few centuries later: 'Let everyone who comes in the name of the Lord be received; but when you have tested him you shall know him, for you shall have understanding of true and false' (Did. 12:1). Solutions to this problem remain much the same today, and are no more satisfactory.

The idea that false prophets come as sheep in wolves' clothing, may come from: 'On that day (when the Lord comes) every false prophet will not put on a hairy mantle to deceive' (Zch. 13:4); and: 'The scion of David, the messiah, will come only in a generation which is brazen-faced like a dog, full of impudence and deserving to be exterminated. After a period when one generation after another curses and blasphemes, the messiah will come' (Cant.R. 2:13-14).

The disciples must expect trials and tribulations: 'Evils have encompassed me without number ... they are more than the hairs of my head' (Ps. 40:12); 'More in number than the hairs of my head are those who hate me without cause' (Ps. 69:4) and God knew everything, even the number of hairs on their heads. They must trust that God would not let them be destroyed even though it may appear that they had been abandoned to the forces of Satan. We cannot know the reason for the evils which fall upon us, but God does: 'Of them that love me and keep my commandments, refers to those who ... risk their lives for the sake of the commandments' (Mek.Bah. 6); and: 'Not a bird dies apart from heaven' (j.Sheb. 31b) was rabbinical teaching.

Baptism was also a rite of passage, of transition, and the baptism of fire which Jesus is said to wish so much to have passed through, may refer to the establishment of the new kingdom. In the O.T. the baptism of fire is necessary: 'Who can endure the day of his (the Lord's messenger) coming? For he is like a refiner's fire ... and he will purify the sons of Levi ...' (Mal. 3:2-3); 'When you pass through the waters I will be with you, and through the rivers, they shall not overwhelm you, when you walk through fire you shall not be burnt and the flames will not consume you' (Is. 43:2).

This passage may be compared with that of J 3, in which similar prophecies are given. Matthew includes much more than Mark and Luke, and says that the day of Judgement will have come before the apostles have gone through the towns of Israel. Many think this was not originally part of his gospel.

* * *

E 17. Other disciples - Mt. 12:30. Mk. 9:38-40. Lk. 9:49-50; 11:23.

The disciples had tried and failed to cast out the evil spirit in the boy possessed by a demon (see I 2), and then they had come across someone outside the "inner circle" who was successfully practising exorcism in Jesus' name.

> "Master", said John to Jesus, "we saw a man driving out demons in your name, but as he wasn't one of us, we forbade him to do so."
> Jesus said, "No, don't forbid him! No one who does such works in my name can be ready to speak evil of me. He that is not with me is against me, and he who does not gather with me scatters."

To do something in Jesus' name was to invoke Jesus' name by saying it aloud, and was thought to promote a transfer of power from one exorcist to another. It was accepted practice, in any case, that one teacher always based his teaching on the authority of other teachers. Herod's reign had 'scattered' the Law according to Hillel and it should be gathered in.

The concept of the power of a name was a common one. The name of God was so powerful it had to be circumvented and in rabbinical times the name YHWH was used only within the Sanctuary (b.Sot. 7:6).

Jesus says the man is not likely to abuse the spirit by which he cures, and those who follow Jesus' teaching are those who will enter the kingdom of God, not necessarily those who belong to the twelve. In the story of Eldad and Medad, they prophesied, although they did not join the seventy elders called together for that purpose. John reminds one of Joshua who thought this was wrong but was corrected by Moses: 'Now two men, Eldad and Medad, remained in the camp and the spirit rested upon them ... and they prophesied in the camp. A young man ran and told Moses ... and Joshua ... said, "My lord, forbid them." But Moses said to him, "Are you jealous on my account? Would that all the Lord's people were prophets, that the Lord would put his spirit on them all."' (Num. 11:26-29).

That was Jesus' viewpoint, too: the more following God's word, the better, wherever or whoever they were! Some encouraged others to hear, and understand the gospel he taught. They gathered them into the kingdom; others drove them away and scattered them.

This passage may be compared to B 2 in which those who had done miracles (in their own names?) were refused entry into the kingdom.

* * *

E 18. The right priority - Lk. 10:38-42.

This passage is really a play on the meaning of 'bread'. Was the food Martha was so busy with more important than the food Jesus was giving?

There was an occasion when Jesus was invited into the home of Martha and her sister Mary. Martha was distracted with much serving.

"Lord", she said, "don't you care that I am having to do all the serving? Tell Mary that she may help me!" "Martha, Martha, you are fussing and fretting about many things, but one thing is necessary. Mary has chosen the good portion and it shall not be taken from her," said Jesus.

To call someone by their name twice was to emphasise the nearness of God and his encouragement; for example when God called Abraham: 'The Angel of the Lord called to him from heaven and said, "Abraham, Abraham"' (Gen. 22:11); or when Moses was called: 'God called to him out of the bush, "Moses, Moses"' (Ex. 3:4); and Samuel: 'Then the Lord called, "Samuel, Samuel"' (I Sam. 3:4).

By this means Jesus is portrayed as recalling Martha to the most important matter, and that she should respond to God's call. The one thing that mattered was what Jesus was offering. It was he who was the host and Martha and Mary were the guests at his table, and the food he would give them was God's word. Martha had her priorities wrong and thought material things had to come first: '... and the Lord fed you with manna ... that he might make you know that man does not live by bread alone, but that he lives by everything that proceeds out of the mouth of the Lord' (Dt. 8:3).

In the Temple, the priests serve the Lord and receive a portion of their service. Mary, by listening attentively serves Jesus and his words and also acquires a portion of them. Sitting at his feet, as a disciple would, she put servicing the word as top priority. The last thing God would want would be for Mary to stop doing that to help Martha servicing the worldly things. It was better to obey God than to offer sacrifices: 'To listen (to the Lord) is better than the fat of rams' (I Sam. 15:22) and as the rabbis said: 'May your house be a meeting place for the wise; sit amid the dust of their feet and drink in their words' (m.Avot.1:4). Martha really put her foot in it by suggesting Mary should leave her good choice and help her sister.

* * *

162

Those who would be counted as belonging to God's people in his realm, were those whom God had been able to forgive because they have forgiven others. No retribution or recompense would be expected of them, and they would do his will at all times, giving to the poor any superfluity they possessed.

Service of others was the hall-mark of God's followers, because there was no distinction between that and serving God. Even those who began to do so only when force of circumstances presented a special opportunity were counted as righteous. Neither was it enough to do miracles nor to be one of the twelve. Nothing could take priority over doing God's will which his followers would learn from him in their hearts. All would be equal in his kingdom - there would be no hierarchy of importance. Such followers would show the light of God's rule, would be able lovingly to reprove a brother. They would pray to God in full confidence that God would hear and that on the day of Judgement, God would call them from the grave to eternal life.

God's capital must be used for God's benefit and no slave could give back to God anything equivalent to the gifts God had given him, but a whole-hearted commitment is acceptable instead.

Some things had to be avoided. None should mislead the 'little ones' and all bad inclinations are known to God and must be combated. God's will guides the good inclination and this will be enough in times of trial and persecution. All must make a full commitment to God's rule, loving all, craving no vengeance on evil doers and giving and lending without expectation of repayment. No statement should be deceptive so that oaths were banned as superfluous.

The passages of E 12 and E 13 are almost wholly from Matthew's gospel and it is striking that nothing of them is found in Mark, and in Luke what little there is, is probably derived from Matthew. The sermon on the mount, on which so much of this section is based, can be seen as extended teaching on three basic matters: the Law, the practices of the new community, the emerging Christian church and the requirement to trust God selflessly.

These three issues are parallel to the three principles of Rabbi Simeon the Just: 'The world stands upon three things: upon the Law, upon service of the Temple and on social or religious deeds of loving kindness'. Matthew presents Jesus as saying that anger and hatred are as bad as murder, lascivious thoughts are as bad as fornication and promiscuity, and oaths are improper. All must make a full commitment to God's rule, loving all, craving no vengeance on evil doers and giving and lending without expectation of repayment. Many think that Matthew formulated some of these passages himself.

In another of the passages (E 2) vicarious suffering for another's sins, and the death of an innocent sacrifice to atone for the sins of others and of Israel, are advocated.

These ideas do not fit with much else of gospel teaching; sacrifices are condemned (G 1) except of one's own self (F 11); nor can one person's merit or sin be transferred to another (B 3); and Isaiah 53 is not to be understood as a prophecy of a perfect victim to atone for all.

F. Jesus' message - mainly to followers.

F 1. Jesus and his family - Mt. 12:46-50. Mk. 3:20-21, 31-35. Lk. 8:19-21; 11:27-28.

Jesus went into a house, but there was such a large
crowd gathered round them, it was not even possible to
recline to eat! When those with him heard of it they went
to seize him for they said, "He is out of his mind."

Then his mother and brothers arrived and sent
a message in to him, while they waited outside. "Your
mother and brothers are outside and want to speak to
you," Jesus was told. "Who is my mother, who are my
brothers?", he replied. Looking at those sitting around
him, he said, "Here they are: those who hear the word of
God and do it are my mother and my brothers."

On another occasion, a woman in the crowd raised
her voice and said to him, "Blessed is the womb that
bore you and the breasts you suckled!" But Jesus said,
"Blessed rather are those, hearing and preserving God's
word, keep it."

This is a difficult passage, since the versions of the evangelists are not the same. Those whom Mark says accompanied Jesus could have been his other relatives, which Matthew and Luke say were his mother and brothers.

This passage is usually understood as meaning that Jesus' family thought he was mentally disturbed, a serious sign of God's displeasure, and that they therefore came to take him away. The implications are considerable. Some have tried to avoid this meaning by saying that the original language suggests that it was the disciples who went to restrain the crowd, for they said it was going crazy with excited enthusiasm. Others have seen the passage as confirming the antagonism between those of the family of Jesus who became the leaders of the Jerusalem church after his death, and the largely Gentile churches which grew up as a result of the work of Paul and which were led by the apostles. (See E 14.)

In any case Jesus' reply was hardly in accord with O.T. and rabbinical teaching: 'He who reviles or insults his father or his mother shall be put to death' (Ex. 21:17). Rabbinical teaching also touched on the position of the Gentiles: 'If one who is commanded to honour his parents and does so is rewarded, one who is not commanded and does so deserves a greater reward' (b.Kid 31a). Here to honour them meant to provide them with food, shelter, etc., when they could no longer look after themselves. Some thought that honouring one's parents, both mother and father, was more important than honouring God and to 'fear' one's father meant to defer to his opinion: 'Thus said my father, my teacher, for whose resting place may I be an atonement, but only for twelve months after his death' (b.Kid. 31b).

Something which all Jews could subscribe to was the ideal that under God's rule, all were members of one family. They paid lip-service to this but it was not observed in practice. Jesus on the other hand would make practice the same as the ideal.

* * *

F 2. A father's love and a brother's lack of it - Lk. 15:11-32.

How would those who had not followed God's rule get on, if they repented of their mistakes, and wished to return to God's kingdom? It was thought by many that repentance was not enough to redeem the sinner in God's eyes, but only after chastisement or penance could the sinner hope for reinstatement: 'Know then in your heart that as a man disciplines his son, the Lord your God disciplines you' (Dt. 8:5-6); 'Your love is towards the seed of Abraham, the children of Israel. Your discipline is upon us as upon a first-born, only begotten son, to turn back the obedient soul from folly, wrought in ignorance' (P.S. 18:4).

Jesus preferred the attitude that God's love could rejoice in the repentant sinner without demanding any retribution first. This is in line with much O.T. teaching: 'Let the wicked forsake his way ... let him return to the Lord, that he may have mercy of him, and to our God, for he will abundantly pardon' (Is. 55:7); 'If my people, who are called by my name, humble themselves and pray and seek my face and turn from their wicked ways, then I will hear from heaven and will forgive their sin and heal their land' (II Chr. 7:14). The story is an illustration of the O.T. verse: 'As a father has compassion for his children, so the Lord has compassion for those who fear him' (Ps. 103:13).

It is also very like the story in the O.T.: 'And the men ... arose and took the captives and with the spoils [after a battle] they clothed all that were naked among them; they clothed them, gave them sandals, provided them with food and drink, and anointed them; and carrying all the feeble among them on asses, they brought them to their kinsfolk at Jericho ...' (II Chr. 28:15).

It may be helpful to explain first something of the background to the parable. The laws about inheritance were given in the O.T.: '(A father) shall acknowledge the first-born son ... by giving him a double-portion of all that he has ... the right of the first-born is his' (Dt. 21:17). The eldest son would take over the ownership of the father's farm as a joint project, the younger son remaining to help him run it, and both had an imperative duty to care for their parents when the latter were too old to work: 'Every one of you shall revere his mother and his father ...' (Lev. 19:3); 'Honour your father and your mother as the Lord God commanded you ...' (Dt. 5:16 and Ex. 20:12); and in rabbinical writings: 'A man must honour his father in life and death. In life he should do deeds "for my father's sake". In death, he should speak of what his father said by saying: "Thus said my father, my teacher for whose resting place may I be an atonement." But only in the year after death. Thereafter he must say: "His memory for a blessing in the world to come"' (b.Kid 31b) [That is, the possibility for punishment in the next life does not last longer than one year.]; 'There are things, the fruit of which man enjoys in this world, while the principle remains for him in the future world: honouring one's parents, loving deeds, making peace between man and neighbour ...' (b.Kid. 40a).

At the time of Jesus, the law had been modified. A father during his own life-time retained an interest in any property given to his son, that is, both had an interest in it and benefited from it, while neither could dispose of it. It was not essential to wait until the father's death for a son to acquire his inheritance, but normally he would be allowed to have only a part of it. It would be a foolish father who gave his younger son the whole of his share of the estate: 'Give not your goods to another ... for it is better for your children to ask of you, than that you should look to the hands of your sons ... In the day of death, distribute your inheritance' (Sir.33:19-23). Indeed, had the son asked for his share, it would have been equivalent to wishing his father was dead. It was not necessary for the father to give him anything, but the father in this story was understanding, and perhaps a little indulgent. He was willing to let the lad sow his wild oats (something which was quite normal then, as now), and he was willing to give him a portion of his inheritance.

The elder son thought of the younger brother as stubborn and rebellious as many other second sons had been but his behaviour, while foolish, was not deserving the punishment prescribed in Dt. 21:18-21. There are many examples in Judaism in which the younger son achieves greatness and often migrates to try his luck such as Elam elder brother of David (ISam. 17:28-9); Adonijah elder brother of Solomon. He tried to assert his primageniture as king but David had decreed Solomon should succeed him as king.

The elder son also acted as though his father was his employer and is alienated from him. He would also be concerned lest the younger turned up later and claimed he had had nothing from the estate although there would almost certainly have been a written document specifying the portions each son would eventually get. If the younger son did return, it was fully within the father's right to accept him as his son, although he had lost the worth of what he had wasted.

Jesus said, "There was once a man who had two sons and the younger asked his father to allow him to have a share of the estate. So his father divided the estate between the two sons, and shortly afterwards the younger son left home and set off on his great adventure.

Unfortunately he scattered his inheritance in prodigality, until he had nothing left. Then a severe famine swept the land, and the only way he could survive was to take a job with one of the local landowners who sent him out to feed the pigs. He longed to fill his belly with the food the pigs ate, but no one gave him anything.

Then he took stock of himself and his situation. "How many of my father's servants have more bread than they need and here I am, starving to death. I will go to my father and say, 'Father, I have sinned against God and against you; I am no longer fit to be your son, but treat me as one of your paid servants." So this is what he did.

While he was yet far from his old home, however, his father saw him and was moved with compassion. He ran towards his son and flung his arms around his neck and kissed him warmly. The son said, "Father, I have sinned against God and against you. I am no longer fit to be called your son, but..." His father interrupted him and called to his servants, "Quickly, bring the best robe,

sandals for his feet, and a ring for his finger. Kill the
fatted calf so we can have a family feast to celebrate
my son's return. This son of mine was lost to me, he was
dead, but now he is found again, he is again alive."

But listen. The elder son was working out in the
fields and, returning to the house, heard the music of
the festivities. He enquired of one of the servants what
was happening. "Your brother has come home," answered
the servant, "and your father has killed the fatted
calf, because he has returned, alive and well."

The elder brother was angry and would not go into
the house. His father went out to him and tried to
persuade him but he was adamant. "I have served you all
these years, and never once have I transgressed one of
your commandments, yet you never gave me so much as a
kid to have a party with my friends. Now, when this son
of yours turns up after wasting your money living with
harlots, you have killed the fatted calf for him!"

"My dear boy," said his father, "you are always
with me and all my things are yours. How could we not
celebrate this event? It is your brother, who was lost
as though dead and now he is found and is alive again."

The story implies that the younger son was unhappy at home since in those
days the sons would work the farm, first with the father and later together, after the
father's death. The younger son's sin was not that he wasted some of his inheritance
- that was not exceptional: 'A lover of wisdom brings joy to his father, but one who
keeps company with harlots squanders his wealth' (Pvb. 29:3). The Jewish writer
Philo (a contemporary of Jesus), describes how a Jewish father could give his sons
a portion of his wealth to speculate with. Some would end up with a good profit,
while others lost money on unfortunate investments. A strictly just father would then
leave things as they were, but a father loving his sons equally, would take the whole
account together, and redistribute the money in equal amounts again. Likewise God
shows mercy to all the repentant, however unsuccessful and foolish they had been. It
was those who had forgotten the primacy of love for God who refused to accept the
invitation to enter the house and join in the festive banquet. The parable shows the
younger son had wanted to be free from God and the elder thinks he has a right to
God's reward because of his status.

The law required all sons to support their parents as they got older and could
not work properly to support themselves. The younger son's sin was that he had had no
thought for his duty to support his father. He had been selfish and by leaving his own
people and 'going away', he was considered to be dead. When he repented, perhaps
he remembered the Jewish saying that when a son goes barefoot, he remembers the
comfort of his father's house; which shows the situation was not unfamiliar to Jesus'
listeners.

His confession to his father is found in the Jewish service of Atonement Eve,
and in I.T. writings: 'My father ... forgive me my folly and I will serve in your house,

168

tend your horses, sweep up the dung of your cattle and feed your sheep; for I am the wicked and you are the righteous; I am the guilty and you are the forgiving' (Ahk. 8:29,34). It also echoes the O.T.: 'I have sinned against the Lord your God and against you. Now therefore forgive my sin ... and entreat the Lord your God only to remove this death from me' (Ex. 10:16). He offered to act as a hired servant, perhaps so that he could earn some money and have the chance to repay his father. He showed he had lost his pride and had grown up, and was willing to take on his proper responsibilities, even an unprivileged position in order to remain part of the household.

The father's response proclaims the young man's status as his son but the language used shows that the father sees the son coming and actively goes to receive him, even before the son realises he has been seen. He shows his compassion before he hears the boy's confession. His actions mirrored those of Esau: 'Esau ran to meet him, embraced him, fell on his neck and kissed him' (Gen. 33:4). The robe and the sandals have several connotations: you are not on holy ground, mourning is over, rejoice, be glad, and be ready for action. The signet ring was a symbol of family relationship or son-ship.

That the father killed a calf to celebrate was not to take anything from the elder brother since the father had a share of the profits of the farm by right. It was hardly possible for the father to have refused the elder son a kid to have a party with his friends, had he asked for one. His 'reason' is an excuse. He is hard-hearted; he calls the other 'your son', and refuses to say 'my brother', although the younger son's return does not reduce in any way the elder's rights and wealth.

Jesus tries to show that when a sinner repents, that is enough. There is no place for men, however pious, to put him on trial and demand penances. God will welcome him at once. The eldest son's reaction was loveless, self-righteous, joyless and thankless. Some religious leaders had made God in their own image and were not willing to greet those who, having lost their way, had found it again: who had been dead, but now were restored to life.

A rabbinical story has some similarities to this parable: 'A king's son fell into evil ways and his father sent to him and said, "Repent, my son; come to yourself." But the son replied, "With what face can I repent and return to you? I am ashamed to come before you.' Then the king sent again to him, saying, "Can a son be ashamed to return to his father? If you return, do you not return to your father?" Likewise God said to Jeremiah: "Go, tell my sons to repent and return." And they replied, "With what face can we return to God?" So God sent again to them, saying, "My sons, if you return, is it not to your Father that you return?"' (Dt.R. 2:24).

Paul used the idea of the second taking precedence when he says that the budding Christian church was the second son and Judaism was the first. True the first born takes precedence over the second but God had elected the second over the first and therefore Christianity is above Judaism (ICor.1:20-29).

In a Buddhist passage translated into Chinese in the third century C.E. a similar story tells how when the son asked for his inheritance he had to submit to careful questioning to find out if he was fit to enjoy the wealth he was asking for.

* * *

F 3. Great and small commandments; the good Samaritan - Mt. 22:34-40.
Mk. 12:28-34. Lk. 10:25-37.

A frequent topic of discussion concerned which Laws were difficult to keep and which were easier, but one Law of the Torah was not more important than another: 'Be as careful about a light precept as of a weighty one, for you do not know the recompense or reward of each precept. And reckon the loss necessary for the performance of a commandment against its reward, and the reward that comes from a transgression (its pleasure) against its loss' (m.Avot. 2:1); 'Be as swift to fulfil a light precept as the weightiest...' (m.Avot. 4:2); 'If you transgress a minor commandment, you will soon transgress a major one' (Sif.Dt. 187).

On one occasion, Jesus came into discussion about this topic and one of a group of lawyers asked him how a person could attain to eternal life. "Tell us, Sir, which is the first and greatest commandment? By doing what shall I gain eternal life?"

Jesus answered, "What is recited at worship? Is it not: 'Hear, O Israel; the Lord your God is the only Lord; love the Lord your God with all your heart, with all your soul, with all your mind and with all your strength.' This is the first commandment, and the second is like it: 'Love your neighbour as yourself.'

"Quite so," said the questioner. "God is indeed one and to love him with all your heart, sagacity and strength and your neighbour as yourself - that is far better than any burnt offerings or sacrifices."

Jesus noted his intelligent answer and said, "You are not far from God's reign in his kingdom. Do that and you will live. No commandment is greater than these."

The question of the lawyer, biblical scholar or theologian, touches on the problem of whether one must obey all the commandments equally or not. Officially, all commandments were of equal weight, although there were minor ones and major ones. The danger was that neglecting the minor ones would lead to neglect of the major ones: 'God has not revealed to men the particular reward for each command. One command leads to another and one transgression leads to another. The reward for a commandment carried out is another one to be carried out. The reward for a transgression is another transgression' (ARN 25).

The question is also equivalent to how one gains admittance to the kingdom but the lawyer should have known the answer: 'You shall not do as they do in Egypt ... nor as they do in Canaan ... You shall do my ordinances and keep my statutes and walk in them ... by doing which a man shall live.' (Lev. 18:3-5); 'Do this and you will live ...' (Gen. 42:18). The answer given was in fact one well known in Judaism: 'Does the Lord desire offerings and sacrifices as he desires obedience? Obedience is better than sacrifice and to listen to him better than the fat of rams.' (I Sam. 15:22); 'Love the Lord and your neighbour' (T.Iss. 5:2); 'Love the Lord through all your life and one another with a true heart.' (T.Dan 5:3).

The two commandments cited by Jesus would have been expected: 'Hear O Israel: the Lord your God, one Lord; you shall love the Lord your God with all your heart, and with all your soul, and with all your might.' (Dt. 6:4-5); and: '... you shall love your fellowman as yourself.' (Lev. 19:18). These two statements were accepted by all Jews as a summary of all the other commandments.

The word translated 'heart' signified not feelings, nor emotional responses, but intention in life, based on understanding, discernment and intelligence. The heart was the seat of reason, of the ability to commit oneself to good or bad conduct: the good and bad inclinations. The meaning includes both of these. Some bad inclinations could be devoted to loving God too, because although they were sometimes responsible for evil deeds, they could also be used to promote God's kingdom. For example, the sexual drive, which was necessary for the continuance and extension of Israel, could be abused in many ways. In rabbinical writings a commentary on 'God saw everything that he had made was very good' (Gen. 1:31) says: 'Everything in the world is useful - death, hell, evil and good desires, sleep, suffering, Paradise, and punishment.' (Gen. R. 9:5-9); and 'Man is bound to bless God for the evil as for the good, for it is written: "You shall love the Lord your God with all your heart, with all your soul and with all your might." "With all your heart" means with both good and bad inclinations. "With all your soul" means even if God takes away your soul. "With all your might" means with all your wealth' (Sif.Dt.on 6:4).

The word 'power' meant not just strength, but wealth, status and prestige as well, while 'soul' refers to both the physical and spiritual being, since Judaism does not accept a body/mind or body/spirit duality. It includes emotions and desires which the heart must control.

In other rabbinical books similar ideas are expressed: 'Charity and deeds of loving-kindness are equal to all statutes of the Torah' (t. Peah 4:19); 'He who occupies himself only with study of Torah, is as if he had no God. Acts of kindness are also essential' (b.A.Z. 17b); this is rather contradicted by: 'He who humbles himself in this age for the word of Torah will be made great in the future age and he who is a servant to the study of Torah in this world becomes free in the next' (b.B.M. 85b).

This is illustrated in the following story: 'The matter is like a king who hired labourers to work in his orchard, without telling them beforehand that some tasks would be rewarded with greater pay than others. All worked well until the evening, when the king called them to him to pay them.

"Which tasks did you have?", he asked the first labourer. "I worked under the pepper tree," he replied. "The wages for tending that tree are one whole gold piece," said the king. To the next he said, "Under which tree did you work?" "Under the one with white blossom," said the second. "That job is worth half a gold piece," said the king.

To the third who said he had worked under the olive tree, the king gave only a few shekels. "Shouldn't you have told us that we should get different wages for different jobs?", they grumbled. "Had I told you that," said the king, "how could I have had the whole of my orchard equally well tended?"' (Dt.R. 6:2).

The last sentence of the gospel passage is different in Matthew's version: 'On these two commandments depend all the Law and the Prophets.' This could also be written, 'Everything in the Law and the Prophets can be derived from these two commandments.' It is said the Rabbi Hillel, a contemporary of Jesus, maintained that from two precepts or commandments, which shared an important concept (here 'Love of...'), it was possible to construct a 'family-tree' of scriptural verses. In this way the whole of the Law and the Prophets could be said to depend on the two commandments. It seems likely that Matthew's statement is secondary and was intended to bring out the respect of the early Christian community for the Jewish Law.

Alternatively, it is significant that there are O.T. texts in which the whole of Israel is said to hang on a nail or peg, and that Israel will fall: 'I will fasten my servant Eliakim like a peg in a sure place and he will become a throne of honour to his father's house. And they will hang on him the whole weight of his father's house (Israel) ... In that day, says the Lord of Hosts, the peg that was fastened ... will give way ... and the burden that was on it will be cut off ...' (Is. 22:23-25).

This is confirmed by the Aramaic version of this passage: 'I will appoint Eliakim as a faithful governor, in a sure place, and he shall be for a throne of glory to his father's house. All the nobles of his father's house shall support themselves on him ... priests clad with the ephod and Levites that handle the harp. At that time ... he shall be removed, torn down and fall, and the oracle concerning him shall be cancelled, as decreed by the presence of the Lord.'

After this, a new law-giver for Israel will arise, a shepherd, or the Messiah, whose words are the 'nails' - fixed supports for the whole of the Law and Prophets: '... the collected sayings given by one Shepherd are like nails firmly fixed' (Ecc. 12:11). Jesus' message needed just two of them, although it would be more correct to say just one; it is impossible to separate love of God and his will from love for one's fellowman, and although it is usual to speak of them as two, they constitute a single precept enshrining God's will (see the rabbinical comment in the introduction above).

It was a natural desire to discover Jesus' viewpoint in the dilemma which Jews felt in their dealings with non-Jews. In theory, God was God of all mankind, but Jews were the chosen people with whom God had made a covenant, and therefore were not as non-Jews. The Torah prescribed love in a negative form: 'You shall not nurse hatred against your brother ... You shall not seek revenge, or cherish anger towards the sons of your own people, you shall love your neighbour as a man like yourself' (Lev. 19:17-18). With reference to an alien settled amongst Jews, the precept is: 'You shall not oppress him. He shall be treated as a native-born among you, and you shall love him as a man like yourself' (Lev. 19:34).

Thus it was not surprising that one of the lawyers in the group who had heard Jesus answer the question about which commandment was the greatest, wanted to ask another question.

"You tell us," he said, "to love the Lord our God with all our heart, soul and strength and our neighbour as ourselves. What I would like to know is, who is my neighbour?"

"Let me illustrate it this way," said Jesus, taking up the question.

"One day a Jew was going along the road from Jerusalem to Jericho, when robbers descended on him, beat him senseless, robbed him and made off, leaving him lying half-dead by the edge of the road.

Soon after a certain priest, and then a Levite came by, but they each looked at him and went by on the far side of the road. Then a Samaritan came by, riding on his donkey. When he saw the poor fellow lying there, he was moved with pity for him. He dismounted, put some wine into his wounds, poured some oil over them and bandaged him as best he could. Then he laid him over his donkey, and took him to the inn, and attended to him. Next day, he paid two denarii for the man's stay at the inn while he recovered, and said to the innkeeper, 'Care for him and I will settle any account outstanding when I return.'

Now then, which of these three, the priest, the Levite or the Samaritan, proved himself to be the poor Jew's neighbour?"

The lawyer had to admit that it was the one who showed the victim kindness - the Samaritan.

"Quite so," said Jesus. "Go and do you likewise."

Jesus answered the jurist's question indirectly. The answer expected might have been a story in which a Jew showed kindness to, for example, one of the poor, or a story in which a Jew was magnanimous enough to show kindness to a Samaritan. The answer given reversed the roles and the expert in the Law was made to imagine himself as the victim, helped by one whom he considered outside decent society, an infidel, a Samaritan.

Oil had been recognised as a soothing agent for centuries, and wine would have been more sterile than water probably; both were forbidden to the pious Jew if obtained from Samaritans because they had not paid tithes on them. There is nice irony in the thought of the unconscious Jew waking up to the horror of his supposed pollution from the kindness of his rescuer, a beautiful way of showing the barrenness of the teaching of many of the pietistic groups.

That this is not just idle speculation may be seen from the story of Rabbi ben Dama. When he was bitten by a snake, a disciple of Jesus was thought to have a secret remedy known only to Christians, and the rabbi sent for him. His uncle remonstrated with him, saying that he was in danger of being unfaithful to the Torah. Ben Dama died before the Christian reached him, but his uncle was glad: 'Blessed are you, ben Dama, that you have gone in peace ... and have not broken down the fence of the wise' (i.e. not gone beyond what the Torah permits) (b.A.Z. 27b).

The reference to oil and wine reminds us of their use by the priests and Levites in the Temple rituals for burnt offerings, i.e. sacrifices, and the passage is an illustration of: 'I desire mercy, not sacrifice' (Hos. 6:6). Another connection between this passage and Hosea is: 'Like robbers waylaying a man, so the priests are banded together; they murder on the road to Shechem (Samaria) - their deeds are outrageous' (Hos. 6:9).

It was accepted that an injured man would reimburse his benefactor for the expenses he had incurred. Between two Jews that was not only a moral duty, but the courts would enforce it. For a Samaritan, there was no possibility of compulsory reimbursement from a Jew, so the Samaritan in the story pledged his credit to the inn-keeper, knowing that the Jew could exploit the situation if he so chose, with only moral condemnation to follow. Without this pledge, the Jew could have been detained until any further debt had been paid.

There is more than one opinion about this story. Some think that the priest and the Levite had very good reasons for doing what they did, behaving correctly according to their understanding of the Law. The regulations about purity were mainly concerned with preserving the Temple in a state of purity appropriate for the dwelling of the Lord and thus no one could enter it in a state of impurity. A priest who became unclean meant he could no longer receive tithes and support his family.

If a priest came within several feet of a corpse, or cast his shadow on it, or touched it with a stick, he became ritually polluted and thus unable to enter the Temple, and above all, he would have contravened the Law which says he must keep himself holy: 'You shall be holy, because I, the Lord your God am holy' (Lev. 19:2). He would not dare to come near to a tomb, even of his parents, and prayed for them away from their grave.

The Levite was in an analogous situation. That the unconscious man was not dead, was something which could only be decided by getting close to him, and they did not dare risk finding that the man was in fact dead. In any case being half-dead almost always meant death would follow, although generally, saving life took precedence over all other commandments.

The Torah allows for uncleanness in order to bury the dead and the parable attacks the extension of this law by the orthodox, in violation of the primary commandment of loving-kindness. According to some rabbinical teaching, any unburied corpse had to be buried by the person to find it, be he priest or Levite or even the High Priest (b.Sot. 47a) and the moral of the story is that important persons can behave more selfishly that one of humble origin, the Samaritan. Nevertheless, priests and Levites would rely on: 'The Lord said to Moses, "Say to the priests ... a priest shall not render himself unclean for the death of any of his kin except for a near blood-relation."' (Lev. 21:1), and a priest was not to enter a cemetery even if an animal had fallen and help was needed to right it again: 'One should help to lift up a fallen animal with its load and its driver, but if it is in a cemetery a priest should not defile himself to help' (Mek.Kas. 2). It was easy for a lay person to become ritually pure again, while for the priest and Levite, it was much more difficult.

Samaritans also acknowledged pollution by the dead, but in the parable the Samaritan was not a priest or Levite and his compassion for another overrode the difficulty. That is how the other two failed. Because of their lack of understanding of what God's will really required, they followed what they saw as the essentials of the Law, which prevented their showing the loving-kindness they ought to have shown.

In spite of being outside the covenant community, and not subscribing to all the beliefs of God's chosen people, the Samaritan did God's will. He shows this by his compassion and love. Binding up wounds caused by robbers is part of God's work: 'I kill and I make alive; I wound and I heal; and there is none that can deliver out of my hand' (Dt. 32:39); 'Happy is the man whom God rebukes! Therefore do not reject the discipline of the Almighty. For, though he wounds, he will bind up, the hand which smites, will heal' (Job 5:17-18); 'I will cause new skin to grow and heal your wounds, says the Lord ...' (Jer. 30:17); 'Come let us return to the Lord; for he has torn us and will heal us; he has struck us and he will bind up our wounds' (Hos. 6:1).

Jesus clearly approved the Samaritan's actions without any hint of complaint that he belonged to the 'wrong' sect. The results of the Samaritan's kindness, by which he did all he could within his power, showed he was following God's will, heretic though the Jews considered him. Attention to the details of their ritual duties led the religious leaders to smother all thoughts of compassion. They so often excluded righteous ends by emphasis on 'proper' means. This passage is one of several which could be taken to indicate that Jesus did not condemn the Samaritans or even that he approved of them.

* * *

F 4. Riches and the kingdom of God - Mt. 10:37, 19:16-29. Mk. 10:17-30. Lk. 14:25-26; 18:18-30; 22:28-30.

Riches had come to be seen as a sign of God's blessing in Judaism, although it was also acknowledged that wealth brought responsibilities and temptations with it. Poverty was an affliction but wealth was a burden and the analogy with the camel in the following passage was very apposite. It is a good example of play on words which is found in so many places in the gospels: the words for 'merchant' and 'camel' were nearly the same. They both bear burdens and by a play on the Hebrew, the camel was supposed to shed some of its burden at the door of the poor man, just as the rich man should share his wealth. The word for 'eye' is another example. It can also mean 'cave' or 'cavern' where a camel would have to be unloaded to get it in, just as the willingness to shed one's wealth is both a prerequisite and a result of entry into the kingdom (see also B 2). Moreover, the camel was to be the bearer of the gospel to other places: 'A multitude of camels shall cover the land ... and they that come with them shall proclaim the praise of the Lord' (Is. 60:6). A rich man could do the same by his beneficence.

A rich man came before Jesus and asked him, "Good teacher, what must I do to gain eternal life?"

"Why do you call me good?", asked Jesus. "No one is good except God alone. You know the commandments: do not murder, do not commit adultery, do not steal, do not give false evidence, do not defraud, honour your father and mother."

The man said, "I have kept all these commandments since I was a boy. Where do I still fall short?"

"One thing you lack if you would be a completely righteous man", said Jesus. "You must sell all your possessions, everything you have, and give to the destitute. Then you will have riches in the kingdom of God, and you will be welcome to come and follow me."

On hearing Jesus' words, his face fell, and he went away grieving because he had great wealth. Jesus saw his reaction and exclaimed, "How hard it will be for the wealthy to enter the kingdom of God! Certainly, it is easier for a camel to pass through the eye of a needle than for a rich man to enter the kingdom of God."

The disciples were greatly astonished. "Who then can be saved?", they said. Looking seriously at them Jesus said, "Children, it is impossible for men, but everything is possible for God."

Peter said, "What about us? We gave up everything to follow you!"

Jesus replied, "I tell you this: if anyone comes to me and does not reject his father and mother, wife and children, brothers and sisters, even his own life,

he cannot be a disciple of mine. Yet all who have left
house, brothers, sisters, mother, father or children,
or land, for the sake of the kingdom of God, will
receive in this age a hundred times as much houses,
brothers, sisters, mothers and children, and land -
and be harassed too! And in the age to come, they will
have eternal life. At the resurrection, on the day of
Judgement, when the son of man is seated on his throne
in heavenly splendour, you who have stood firmly by me,
you shall eat and drink at my table in my kingdom and
sit on thrones of your own as judges of the twelve
tribes of Israel.

The man asked Jesus for a formula to achieve eternal life. Jesus responds by
picking up the questioner's suggestion that Jesus was good, when all Jews knew it
was God alone who should be called good. A rabbinical comment on Pvb. 4:2 is that
only God is good, and yet because the Torah contains God's will it is good: 'Good is
nothing else but the Law, for it is written, "I give you good doctrine; forsake not my
Law"' (Lam.R. Proem 2).

The man claimed that he had followed all the commandments which Jesus
quoted from the Torah. Mark includes one not in the O.T., namely, not to defraud, and in
some manuscripts, a further one also not in the O.T.: 'Do not practise prostitution.'

The man said he had followed the Law since he was a youth and yet he was
humble enough to recognise he had not attained the best. He wished to be accepted as
a fully righteous Jew, and Jesus realised what was wrong: he had retained for himself
more than he needed: 'The necessities of life are water and bread, a house and clothing
to cover one's nakedness' (Sir. 29:21); 'Store up for yourself treasure of righteousness
and love and it will benefit you more than gold. Let alms-giving be the treasure in your
strong room and it will rescue you from every misfortune' (Sir. 29:11-12); 'Happy is
he whom God remembers in a due sufficiency with righteousness, for the blessing
of the Lord then becomes abundance' (P.S. 5:18-20); 'Give some of your food to the
hungry and some of your clothing to the naked. Give all your surplus in alms and do
not let your eye begrudge your giving' (Tobit 4:16).

He could not have kept all the commandments since his youth if he had
much to dispose of, which he should have shared with his less fortunate brethren.
The same reaction is found in a similar story, in the Gospel of the Hebrews: 'The rich
man began to scratch his head, for Jesus' answer did not please him. So the Master
said to him, "How can you say you have carried out the Law and Prophets, since it is
stated in the Law that you are to love your neighbour as yourself, and there are many
of your brethren, sons of Abraham, clad with dung, dying of hunger and your house
is full of many good things and nothing goes out of it to them?"' The accepted view
of the day was that one should give not more than one fifth of one's possessions to
avoid becoming a liability to family and society. Thus Jesus' demand was extreme but
it clearly pinpointed the man's weakness - his love of his wealth.

The last paragraph of the passage describes a vision of the situation which
will arise on the day of Judgement when all will be caused to live again, be resurrected.
A rabbinical passage has similar ideas: 'They that have been born are destined to die,

and they that are dead are destined to be made alive and they that are made alive again are destined to be judged ... Do not let your evil inclination persuade you that your grave will be a refuge; despite yourself you were formed, despite yourself you were born; despite yourself you live, despite yourself you shall die and despite yourself you shall hereafter give account and reckoning before the king of kings, the Holy One, blessed be he' (m.Avot. 4:22).

There were several speculations about how the day of Judgement would take place, but some at least thought that the twelve tribes of Israel would sit in judgement with God or his Messiah: 'In the moment of God's coming ... they will be judges and rulers over the nations of the world and the Lord shall be their king for ever' (W.S. 3:7-8). In Matthew the disciples, instead of the twelve tribes, are pictured as sitting on thrones as judges alongside the Messiah.

There were different opinions about who would sit on thrones in heaven. Some said there was one for God and one for David; others said one for justice and one for mercy; or one for justice and one for charity. A third idea was that: '... only God had a throne; any other was God's footstool' (b.San. 38b). Yet others believed that there were thrones only for God and his son the Messiah, but they would be helped by the 'Holy Ones' and possibly this was the role the disciples envisaged for themselves. There are many passages which say this, including I.T. and rabbinical literature: 'They shall judge nations and have dominion over peoples' (W.S. 3:8); 'God will rule nations by the hand of his Elect' (DSS Habb. 5:4).

Disciples who are fit for such important work could thus, it may be implied, begin to administer discipline now, in the early church. They had to accept only a modest compensation for their preaching, relinquish their possessions and in this way both rich and poor would become an equitable brotherhood. Once again, the theme is to forget one's own needs in God's service.

* * *

F 5. Hoarding worldly wealth or heavenly treasure - Mt. 6:19-20, 25-34. Lk. 12:13-34.

Jesus was asked to arbitrate in a dispute between two brothers. One felt he wasn't getting his rightful share, and it was not in the least uncommon for a respected holy man to be asked to arbitrate. Indeed it was considered to be a fine work if two could be reconciled and brought to be at peace with one another. Although this was an important duty for all who follow God's rule, Jesus refused to do what they wanted. They were less interested in peace between them than in getting all they could. Jesus viewed the matter from another angle. He also added a warning and told a parable to illustrate his viewpoint.

A man said to Jesus, "Master, tell my brother to divide the inheritance with me." Jesus replied, "Who appointed me judge, to divide or arbitrate between you?" Turning to those standing listening, he added, "Be on your guard against the least inclination to greed. Life is not in the abundance of things existing to him, his possessions." He went on to tell them this story.

"There was once a rich man whose land yielded heavy crops. He was in a quandary, calculating what to do, because he had no room in his barns to store all his produce. 'This is what I will do,' he said to himself. 'I will pull down my present barns and build bigger ones. I will collect together all my corn and goods, and then say to my soul, Soul, you have enough good things in store to last for many years: take life easy, relax, eat, drink and enjoy yourself.'

But God said, 'What a fool you are! Even this very night you must surrender your soul. Yes, you have acquired much, but who will enjoy it now?'

That is how it is with the man who amasses wealth for himself and remains a pauper in the sight of God."

On the surface this passage has a clear moral message: true peace comes not from partition but reconciliation leading to unity. If a man bequeathed all his estates to one son of several, that son was considered to be a trustee and held the property for the benefit of all the sons equally, unless a specific clause denying this interpretation was included. Thus even on a worldly level, dividing an inheritance sometimes led to one or both becoming destitute.

Jesus rejects their opinion of him as judge, following rabbinical opinion: if a person arbitrates he is to be condemned because he acts as if he was so good he is like God in disputes: 'It is forbidden to arbitrate in a settlement' (b.San 6b); 'Judge not alone for none may do so save One. And say not, "Receive my opinion", for it is for them to choose and not for thee' (m.Avot. 4:8). Moses had been asked: 'Who made you a prince and judge over us?' (Ex. 2:14). In I.T. books too: 'Arbitration does not determine guilt or innocence and therefore is against justice and the Law.' (Sif Dt. on

179

1:17)

Jesus was to be seen as a healer not a divider. He was concerned for their spiritual welfare and he warns against greed, by which is meant longing for more than that which is necessary. The latter attitude is not compatible with life in the kingdom of God! The brothers already had assets to live on: 'The necessities of life are bread, water, a garment and a home with decent privacy' (Sir. 29:21), and it was unrighteous to be trying to get even more - an even greater superfluity. They should be giving their excess to charity: 'If you feed the hungry from your own plenty and satisfy the needs of the wretched, then your light will rise like dawn out of darkness' (Is. 58:10). It would have been immoral of Jesus to have helped the brothers in the way they wanted. He tried to help them to see the matter correctly and follow the spirit of the Law honestly.

In the New Era, boundaries and partitions were abandoned, and each person was one in a society whose merit was not derived from the patriarchs Abraham, Isaac and Jacob, but from the good deeds its members performed. The true inheritance of such a society was not in worldly goods but in the eternal treasure in heaven. Life on earth did not depend on excess: 'He who rejoices in his lot is rich. When you eat the labour of your hands, happy are you (in this world) and it shall be well with you (in the next)' (m.Avot. 4:1), and life in the kingdom of God was prevented by it: 'Because you trusted in your strongholds and your treasures, you shall be taken to destruction' (Jer. 48:7). Those who have more than enough should give their excess to the poor: 'When one of your fellow-countrymen ... becomes poor, do not be hard-hearted or close-fisted ... Give generously to him and do not begrudge him your bounty, because it is for this bounty the Lord will bless you in everything you do' (Dt. 15:7-10). Likewise in I.T. books: 'Woe to you, you rich, for you have trusted in your riches and from your riches you shall depart because you did not remember the Most High ...' (I En. 94:8).

In this way those better off will get spiritual profit, because God was imagined as a banker, keeping note of all the good deeds of each person who could thereby accumulate credit. This bank account could not be overdrawn, but adding to it benefited the poor as well as oneself. Indeed the more the rich reduce their needs to the essentials, and give the rest to the poor, the greater will be their treasure under God's reign: 'Do not reject the appeal of a man in distress or turn your back on the poor ...' (Sir. 4:4); 'Do not be intent on wealth and imagine you are thereby independent' (Sir. 5:1); 'Work righteousness on earth that you may have it as treasure in heaven' (T.Lev. 13:5). The same idea is held today: a famous scholar rabbi at the time of the six-days war in 1967 declared with reference to the army and people of Israel: "The Lord is also a banker. He has invested so much in our people's history that He can no longer turn away from them without forfeiting His capital."

The rich man is called a fool; he was a man who did not consider the world to come. He hopes to pile up his fruits in a worldly treasury, and enjoy them, but his death puts an end to his dream: 'The impious fool says in his heart, "There is no God"' (Ps. 14:1); 'The righteous ... shall laugh at him, and say "See the man who would not make God his refuge, but trusted in the abundance of his riches and sought refuge in his wealth"' (Ps. 52:7); 'When a man says, "I have found rest and now I will enjoy my goods," he does not know how long it will be before he must die and leave his wealth to others' (Sir. 11:19).

There are similar stories in Judaism. One story, for example, tells of a man who said to his friend, 'I have a thousand measures of grain, a thousand of oil and a thousand of wine. His friend replied, "That's fine, but have you storehouses for it all? If so, all is well; if not, then you possess nothing."' The interpretation given is that one may learn all Judaism but if one has no fear of sin, he or she has nothing (Ex.R. 30:14).

An alternative understanding of the passage seeks a deeper understanding of the first paragraph. The language suggests there may be a reference to the division and destruction of Israel's inheritance of the land of Canaan: 'In the meantime, you are to allot all this to the Israelites for their patrimony, as I have commanded you. Distribute this land now to the nine tribes and half the tribe of Manasseh for their patrimony' (Jos. 13:6-7). Before doing this Joshua sent out men to survey the land: 'How much longer will you neglect to take possession of the land which the Lord God of your forefathers has given you? Appoint three men from each tribe ... send them out ... through the whole country. They shall make a register showing the patrimony suitable for each tribe ...' (Jos. 18:3-4).

Jesus also sent out his disciples, an action which could have given rise to messianic expectations, leading the crowd to thoughts of the ejection of Rome and political freedom for Israel. For Jesus there was probably a constant pressure to appear as the kind of Messiah many of the Jews looked forward to, with Israel, God's chosen, receiving homage from all other nations. He is shown rejecting this in his temptations, in his very abrupt rejection of Peter's concern for his prospective suffering, and here, as judge and divider of Israel's inheritance. Jesus' vision may have been the inheritance of the kingdom of God by all, and he will have nothing to do with the Zealot line of resistance for political power.

Jesus continued, "Have no fear, little flock, for your Father has chosen to give you the kingdom. Sell your possessions and give in charity. Do not bother to accumulate treasure here on earth, in material things that go rusty or get moth-eaten or stolen by thieves. Store up treasure in heaven; there is no rust there, and no moths either. And where your treasure is, there will your heart be also.

Put away anxious worries about food and drink to keep you alive, and clothes to cover your body. Life is more than food and the body more than clothes. Think of the ravens - they do not sow and reap and store in barns, yet your heavenly Father feeds them. Do you not excel them? Is there a man among you who by anxious striving can add a foot to his height or increase his life-span? And why give anxious thought to clothes? Think of the lilies which grow in the fields, they neither ret nor spin nor weave, yet not even Solomon was so splendidly attired. If God can clothe the flowers of the field, which grow today and tomorrow are taken and burnt, how much more will God clothe you! What little faith you have!

You are not to set your mind on food and drink, nor what you shall wear. The heathen chases after such things, but your heavenly Father knows you need them all. No, set your mind on the kingdom of God's righteousness before everything else and all the rest will come to you as well. Do not be anxious about tomorrow; tomorrow will take care of itself. Each day has troubles enough of its own."

Some have suggested that the teaching was preserved in this form because during Jesus' lifetime and in the earliest years of the early church, it was believed that the day of Judgement would come at any moment. Thus hoarding was pointless.

The sentiments are, however, thoroughly Jewish: 'Cast your burden on the Lord and he will sustain you, he will never permit the righteous to be moved' (Ps. 55:22); 'If I have made gold my trust or called fine gold my confidence, if I have rejoiced because my wealth was great ... this would be an iniquity to be punished by the judges, for I should have been false to God' (Job 31:24,28); 'Whoever spends gold and silver for his brother's sake, will receive ample treasure in the world to come' (II En. 50:5); 'The righteous justly hope for the end and depart from this world without fear, because they have a store of deeds preserved in treasuries of heaven' (II Bar. 14:12); 'Lose your silver for the sake of a friend and do not let it rust under a stone and be lost' (Sir. 29:10).

Some rabbinical sayings are of interest too: 'Did you ever see an animal or bird with a trade? They support themselves without trouble. Were they not created to serve me and I to serve my maker? Does it not follow I shall be supported without trouble!' (m.Kid. 4:14); 'He who has bread in his basket and says, "What shall I eat tomorrow?", lacks faith; for it is said, "The day's portion every day"' (b.Sot. 48b).

A rabbinical story points the same lesson: 'King Monobaz distributed all his treasures to the poor in the year of famine. His brothers sent to him and said, "Our fathers gathered treasures ... and you have dispersed both your own and theirs." Monobaz said to them, "My fathers gathered treasures for below; I have gathered treasures for above. They stored treasures where the hand of man can rule, but I have stored treasures where the hand of man cannot rule. My fathers gathered treasures which bear no fruit; I have gathered treasures which bear fruit. My fathers gathered treasures of mammon; I have gathered treasures in souls. My fathers gathered treasures for others in this world, but I have gathered treasures (also) for myself in the world to come' (b.B.B. 11a; t.Peah 4:18).

The same thought is found in the O.T and in even older literature: 'Lie down not at night being fearful of the morrow. Man knows not what the morrow is like', which is similar to: 'Do not boast about tomorrow for you do not know what a day may bring forth' (Pvb. 27:1). Instead of being anxious about food and clothing one should seek or search for, the coming kingdom.

There are several levels of thought behind the passage. Firstly, the O.T. proclaims that this world is God's creation and all living things - plants, animals and mankind - are his creatures. He feeds them: 'You cause the grass to grow for cattle and plants for man to cultivate, that he may bring food from the earth. ... All (creatures) look to you to give them their food in due season' (Ps. 104:27); 'You make springs gush forth in the valleys ... they give drink to every beast of the field ... By them the birds of the air have their habitation: they sing among the branches' (Ps. 104:10-12). This even applies to the 'unclean' ravens and vultures which feed on dead remains: 'He makes grass grow on the hills, he gives forth to the beasts and the young ravens which cry ... The Lord takes pleasure in those who fear him, in those who hope in his steadfast love' (Ps. 147:8-9,11). It may also be that the reference to rust and moths is connected with: 'For the moth will eat them up like a garment, and the worm eat them like wool' (Is. 51:8).

Secondly, mankind is nonetheless thought to be different from other creatures. Plants grow and man can use them. He benefits from them or they are there for his benefit, but he has to work on them himself. He was not expected to be indolent. Corn grows, but man must sow, tend, reap, thresh, grind and bake his bread; from flax ('lilies' could also mean herbaceous plants), he must prepare linen by retting the plant, spin and weave his cloth; he must look after his cattle and so on: 'Ask the beasts and they will teach you; the birds of the air and they will tell you; or the plants of the earth and they will teach you ... the hand of the Lord has done this. In his hand is the life of every living thing and the breath of all mankind' (Job 12:7-10).

At the same time, man remains totally dependent on God. He has no possibility of increasing his height or his life-span: 'Man and his portion lie before God in the balance; he cannot add to and enlarge what has been prescribed by God!' (P.S. 5:6). God had given Hezekiah some extra years, because of his righteousness and prayers, but his case was exceptional: 'Thus says the Lord ... I have heard your prayer and seen your tears. Behold I will heal you and add fifteen years to your life' (II Kgs. 20:5-6). Only God knows the date of one's death and only he could change it. Note that 'length of days' is closely connected with being a faithful servant of God: 'Loving the Lord your God, obeying his voice ... means life to you and length of days' (Dt. 30:20).

Thirdly, those who seek after the one important matter would receive all other necessary things as well, as Solomon discovered: 'The Lord appeared to Solomon in a dream ... and said, "Ask what I shall give you." And Solomon said ... "Give your servant an understanding mind to govern your people, that I may discern between good and evil ..." And God said, "Because you have asked this ... behold I now do according to your word. I give you a wise and discerning mind ... I give you also what you have not asked, both riches and honour ... and if you walk in my ways ... I will give you long life"' (I Kgs. 3:5-14). The reverse is not true and those whose lives are devoted to excesses of this world's goods have all the merit and reward they ever will get. 'The mouth of the furnace of God's wrath awaits them.'

Fourthly, there are hints in the language of the life to come. The flowers appeared, only to 'die' and disappear, but next spring God's breath quickened them and they were 'resurrected' to a new life: 'When you take away their breath, they die and return to their dust. When you send forth your Spirit they are (re-)created and you renew the face of the ground' (Ps. 104:29-30).

This is one of few passages in which the moral is the opposite to one in the O.T. In the book of Proverbs, the very active and busy ant succeeds by its hard work and industry: 'Go to the ant, O sluggard; consider her ways, and be wise. Without having any chief, officer or ruler, she prepares her food in summer, and gathers her sustenance in harvest' (Pvb. 6:6-8). In the N.T. parable the flowers receive from God much more than could be acquired by any amount of busyness.

In the New Era, the trees would shelter the little birds, whose song would gladden the hearts of the faithful, life would be without troubles because food and water would always be available and clothing would be imperishable; all as it had been in the wilderness before Israel abandoned the covenant which Jacob had sworn with God: 'Behold I (the Lord) am with you and will keep you wherever you go ... Then Jacob made a vow, saying, "If God will be with me and will keep me in the way that I go, and will give me bread to eat and clothing to wear, so that I come to my father's house in peace, then the Lord shall be my God ..."' (Gen. 28:15-21). God would supply all that was necessary in boundless measure, and concern for material needs would be pointless.

Yet Jesus says his disciples are already in the burgeoning kingdom. As Solomon chose wisdom and found God showered him with all sorts of other gifts, so the faithful would make the kingdom of God their life's priority. Their commitment would be thorough and without deviation. They could have no other concern in life, and therefore to keep superfluities, to encumber themselves with more than necessary, was faithlessness. What they had, what they acquired, what they saved, what they inherited, had to be used for practising God's rule - love of God and others. Nothing else mattered, and God would not let them down: 'The Lord knows the days of the blameless ... they are not put to shame in evil times, in the days of famine they have abundance' (Ps. 37:18-19).

* * *

F 6. Invite the poor to your party - Lk. 14:12-15.

The exact reciprocation of obligations of all possible forms was a major principle of Jewish society, but spiritual merit is earned by hospitality which cannot be returned.

"When you give a party," said Jesus, "do not invite your friends, brothers or relations, nor your rich neighbours. They will only ask you back again and so repay you. No, when you give a reception and banquet, invite the poor, the crippled, the lame and the blind. Then you will find happiness. They cannot repay you, but you will be rewarded when the righteous rise up again."
'One who was at table with them said, "Blessed is he who eats bread in the kingdom of God."'

The passage has a clear indication that the reward comes in the next life, after the day of Judgement when the dead rise again. The passage echoes several remarks in the O.T.: 'Those who are generous are blessed, for they share their bread with the poor' (Pvb. 22:9); 'He who is kind to the poor lends to the Lord, and he will be repaid for his deed' (Pvb. 19:17); 'If you pour yourself out for the hungry and satisfy the desire of the afflicted then your light shall rise in the darkness and your gloom be a noonday' (Is. 58:10). The same is found in rabbinical literature too: 'Let your house be opened wide and let the needy be sons of your house ...' (ARN 14); also in I.T. writings: 'Receive the homeless into your house' (P.Ph. 24).

* * *

F 7. Known by their fruits - Mt. 7:16-20; 12:33-37; 13:51-52. Lk. 6:43-45.

The wilful inclinations within a person for good and evil, are likened here to good and bad fruit, which show from what sort of person they have come. It was rabbinical teaching that reward is given for setting out to perform a religious duty as well as for actually doing it: 'Once a man undertakes to do something, it is accounted to him as if he had already done it' (Mek.Pis. 12)

Jesus said, "No good tree produces corrupt fruit and no corrupt tree produces good fruit. Can you gather figs from thistles or grapes from thorns? No, a good tree bears good fruit and a corrupt tree corrupt fruit. The words men say come from their hearts, and a good man produces good from the store within himself while a wicked man produces evil from the evil within; thus you can recognise men by the fruit they bear. Therefore every teacher of the Law, who becomes a disciple of the kingdom of God, is like a householder who produces from his treasury both the new and the old.

When a tree becomes corrupt and no longer bears good fruit, it is cut down and burnt, and every unpropitious word bearing no fruit will have to be accounted for on the day of Judgement. You will either be justified or condemned by your own words."

The last sentence of the passage, found only in Matthew, may be compared with: 'I shall not pass sentence, for it is each man's intention which is examined' (P.Ph. 52); 'Honour or shame can come through speaking, and a man's tongue may be his downfall' (Sir. 5:13).

Fruit showed the value of the plant; the fruitful and honourable olive, fig and vine trees, are contrasted with the fruitless and deceitful thorn (Judges 9). Other O.T. passages are similar: 'But godless men are all like thorns that are thrown away' (II Sam. 23:6); 'Like thorns they (God's foes) are entangled; like dry stubble they are consumed' (Nah. 1:10).

A rabbinical story tells of trees with edible fruit who were asked why they were silent: "We have no need to speak", they said. "Our fruits are our witness." Then the trees without fruit were asked why they made such a noise. "Would that we could make our voices louder still, so we might attract attention", they replied' (Gen.R. 16:3). Just as a man's utterances express his nature, so the tree "utters" its fruit, good or bad: 'As the fruit of a tree shows how it has been cultivated, so the utterance of a man's thought reveals his heart' (Sir. 27:6).

The concept of a store with 'old' contents is found in several contexts: 'You shall eat of the long-kept produce in the old store' (b.B.B. 91b); 'You shall eat old grain long stored and you shall have to clear out the old to make room for the new' (Lev. 26:10). It was also thought of as the treasure of the Law stored in the scribe's store. Jesus is not shown rejecting this, but accepting it alongside the 'new' of his teaching. This is typical of Matthew's gospel.

186

A rabbinical story is similar: 'A king had an orchard and he built a treasure house there. He decreed that those who work conscientiously in the orchard may enter the treasure house ... Thus for him whose religious acts and good deeds are saved in the treasure house, he will enter Paradise' (Gen.R. 9:9). The idea of fruit as the interest on the capital fund of one's merits is found in much rabbinical teaching: 'Things of which the fruits are enjoyed in this world while the capital remains for the world to come are honouring of parents, benevolence, restoring peace between fellowmen and study of Torah, which is equal to them all [put together]' (m.Peah 1:1).

* * *

F 8. Fate and guilt - Lk. 13:1-5.

Reference to the O.T. is necessary to understand this passage. There were precedents for the murder of people in the Temple; the instruments were human, but the ultimate cause was thought to be God's anger with the faithless, idolatrous Jews. The prophets had made it quite clear: 'The Lord said to the man in linen, "Go through the city of Jerusalem and put a mark on the foreheads of those who sigh and groan over all the abominations that are committed in it." To others he said, "Pass through the city after him and smite; your eye shall not spare, and you shall show no pity. Slay old men outright, young men and maidens, little children and women, but touch no one upon whom is the mark. Begin at my sanctuary. Defile the Temple and fill the court with slain; then go out into the city and kill"' (Ezk. 9:4-7).

Other prophets had said the same: '... the Lord will suddenly come to his Temple... But who can endure the day of his coming ... for he is like a refiner's fire ... and he will purify the sons of Levi' (Mal 3:1-3); 'The Lord has destroyed (Zion) without mercy ... he levelled it with the ground and desecrated the kingdom and its rulers ... In fierce anger he has cut down all the might of Israel ... The Lord spurned his own altar and laid a curse on his sanctuary ...' (Lam. 2:2-7); 'Behold, the inescapable Day of the Lord is coming, of wrath and anger, to make the world desolate and to destroy the sinners out of the land' (Is. 13:9,LXX).

Some of the crowd spoke to him about the Galileans whose blood Pilate had mingled with their sacrifices. Jesus answered, "It was not because these Galileans were more sinful than others, that this happened to them; any more that the eighteen, who were killed when the tower at Siloam collapsed on them, were more guilty than all the others living in Jerusalem. But unless you all repent you will all perish likewise."

The incidents described by Luke were used by Jesus to point out once again his message: follow God's rule. The signs of the times show that there could be a cataclysm of destruction loosed on Israel because of her intransigent arrogant indifference to the true meaning of God's word: 'Your prophets have seen false visions, they did not bring home to you your guilt and so restore your fortunes' (Lam 2:14). That Jews were killed in the Temple was a sign of impending disaster, and towers would fall down on the day of slaughter: '...in the day of great slaughter, when the towers will fall...' (Is. 30:25). Jesus had healed and restored to life like the prophets of old, and his prophecy was very like theirs. No one could offer the excuse that they had not been warned.

It is not unlikely that the killing of those sacrificing in the Temple was interpreted in other ways, in accordance with the O.T., and the beliefs of Judaism. The story of Jehu who killed the priests in the temple for their idolatry was a good parallel. Jehu, like Pilate, was no faithful Israelite, but was seen as having been used by God to eradicate, by a deceitful stratagem, all the priests of Ba'al: 'Jehu sent throughout all Israel after the worshippers of Ba'al, and they entered the house of Ba'al ... Jehu had stationed eighty men outside and Jehu said to them, "Go in and slay them; let not one escape." Thus Jehu wiped out Ba'al from Israel.' (II Kgs. 10:21-28).

There was no point in blaming Pilate. In Judaism, what he did was wicked and he would be punished, yet he was God's means to warn his people that they had not infinite time to repent, before they and their rottenness were wiped out: 'Repent, therefore, to avoid coming to the same end as those killed in the Temple or under the tower.'

There are several aspects of this passage which are even more unexpected. Sacrifices of animals were seen as symbolising the desire on the part of the worshipper of sacrificing himself to atone for his sins. In being killed in the midst of this, those who had died had become their own sacrifice and it was thought likely that they would enter paradise quite sinless.

The Jewish historian Josephus, tells of worshippers murdered in the Temple and synagogues, but some believe that the alleged atrocity ascribed to Pilate is untrue, and that the question was put by *agents provocateurs*, who were trying to find out if Jesus would advocate or support a revolt against Rome. Jesus' reply is then taken to imply that if suffering were apportioned according to sinfulness there would be a great deal more suffering about. In rabbinical teaching some thought that: 'There is no death without sin and no suffering without iniquity. The soul which sins shall die. The son shall not bear the iniquity of the father nor the father the iniquity of the son' (b.Shab.55a). That this is not the full story is obvious. It should also be noted that the passage is not a prophecy of the destruction of Jerusalem by the Romans, although this may have been taken as another example of the same process. The lesson is that those who do not turn and follow God's rule will perish. It is as applicable to the time before the sack of Jerusalem as after it.

It was thought in Judaism that sacrifices of lambs 'cleanse the sins of Israel and make it as an infant in its first year' (PR 16:7).

* * *

F 9. Correcting your brother - Mt. 7:1-5. Mk. 4:24. Lk. 6:37-38, 41-42.

"Pass no judgement, and you yourselves will not be judged; do not condemn and you will not be condemned; forgive and you will be forgiven; give and you will receive gifts in plenty - good measure, pressed down and topped up. Take heed of what you hear: whatever measure you deal out to others will be that which you will receive in return, with something more besides.

Why do you observe the bit of chaff in your brother's eye, without even thinking about the log in your own eye? How can you say to your brother, 'Dear brother, let me take the speck out of your eye', when all the time there is that pole in your own? Hypocrites! First get the log out of your own eye, then you will see through to take the speck out of your brother's."

This apparently simple passage hides many associations which must have awakened the interest of Jesus' audience. The first part of the passage suggests that one should neither judge another's conduct nor reprove him if he does wrong. While this would not apply to those belonging to the land of Israel, it may apply to foreigners: 'A stranger you shall not vex, neither shall you oppose him, for you were strangers in the land of Egypt' (Mek.Nez. 18), but some think that originally it meant that no one should judge or condemn another in such a way that God would disapprove: 'Judge not alone, for none may judge alone save God' (m.Avot. 4:8).

In rabbinical writings it was argued by some that: 'The majority must be followed. When the majority declare it is forbidden it is not allowed; when they declare it is permitted it is allowed' (j.San. 22a). It was also important that preventing wrong-doing was a duty: 'Anyone who has the power to prevent another from wrong-doing and does not prevent it, is punished for this' (b.A.Z. 18a)

In other Jewish writings the first part of the passage is also understood as referring to the granting of rewards in the world to come: 'The measure a man gives will be measured unto him' (Tg.Is. 27:8); '... on the day of judgement ... every one shall learn his own measure and according to his measure shall take his reward' (II En. 44:5); and in rabbinical thought: 'Remove the stubble from your own eyes before you remove it from others' (b.B.B. 60b); 'Do not reproach your fellow man with a fault which is also your own' (Mek.Nez. 18).

The second part of the passage is a precept known in many cultures including Judaism. No one likes to be corrected by someone with a greater measure of the same fault, and few like to be corrected at all. The O.T. passage: 'You shall not hate your brother in your heart, but you shall reprove your neighbour, lest you share in his sin. You shall not seek revenge nor cherish anger towards your kinsfolk' (Lev. 19:17-18), or, as rabbinical writing has it: 'You shall surely rebuke and if he does not accept it he must be rebuked again. You shall not bear sin because of him' (b.Arak. 16b). This is the basis of the N.T. passage.

There is also a rabbinical saying: 'Judge not your neighbour until you come into his place' (m.Avot. 2:5) Only those who have committed themselves to humble service in God's realm can have any possible justification for looking for bits of chaff in another's eye. First they must submit themselves to God so he can take away their own 'poles'. Then they will not be so ready to judge and condemn others and they will still less seek revenge on their own behalf. 'Create in me a pure heart, O God, and give me a new and steadfast spirit; do not drive me from your presence or take your Holy Spirit from me' (Ps. 51:10-12).

At the same time, it may be necessary to rebuke and reprimand those who thwart God's rule, because for the Jew, society was a unit and all Jews were one family. Each was responsible for the other's sinfulness: 'Confront your friend with gossip about him; he may not have done it, or if he did it, he will not do it again' (Sir. 19:13). Evil comes when good men do nothing to stop it, and every society needs some ascetics to provide the optimum norms of conduct. Reproving must be such as to earn God's approval; one's motive must be pure, and one must: 'Judge all men with the scale of innocence' (m.Avot. 1:6). See also C 6.

There must be no ulterior motive, no desire for any kind of domination and the motive must be purely one of love. It is the disposition, or inclination, of each person which is crucial, and those who think they are always able to judge the motives of others are those who need to lose their 'logs' first. Those who ignore this preliminary redemption should note that as they treat others so will they be treated, with positive or negative bonuses as appropriate.

For the Jews the time in the wilderness and the conquest of Canaan were constantly remembered. They were required to drive out the original inhabitants: 'If you do not drive out the inhabitants of the land as you advance, any whom you leave in possession will become a barbed hook in your eye and a thorn in your side' (Num. 33:55); nevertheless 'They did not destroy the peoples round about but ... they worshipped their idols and were ensnared by them' (Ps. 106: 33-34).

This involved building defensive palisades and the word for log or beam also can be used for stakes which strengthen thorn-hedges round a settlement. Idols were called 'thorn-eyes', seductive false gods, so there is an association with eyes. Sins were also called thorns.

* * *

F 10. Commitment to the new life - Mt. 8:18-22. Lk. 9:57-62.

The obvious meaning in the following three passages is that those who will follow Jesus must be prepared to cut their ties with their earlier lives, and accept the consequences. It would seem that these were very unpleasant: nowhere to rest, no home, no connection with one's family, not even permission to bury one's dead father, although this was a filial duty of great importance in Judaism. Why did Jesus seem to offer only misery, hardship and unnatural separation from loved ones? Not even time to say goodbye! It seemed a most unattractive invitation. He wouldn't win many followers talking like that !

A doctor of the Law came to Jesus and said, "I will follow you wherever you go." "Will you indeed," said Jesus. "Jackals have their lairs, and vultures their roosting- quarters, but the son of man has no place to lay his head."

On another occasion, one of his disciples said to Jesus, "Let me go and bury my father first." Jesus replied, "Leave the dead to bury the dead; you must follow me and go to proclaim the kingdom of God."

Another time a man came and would follow Jesus. "Just let me go first and say goodbye to my people at home." "No", said Jesus. "No one who sets his hand to the plough and keeps looking back, is fit for the kingdom of God."

O.T. prophecy, as so often, lies behind Jesus' teaching. Jesus and his followers would welcome the full inauguration of God's rule on the day of Judgement, but to do so they must be as devoted as the High Priest or the Nazirites. They could have nothing to do with a corpse or a burial: 'The High Priest shall not enter the place where any dead body lies, not even for his father or his mother shall he render himself unclean' (Lev. 21:11); 'When either a man or a woman makes ... the vow of a Nazirite ... all the days that he separates himself to the Lord, he shall not go near a dead body; neither for his father, nor his mother, nor brother nor sister, if they die, shall he make himself unclean' (Num. 6:2,6-7). Nevertheless in rabbinical books, it is said that: 'Even a High Priest ... must bury a corpse if nobody else is available to do it' (Sif. Num. 26:9).

The prohibition against the man going to say goodbye to his family is similar to that in the O.T. story about the calling of Elisha who was ploughing with twelve yokes of oxen: 'Elijah passed Elisha by and cast his mantle over him, and Elisha left his oxen and ran after Elijah. "Let me kiss my father and my mother and then I will follow you." Elijah said to him, "Go back again; for what have I done to you?" Elisha returned to the oxen, killed them ... and gave to the people ... Then he arose and went after Elijah and ministered to him' (I Kgs. 19:19-21).

Casting his mantle over Elisha was to symbolise the transfer of Elijah's rights and authority, and when Elijah was carried up into heaven his cloak fell to earth and Elisha used it instead of his own (II Kgs. 2:13). Elisha was allowed to return for a last visit and to be rid of his oxen and their yoke but Jesus' rule was stricter than that of Elijah.

Similarly, Moses had asked God to bless Levi in spite of the fact that he had left his family: 'Of Levi, who said of his parents, "I do not know them", and who did not acknowledge his brothers nor recognise his children' (Dt. 33:9). And in I.T. books the same priority is found: 'Their anxiety about wives and children as well as brothers and kinsfolk, weighed less with them than their chief anxiety about the consecrated sanctuary' (II Mac. 15:18).

The passage creates a picture of Israel as rotten as it had been when God punished her by imposing exile in Babylon, and in the New Era God would again punish Israel. There would be total destruction, and those who did not take steps to prevent it, would be destroyed too: '"The men of Judah have done what is wrong in my eyes," says the Lord ... "A time is coming when ... the bodies of this people shall become food for the birds of the air and the wild beasts, and there will be no one to scare them away"' (Jer. 7:30,33). That is, it would be even worse than in Abram's time: 'Birds came down upon the carcasses, even upon the divided parts of them, and Abram drove them away' (Gen. 15:11 LXX).

'For the Lord has a day of vengeance, a year of recompense for the cause of Zion ... From generation to generation it shall be waste: none shall pass through it for ever. They shall name it 'No kingdom'. It shall be the haunt of jackals ... there shall the vultures gather one after another' (Is. 34:8,10,12-15); 'Man, these are the words of the Lord God: "Cry to every bird that flies and to all the wild beasts; come assemble ... to the great sacrifice ... on the mountains of Israel, eat flesh and drink blood, the flesh of warriors and blood of princes ... At my table you shall eat your fill ... The nations shall know that the Israelites went into exile for their iniquity, because they were faithless to me. So I hid my face from them ... and they fell every one of them by the sword. I dealt with them as they deserved, defiled and rebellious as they were ..."' (Ezk. 39:17-24).

In this passage the words 'son of man' refer to Jesus as he travelled and taught throughout the countryside, but the saying that man has no place to rest his head was well known in other literature of the time, and it reflects the uncertainty of life then.

Those who understood the barrenness of Israel must separate themselves in order to carry forward God's message. Jesus and his followers were fulfilling that role. They would be spared. Thus to be counted among Jesus' followers may be uncomfortable, even arduous, in this life, but it was they who were the servants of God. They should not mourn for the dead of the unrighteous, those of a new Sodom. Israel needed to repent and get back to observing the true covenant. Otherwise the 'dead' would bury the dead and the jackals and vultures would see off the others.

Jesus message did demand sacrifices on the part of his disciples; it was a message of hardship, measured by worldly standards, but for any who hoped to enter God's kingdom, either on earth or in heaven, the hardships were trivial compared to the bliss to come. Some scholars think that only (specially chosen) disciples were required by Jesus to adopt his rigorous and uncertain way of life.

* * *

F 11. Take up your cross - Mt. 10:32-33, 37-39; 16:24-28. Mk. 8:34-9:1
Lk. 9:23-27; 12:8-9; 14:25-27, 33; 17:33.

In Judaism, the 'self', the person, was often thought of as a unity, body plus spirit or soul, with the rational mind or reason able to observe, and ideally to control, the 'self'. This reason could be devoted to God's purposes or to Satan's. It was the source of the 'inclinations' either for good or for evil: 'Let us not fear him who thinks he kills, for a great struggle and peril of the soul awaits in eternal torments those who transgress the ordinance of God. Let us then arm ourselves with divine reason's mastery of the passions' (IV Mac. 13:14-16); 'We can recognise that reason is the master over the passions and affections (inclinations). For the Law ranks above affection for parents, so a man may not surrender his virtue for their sakes; it overrides love for a wife, so if she transgress a man should rebuke her; it governs love of children, so if they are naughty a man should punish them; and it controls the claims of friendship, so a man should reprove his friends if they do evil' (IV Mac. 2:9-12).

The 'self' was imbued with good and bad inclinations: 'God has given two ways to men and two inclinations and two kinds of action' (T.Ash. 1:3); 'A man set on righteousness finds life, but the pursuit of evil leads to death' (Pvb. 11:19); 'I offer you the choice of life or death, blessing or curse. ... Love the Lord, obey him and hold fast to him: that is life for you...' (Dt. 30:19-20). Bad impulses led to worldly prestige, status and success, but thereby to exclusion from the kingdom of God: 'God created man from the beginning and placed him in the hands of his 'inclinations' (Sir. 15:14). It was accepted in Judaism that one must bless God for evil inclinations as one blesses God for the good, because to love God with all one's heart meant with both good and bad impulses (b.Ber. 33b) and, 'If I bring good to you, give thanks and when I bring suffering to you, give thanks' (Ps. 116:3-4; Job 1:21). Nevertheless, 'God admitted to Elijah that he had made a mistake in creating sinners' evil intentions' (b.Ber.32a).

Jesus spoke to the crowd of people with him, including his disciples and said, "If anyone will be a follower of mine, he must deny his 'self', take up his cross and come with me. Whoever tries to save or spare his 'self' shall lose it, whoever loses it (for my sake and my gospel's) shall preserve it alive. What does a man gain by acquiring the whole world, if he thereby forfeits his 'self'? With what could a man buy back the 'self'?

If anyone comes to me and does not reject his family, he cannot be my disciple. If anyone disowns or is ashamed of me, my words and my followers, the son of man will be ashamed of him when he comes in the glory of his Father and his angels. Those who confess or acknowledge me before other men, the son of man will confess or acknowledge before the angels of God. For the son of man is to come in the glory of his Father with his angels and then he will give each man the due reward for what he has done.

Any who hoped to enter the kingdom of God had to utilise his good

194

inclinations: 'Persevere in right conduct and loyalty and you shall find life and honour' (Pvb. 21:21); 'If a wicked man turns from his wicked ways and does what is just and right, he will save his life' (Ezk. 18:27). To follow Jesus and his teaching was the best way to do this. There are good reasons for thinking that the Aramaic which presumably underlies the Greek text in the first sentence is more accurately given as: 'Anyone willing to follow after me, he must know and understand his 'self', and take my yoke upon him.'

The cross was the yoke of duty and obligation that a follower of Jesus had to accept, and it was not that he should deny or despise himself. He had to know his own self to recognise and see himself for what he was. Then he could love his neighbour as himself. This yoke could bring suffering, it could mean rejecting family ties, but there was no possible way to regain one's 'self', if this was lost in worldly success: 'Also no man can ever ransom himself nor pay God the price of his 'self;' the ransom would cost too much ... that would let him live for ever and never see the pit of destruction' (Ps. 49:7-9); 'No man can by any means redeem his brother nor give to God a ransom for his soul ... But God said half a shekel is enough' (PR 16.7). [Half a shekel was the Temple tax.]

The saying, 'Whoever tries to save or spare his 'self' or life will lose it, and whoever loses his life will save it', is almost certainly derived from: 'Everyone who rescues his 'self' shall lose it, and everyone who loses his 'self' shall rescue it.' Striving for long-term security leads to only short-term benefits; God gives both short- and long-term benefits. However, some think that the word translated 'it' should be 'her', and refer to Wisdom, which is feminine in gender, so that the saying becomes similar to: 'Wisdom is near to those who seek her and he that gives his 'self' or soul to her, finds her' (Sir. 51:26).

Other approaches to this concept are the sayings in Jewish literature: 'If you wish to live, become dead, so you may care neither for the reviling of men nor for their praise, for the dead care for nothing; in this way you can live', and 'Everyone who keeps a precept (of the Torah) keeps his own soul (life), and everyone who destroys one precept of the Law, destroys his own soul' (Sif.Num. 15:1-15).

Those admitted to the kingdom were those who were so concerned for their acceptance by God that this outweighed everything else. Nothing else could have any influence over their judgement as to what was good and what was evil. Admittance to the kingdom was their only worry, and this they could achieve by becoming Jesus' followers, obedient to God's rule: 'They will see the age which is now invisible to them and see the time which is now hidden from them' (II Bar. 51:8).

Similar sayings are found in the O.T. and I.T. books: 'For you, O Lord, requite a man according to this works' (Ps.62:12); 'I will put my neck in the noose and take my life in my hands. If he would slay me I should not hesitate ... This at least assures my success: that no godless man appears before him' (Job 13:14-16); '... the forgiven Israelites will see the sovereignty of their messiah' (Tg.Is. 53:10); '... they who are put to death for the Lord's sake shall awake to life' (T.Jud. 25:4).

There are many associations with the word for 'cross'. To take up one's cross had nothing to do with death by crucifixion, which was reserved for political offences, rebellion, treason, etc. Heretics were stoned to death and the body was then hung from a tree. It meant, in the O.T., the staff of Moses and it also referred to the stakes carried by soldiers to build a defensive palisade when on a campaign. These stakes could be used to kill their bearers by impalement if they were defeated in battle. (They were sometimes used as punishment for idolatry too.) It could thus imply an invitation by Jesus to those who would enlist in his campaign and go with him into battle against the forces of evil, so rampant in the world.

It is important to realise that in Judaism, 'hanging' or 'crucifixion' was used for corpses. It was not used as a means of putting someone to death, as in Roman practice, and would never be advocated for that purpose - least of all by Jesus. For heretics, stoning or strangulation was used and anyone' hung on a tree' was considered to be under God's curse (Dt. 21:22-23).

The meaning of the saying is that one must not let the prospect of loss and hostility deter one from seeking immortality, nor reject the prospect of immortality in favour of immediate comforts. Attachment to secular values hinders the utilisation of the potential in each one for eternal life or life in the kingdom of God. A degree of simplicity and asceticism is discernible in this passage, but it does not suggest that deliberate abandonment of property to destitution, or life to martyrdom, are required.

Consecration of one's life and discipline of the 'self', under the guidance of God's word, indifferent to, or defying the world and its evil values, will result in resurrection and eternal life in the kingdom. Only those willing to take part in the battle with God's enemies could be guests at the heavenly banquet after victory. Willingness to carry his stake, his cross, reminded the disciple of this.

There is probably a link between the last sentence of the passage and Psalm 20: 'Now I know the Lord will help his anointed, he will answer him from his heaven with mighty victories by his right hand. Some boast of chariots and some of horses; but we boast of the name of the Lord our God. They will collapse and fall; but we shall rise and stand upright' (Ps. 20:6-8).

* * *

F 12. Blasphemy against the Holy Spirit - Mt. 12:31-32. Mk. 3:28-30. Lk. 12:10.

"Most certainly I tell you, men can be forgiven all their sins, and no blasphemy is beyond forgiveness except blasphemy against the Spirit of holiness. That can never be forgiven, either in this age or in the next." For they had been saying that Jesus' power came from a demon by which he was possessed.

Generally, Jesus as well as the O.T. says that forgiveness is readily available to those who repent and turn to God: 'I am he who blots out your sins for my own sake and I will not remember your sins' (Is. 43:25); 'You forgive the iniquity of your people and pardon all their sin' (Ps. 85:2); but it is logically impossible to ask God or the Holy Spirit for forgiveness when one rejects the very concept of either: 'If a man sins against a man, God will mediate for him; but if a man sins against the Lord, who can intercede for him?' (I Sam. 2:25). There can be no healing, no release from the guilt of sin if a man denies God and his Spirit. God is powerless in the face of human refusal.

That this was not the only sin for which no repentance was thought possible is shown by the rabbinical saying, 'He who makes many to sin, to him shall be given no means for repentance' (m.Avot. 5:3). It is also found in the O.T.: 'Whoever curses his God shall bear his sin. He who blasphemes the name of the Lord, shall be put to death' (Lev. 24:15). Some similar passages are found in I.T. books: 'Wisdom is a spirit that loves man, but she will not hold a blasphemer guiltless for his lips, because God is witness of his inmost being and is a true overseer of his heart, and hearer of all he says' (W.S. 1:6); 'Woe to those who pronounce fierce curses which cannot be reversed' (I En. 95:4).

Nevertheless, some rabbis said that even if the iniquity of Israel went so far as to deny the Root of the Universe, he would accept their repentance and let them return to him. This idea of forgiveness by God is made clear in a comment on an O.T. text: 'By the verse, "Open to me" (S.S. 5:12), the Holy One meant: Make for me an opening in you, an opening as narrow as the eye of a needle and I shall make the opening so wide that camps full of soldiers and siege engines could enter it' (PRK 24:12).

It was an accepted principle of Jewish law that ignorance of the Law and its interpretation was a mitigating factor in assessing the punishment the perpetrator should suffer, with one exception. Those who transgressed against the Jewish religion, that is who were guilty of sacrilegious actions, especially profanation of the name of God, were liable, whether the prohibitions were known to them or not. It was thought self-evident that abuse of God, blasphemy and sacrilege, that is idolatry, were unacceptable (a comment on Num. 15:22-31).

In another passage it is said: 'To profane God's name was the worst sin; those guilty of this are without forgiveness and there is no redemption short of death' (b.Yoma 86a); and 'One who profanes God's name in secret will suffer the penalty publicly' (m.Avot. 4:4).

* * *

In Judaism, the word salt was a symbol for several things: Israel, peace and prudence, for example. Elisha had to purify the spring with salt. 'Elisha went out to the spring and, throwing salt in it, said, "This is the word of the Lord: 'I purify this water. It shall cause no more death or miscarriages'"' (II Kgs. 2:21).

Salt was also necessary for the correct sacrificial offerings. 'Make an incense blended as by the perfumer, seasoned with salt, pure and holy' (Ex. 30:35); 'Every grain offering shall be salted; you shall put the salt of your covenant with God on your grain-offering. Salt shall accompany all offerings' (Lev. 2:13); 'On all your oblations you shall strew salt and let not the covenant of salt be lacking' (Jub. 21:11).

A rabbinical comment on: 'it is a covenant of salt for ever before the Lord for you and your descendants as well' (Sif.Num. on 18:19), refers to the covenant God made with Aaron understood as something wholesome and which will last, since salt is a preservative (b.B.K. 110b). Another, but more obscure, statement is: 'How are we to understand the case of the salt? If its owner has renounced it, would not the scattering constitute an addition to the structure? And if he did not renounce it, would it not constitute an unlawful imposition?' (b.Erub. 104a). To scatter salt would be to do work forbidden on the sabbath but this does not elucidate the intention and meaning of this statement.

"Salt is good but if the salt has lost its saltiness, how can it recover its savour? It would be worthless and fit only to be thrown out and trodden underfoot. Have salt in yourselves and be at peace with each other."

The sayings about salt are not easy to understand but the essential meaning seems to be that the gospel is like salt - if it is good, one can taste it; if it has no effect it is good for nothing. To say that salt is useless may also be tantamount to saying that the old Israel should be thrown away; a New Israel is needed. It may also be taken to suggest that followers of God's law must apply salt to themselves and to others so they are preserved and do not decay away.

The eating of salted food was a symbol of a sacred bond between Arabs, at least until recent times. It was an acknowledgement of peace among those taking part. Mark's version mentions keeping the peace between men and in rabbinical literature a man who is salty is prudent and held up as worthy of imitation.

More prosaically salt from ancient times has had several domestic uses. Its use as a seasoning is well known and it was used as a food preservative in the form of brine. This would extract the water from the food, so that gradually the brine would become diluted and ineffective. In ancient times salt was also used to sterilise the land: 'And Abimelech ... razed the city and sowed it with salt' (Jdg. 9:45).

If the salt had lost its saltiness or the brine had become diluted it was useless for these and all other purposes and it was fit only to be cast on the rubbish heap or trodden underfoot.

Salt was sometimes put beside the flame of a lamp to make it shine more brightly. Anyone who has thrown salt on to a fire knows the intense yellow colour which results. If salt was added to incense, it, too, would glow brightly when burned on the altar or in a censer.

In rabbinical books the salt used in sacrifices was special: 'The scripture declares a covenant with Aaron with a substance which does not decay' (Sif.Num.18 on 18:19). So there is the idea here that followers of Jesus must apply this sacrificial salt to themselves and to others so they do not decay away.

* * *

F 14. Pearls and pigs - Mt. 7:6.

"Do not give dogs what is holy; do not throw your pearls before pigs: lest they trample on them under their feet; and turning may tear you to pieces."

This is a difficult saying and many explanations have been offered. It has been thought that the first clause suggests that the holy in Judaism should not be given to the unrighteous: 'If any one ... approaches the holy things ... that person shall be cut off from my presence: I am the Lord' (Lev. 22:2-3). Those fit to receive the holy things were holy: 'They shall be holy to their God, and not profane the name of their God ... therefore they are holy' (Lev. 21:6). The second is taken by some to mean that by exposing their knowledge, the members of the early community, in conflict with strict Jews and others, had their arguments torn to pieces and trampled on. 'Pearls' may also refer to pearls of knowledge or wisdom which are not to be given to 'hogs', that is the Romans who had wild boars as their emblem on their banners in Palestine at the time. The word could also mean crumbs of the Eucharist bread which were not to be cast to swine.

According to this explanation, the early community was instructed here to keep the sacred from the wicked and not to share their secrets and wealth with the wicked generation. Their alms and/or their knowledge were to benefit members of the community, not non-believers. Similar sayings are known from the time of Jesus such as: 'You have put before your opponents your golden words, who have trampled on them as swine trample on pearls;' and in the rabbinical literature: 'Do not expose the Holy to let dogs eat it' (m.Tem. 6:5).

There are problems with this interpretation. The word used for 'dogs' refers to the ownerless, wild dogs which were a common feature of the towns of the time. It was forbidden to feed them (they ate refuse and carrion) and they could be dangerous to humans.

The word used for swine or pigs, refers to pigs herded by their owner, and perhaps fattened up with plenty of food. They were not such as would recognise the value of pearls cast before them! Furthermore, the word 'holy' is used in the O.T. to mean the meat of the flesh-offerings of the Temple. The point of the saying, which has parallels in the Jewish, Arabian and Greek literatures of the day, could be that by doing the wrong thing - feeding wild dogs with holy food, or throwing pearls before pigs - the result is the reverse of that hoped for: the dogs will attack you, and the pigs will trample the precious pearls in the mire. Jesus uses this bit of secular wisdom to point out that false relationships and actions return to plague those who are responsible for them. He tells his listeners that they had the knowledge required to do righteous deeds, and if they did the opposite, they would be delivered to God's justice.

* * *

F. Summary.

All in God's kingdom are members of the same family, both Jews and Gentiles, and there is no need to worry about material possessions and provisions. God will give all that is necessary to those enjoying his reign.

Any repentant sinner is welcomed by God without requiring penances, but without love for others no repentance is possible.

God's soldiers receive eternal life; they are those whose fruits show their source - the good inclination. They do not expect any return for good deeds, but can rely on God to reward them in the New Era.

Riches, pious observances of the correct rituals, and subscription to the 'proper' beliefs, are of no importance. Only doing God's will counts and gives merit in God's realm.

G. Jesus' message - mainly to opponents.

G 1. The cleansing of the Temple - Mt. 21:12-16. Mk. 11:15-18. Lk. 19:45-46.

Jesus' behaviour, described in this passage, was in accordance with the belief of the time that the Messiah would come to the Temple to find out if it were fit for the nations of the earth to gather to worship God. His actions were like that of Nehemiah who cleansed the Temple in his day when he discovered it had been misused: 'Then I discovered what wicked thing Eliashib had done in providing Tobiah with a room in the courts of the house of God. I was very angry and threw out all Tobiah's things from the chamber. I gave orders that the chamber be purified, and I brought back the vessels of God ...' (Neh. 13:7-9) [Tobiah was a Gentile businessman.]; 'Both prophet and priest are ungodly; even in my house have I found their wickedness' (Jer. 23:11).

Jesus went into the Temple in Jerusalem and began to drive out the traders, those buying and selling in the Temple precincts. He overturned the tables of the money-changers and the seats of the sellers of pigeons and he would not allow anyone to carry any implements or vessels through the Temple court, using it as a thoroughfare. He said to those present: "Is it not written, 'My house shall be called a house of prayer for all nations'? But you have made it a thieves' den."

Jesus here combines two passages one from the O.T.: '... for my house shall be called a house of prayer for all peoples' (Is. 56:7) and 'Has this house ... become a den of robbers in your sight?' (Jer. 7:10). What did Jesus intend by his actions? This question has been answered in several different ways, though it is agreed that his action was not simply demonstrative but also symbolic.

Some have thought his aim was to remove from the Temple the commercial transactions associated with sacrifices. Although sacrifices were a traditional part of Judaism for which the Temple existed, the whole sacrificial system had been condemned by the prophets, who had proclaimed God's wish for Israel to follow his will instead: 'I hate, I despise your feasts, and I take no delight in your solemn assemblies. Even though you offer me your burnt-offerings and cereal-offerings, I will not accept them ...' (Am. 5:21-22); 'Thus says the Lord of Hosts, the God of Israel: "Gather your burnt-offerings with your meat-offerings and eat the flesh (yourselves). For in the day that I brought them out of the land of Egypt, I did not speak to their fathers nor commanded them concerning burnt-offerings and meat-offerings. But I commanded them this: obey my voice and I will be your God and you shall be my people and walk in all the ways that I command you, that it may be well with you"' (Jer. 7:21-23).

Although these and other quotations show that the prophets and others opposed the use of sacrifices as a substitute for right conduct, many Jews believed that they were required by God in the Torah and therefore they had to be carried out, whatever men thought about them. Nevertheless some at least were clear that sacrifices had to be properly made: 'The Most High is not pleased with the offerings of the ungodly and iniquity is not atoned for by a multitude of offerings' (Sir. 34:19).

Jesus will remove the abuses and recall the priests to their proper concerns, studying the Torah and serving Israel by being an offering to God: '... my house shall be called a house of prayer for all nations.' (Is. 56:7); 'You chose this house to bear your name, to be house of prayer and supplication for your people' (I Mac. 7:37). The Temple was valueless because what God wants is righteousness not sacrifices and Jesus is shown as creating a disturbance signifying this: 'The Lord spurned his altar and laid a curse on his sanctuary ... a clamour was raised in the house of the Lord' (Lam. 2:7).

Others have suggested that Jesus' action was an attack on a corrupt priesthood, and no doubt there were grounds for complaint. The O.T. tells of the results of their misdeeds and like the Lord's messenger, Jesus came to the Temple: '"Behold, he is coming", says the Lord of Hosts. But who can endure the day of his coming ... for he is like a refiner's fire ... he will sit as a refiner and purifier of silver, and he will purify the sons of Levi and refine them as gold and silver, till they present right offerings to the Lord' (Mal. 3:1-3); 'Hear the word of the Lord, all ... who enter these gates (of the Lord's house) to worship the Lord. Amend your ways and your doings and I will cause you to dwell in this place. Do not rely on the words, "This is the temple of the Lord" ... If you truly change your ways and your doings, if you truly execute justice with one another, if you do not oppress the alien, the fatherless, the widow or shed innocent blood here and if you do not go after other gods ... then I will cause you to dwell in this place ...' (Jer. 7:2-7); 'You steal, murder, fornicate, burn sacrifices to Baal ... then you come and stand before me in this house ... and say, "We are safe!" - safe to carry on all these abominations. Do you think this house, my house, is a robber's cave?' (Jer. 7:9-11). As a robber secures his spoil in his den, so the Israelites intend to secure their debauched and rapacious life in the Temple cult.

In another pasage, Jesus prophesied that the Temple would be destroyed (see J 3), being smitten with 'leprosy', as a result of devotion to money, profit, worldly prestige and so forth. Both passages show Jesus finding the staff and practices of the Temple beyond hope of redemption.

However, the priesthood had been established by God: 'The Lord said to Moses, "Behold, I have taken the Levites from among the people of Israel ... The Levites shall be mine ... And Eleazar the son of Aaron the priest was to be chief over ... the Levites and to have charge of the sanctuary (Num. 3:11-12,32), but they had become corrupt. The lips of a priest should guard knowledge and men should seek instruction from his mouth, for he is the messenger of the Lord of Hosts. But you have turned aside from the way; you have caused many to stumble by your instructions, you have corrupted the covenant of Levi," says the Lord of Hosts' (Mal. 2:7-8).

The priesthood, and the Levites, had abused their privileged status and perhaps were too concerned with the profits from the trading for the sacrifices, of which they would take a share. It was not the first time corruption of the priests had led to their downfall. This happened to the house of Eli: 'Therefore I (the Lord) swear ... that the iniquity of Eli's house shall never be expiated by offerings or sacrifices' (I Sam. 3:14); 'After their punishment ... the priesthood shall fall. Then the Lord shall raise up a new priest ... He shall open the gates of paradise ... he shall give to the saints to eat from the tree of life and the spirit of holiness shall be on them' (T.Lev. 18:1-2,10-11).

Another opinion is that Jesus was acting as a prophet following the words of the O.T. prophets: 'There shall no longer be a trader in the house of the Lord of hosts on that day (when the Lord comes)' (Zch. 14:21); 'Because of the wickedness of their deeds I will drive them out of my house' (Hos. 9:15). The same idea is found in I.T. books: 'He [the son of David] shall glorify the Lord in a place to be seen by all the earth and purge Jerusalem making it holy as of old' (P.S. 17:32-33).

As God's servant armed with spiritual power, Jesus dealt with his enemies: 'The works of men are works of iniquity and deeds of violence are in their hands. Their feet run to evil, and they make haste to shed innocent blood ... the way of peace they know not, and there is no justice in their paths ... He will come to Zion as Redeemer, to those in Israel who turn from transgression ...' (Is. 59:6-8,20).

The word for 'table' could also mean 'altar' and as such their use for buying and selling and changing money was wholly inappropriate and the only 'chairs' were those of the chief teachers and leaders. Jesus is shown casting them down, and later on he himself begins to teach those in the Temple. A prophet was to be obeyed even against the Law. 'The Lord your God will raise up for you a prophet like me from among you ... Him you shall heed' (Dt. 18:15).

In rabbinical literature, the comment on this verse is, 'Even if he bids you transgress one of the commands in the Torah, as Elijah did on Mt. Carmel, yet according to the need of the hour, listen to him' (Sif.Dt. 107b). He was entitled to decide what was lawful and what was not: 'I have made you an assayer and tester among my people ... They are stubbornly rebellious ... all of them act corruptly ... In vain the refining goes on, for the wicked are not removed. Call them spurious silver, for the Lord has rejected them' (Jer. 6:27-30); 'They laid up the stones (of the altar) ... until a prophet should come to decide what should be done with them' (I Mac. 4:46); 'The Jews and priests were pleased that Simon should be their leader and high priest ... until a faithful prophet should arise' (I Mac. 14:41).

O.T. and I.T. books contain many passages looking forward to an improvement in the Temple which existed, and to a second Temple: 'I will set your stones in antimony and lay your foundations in sapphires. I will make your pinnacles of agate, your gates of carbuncles and your wall of precious stones' (Is. 54:11-12); 'I, the Lord, am your saviour and redeemer, the Mighty One of Israel. Instead of bronze I will bring gold; instead of iron silver; instead of wood, bronze; instead of stones, iron' (Is. 60:16-17); '"I will fill this house with splendour", says the Lord of Hosts. "The silver is mine, the gold is mine," says the Lord. The latter splendours of this house shall be greater than the former' (Hag. 2:7-9).

Others hoped for the fulfilment of Isaiah's: 'God will make a new heaven and new earth' (Is. 66:22). They looked for the obliteration of the old Temple and its replacement with one of the new kingdom from heaven: 'I stood up to see till they folded up that old house, and carried off all the pillars, all the beams and ornaments ... And the Lord ... brought a new house, greater and higher than the first and set it up in the place of the first that had been folded up' (I En. 90:28-29); 'There has come from ... heaven a blessed man with the sceptre in his hand which God has committed to his grasp ... He has destroyed every city ... and the city beloved of God he has made ... as the jewel of the world, and has made a temple, exceeding fair ...' (S.O. 5:414,419-423).

When that day came, God would provide a new Temple, and all Jerusalem would be holy: 'The pots in the house of the Lord shall be as bowls before the altar - holy. Every pot in Jerusalem and Judah shall be holy to the Lord of Hosts.' (Zch. 14:20-21).

The interpretation of this event as a prophet predicting the replacement of the man-made Temple with a Temple from God in the new kingdom after the day of Judgement, is supported by other passages, see for example J 3, but it may be valid to suggest that the report of Jesus' action has elements of all of the interpretations proposed: he was a prophet, the time for the establishment of the new kingdom was nigh, when the Temple would be replaced by a heavenly one, commercial transactions for profit did not belong within the Temple precincts, and the priesthood was guilty of promoting and maintaining the belief that sacrifices were sufficient rather than the practice of steadfast loving-kindness. It may be that Mark associated this passage with that of the 'cursed' fig tree (C 5) in order to emphasize that like the useless tree, the Temple was also withered from its roots and was bound to be destroyed by God.

By driving out the animals rather than leading them, Jesus avoided technically stealing them. By tipping over the tables and the money-bags on them, he also avoided being accused of stealing the money by lifting it. It was fully accepted at the time that the Temple was God's house. No one should carry a vessel into the Temple nor use it as a thoroughfare or short-cut, any more than they should use the Temple precincts for profit, but a blind eye was turned to it.

The blind and lame came to him in the temple, and he cured them. But when the chief priests and the scribes saw the amazing things that he did and heard the children crying out in the temple, "Hosanna to the Son of David", they became angry and said to him, "Do you hear what these are saying?"

Jesus said to them, "Yes; have you never read, 'Out of the mouths of infants and nursing babies you have prepared praise for yourself'?"

The quotation echoes the O.T.: 'Out of the mouths of babes and infants you have founded a bulwark because of your foes, to silence the enemy and the avenger' (Ps. 8:2).

The reference to the blind and lame here, as elsewhere in the N.T., may imply sinners or exiles, as they often did in the O.T. 'David had said...Whoever would strike down the Jebusites, let him ... attack the lame and blind, those whom David hates' (2 Sam.5:8). The response of Jesus was rather different. He wanted all to be restored to full health or faithfulness: 'I will save the lame and gather the outcast, and I will change their shame into praise and renown in all the earth' (Zph. 3:19); 'To the eunuchs who keep my sabbaths ... and hold fast to my covenant, I will give a monument and a name better than sons and daughters; ... and the foreigners who join themselves to the Lord to minister to him ... to be his servants ... and hold fast my covenant, these I will bring to my holy mountain and make them joyful in my house of prayer' (Is. 56:4-7). Many believed such conditions must be achieved before the Kingdom of God could be fully manifest.

* * *

G 2. Fasts and feasts - Mt. 9:14-17. Mk. 2:18-22. Lk. 5:33-39.

Fasting was required by the Law only on the day of atonement: '... it is a day of atonement ... on your behalf before the Lord your God. For anyone who does not fast during the entire day shall be cut off from the people' (Lev. 23:28-29). Fasting was common in time of sorrow and was sometimes used to show contrition before God, or to avert God's wrath. 'I have kept a fast: count my loss of fat and blood as a sacrifice' was a prayer in the rabbinical literature (b.Ber.17a)!

Fasting was forbidden on Sabbaths and festival days and was not considered to be part of God's will for his people. Most Jews rejected any idea of excessive asceticism. They said that the world and its blessings were given by God and man should not refuse them: 'Rejoicing at a feast is a religious duty' (b.Pes. 68b). Some even went so far as to say such refusal might be sinful: 'He who fasts and makes a display of himself to others, to boast of his fasting, is punished for this' is a rabbinical saying (m.Avot. 1:13, 4:7).

Once when Jesus and his friends were having a feast with Levi, some people came to him and asked, "Why do not your disciples fast when John's disciples and the Pharisees are fasting?"

Jesus replied, "Can you expect the bridegroom's friends and wedding guests to fast in mourning while the bridegroom is with them? The time will come when the bridegroom will be taken away from them; then they will fast."

The evangelists tell this story as if Jesus and his disciples were analogous to God and the Israelites in Egypt. God called the Israelites to partake of a feast with him in the wilderness: 'Afterwards Moses and Aaron went to Pharaoh and said. "Our Lord, the God of Israel, says, 'Let my people go, that they may hold a feast with me in the wilderness'"' (Ex. 5:1). This was the first time they had had such a feast, which became the first Passover feast, the feast of redemption. It was celebrated the night before the "wedding" of God and his "bride", Israel. God had offered all Israel his covenant and had saved them from their slavery in Egypt.

Ever since, Passover had celebrated the separation of the righteous Israel from the unrighteous Egypt: 'You shall eat it (the Passover lamb) in haste. It is the Lord's Passover ... This day shall be for you a memorial day and you shall keep it as a feast to the Lord, throughout your generations you shall observe it as an ordinance for ever' (Ex. 12:11,14). The Israelites' happiness was Egypt's sorrow. Since then, Israel had debased her obedience to God, beginning with the time when she mixed with the heathen tribes in Canaan.

According to this passage, Jesus had come to offer those who would turn from these false gods, those who repented of their sinfulness, a new (marriage) covenant. They could begin again and live in God's realm. Even during an ordinary wedding fasting was excluded, but during this, the equivalent of the greatest of all feasts in Israel, fasting was unthinkable.

It may also be significant that the word translated 'bridegroom' is the same as that of the man described in the Song of Solomon as he whose name is like perfume poured out or spread over, namely the anointed one, the Messiah. As the bride in the Song of Solomon yearns for her bridegroom: 'I sought him but found him not, I called him, but he gave no answer' (S.S. 5:6), so the new Israel would mourn when the Bridegroom was taken from her (the Bride).

This passage shows Jesus agreed with neither the practices of the Pharisees nor those of John the baptizer, who seemed to have extended the single biblical fast once a year to many, and later on, one or two a week.

These ideas are intertwined with the later events of Jesus' death on Passover eve, which, in the early church, seems to have been seen as an atonement for the sins of Israel. Like the Israelites who failed to fulfil God's wishes, there would come a time when feasting would come to an end and mourning would be necessary: 'The people ... mourned in mourning apparel, for the Lord said to the children of Israel, "You are a stiff-necked people ... So now put off your ornaments and your glorious apparel ..."' (Ex. 33:4-5). The situation was repeating itself; Jesus and his followers were the happy righteous ones of the New Israel, while the leaders of the Old Israel were the unrighteous 'Egyptians' of their time who ought to be most unhappy!

Jesus continued, "It is no use trying to mend old clothes with a piece of unfulled material[1]: it will only shrink and make the tear worse, and the two pieces won't match anyway! Again, no one would use old wineskins for new wine. The skins would burst and both skins and wine would be lost. Fresh skins for new wine!

The passages describe a time when Jesus and his friends were eating together, and at a feast torn garments were not appropriate. A tear meant mourning and sorrow: 'When King Hezekiah heard it (the threat of the besieging Assyrian king), he rent his clothes and covered himself with sackcloth' (Is. 37:1); 'Then Jacob rent his garments and put sackcloth on his loins and mourned his son many days' (Gen. 37:34), and in many cases even a patched garment would be unacceptable. Once torn for mourning, a garment was to be discarded.

The second of the two passages suggest that the content and practice of Judaism by the religious leaders of the time should be discarded and the new covenant of Jesus followed instead. Using new material to try to mend an old garment was not sensible and to put fermenting new wine into old stiff wine-skins was asking for trouble. They would burst and both wine and the skins would be lost. The 'Old Israel' cannot contain the message and deeds required in the New Era.

A further sentence, found only in Luke says:

No one wants the new wine after drinking the old, for he thinks the old is better.

This implies that the old covenant was better than the new - a most unlikely interpretation. One suggestion is that Luke was pointing out how those used to the old refuse to change their opinion - they show their prejudice in favour of what they know rather than being willing to try something new. Another explanation is that Jesus was referring to the first covenant with Adam in the Garden of Eden before it was corrupted by his sin, and which Jesus was proclaiming. It is not possible to be certain at the present time what Luke intended.

In rabbinical writings, there is a story that the Egyptians were blown up and ready to burst like wine-skins containing fermenting wine, and that is why they floated on the water when they tried to pursue the Israelites at the Exodus (Mek. Shir. 2:51). 'Elihu felt the same: 'Elius (Elihu) said, "I will again speak for I am full of words, for the spirit in my belly destroys me. My belly is as a skin of new sweet wine tied up and ready to burst or as a brazier's bellows'" (Job 32:17-19). They could not cope with the ferment of the Lord in their bellies. The same applied to Jesus' situation: the new wine of the message was too strong for the skins of Old Israel.

[1] Unfulled material has not been treated to stop it shrinking.

* * *

G 3. The (un)scrupulous bailiff - Mt. 6:24. Lk. 16:1-15.

In attempting to understand this parable, it is useful to have some knowledge of the relation between a master and his bailiff or steward at the time of Jesus.

In a rich household there would be slaves, servants and one or two trusted bailiffs. A bailiff was the agent of the master and could act on the master's behalf, incurring or cancelling debts, fixing prices, setting times for debt repayment and giving loans. If he was dishonest, a bailiff could prove a serious problem to his master. However, he could also be dishonest with the master's approval or even under the master's instruction, a situation which was fraught with difficulty for the bailiff, since only he suffered from the sin involved. The master was exonerated!

Usury was contrary to the Torah, the Law, and was therefore sinful; unfortunately it was also almost inevitable for poorer people to need a loan, especially at times such as spring-sowing, when it was necessary to get seeds etc.: 'Lend to your neighbour in his time of need; repay your neighbour punctually' (Sir. 29:2). Few were willing to lend without security and without interest, and a system grew up of 'deaf' or 'silent' usury. This was permitted by the religious leaders if the arrangement benefited both parties, the poor farmer who needed to buy seed and the richer man who needed to safeguard his credit by charging interest.

Interest rates of between 30 and 100% were common at the time, depending on the commodity borrowed. In an agreement between a lender and a borrower, dating from 34CE, no interest is mentioned because it was simply added by the lender to the debt. There was also an extra penalty of 50% of the total amount for not repaying it by the due date (P.Oxy. 3351). Often the time for repayment would arrive before the crop could be harvested, and it is no wonder that many of the poor were chronically indebted to richer persons.

There were many dodges to avoid appearing to transgress the Law of usury. The contract could say that the lender had lent more than he in fact had, so that principle and interest were included in the amount the borrower had to pay back. Another way was not to specify the date of repayment. This permitted endless postponement for repayment of the capital but constant interest for the lender. Thirdly, the religious leaders said that interest on loans of goods such as corn, oil, salt etc., was not usury. So loans of money could specify repayment in goods such as corn, oil, or salt to a greater value than the loan, theoretically without incurring usury. Similarly, it was accepted that one who lent some oil or meal to his neighbour did not transgress the law of usury even though the value of the oil or meal to be returned was much more than the value of the original loan.

Judaism was riddled with such devious thinking although there are rabbinical texts which condemned usury: 'Usurers are comparable to shedders of blood' (b.B.M. 61b), and usurers were not allowed to give evidence in a court of law (m.San. 3:3).

How did Jesus react to all this? As so often, he fought against the arrangement created by the religious leaders which modified and nullified the Law.

"There was a rich man", said Jesus, "who had a bailiff to look after the affairs of the estate. The master heard rumours that things were not as they should have been; he had been told the bailiff was squandering the estate's possessions.

So the bailiff was sent for, to give an account of his dealings. His master told him he could not continue in his service and that he must produce his accounts.

'Whatever shall I do when I am removed from my stewardship', he said to himself. 'I'm not a labourer and I am ashamed to be a beggar! I know what to do when I leave my position, so that people will receive me into their houses!

He summoned one by one those who owed money to his master and to the first he said, 'How much do you owe my master?'

'I owe for a hundred barrels of oil', replied the man.

'Right', said the bailiff. 'Quickly take your bill and make out a new order for fifty barrels.'

To the next he said, 'How much do you owe my master?'

'Well', said the man, 'I owe for a hundred sacks of wheat.'

'Very well', said the bailiff. 'Take your bill and write out a new one for eighty.'

The master praised the bailiff for his actions: he acted shrewdly as the worldly do in dealing with their own kind. The sons of this age are more shrewd in dealing with their own generation than are the sons of light.

So I tell you this: make friends for yourselves by means of unrighteous ill-gotten wealth so that when it is gone they may receive you into the eternal tabernacles."

It was not unusual for a rich man to live part of the time abroad and to leave his estate in the care of a bailiff or steward; and there were no auditors to check the books! For the purposes of this parable, the bailiff fell out of favour because of his supposed dishonesty. He is called to account and is told he is to be dismissed. He has to make up his books and produce them for checking so that his replacement could take over. Perhaps it was harvest time when the accounts of the year were due to be completed.

The situation was critical for the bailiff. Unemployment was rife at the time and a dishonest bailiff was unemployable. He had to find a solution.

The last part of the passage seems to tell those who follow God to make sure they win friends with their money and that is how to reach the kingdom of God! This was not unknown in Judaism: 'If a person is wise to his own advantage, the fruits of his good sense will be praiseworthy (trustworthy)' (Sir. 37:22).

Some have thought that was a call to prepare for the next life, while others have pointed out that to give alms was supposed to be a sign of repentance so that God will accept the giver into his realm. Certainly, any money from usury was 'unclean' and it could not legitimately be used for the benefit of the usurer, nor given to the Temple. Its only use was to give it to the poor. Thus when a worldly person does improperly practise usury, to give it away as alms is the best use for it.

Some think this passage has connections with: 'You shall not surrender to his master a slave who has taken refuge with you. Let him stay with you anywhere he chooses in any one of your settlements, wherever suits him best; you shall not force or oppress him' (Dt. 23:15-16).

One explanation of the bailiff's behaviour is that he hit upon the idea of releasing the debtors from any usury on their debts, a nice example of the Jewish saying: 'The wine belongs to the master but the butler receives the thanks!'; 'Everyone ... that withholds his hands from receiving a bribe ... his dwelling place shall be ... the sanctuary' (Tg.Is. 33:15-16); 'Woe unto ... men of wealth ... which justify the guilty because they receive unjust gain from them' (Tg.Is. 5:22-23). This would cause them to be grateful to him, but it would also absolve him from the sin of exacting usury too. Through force of circumstance he adopted a righteous mode of action. At this level, the parable teaches that a good action remains good even if it is brought about by force of circumstances, the same lesson taught by the passage of E 4.

Others think that the release of part of the debt relates to Jubilee years when creditors were to cancel debts.

The master, when he found out, praised his bailiff. Actually he could do little else unless he wished to stand out and admit he approved of sinfully violating the Torah. The bailiff's righteousness also prevented the master from spreading slanderous rumours about the bailiff. The master realised that the steward had had a change of heart, excusing the debtors the usury they had hitherto been charged, and he had to accept the situation and act as though he approved.

This understanding means the teaching of this parable is similar to that of other passages in the gospels. God was anxious to cancel or scale down the debts of those who repented (see E 6). Worldly people may do wrong things, but when they change and wish to follow God, they are not held back by inappropriate scruples nor disingenuous juristic subtlety. The disciples should not reject others even though polluted with worldly wealth: 'sharing wealth could lead to sharing heavenly things which are true.'

The religious leaders were largely concerned to avoid any apparent transgressions of the Law so that they could retain their prestige among men for their apparent piety but they also evolved ways of diluting God's laws so that small transgressions were accepted for comfort and convenience. These small deviations from the law were called "dusts" of laws, for example the laws of usury, using money borrowed from a neighbour; agricultural activity not expressly forbidden in the sabbatical year; idolatry, doing business with neighbours during a heathen festival; and slander, by gossiping about neighbours (b.Suk. 40b). Such convenient small deviations from the law mitigated the rigour of some of the precepts of the Torah, and were accepted and practised in Jewish society. They were not what Jesus advocated. The lesson to be learned was that another kind of disaster was approaching, far worse than any concerned with material well-being. Those who did not take drastic action now to change their ways would be excluded from God's realm.

Several have found this explanation unsatisfactory. Some have suggested that the sentence in which the master praises his bailiff should be a question: 'Did the master praise the unfaithful bailiff for his actions?' The expected answer would be 'No', which would accord with the sentiment of the second group of verses given below.

There is unfortunately also no agreement that the Greek means that is was the master rather than Jesus who praised the bailiff. If the latter were the case, it seems incredible to suppose Jesus wanted to encourage dishonest conduct and to approve the worldly children rather than the children of light. This has led some to suggest that the 'mammon of unrighteousness' may be used wisely for the benefit of the down-trodden and poor, and the story shows God (the Lord) as a gracious and demanding master who praises skilful generosity.

Nonetheless, it seems possible that it could be a cry of despairing irony: 'Yes, follow the worldly ones: those who think they can buy themselves out of trouble will receive their reward. They'll surely end up in the eternal dwellings of the worshippers of mammon!' In some ways this is rather like the cry, 'You faithless and perverse generation, how much longer must I be with you and bear with you?' (I 2).

Then follow several more verses:

"One who can be trusted in little things can be trusted also in great; a man dishonest over small matters will be dishonest over great things. If then you have not shown yourself trustworthy with unrighteous mammon, how can you be trusted with real wealth? If you have proved unfaithful with another's belongings, who will give you what is your own?

No servant can serve two masters. Either he will hate the one and love the other, or vice versa. You cannot be the servant of God and money at the same time."

This passage teaches about the danger of slight deviations from the true path soon lead to bigger ones. As the rabbinical literature has it: 'One commandment leads to another and one transgression leads to another. The reward for a commandment carried out is another one to be carried out. The reward for a transgression is another transgression' (ARN 25).

'Every word of God proves true; he is a shield to those who take refuge in him' (Pvb. 30:5). This was understood as meaning that God tests a man with a small task and if successful he would be given a greater. The passage demands allegiance to God's rule, rather than allegiance to worldly wealth, although the first part of this section and the parable of the use of resources (E 7) show that even worldly wealth can be used for God's benefit. Attention, though, must not be divided between money and God's purposes. 'Beware ... of promiscuity and the love of money ... for these things withdraw you from the Law of God' (T.Jud. 18:2-3). There was only one master to obey: 'You shall serve the Lord your God ... You shall not go after other gods' (Dt. 6:13-14); 'I am the Lord your God. You shall therefore keep my statutes and my ordinances, by doing which a man shall live' (Lev. 18:4-5).

Finally there is a paragraph which is included here as well as in the parable of the foolish rich man because it is not clear whether it is the end of the passage of G3 or the beginning of G 4.

> **The Pharisees who loved money[1], heard all this and scoffed at Jesus. He said to them, "You justify yourselves before men but God sees through you and knows your hearts. What is exalted among men is abomination in the sight of God."**

This is a severe denunciation of those who are so perfidious they are worse than those who are simply worldly. They are the pious ones who are concerned not openly to transgress the Law by one iota. The pride lying at the heart of this passage is idolatry, an abomination to God: 'Every one who is full of pride is an abomination to the Lord' (Pvb. 16:5); 'Our souls are full of money from the exploitation of others; it does not save us from descending into oppressing Sheol' (I En. 63:10); 'Trust not in unrighteous mammon, for it shall profit you nothing in the day of wrath' (Sir. 5:8).

[1] It is not true that most of the Pharisees were particularly lovers of money, unlike the Sadducees. Many think it was the Sadducees who scoffed at Jesus' ideas about mammon. The language plays on the name Sadducee and the phrase 'to justify oneself'.

* * *

G 4. The rich man and Lazarus - Lk. 16:14-15, 19-31.

A group of Pharisees had been pouring scorn on Jesus' demand for honesty in full accordance with the Law, in matters of money. They laughed about it and Jesus warned them by saying, "You justify yourselves before men, but God sees through you and knows your hearts. What is exalted among men is abomination in the sight of God."

He continued, "There was once a rich man, a reveller, feasting in great extravagance every day, dressed in fine linen and a purple cloak. At the entrance to his house there lay a crippled beggar named Lazarus, cast down in the street. He was always hungry and wished to eat even the things which fell from the rich man's table. Poor Lazarus was covered with sores, but sometimes the dogs would come and lick them for him.

Lazarus died and was carried away by angels to be with Abraham. The rich man also died and was buried. In Hades he was in torment, and looking up, far away he saw Lazarus standing with Abraham. 'Father Abraham', he called, 'please take pity on me! Let Lazarus dip the tip of his finger in the water to cool my tongue, for I am in agony in this fire.'

But Abraham said, 'Remember child, all the good things you had when you were alive, and all the misery Lazarus suffered; now your fortunes are reversed. He is in comfort here and it is you who suffer the torments. In any case, you know it is impossible to cross the divide between you; none can pass from the one side to the other.'

'Then father Abraham', said the rich man, 'Please send Lazarus to my five brothers to witness to them about my fate, that they do not come to this place of torment.' 'No', said Abraham. 'They have Moses and the prophets to guide them. They should hear them.'

'But if someone from the dead goes to them with the message, they will listen and repent', said the rich man.

Abraham replied, 'If they do not listen to the scriptures they are the sort of people who will not believe even if someone rose from the dead.'

The rest of the story about Bar Ma'jam and the poor scholar (given in connection with the story of the great feast, E 4), is similar to this passage and is as follows: 'One of the poor man's friends saw in a dream the poor scholar in paradise, watered by a stream of sweet water, while Bar Ma'jam stood trying to reach the water, but he could not.'

This story is derived from a popular Egyptian folk-tale, known from several centuries before the time of Jesus, but there are closer parallels with some of the writings of some Greek philosophers, the Cynics. They emphasized that it was the hedonism, the unbridled immorality, which their wealth permitted, which condemned rich people.

In this passage the contrasts are exaggerated. The rich man, sometimes (incorrectly) called Dives, feasted everyday in extravagant luxury, while the Law said six days were to be used for labour and the seventh for rest and feasting. Lazarus, on the other hand, was so decrepit, the dogs licked his suppurating sores! He belonged to one of those groups said in rabbinical writings to be the three groups of people who have no life worth living: 'He who depends on the table of another for food, he who is ruled by his wife, and he who is burdened with sufferings' (b.Bez. 32b).

The rich man symbolized those who, like his brothers - that is like some of the religious leaders - knew of the Torah and Prophets but did not behave as God's word demanded. They were not ignorant of the covenant; they deliberately chose to be selfish and secular, and there was no likelihood that such people would change their wicked wilful inclinations, even by a person returning from the dead. Like so many, the very fact that they will have an unambiguous sign shows they will not accept God's word by faith.

Lazarus had to suffer at his gate where his only kindness was from dogs, which the Jews considered were unclean. That an excess of material goods, or wealth, should be shared with less fortunate brethren and that the rich are destined for hell-fire, were a common ideas in the O.T. and I.T. writings: 'Untie every burden of iniquity ... set the bruised free and cancel every unjust account. Break your bread to the hungry and lead the unsheltered poor to your house' (Is. 58:6-7 LXX); 'Woe to you who devour the finest wheat, and drink wine from large bowls and tread the lowly underfoot with your might' (I En. 96:5); 'They that have died in prosperity and wealth ... their souls will ... descend into Sheol ... into darkness and chains and a burning flame, where there is grievous judgement ...' (I En. 103:6-8), but the righteous would go to paradise: 'The spirits of you who have died in righteousness shall live and rejoice' (I En. 103:4).

The name 'Lazarus' is a Greek version of the Hebrew name Eliezer meaning 'the one whom God helps'. Eliezer was Abraham's heir before Abraham got children of his own and was considered to be Abraham's agent. One implication of this is that he was sent from heaven to investigate the rich man's moral life. The rich man's spiritual 'door-keeper' (see B 1), had had wrong instructions from his master, namely to exclude any hint of the need for compassion and to allow his 'servants' full rein. The result was a gross display of sensuality with no thought for others worse off than himself.

Thirst is a characteristic of the torments of hell while fresh water belongs in paradise: 'A part has been made for the spirits of the righteous in which there is the bright spring of water. And a section has been made for sinners when they die and are buried ... Here their spirits shall be set apart in great pain till the great day of Judgement' (I En. 22:9-10); 'They despised the Most High and scorned his Law ... so thirst and anguish await them' (IV Ezr. 8:56,59). After Judgement, the righteous would be summoned to heaven and the wicked would be dismissed to hell's fires and torments. Only the most saintly would ever go straight to heaven as Lazarus is made to do.

In paradise Lazarus is elevated to lie on Abraham's bosom, in other words to sit in one of the places reserved for those of greatest honour, and, as in much of Jewish literature, the good and the evil could see each other after death, the former in paradise enjoying blessings and the latter suffering torments in hell: 'You shall look from on high and see your enemies (in Gehenna) and you shall recognize them and rejoice ...' (A.M. 10:10); 'I will give them over into the hands of My Elect, as straw in the fire they shall burn before the face of the holy' (I En. 48:9); 'In those days Sheol shall open its jaws and they shall be swallowed up therein ... and it shall devour the sinners in the presence of the elect' (I En. 56:8); 'The pit of torment shall appear and opposite it shall be the place of rest; and the furnace of hell shall be disclosed and opposite it the paradise of delight' (IV Ezr. 7:36). There is an abyss between them, like that found in the O.T.: 'For the Lord, high as he is, cares for the lowly, but from afar he humbles the proud' (Ps. 138:6).

This belief allows no room for forgiveness after judgement, a viewpoint wholly in agreement with some rabbinical thought: 'There may be two sinners in partnership in this world; one repents before his death, the other does not. One joins the company of the righteous, the other the company of the wicked...This is the gate of the Lord, and only the righteous shall enter therein' (Ruth.R. 3:3, a commentary on: 'The crooked cannot be made straight, and what is lacking cannot be supplied.' in Ecc. 1:15). Others took a kinder view: 'There will be on eternal punishment in Gehenna' (b.B.M. 58b).

* * *

G 5. The children in the town square - Mt. 11:16-19. Lk. 7:31-35.

Jesus, exasperated and saddened by the perverse resistance of the religious leaders to his teaching, remonstrates with them.

How can I describe this generation? You are like a lot of children who sit in the main square pronouncing judgement: 'We played our flutes and you would not dance; we lamented and you did not mourn.'
John the Baptizer has come neither eating bread nor drinking wine and you say, 'He is possessed'. Then the son of man has come eating and drinking and you say, 'Look, a glutton and drunkard, a friend of tax-collectors and of sinners!'
Yet Wisdom is justified by all her children.

There is here a reference perhaps to the O.T.: 'This son of ours is stubborn and rebellious, he will not obey our voice; he is a glutton and drunkard. Then all the men of the city shall stone him to death with stones' (Dt. 21:20-21).

In every town or city there was an open area, with a raised platform at one point, where people would congregate for town business, festivities, court trials and the issue of judgements. The picture is of play-acting children who sit and play their pipes or wail and lament. They expect others to respond, the boys by dancing the round dance and girls by acting out a funeral: 'Teach your daughters to lament, let them teach one another this dirge; death has come in through the windows, it has entered our palaces' (Jer. 9:20-21). They do not get up themselves to do anything, but they complain others do not do what they tell them.

The religious leaders are pictured sitting there, pronouncing judgement on their contemporaries, but they are like petulant children. They adopt postures of dignity and importance, but what sort of judgements do they give? They said John who fasted was mad, and Jesus who ate like ordinary folk, was a glutton and drunkard, deserving stoning! They rejected John and Jesus, who had come to warn them; the 'Old' Israel did not see what was going to happen and that it would go down to destruction.

In the messianic age discerning men who can read the signs of the times are needed, as men of the tribe of Issachar had done in the time of David: 'Of Issachar, men who had understanding of the times to know what Israel ought to do ...' (I Chr. 12:32). Nor had they remembered God's words to Isaiah if they would change their ways: 'The Lord God will swallow death for ever. He will wipe away the tears from every face and remove the reproach of this people from the whole earth' (Is. 25:8). They were avoiding God's call and lost the future offered by God, by attempting to control it.

The kingdom of God had already dawned in Jesus' ministry and those who failed to see this were spiritually hard or dead. The very judgements of these charlatans demonstrated their silliness, and that they knew nothing of Wisdom and her children. It was the actions and teachings of John and Jesus and their followers which showed that they were the true children of Wisdom and who did her work.

In Judaism, Wisdom was thought of as God's Son or Wife; in the last chapter of Proverbs for example, Wisdom is described as a perfect wife, mother and mistress of the household (Pvb. 31:10-31). She is also sometimes the Torah: 'Wisdom is the book of the commandments of God, the Law that stands for ever. All who hold fast to her shall live, but those who forsake her shall die. Return Israel, because we know what is pleasing to God' (I Bar. 4:1-4); 'Hear how Wisdom lifts her voice and Understanding cries out' (Pvb. 8:1); 'Blessed be God's name ... for all wisdom and power are his ... he gives wisdom to the wise, and all their store of knowledge to the men who know' (Dan. 2:20-21); 'The fruits of Wisdom's labours are the virtues of temperance, prudence, justice and fortitude' (IV Mac. 1:18). On the other hand, some said God's first born was Israel: 'Have mercy O Lord ... on Israel whom you have named your first born' (Sir. 36:17). God was head of Israel: 'I [God] have forsaken my house' (Jer. 12:7); 'One like a vulture is over the house of the Lord because Israel has broken the covenant ...' (Hos. 8:1).

* * *

G 6. The wicked vineyard tenants - Mt. 21:33-46. Mk. 12:1-12. Lk. 20:9-19.

This parable assumes a certain acquaintance with Jewish custom and law, something which Jesus' listeners would be very familiar with and which they would notice in the course of the story.

To start up a vineyard was a complex process, a speculative project for a rich man to indulge in. It required equipment for pruning and training the trees, and it required skilled people to tend them. All boundaries also were to be clearly marked, otherwise someone might eat of the fruit in the first three years, before the fruit was tithed in the fourth year: 'When you come into the land (of Canaan) and plant all kinds of trees for food, then you shall count their fruit as forbidden; three years it shall be forbidden to you, it must not be eaten. And in the fourth year all their fruit shall be holy, an offering of praise to the Lord. But in the fifth year you may eat of their fruit, that they may yield more richly for you' (Lev. 19:23-25).

The situation became even more complicated when there was a Sabbatical year. Crops, grapes, olives and other fruits which are not ready at the end of the sixth year can be harvested at the beginning of the seventh (Sabbatical) year. Crops which grow in the Sabbatical year but which are ready for harvesting after the beginning of the first year may not be harvested, as they have grown during the Sabbatical year.

There were many laws regulating the relation between tenants and owner; in summary the expenditure involved in the first few years would outweigh the returns from the vineyard, and would be borne by the owner, but any small profit from, for example, vegetables grown while the trees were small, had to be shared between the tenants and the owner.

It was essential for the owner to claim his share each year, trivial though it might be. If he did not, it could be construed as lack of interest in the vineyard. Were this to happen for three successive years, or four if the owner was abroad, the tenants could become the owners.

To fetch the share due to him, the owner could send a slave. To assert his ownership against intransigent tenants, he himself, or an agent with full powers, such as his son, had to visit them.

"Let me tell you a story", said Jesus. "A man planted a vineyard, put a fence round it, dug out a pit for the winepress and wine vat and built a tower. He then let it out to vine-growers and went to live abroad. When the time came to claim his share of the produce, he sent one of his slaves to collect it. The tenants beat the slave and sent him back empty. The owner sent a second slave and then a third, but they too, were badly beaten, wounded and disgracefully treated and sent back empty.

The owner then said, 'What am I to do? I will send my own dear son. They will respect him.' However, the tenants supposed the son was now owner of the vineyard. 'Let us kill him', they said. 'Then the vineyard will be ours.' They took the son, killed him and threw his body outside the vineyard.

What would the owner of the vineyard do to them? He will come and destroy the tenants and put others in charge of the vineyard."

On hearing this those listening said, "Far from it: that shall not happen!"

Jesus said to them, "Have you never understood the text, 'The stone which the builders rejected has become the main corner-stone'? Any man who falls on that stone will be dashed to pieces and if it falls on a man he will be crushed by it."

The chief priests and doctors of the Law saw that the parable was aimed at them and began to seek a method of getting rid of Jesus, but they were afraid of popular feeling, so they left him and went away.

The tenants were rapacious and wanted to steal the vineyard for themselves, behaviour which was by no means unknown at the time. They beat the first slave sent by the owner and took from him his sandals and cloak ; they sent him back 'empty'. This was a sign from the tenants that they asserted that the owner owed them money, rather than the other way round. They did the same the following year and the year after that too.

By the fourth year the owner had to act, and he decided to send his son. The tenants acted as if they supposed the father had died, so that those occupying his property would become its owners if they got rid of the son. They took the risk, killed the son and dumped the body outside the vineyard. This was to avoid polluting the vineyard with a corpse; otherwise they could never sell either grapes or wine from the vineyard. The owner was not dead though, and decided to exact retribution on the wicked tenants. He came to the vineyard and cast out the wicked tenants, and let others take over.

At this level, the parable is a warning against dishonesty and avarice, and depicts how a little dishonesty in calculating how much the tenants owed the owner and how much the owner owed the tenants, at the end of the first year - how this dishonesty and greed grew each year, culminating in murder and total depravity. This concept is found in the O.T. and rabbinical writings: 'The wicked man will be trapped by his iniquities; he will be caught by the ropes of his sin' (Pvb. 5:22). In a comment on 'You who drag iniquity along with cords of falsehood, who drag sin along as with cart-ropes' (Is. 5:18), it is written: 'The beginning of sin is as thin as a strand of a spider's web but its end is as thick as a cart-rope' (b.Suk.52a). See also G3.

Allegorically, the vineyard's owner may represent God, the vineyard his creation, the world, the son the Messiah and the tenants the Jews who should cultivate God's word, the Torah: 'You, Lord, brought a vine out of Egypt; you drove out the nations and planted it. You cleared the ground, it took deep root and filled the land ... Turn again O God of Hosts! Look down from heaven and see; have regard for this vine, the stock which your right hand planted, and on the son (Israel) whom you have reared for yourself' (Ps. 80:8-9,14-15).

Since the days of the creation and the Garden of Eden, God had been away, 'abroad', Israel had become more and more disobedient to the original contract, the covenant. 'The wicked plundered the holy things of God, as though there was no one to inherit and redeem them' (P.S. 8:11). They had usurped God's authority in favour of their own, but God would reassert his ownership and throw out the corrupt (present) tenants and give the vineyard to others who could be trusted to be obedient.

The story has other affinities with the O.T. in which the prophets had called Israel to recognize her sinfulness: 'My beloved had a vineyard on a very fertile hill. He dug it and cleared it of stones and planted it with choice vines and built a watchtower ... and hewed out a wine-press and vat in it. He looked for it to yield (good) grapes but it gave only wild grapes... Why ... did it yield wild grapes? ... I will take away the fences and let it be burnt, I will break down the walls and let it be trampled under foot, and I will leave it derelict ... For the vineyard of the Lord of Hosts is Israel and the men of Judah are the plant he loved; he looked for justice, but behold, bloodshed; he looked for righteousness, but behold, cries of woe!' (Is. 5:1-7). The Aramaic form of these verses is: 'And I sanctified them (the Israelites) and honoured them and established them like ... a chosen vine. I built my sanctuary among them. I gave them my altar to make atonement for their sins ... I will take my presence from them and they shall be for booty; I will break down their sanctuaries and they shall be for trampling underfoot' (Tg.Is. 5:2,5). At the time this song of the vineyard meant that it was the Sadducees who were failing the Temple and should be removed and the immediate response by the religious leaders shows that they were fully aware of the thrust of the parable.

The wine-press of Isaiah was supposed to represent the channel which took the liquids from the sacrifices on the altar to outside the Temple. These liquids were the wine of the Lord, which accounted for the prophecy: 'The leaves of all kinds of trees will not wither nor their fruit fail, but they will bear fresh fruit every month, because the water for them flows from the sanctuary' (Ezk. 47:12).

The passage would also remind the hearers of the garden of Eden, which in Ezekiel's words is God's garden: 'You were in Eden, the garden of God ... on the holy mountain of God' (Ezk. 28:13-14), that is the Temple and the Temple mount.

The tenants of God's garden or vineyard betrayed his trust in them and they had to be removed. God is not bound unconditionally to his covenant people, when they are so unfaithful and do not keep their side of the bargain. God could bring destruction, take away the Temple and the altar, and replace the institutions intended to guard them: 'The Lord opens the indictment against the leaders of this people and their officers: you have ravaged the vineyard ...' (Is. 3:14); 'I planted you as a choice red vine, true stock all of you, yet now you are turned into a debased and worthless vine' (Jer. 2:21); 'Israel is like a rank vine ripening its fruit; the more fruit, the more altars were built; the better the land becomes, the more beautiful become the sacred monuments. They are false and must bear their guilt. God will break down their altars and destroy their pillars' (Hos. 10:1-2).

In I.T. books also: 'I will recall the time that was before the creation of the world when man did not exist and there was no wickedness in it, when I said that the world would be created and those who would come into it would praise me. I would plant a great vineyard, and from it I would choose a plant; and I would care for it and call it by my name and it would be mine for ever ... Nevertheless my plant, that was called by my name, did not recognize me as its planter but destroyed its own fruit and did not yield up its fruit to me' (P.P. 28:4).

This allegorical understanding is not the only one possible. There are grounds for thinking that the parable may have been told in connection with the attempt of the Temple priests to challenge Jesus' right to teach others, during which Jesus puts the question as to how they judge John's baptism (see H 8). Then the owner of the vineyard represents God, the tenants were the contemporary religious leaders and the son, John the Baptizer, whom Jesus called the last of the prophets. He had been rejected by the chief priests and elders, and killed by Herod. The questioners themselves were among the guilty, unfit to care for God's vineyard any longer.

At least some of the audience were alarmed at the idea and protested. Jesus then quoted, 'I will praise you, for you answered me and have become my deliverer. The stone the builders rejected, it became the head of the corner. This is the Lord's doing; it is marvellous in our eyes' (Ps. 118:21-23). Jesus uses the quotation to drive home his assessment of the attitudes of the religious leaders as totally misleading and wrong. They think they have chosen the foundations, the walls and the headstones of the quoins, but the corner-stone they had rejected was in fact God's word.

Moreover, the word for builders also could mean scholars, while 'corner-stone' could mean 'leader of the people'. Thus the story could be intended to mean also that Jesus tells his listeners that they, the scholars of the Law, have rejected the correct leader of Israel and become false leaders themselves. They were deaf to the warning of Jeremiah: 'No stone shall be taken from you (Babylon) for a corner and no stone for a foundation, but you shall be a perpetual waste, says the Lord' (Jer. 51:26). No wonder they plotted to be rid of someone who dared to say such things about them.

The head or corner stone stands on the intersection of two walls, adding weight to the angle, binding the walls together. In some cases the term refers to a foundation stone: 'These are the words of the Lord God: I am laying a stone in Zion, a tested block of granite, a precious corner-stone for a firm foundation' (Is. 28:16); 'Where were you when I laid the earth's foundations? On what do its supporting pillars rest? Who set its corner-stone in place?' (Job 38:4-6). The stone which will crush when it falls may refer to Daniel's prophecy: '... the God of heaven will set up a kingdom that shall never be destroyed ... It shall crush all these [other] kingdoms ... just as ... a stone cut from the mountains not by human hands, ... crushed the iron, the bronze, the clay, the silver and the gold' (Dan. 2:44). The idea of stumbling over it, that is to sin, is also found in the O.T.: 'But the Lord of hosts, him shall you fear, and let him be your dread. And his presence will be among you to be a stone of offence and rock of stumbling to both houses of Israel, a trap and snare to the inhabitants of Jerusalem, and many shall stumble thereon; they shall fall and be broken, they shall be snared and taken' (Is. 8:13-15). This passage is an example of the differences which sometimes are to be found in the Greek version, the Septuagint: 'Sanctify the Lord himself; and he shall be your fear. If you shall trust in him he shall be to you a sanctuary; and you shall not come against him as against a stumbling-stone, neither as against the falling of a rock: but the houses of Jacob are in a snare, and the dwellers in Jerusalem in a pit. Therefore many among them shall be weak, and fall, and be crushed ...' (Is. 8:13-15 LXX).

In Jewish commentaries, the head-stone at the corner refers to David and the builders are Samuel and Jesse who rejected him. This idea is also found in the documents of Qumran relating to Psalm 151. There is a play on Hebrew words: ben (son), banim (sons), bonim (builders), even (stone), avanim (stones) and the religious leaders sometimes called themselves 'builders'.

A story in rabbinical literature is similar: 'A king had a field which he leased to tenants. When they began to steal, he leased the field to the tenant's children. They were worse than their fathers, so the king leased it to the grandchildren. They were equally bad. In the end the king took back the field and gave it to his son.'

This story is interpreted as showing that God was not satisfied with Abraham, nor Ishmael, nor Isaac, nor Esau, but God accepted Jacob/Israel as his son to cultivate the world and be the corner-stone of God's kingdom (Sif.Dt. on 32:9 and Midr.Ps. 118:20-22).

* * *

G7 a. Unclean hands.

This is the first of four passages describing encounters between some of the very pious Pharisees and Jesus. They were particularly concerned with ritual purity and may have thought that any one acting as a holy man, sage or prophet ought to be as punctilious as they were. It is thought that some of them were so concerned about protecting themselves from any transgressions of the law, they formed a society of those who could be relied upon to be ritually clean, serve ritually clean food and follow all the precepts accurately. Naturally, they would never sit at the table of one suspected of 'uncleanliness'.

The evangelists say it was simply a tradition and not a biblical requirement to wash or rinse one's hands except in special circumstances; when one had had a discharge, for example, (Lev. 15). The requirement of washing of the hands before eating was derived from the Torah and priests had to wash their hands and feet before approaching the altar: '... Aaron and his sons shall wash their hands and feet ... when they come near to the altar to minister or to make an offering by fire to the Lord' (Ex. 30:19-20).

In rabbinical literature, 'To eat bread without washing hands first is as though he has sinned with a harlot' and, 'Whoever makes light of washing of his hands will be uprooted from the world' (b.Sot. 4b); 'Hands must be washed at once when getting up in the morning. They remain in a dangerous (i.e. ritually impure) condition until they have been washed three times' (b.Shab. 108b); '...cleanliness leads to restraint, restraint leads to purity, purity leads to holiness, holiness leads to meekness, meekness leads to fear of sin, fear of sin leads to saintliness, saintliness leads to possession of the Holy Spirit and the Holy Spirit to eternal life' (b.A.Z. 20b). It was also accepted that one possessing the Holy Spirit is endowed with the power of restoring life to the dead.

After the Temple had been destroyed, there was no altar to approach but it was thought necessary to retain the precept among the righteous, even if they were not priests. The admonition was often used before prayers and was thought to signify innocence: 'I wash my hands in innocence and go round your altar, O Lord' (Ps. 26:6).

It was very common to practice bathing immersion and the remains of many immersion pools have come to light in recent years in places where Jews lived in Palestine and surrounding areas. Washing or bathing in the sea was thought to be especially valuable.

The Pharisees and the Jews generally never eat without washing their hands in obedience to the traditions of the elders, and their hands are always rinsed before they eat when they come in from the markets. They maintain several other traditional practices, such as immersing cups and bowls and bronze vessels.

One day a group of Pharisees and doctors of the Law from Jerusalem approached Jesus and asked him why his disciples did not wash their hands but ate their food with polluted hands.

Jesus replied, "You Pharisees neglect the commandments of God in order to maintain the traditions of men. Isaiah was right when he said, 'This people pays me lip-service, but their heart is far from me, their worship of me is in vain, for they teach as doctrines the commandments of men.'"

The regulations about rendering hands ritually clean were extensive and extremely detailed. The traditional ritual was to pour about half a cup of water over each hand as far up as the wrist. The water was reckoned as efficacious if it had collected naturally or had been mixed with a small amount of natural water. Behind the rite was the idea that unrinsed hands were desecrating, and that after the rinsing ritual, the person was pure enough to ask God's blessing before eating. It is important to realize that in Judaism, it was not sinful to become ritually unclean. This was inevitable for ordinary people, and sin occurred only if one in the polluted state defiled a holy place or holy food.

The quotation is from Isaiah: 'The Lord said, "This people draw near me with their mouth and honour me with their lips, while their hearts are far from me, and their fear of me is a commandment of men learned by rote ..."' (Is. 29:13). Another equally appropriate quotation is: 'They remembered that God was their rock, the Most High God their redeemer, but they flattered him with their mouths and lied to him with their tongues.' (Ps. 78:35-36). Jesus, on this view, also thought that God's followers would come to no harm and that pietistic practices should in no way inhibit his fellowship with his disciples, nor his contact with the ordinary people. It should be noted that the Torah gives the rules which applied only to the priests, not to the ordinary laity, and Jesus was not defying the Law by doing what he did.

* * *

G 7 b. Unclean food.

On one occasion Jesus spoke to the crowd and said, "Listen to me and get this clear. Nothing that goes into a man from the outside can pollute him. No, it is the things that issue from a man that defile a man.

Then the disciples came to Jesus on their own and said, "Explain your parable to us." Jesus said, "Are you as lacking in discernment as the others? Do you not understand that whatever goes in by the mouth does not enter the heart but passes into the stomach and then is discharged into the drain? Thus are all the foulnesses of foods purged from the body.

But what comes from the mouth arises from the heart (mind). That is what defiles a man: wicked thoughts, murder, fornication, theft, perjury, blasphemies and so on. These evil things which come forth from within, these are what defile a man."

Today one wonders why the disciples needed to ask for an explanation and Jesus' reply seems to be an example of his irritation with their dullness (see also E14). They are shown as not having grasped Jesus' attitude and attention to the inner source of right and wrong conduct - the inclinations which are manifest in deeds. Some think that Jesus in this passage was not directly concerned with the question of whether the dietary laws should be abolished or not. The passage does not say all foods are ritually pure; men are not defiled by what is expelled out of them, but by what arises in their hearts and inclinations. What was important was to prevent them being used to create a barrier between supposedly righteous Jews and others.

What one eats may be defiled and defiles the gut, but then it is expelled. Such pollution was only temporary, Jesus implied. It was evil motives, which bring pollution lasting as long as the person is unrepentant and which cannot be removed by any amount of ritual purification, which were the problem. Jesus does not deny the Torah but goes deeper and asserts, with a prophet's authority, that the only defilement which could be in any way significant was moral defilement.

It has often been supposed that this passage shows Jesus rejecting one of the main prohibitions of the Torah. This is not correct and is contrary to everything else in his teaching recorded in the gospels, and this passage could originally have been associated with the argument with the religious leaders about washing of hands since Mt. adds: '... but to eat with unwashed hands does not defile the person' (See G 7a).

A similar viewpoint is found in I.T. writings: 'Just as the sun is not defiled by shining on dung and mire, but dries them up and drives away the vile smells, so the pure mind, though surrounded by defilements, cleanses them and is not itself defiled' (T.Ben. 8:3). In rabbinical books it was thought that care of the body was essential for the care also of the soul. Regular motions, and purgations helped moral health: 'Physical cleanliness leads to spiritual purity' (b.A.Z. 20b) and: 'Whoever wishes to receive the yoke of the kingdom of heaven in perfection should first have evacuation, wash his hands, put on phylacteries[1] and offer his prayers' (b.Ber. 15a).

Amusingly enough, in rabbinical writings is found the idea that if a righteous man dies of diarrhoea, he passes out of this world purged of uncleanliness! (b.Ket.103b). On the other hand, excrement was not considered to render a hand ritually unclean (b.Shab. 25b; b.San. 17b).

Among the laws given in the bible are those about which animals are 'unclean' and not permitted to be eaten. Should any one of these animals, which include nearly all insects, die and fall on to moistened food, the food became impure. This law was almost impossible to apply and generally it was accepted that an animal less than the size of a lentil did not count. One larger polluted the food.

The levitical rules were probably originally intended to prevent contamination of the Hebrews by the pagans of Canaan, and it has been suggested that the prevalent attitude of the pietists and pedants among the lawyers was that exact conformity to these rules was what mattered, as though God could be deceived by outward show. They had forgotten that when their ancestors had entered Canaan, after wandering in the wilderness, they were very glad to eat the 'unclean' produce, grown by the pagans, which they found there. Earlier prophets like Elijah and Elisha ignored the prohibition too. They were fed by the non-Jew, the widow of Zarephath, and Naaman was pronounced clean, that is ritually acceptable, even though he was not a Jew (I Kgs. 17 and II Kgs. 5).

The rule about not eating blood is rather different from the rest. It is derived from the idea that blood was the life of the animal. It had to be returned to the earth from whence it had come, so that new life could arise: 'Any ... who takes in hunting any beast or bird that may be eaten shall pour out its blood and cover it with dust. For the life of every creature is the blood of it. Therefore ... you shall not eat the blood of any creature' (Lev. 17:13-14). This law is not contradicted by the teaching of Jesus as recorded in the gospels. (See also D 3.)

[1] Phylacteries were the tefillim bound to the head and arm. See also G 9.

* * *

G 7 c. Unclean utensils.

"Alas for you Pharisees and lawyers," said Jesus. "Impious ones who clean the outside of cup and dish but are filled with plunder and evil. Conceited, foolish Pharisees! Clean the inside of the cup first, then the outside will be clean also. Did not he who made the outside make the inside too? Give what is in the cup for alms and all things are clean to you."

There are several obscurities in this passage, and it has given rise to much discussion among bible scholars. One of the words used in the text means a side-plate used only on festive occasions, especially Passover, and one possibility is that the vessels Jesus was thinking of were those of the Temple. They had to be clean inside and that meant that after washing them normally, they were dipped (baptized) in ritually clean water. Thus if the insides were ritually clean the outsides would be too, since there was no way of immersing the inside without also immersing the outside.

In rabbinical teaching: 'The cleanliness applies also to vessels used during the meal; rinse the cup before and after drinking' (b.Tam. 27b).

Nevertheless pollution of vessels and utensils occurred when a crawling animal such as an insect fell into moistened food and died. Because this requirement of the Law was quite impractical, the Pharisees said that if the creature was smaller than a lentil, like a gnat, it did not count. If it was larger, like a fly, the food could not be used and the vessel had to be broken, unless it was made of stone, which could not become impure. Metal vessels had to dipped in purifying water.

Jesus used the point of the passage metaphorically, playing on the idea of men as a vessel made by a potter. 'You are our Father, O Lord; we are the clay and you are the potter; we are all the work of your hand' (Is. 64:8); 'Behold, you desire truth in the inward being, teach me wisdom in my secret heart. Purge me with hyssop and I shall be clean, wash me and I shall be whiter than snow' (Ps. 51:5-6). The pots could be full of uncleanliness - greed and selfishness - and to scrub that out from their insides was what mattered. Only then were men fit to serve the Lord in the Temple and they would show their consecration by giving the superfluities they had accumulated to the poor. Not only that; God's servants had to be pure throughout and like the holy vessels there was no question of one side being pure and the other not.

* * *

G 7 d. Unclean tombs.

"Woe to you Pharisees and lawyers. You are like tombs covered with 'whitening': they look well from outside but inside are full of dead men's bones and rottenness. You are the same; outside you look like honest men but inside are full of ungodliness and crime. You are like unmarked graves over which men may walk without knowing it. You are the people who impress your fellowmen with your apparent righteousness but God sees through you. What sets itself up to be admired by men is idolatry in the sight of God."

After death, the bones of the deceased were put into vaults or ossuaries which were covered by a mixture of ground marble and lime giving a rich sheen to them. This was the 'whitewash' referred to, and it was renewed each year as part of the preparations for Passover. That they were full of dead men's bones was not only obvious, but was a common remark at the time. To say that someone's outside is fair but inside is foul, is a reference to the person's duplicity. At the same time, white was the colour of the clothes of the redeemed, so those who whitewashed one another were indeed wolves in sheep's clothing. Outwardly sons of God's kingdom; inwardly anything except that.

There are indications in the language of the passage that tombs were thought of as having openings which were fair and enticing, but which led straight to hell. Many of the religious leaders were similar. Their mouths gave forth perfectly ripe, attractive words, but they led straight into an interior full of hypocrisy and unlawfulness: 'Their throats are an open sepulchre and smooth talk runs off their tongues' (Ps. 5:9).

In all these passages about uncleanliness there is the tacit implication that when all Israel is 'clean', there can be no further use for the rules of ritual cleanliness. Jesus emphasizes that only when Israel is repentant, can it be thought of as 'clean'.

* * *

G 8. Korban - Mt. 15:3-9. Mk. 7:9-13.

The system of Korban began as a way of honouring God, often by making gifts for the Lord's service at the Temple: 'Honour the Lord with your substance ...' (Pvb. 3:9). Once given, the gift could not be recovered: 'But nothing that a man devoted to the Lord ... shall be sold or redeemed, every devoted thing is most holy to the Lord' (Lev. 27:28). It was extended also to assets which were expected in the future, or which could be realized in the future. These could also be dedicated to God's use and thereby became untouchable.

Problems arose when someone, wishing to deprive a dependant, made a vow of Korban about his wealth. The dependant could then never hope to be able to use those assets, even if he or she was an aged parent or a deserted wife. God had already said that parents were to be honoured which included supporting them when they were unable to support themselves, and the vow of Korban promoted sin not righteousness.

Jesus put a question to the Pharisees and doctors of Law: "Why do you break God's commandment in order to maintain your human traditions! Moses told us God said that a man must honour his father and mother and he who curses them must be put to death. Yet you hold that any one who says to his mother or father, 'Anything of mine which might have been used for your benefit is an offering set aside of God', then he is not permitted thereafter to do anything for them. He has no need to honour them! What impiety, what blasphemy! By your traditions you make God's word null and void and it's not the only example either."

The vow of Korban was unusual in that it was binding even though not using the equivalent of God's name (compare E 13). While the priests might be willing to revoke a vow if someone asked them to do so, they could not force him to do so. Yet O.T. teaching was: 'Honour your father and your mother ...' (Ex. 20:12), that is support them if they require it; 'Every one of you shall revere his mother and his father ...' (Lev. 19:3), and the position Jesus advocates is foreshadowed in: 'He who robs his father or his mother and says, "That is not sin", is the companion of a man who destroys' (Pvb. 28:24); 'Honour God foremost and afterwards your parents' (P.Ph. 8).

Jesus clearly thinks the system of 'korban' leads to such immoral results that the initial vow should be declared null and void. God would prefer to do without some money in the Temple treasury than have the hard-hearted make such a vow, let alone be unable to revoke it. What is due to God belongs to him by right. Men have no authority to make vows which will make God a party to their nastiness.

In rabbinical writings, the regulations relating to this vow of 'korban' occupy a whole chapter of very detailed instructions. One way round the problem by which the first man, regretting his maliciousness during a fit of temper, could give his assets to a friend, on condition that the latter used them to help those who needed them: 'If

230

a man was forbidden by his vow to receive any benefit from his relative and the man was starving, the relative could give food to a third person who then permits the first to eat it.' (m.Ned. 4:6). In other passages some conceded that a man may be released from his vow if it conflicted with a biblical precept, such as the requirement to support his parent or other dependant: 'I had vowed away all my property because my son did not occupy himself with study of the Law. But I went to my colleagues and they freed me from my vow' (b.Shab. 127b).

* * *

The robes of the leaders were finer and had longer fringes than those of the ordinary people. Their tefillim (cubical boxes containing certain verses of the Torah and worn on the head and arm) had broader straps, to draw attention to their 'piety'. The less learned were to greet the more learned when meeting on the street and to defer to them in taking places at table or at gatherings.

The fringes were supposed to remind the person of all the numerous laws in the Torah to which one must attend and obey.

"Beware of the doctors of the Law and the Pharisees. They speak but do not practise what they preach. They do everything for show; they widen the bands on their tefillim and lengthen the fringes on their robes, they want to have the best places at feasts and in the synagogues and to be greeted respectfully in the market squares. These are the men who eat up the property of widows while they say long prayers for appearances' sake. They will get severe condemnation."

When a man died and left a widow or children, it was usual to ask a person of rank to act as trustee and guardian of the estate left by the husband or father. They could claim expenses, but they decided what expenses they had had. They took what they wished in practice, often even though provision was made in the will for them to be given remuneration as well. Those who were chosen to discharge this function of guardianship were those with a reputation for piety. This was deducible from their dress and behaviour; those who went to the synagogue and indulged in long prayers were pious, and the longer the prayers, the more widows' houses and estates would come under their control, and the richer they would become. Even worse, some of them would offer to say long prayers asking God to give the widow or orphan justice, excusing the size of their bill for their 'expert' services.

If it was difficult to bring such rogues to justice in this world, there is a higher court. Jesus reminds them that there they will receive severe sentences for their evil-doing.

This sort of hypocrisy had been rampant for a long time: 'Your princes are rebels and companions of thieves; everyone loves a bribe and runs after gifts; they do not defend the fatherless, and the widow's cause does not come before them' (Is 1:23). (In the Aramaic version: 'They say to one another, "Assist me in my suit, that I may repay you in your suit"'); 'Woe to those...who turn aside the needy from justice and rob the poor of my people of their right, that widows may be their spoil, and that they may make the fatherless their prey!' (Is. 10:2).

In I.T. literature too, we find similar denunciations: 'Destructive and impious men will rule saying they are just ... Devourers of the goods of the poor saying that they do so on the grounds of justice but in reality to destroy them ... Deceitful ... impious, filled with lawlessness and iniquity from sunrise to sunset, saying, "We shall have feasting and luxury ... we shall esteem ourselves as princes." Their mouths shall speak great things, and though their hands and their minds are defiled with unclean things, they shall say, "Do not touch me lest you pollute me..."' (A.M. 7:3-10); 'The profane man is swift to enter every house with cheerfulness as though guiltless ... He lays waste a house on account of his lawless desire ... He deceives with his words saying, "There is none to see and judge", and then his eyes are fixed on the next house; yet with all this, his soul, like hell, is not sated' (P.S. 4:6-7,13-15); and in rabbinical writings: 'A man in whom is hypocrisy brings wrath upon the world and his prayer is not heard. Hypocrites are cursed, and they go to hell' (b.Sot.41b).

It was religious leaders who paraded their virtue, enjoyed the chief places in society and who wore the robes of those distinguished for their supposed piety and learning who deserved such condemnation: 'Extravagant in speech and appearance beyond all men is he that is severe of speech in condemning sinners in judgement. His hand is first upon him (to punish him) as though he was full of zeal, yet he is himself guilty of many sins and wantonness' (P.S. 4:2-3). Jesus could support their citations from the Law and the Prophets, but he condemned the way in which they did not practise what they preached.

There were two groups of Pharisees, Shammaites and Hillelites. The former liked to have longer fringes on their cloaks; the latter were satisfied with shorter ones. If Jesus contended that longer fringes were ostentatious it shows that is this respect he favoured the practices of Hillel.

Hillel also advocated peaceful behaviour; the Shammites would resort to violence at times. Here too, Jesus generally followed Hillel's teachings.

* * *

233

G 10. Jailers of heaven - Mt. 15:12-14; 23:13-24. Lk. 6:39; 11:42, 45-46, 52.

One of the learned in the Law was stung to protest: "Master, when you say things like this to us (see G 9), you insult us too." Jesus replied, "Yes, you lawyers, it is no better with you! For you load men with intolerable burdens but won't lift a finger to help."

To the others listening he said, "You may pay attention to the words of the Pharisees and doctors of the Law - those who sit in the seats of Moses - but do not follow their practices. Woe to you lawyers and Pharisees, you hypocrites: you shut the door of the kingdom of God in men's faces and you have taken away the key of knowledge. You don't go in yourselves and you stop others entering as well. You pay tithes on mint and dill and cummin, but you overlook the weightier demands of the Law - justice, mercy and faith. It is these you should have practised, without neglecting the others. You swallow a camel at one gulp, but use a strainer to get rid of a gnat!

Leave them alone; they are blind guides. Can a blind man guide another ? Will they not both fall into the pit? They say that if a man swears by the sanctuary it doesn't count, but if he swears by the gold in it, he is bound by his oath. How stupid! Is it not the sanctuary which sanctifies the gold? Or again if a man swears by the altar it is not binding, but if he swears by the offering on the altar, then it is a valid oath. How blind that is! Is it not the altar which sanctifies the offering? To swear by the altar is to swear both by it and the One who dwells there, and to swear by heaven is to swear both by the throne of God and by him who sits on it.

Woe to you ungodly blasphemers; you travel by sea and land to win over a foreigner and when you have won him, you make him twice as much a child of Gehenna as you are yourselves."

The disciples said to Jesus, "Do you realize that the Pharisees think what you were saying is a stumbling-block or a trap?" Jesus replied, "Any plant not of my heavenly Father's planting shall be rooted up."

This passage illustrates how far some of the religious leaders of the time had missed the point. They had forgotten the O.T.: 'The altar shall be most holy; whatever touches it shall become holy' (Ex. 29:37), and they had elevated the gold of the sanctuary to the holiness of God's presence there. They were guilty of idolatry by associating the non-holy with the holy and forgetting the distinction. It was also

234

contrary to the teaching of Judaism: 'Whoever vows by the Torah has said nothing; but whoever vows by what is written in it, is liable' (b.Sot. 41b); 'You shall not swear by my name falsely so that you profane the name of your God. For the crimes of vain oaths, false oaths, profanation of the divine name and the desecration of the Sabbath, numerous punishments result' (b.Shab. 33a).

The seat of Moses was the chief one among those reserved for the elders facing the congregation at the end of the synagogue, and the passage shows Jesus as not condemning the Law but condemning those who did not practice it truly. The admonition to listen to their words (read from the scriptures) and practise them, is from the O.T.: 'You shall be careful to do according to all that they declare to you' (Dt. 17:10). What Jesus condemns about the religious leaders is condemned equally well in rabbinical writings also; hypocrites, together with liars, slanderers and mockers, were said never to be able to see the face of the Almighty, that is enter into paradise: 'If one who falsifies the words of his companion is liable to death, so certainly is he who falsifies the word of God' (Sif.Dt. on 13:6).

The severe criticism of the latter part of the passage suggests that those who became converted to Judaism were more Jewish than the Jews, that is they were those most concerned to keep all Gentiles and non-believers out of the kingdom, something Jesus had no sympathy with at all. They are called 'children of hell' rather than children of the heavenly kingdom. Pharisees are blamed for being more concerned to recruit new members into their brand of Judaism rather than working to bring back the 'lost' into Israel.

The passage seems to demonstrate that there was an acrimonious dialogue between the community of Matthew and the orthodox, rabbinical Judaism of the time. Matthew's criticism was aimed not only at the Jewish religious leaders but also those of the developing Christian sect. Leaders were necessary but were expected to function under the threat of the day of Judgement, which would not be long delayed.

* * *

G 11. God's vengeance on the fathers' sons. Mt. 23:29-36. Lk. 11:47-51

"Woe to you religious leaders, you build up the tombs of the prophets and embellish the monuments to the saints whom your fathers slew, and so you are witnesses and approve your father's work: they killed and you build. You say, 'If we had been alive in our father's time we should never have taken part in the murders of the prophets.' Thus you acknowledge you are sons of those who killed them. (That is why the Wisdom of God said, 'I will send prophets and apostles and some of them you will persecute and kill'.) You shall complete the work your fathers began.

I tell you this; this present generation will have to answer for the blood of all the prophets; from Abel to Zechariah, who died between the altar and the shrine of God. You are as wicked as your fathers. Snakes and offspring of echidna[1] you are! I send you prophets, sages and teachers - some you will crucify, others you will flog in your synagogues and hound from city to city. How can you avoid being condemned to Gehenna?"

Jesus denies the religious leaders the right to act as defenders of the memory of the prophets and he mentions Zechariah and Abel. Zechariah was not a prophet but a priest whom the Pharisees pretended was the son of Barachiah to make him a prophet. They were building and embellishing tombs of non-prophets and false prophets, and even today there are near Jerusalem tombs claimed to be of O.T. prophets, which date from the period 300 to 60 B.C.E. long after their deaths.

God sent his prophets and they had been ignored and murdered. 'The Lord ... gave his people commandments through his servants the prophets: but they shut their ears to the prophets and let my precepts become a dead letter' (II Esdras 2:1); 'From the day that your fathers came out of the land of Egypt to this day I have persistently sent all my servants the prophets to them ... yet they did not listen to me ... but stiffened their necks.' (Jer. 7:25-26). Now the descendants of those responsible were putting up monuments and embellishing the "prophets" tombs, showing that they fully acknowledged that they were their fathers' sons. Such descendants of malefactors, who do not repudiate the latter's deeds, bear witness to their own passive participation in those deeds; they proclaim their own guilt, whatever they may say.

The case of Abel is even more interesting. Abel was neither prophet nor priest but he had been murdered and his innocent blood had never been avenged, since his murderer, Cain, had been given immunity. The old covenant was quite inadequate: it even began with an unpunished murder, was without justice and had to be abandoned, and those who continued to support it were themselves guilty of the taking of innocent blood. They were not fit to partake of God's realm. 'The fathers swore to uphold the covenant' (Dt. 7:12), but they did not: 'The Lord forewarned Israel and Judah, by the hand of every prophet and of every seer, saying, "Turn back from your wicked ways and observe my commandments and my laws" ... But they spurned his laws and the covenant he made with their fathers ...' (II Kgs. 17:13,15).

The deaths of the true prophets had not been avenged, but that did not mean that they never would be. Blood-guilt shall be requited, though God's vengeance could come generations later: "For your life-blood I will surely require a reckoning, of every beast ... and of man; of every man's brother I will require the life of man" (Gen. 9:5); "For I the Lord your God am a jealous God, visiting the iniquities of the fathers upon the children to the third and fourth generation ..." (Ex. 20:5); "I sent you my servants the prophets, but you took them and killed them and mutilated their dead bodies. For their murder I will call you to account, says the Lord" (II Esdras 1:32).

This blood must and will be avenged and the current generation were so wicked it would be appropriate for such retribution to fall on them: 'The Lord ... sent persistently to them by his messengers because he had compassion on his people ... but they mocked the messengers of God despising his words and scoffing at his prophets until the wrath of the Lord rose against his people, till there was no remedy' (II Chr. 36:15-16); '... with mocking tongue this people were scoffing at the prophets who prophesied to them' (Tg.Is. 28:11); 'Thus says the Lord of Hosts, "Behold I am sending on them sword, famine and pestilence and I will make them like vile figs which are so bad they cannot be eaten. I ... will make them a horror to all the kingdoms of the earth ... because they did not heed my words ... which I repeatedly sent to you by my servants, the prophets, but you would not listen"' (Jer. 29:17-19): 'And I will send witnesses to them ... but they will slay them and persecute those who seek the Law ... they will not listen' (Jub. 1:12). Those who build the tombs of prophets have complicity in their deaths since the word for builders implies' those who understand and know what they are about'. They are the sons of murderers. 'Both their little ones and their great men ... are robbers of wealth and both scribes and priests, all of them are doers of falsehood' (Tg.Jer. 6:13).

It was a common thought in the O.T. that those who repented could hope for forgiveness: 'If a man begets a son who is a robber, a shedder of blood, who ... defiles his neighbour's wife, oppresses the poor and needy ... commits abominations, he shall not live ... and his blood shall be on himself. But if a man begets a son who sees all the sins of his father and fears and does not do likewise ... does not wrong anyone ... observes my ordinances and walks in my statutes, he shall not die for this father's iniquity, he shall surely live' (Ezk. 18:10-17); 'The son shall not suffer sins of the father, nor the father for the sins of the son. The righteousness of the righteous shall be upon himself; and the wickedness of the wicked shall be upon himself' (Ezk. 18:20).

In rabbinical books some of the bible texts were considered: 'It says in Dt. 24:16: "The children shall not be put to death for their fathers. Every man shall be put to death only for his own sin." This was applied in the courts of law, where it was not permitted for the father to give evidence in relation to the trial of a son and vice versa. But it says in Ex. 20:5, "God visits the sins of the fathers upon the children." This means that he does so only if they hold fast to the deeds of their fathers' (b.San.27b, b.Ber.7a); and: 'In those days they shall no longer say, "Parents have eaten sour grapes and the children's teeth are set on edge." But everyone shall die for his own sins' (Jer. 31:29-30); 'Consider: all lives are the same [says the Lord], the life of the parent and the life of the child are both mine. The person who sins - only he shall die' (Ezk. 18:4).

This passage from Matthew's gospel betrays signs of later editing. Vengeance was not part of Jesus' teaching elsewhere, crucifixion was never a Jewish mode of punishment, and much in the gospels suggests that Jesus did not aim to destroy the Law, but would have it practised with a true spirit. Furthermore, it was not true that the Pharisees of Jesus' day tried to impose their will by coercion, and arguing was part of daily life. Even if they disagreed with the activities of the priests, they were members of the Sanhedrin of the Temple, and took part in what for them were sometimes dubious rituals there.

[1] 'Echidna' could mean a viper, but the word does not occur in any other Hebrew or Aramaic book and some scholars believe it is a mistranslation. It is the leopard, jackal or wildcat which is the usual symbol for a hypocrite in Jewish writings, not a snake. In Greek mythology it was a monster the upper part of its body being a beautiful woman, and the lower part a serpent: a suitable term for enticing but lethal religious leaders.

* * *

G 12. Stripping ears of wheat on the sabbath - Mt. 12:1-8. Mk. 2:23-28. Lk. 6:1-5.

On the second sabbath Jesus and his disciples were passing through a corn field, and as they went along, they began to pluck some ears of corn, rubbing them in their hands in order to eat the grains.

The Pharisees noticed this and drew Jesus' attention to it. "Why are they doing what is forbidden on the sabbath?", they asked.

Jesus replied, "Have you not read what David did when he and his men were hungry? He went to the House of God and was given the bread which only the priests were allowed to eat. And what about the priests? Have you not read in the Law that on the sabbath they break the sabbath, yet it is not held against them.

If you had known what the text means, 'I desire mercy and not sacrifice' you would have not have condemned those who are innocent. The sabbath was made for man not man for the sabbath, and man is sovereign over the sabbath too."

The disciples were not stealing: 'If you go into your neighbour's standing grain, you may pluck the ears with your hand, but you shall not put a sickle to your neighbour's standing grain' (Dt. 23:25). The accusation that the disciples were breaking the sabbath taboos was not one supported by all of the different sects of Judaism at the time. Some extreme groups may have thought it was reaping and therefore forbidden work: 'The seventh day is a sabbath ... you shall do no work' (Ex. 20:10; Dt. 5:14), but it was normally accepted that taking fruit from a plant to eat it, especially when one was hungry or on a journey, was permitted on the sabbath. This was reinforced if the journey were devoted to a sacred purpose.

The sabbath was an important day in history. It was the day when preparations were made to cross the Jordan to invade Canaan and Mark uses the word which meant passing through the wilderness and crossing the Jordan, to suggest that Jesus was a king, who with his disciples was about to reconquer Canaan spiritually.

The sabbath was also a day of rejoicing, feasting and hallowing life, and in many circles fasting on the sabbath was condemned: 'For great is the honour which the Lord has given Israel that they should eat and drink and be satisfied on this festival day and rest thereon from all labour which belongs to the labour of the children of men, save burning frankincense and bringing oblations and sacrifices before the Lord for feast days and for sabbaths' (Jub. 50:10-11); 'No man shall fast of his own will on the sabbath' (Zad. 13:13); 'Observe the sabbath according to the true interpretation: to love every one his brother as himself, to strengthen the hand of the poor, the needy and the stranger and to seek every one the peace of his brother' (Zad. 8:15-17); 'He gave us a great sign, the sabbath day, that we should work six days but keep the sabbath on the seventh day from all work' (Jub. 2:17); 'If you cease to tread the sabbath underfoot, and keep my holy days free from your affairs, call the sabbath a day of joy, the Lord's holy day, a day to be honoured ... then you shall find joy in the Lord' (Is. 58:13-14).

Jesus not only rejects the accusation of the religious leaders but points to the incident in which David and his men ate the bread devoted to the use of the priest: '(David said to Abimelech) "Let me have five loaves, or as many as you can find." The priest answered, "I have no ordinary bread ... only the sacred bread." ... So as there was no other bread there, the priest gave him the sacred ... Bread of the Presence, which had just been taken from the presence of the Lord to be replaced by freshly baked bread...' (I Sam. 21:3-6). The show bread was always baked for the sabbath: 'Every sabbath day Aaron shall set them [twelve loaves] before the Lord' (Lev. 24:8). It is not stated that David received the shew-bread on a sabbath, but it was the only day on which the holy bread would be renewed, the old being taken away to be eaten by the priests.

The succour of David and his men was an act of loving-kindness; it accorded with the primary rule of God: love of God and neighbour, and it was also in accordance with the rule in Judaism that the saving of life took precedence over other considerations. It took precedence over the ritual laws about the use of the priests' bread: 'This is the law of the grain-offering... The priest shall set aside a handful of the flour from it ... He shall burn this token of the grain-offering on the altar ... The remainder shall Aaron and his sons eat ... It shall not be baked with leaven. I have allotted this to them as their share of my food-offerings to the Lord for generation after generation' (Lev. 6:14-18). Jesus thus says that the rule of love is greater than rules of ritual, even though the ritual was concerned with the sanctity of the priests and the altar itself. Also the High Priest was High Priest for David too, so that David's action had received the approval of the highest religious authority of his day.

Jesus adds another example. Some of the practices of the Temple worship entailed breaking some of the sabbath rules by the priests, who did not hesitate to do so, for example, in performing circumcision. Work could also be done in the sanctuary: 'The Sabbath is a holy day outside the sanctuary; for God in the sanctuary, it is a profane day' (Mek.Shab.1) Yet they were not excommunicated or worse. So it is clear that here the ritual rules were greater than the sabbath rules. Thus the commandment of love is greater than the rules of ritual and the rules of ritual can be greater than the rules of the sabbath. Hence the commandment of love outweighs by far the sabbath taboos.

No wonder that Jesus says they ought to find out what is meant by the requirement of mercy (loving-kindness) not sacrifice (Temple ritual): 'For I desire steadfast love and not sacrifice, the knowledge of God, not burnt offerings' (Hos. 6:6). It is the commandment of love which is greater than the Temple and the sabbath is for man to show love to others, not that man is the prisoner of the taboos of the sabbath which one group of Jews wished to enforce on all.

Some have noted other aspects of this passage. There are parallels between the actions of Jesus and his disciples and the Israelites being allowed out of Egypt. The corn eaten by the disciples was the equivalent of the unleavened cakes which the Israelites used on their way out of Egypt (the kingdom of wickedness), on their way to the promised land; the disciples were on a campaign, just as David had been engaged in a mission for his king. This was permitted: 'The king may go through the private domain of any man to make himself a road and none may protest against him' (m.San. 2:4). Given their reasoning, they could claim exemption from the sabbatical prohibitions about taking the corn on a sabbath.

It is the opinion of some scholars that the verses got muddled up at some time, and that they should be rearranged so that the last sentence becomes the first part of Jesus' reply to the Pharisees.

The idea that the sabbath was made for man and not vice versa, is found in rabbinical works: 'The sabbath is holy to you; the sabbath is committed to your hands, not you to its hands' (b.Yoma 85b on Ex. 31:14).

* * *

G 13. The man with the withered hand - Mt. 12:9-13. Mk. 3:1-6. Lk. 6:6-11.

One sabbath Jesus went into the synagogue and a
man there had a withered hand. They questioned Jesus:
"Is it lawful to heal on the sabbath?", so that they
might accuse him.

Jesus told the man to come forward and stand
before the whole congregation. Jesus said to them, "Are
we not free to do good or evil on the sabbath, to save a
soul or to destroy it?

Suppose you had one sheep and it fell into a pit,"
he continued, "is there any one of you who would not
take hold of it and lift it out? By how much does a man
surpass a sheep?"

No one said a word. Jesus looked round at them
with anger and grief at their hardness of heart. He
turned to the man and said, "Stretch out your arm." The
man did so - his arm was restored to normal.

The Pharisees went out and began plotting with the
supporters of Herod to get rid of Jesus.

The man's hand or arm was 'withered' or 'dried', that is paralysed like
Jeroboam's before him: 'Jeroboam stretched out his hand from the altar, saying "Take
hold of him". His hand which he stretched out dried up, so he could not draw it
back' (I Kgs. 13:4); and like Simeon: 'But the Lord restrained me and withheld the
power of my hands, for my right hand was half withered for seven days' (T.Sim.
2:12). Such a 'drying up' or paralysis was often taken as proof of unconfessed sin:
'When I did not admit my sin, my body wasted away ... my strength was dried up as
by the heat of summer' (Ps. 32:3-4). Any physical defect was deplored and a matter
for commiseration (b.San 17a) and this was especially true of sins connected with
sex, since a withered hand could mean impotence - taken as a sure sign of God's
disfavour.

The man was placed in the centre of the synagogue so that there was no hiding
the fact that one of its member was sinful, which meant the synagogue was sinful too,
and should be in sackcloth and ashes, praying earnestly for the sinner to repent and
receive God's pardon and healing. Their ancestors had pledged their allegiance and
accepted God's will: 'All the people answered with one voice and said, "All the words
which the Lord has spoken we will do"' (Ex. 24:3). But some had been unfaithful: 'I
have heard the words of this people which they have spoken to you, Moses, they have
rightly said all they have spoken. Oh, that they had such a mind as this always, to fear
(respect) me and keep my commandments that it might go well with them and with
their children for ever' (Dt. 5:28-29).

Not only was the synagogue unfaithful to its purpose, it was not concerned
about the man's life or soul or self, as it is said, 'When one welcomes a fellowman, it
is as if one had welcomed the Divine Presence' (Mek.Ama. 3). It was this which was
in danger and Jesus' concern, and to his question, there was only one possible answer:
'See, I have set before you this day life and good, death and evil ... I call on heaven

and earth to witness against you this day, that I have set before you life and death, blessing and curse' (Dt. 30:15,19); 'When the Lord made man in the beginning he left him free to take his own decisions ... he has set before you fire and water - reach out and take what you choose. Before man is life and death and which ever he prefers is his' (Sir. 15:14-17).

Jesus longed to restore them to life and let God heal them: 'God said [to Moses], "Put your hand back into your bosom." So he put his hand back into his bosom, and when he took it out again, it was restored like the rest of his flesh' (Ex. 4:7). Jesus, like God, grieved at those who choose evil or death: 'In his love and pity the Lord redeemed them. He lifted them up and carried them all the days of old. But they rebelled and grieved his Holy Spirit' (Is. 63:9-10).

According to Jewish beliefs, when the Torah was originally given to the Israelites on Mount Sinai, there were no cripples - all were perfect. So now the more who chose life and were healed, the more fully was the kingdom of God manifest and when all were perfect the Messiah would come and God's kingdom would be throughout the world (Sif.Num on Dt. 29:2-4). The leaders were not obeying God's will and were behaving as wicked men will: 'The wicked watches the righteous and seeks to slay him' (Ps. 37:32). The consequences of such an attitude had been made clear: 'If your heart turns away and you will not hear ... you shall perish' (Dt. 30:17-18).

The phrase 'hardness of heart' originally meant a heart covered in fat as in Isaiah's prophecy: 'The Lord said, "Go and say to this people, hear and hear but do not understand; see and see but do not perceive. Make the heart of this people fat and their ears heavy and shut their eyes, lest they see with their eyes, hear with their ears and understand with their hearts and turn and be healed' (Is. 6:9-10). The heart for Jews was the seat of understanding, more than the seat of feelings, and for Jesus the people of the synagogue were as useless as those to whom God had sent his prophet long before.

The passage has a parallel in the O.T.: 'Blessed is the man ... who keeps the sabbath and keeps his hand from doing any evil ... To the eunuchs who keep my sabbath ... I will give in my house ... a monument and a name ...' (Is. 56:2-5), especially as 'hand' and 'name', and 'eunuch' and 'withered' were pairs of equivalents. It is about the blindness of the leaders who could not see that making the choice of life and sinlessness could be more important on the sabbath than on other days. It was the very essence of God's work. God does not rest on the sabbath as many believed. True sabbath observance gives no withering but life in abundance.

It is correct that healing was 'work' in the eyes of the Pharisees, but if life was in danger, such work could supersede the sabbath rules. It was a nice point just when life was in such danger that it was likely to be lost, and in rabbinical literature is found the following: 'If in performing the ceremony of circumcision, which affects only one member of the body, one is to disregard the sabbath Laws, how much more should one do so for the whole body when it is in danger!' (Mek.Shab.1). That is true even in self-defence against a burglar. A person saved means he can observe future sabbaths and therefore it is good that his life is saved. The religious leaders were also divided about the correct procedure if an animal fell into a pit. I.T. teaching included: 'Show mercy to your neighbours and ... have compassion towards all, not towards men only, but also towards beasts' (T.Zeb. 5:1). The Qumran community had a positive rule that it should not be rescued on a sabbath.

In rabbinical literature any form of cruelty or pain must not be inflicted on an animal. An animal getting into difficulties must receive support for life, even on the sabbath (b.Shab. 128b) and not only hunting but also any spectator 'sport' such as contests between animals, circuses, or other events in which mutilation was possible, were also abhorred (b.A.Z. 18b). It is even claimed that in Noah's ark, 'We did not sleep but gave to the animals, birds and beasts each its food during the night' (Midr. Ps. 37.1).

* * *

G 14. The woman bent double - Lk. 13:10-17.

One sabbath, Jesus was teaching in a synagogue and there was a woman there, possessed by a demon of weakness. She had suffered for eighteen years; she was bent double, and unable to stand up straight.

When Jesus saw her he said, "You are loosed from your infirmity." He laid his hands on her and at once she straightened herself up and began to praise God.

The president of the synagogue was indignant. Healing on the sabbath! That was work! There were six other days for working and if there were to be healings, they were not to be done on the sabbath.

"What impious, ungodly men you are," said Jesus. "Is there a single one of you who, on the sabbath, does not loosen his ox or donkey from its stall and lead it away to give it water? Yet here is this woman, a daughter of Abraham, kept bound by Satan for eighteen years! Was it not necessary for her to be loosened from these bonds on the sabbath?"

All his opponents were put to shame, but the onlookers were delighted by the blessed things he brought about.

It was a firmly held belief that disease or deformity was associated with sin, either individual or of the nation. This was particularly true in Judaism in which God's servants must be perfect and without blemish: 'You shall be to me a kingdom of priests and a holy nation' (Ex. 19:6) and 'No man of the descendants of Aaron the priest, who has a blemish shall come near to offer the Lord's offerings by fire ... he shall not come near to offer the bread of his God' (Lev. 21:21). It was thought that well-built, tall people were favoured by God: 'God's Spirit rests only on a wise man, a strong man, a wealthy man and a tall man' (b.Shab. 92a);. 'Only men of stature, wisdom, good appearance, mature age and a knowledge of sorcery (and thus able to detect it) can be members of the Sanhedrin' (b.San. 17a).

It is also likely that Jesus, like many others, thought that when sickness and disease were removed, the kingdom of God would be fully present. This process was beginning and helping it along by healing was God's work. His call had been made: 'The Lord has chosen Zion, he has desired it for his habitation; therefore ... her priests I will clothe with salvation and her saints will shout for joy. There I will make a horn to sprout for David; I have made a lamp for my anointed. His enemies I will clothe with shame, but upon himself his crown will shed its lustre' (Ps. 132: 13,16-18); 'But you shall be called the priests of the Lord; men shall speak of you as ministers of our God' (Is. 61:6). The True Israel was becoming triumphant: 'All who are incensed against you shall be put to shame and confounded; those who strive against you shall be as nothing and perish' (Is. 41:11).

The leaders were not so sure; not keeping to the rules they had evolved over the centuries appeared to be very disruptive. They had good arguments on their side too: to keep an animal without water was cruel and therefore against O.T. teaching, but there was no similarity between the woman's case and that of the animals, in spite of the fact that she had suffered for eighteen years. One day longer in her case, was hardly significant, but they had forgotten that that could be against God's wishes and cause 'A tumult from the city, a voice from the Temple, the voice of the Lord rendering recompense to his adversaries' (Is. 66:6).

In this healing, Jesus deals with a woman who, perhaps from a belief in her own unworthiness, was bent over so she could not straighten up. She could not 'look anyone in the face' (she could not receive forgiveness, see G 17) and she was even worse off than the donkey or ox. They at least had to put their heads down to drink when they were loosed from their stalls, and led to water. The passage uses language which plays on the idea that to loosen the bonds of this daughter of Abraham could hardly be considered more wicked than to loosen those of the beasts. Then she could lift her head and receive the 'water' she needed, God's blessing. Perhaps Jesus thought of the rabbinical saying, 'He that is bent down shall speedily be loosed' (Gen.R. 20:10, based on Dt. 3:19 and Ps.145:14).

God could restore the repentant sinner afterwards, and curing a bent back was a divine action. The woman no longer was one of the lost but had become one of the New Israel. God had cured her weakness: 'The Lord... raises up all who are bowed down' (Ps. 145:14); 'He who is oppressed shall speedily be released' (Is. 51:14), and in a rabbinical commentary on Dt. 3:19, to be able to stand upright is taken to be a sign of recovery from illness (Tanh. 76a,b); 'The Lord raises the poor from the dust and lifts the needy from the rubbish heap' (Ps. 113:7).

The woman's infirmity could have had many causes but the evangelist says she had been like that for eighteen years, which the Jews believed was the duration of God's punishment, for example: 'The people of Israel served Eglon, the king of Moab eighteen years' (Jdg. 3:14). Disobedient Israelites were punished by God for their opposition to his will: 'Let their eyes be darkened so that they cannot see; make their loins to tremble continually' (Ps. 69:23), or in the Greek version, '...the back of the sinner is perpetually bowed down' (Ps. 68:23,LXX); 'He will bring on you again all the diseases of Egypt ... Every sickness and every affliction ... the Lord will bring upon you, until you are destroyed' (Dt. 28:60-61).

The rules of the Pharisees, though derived from scripture, were not always God's intentions, and it was these which must be followed. It was not enough to be in acute, immediate danger of being killed; those in the valley of death's shadow needed rescuing too. Satan had tied up this woman and she must be freed from his bonds at once.

* * *

G 15. The man with dropsy - Lk. 14:1-6.

One sabbath, Jesus had been invited to dine at the house of one of the leading Pharisees. There was a man there suffering from dropsy, and Jesus asked the company of doctors of the Law and Pharisees, "Is it lawful to heal people on the sabbath or not?"

They said nothing.

Jesus continued, "If one of you had an ox or a donkey which fell into a well, would you not pull it out even on a sabbath?"

Again they could make no reply against him.

Jesus then turned to the man and healed him.

Dropsy could have been one of several diseases, or even simply a watery discharge, but usually it was used when the body was swollen, either by accumulated liquid or from other causes.

This story is very similar to the two previous passages but Greeks as well as Jews believed a dropsical condition was a result of sin, especially unchastity, and it is said that cases were cured at the temple of Asclepios at Epidauros. 'He who devotes himself to sin, wounds and bruises break out over him ... dropsy is sign of sin' (b.Shab.33a) is a rabbinical saying. In the O.T., too, a dropsical person is under God's curse: 'Therefore may this water that brings the curse, pass into your bowels and make your body swell ...' (Num. 5:22); and in I.T. writings: 'When Nadan heard his uncle's words, he swelled up immediately and became like a blown-out bladder. His limbs swelled, his legs, feet and side, and he was torn and his belly burst asunder, his entrails were scattered and he perished and died' (Ahk. 8:38). When the Israelites were in the wilderness and not tainted by the idolatry of Canaan, they never suffered from swollen feet or legs: 'Forty years you sustained them in the wilderness ... and their feet did not swell' (Neh. 9:21).

In the understanding of the day, a person swollen up was likened to a man in a well or cistern or pit, full of water or mire, except that he was in danger of drowning in the water within him, rather than that outside him: 'Save me, O God, for the waters have come up to my neck ... I have come into deep waters and the flood sweeps over me ... Rescue me, O God, from sinking in the mire; let me be delivered from my enemies and from the deep waters' (Ps. 69:1-3,14).

To fall, or be cast, into a pit was to be punished by God: 'But you, O God, will cast them down into the lowest pit, men of blood and treachery shall not live out all their days' (Ps. 55:23). If they truly repented 'Let neither man nor beast ... taste anything, let them not feed nor drink water, but let man and beast be covered with sackcloth and let them cry mightily to God' (Jon. 3:7), God would pull the sinner out of the pit and save him as he did Jeremiah (Jer. 39:11-14). An animal which falls in is hauled out, and is cared for by God; surely a man should be too! 'We are the people of his pasture, and the sheep of his hand' (Ps. 95:7).

But there was hope. God will not punish the sinner for ever: 'I will not contend for ever, nor will I always be angry ... I will heal him, lead him and requite him with comfort' (Is. 57:16,18); and: 'Your healing shall spring up quickly' (Is.

58:8). Jesus' actions speak louder than his words. By healing so boldly on the sabbath and in a synagogue, he proclaimed that the yoke of divine punishment was lifted, the kingdom of God was come, and with the New Era beginning, freeing and healing were fully appropriate. If the synagogues and their leaders had not been so bound by their interpretations of the Law, and therefore unable to help in any way, things would have been very different: 'Thus says the Lord God, who gathers the outcasts of Israel, I will gather yet others to him, beside those already gathered' (Is. 56:8).

In any case, Judaism was very clear about this point. Animals had to be cared for: 'I will give grass in your fields and for your cattle and you will eat and be filled. This teaches us that one may not eat until it is sure the beasts have their food' (b.Git. 62a on Dt. 11:15). A story in the rabbinical books illustrates this point: 'Rabbi Judah was out one day and a terrified calf ran and hid under his robe. He showed no compassion, merely telling the calf that it was there to be slaughtered. From that time he suffered several painful illnesses. Later the maid disturbed a nest of young weasels and R. Judah told her to leave them alone. He quoted Ps 145:9, "His mercies are over all his works". As he was compassionate towards the animals, heaven was kind to him and his pains left him' (b.B.M. 85a); 'Show kindness to your neighbours and have compassion towards all, not only humans but also towards beasts' (T.Zeb. 5:1); 'If an animal falls into a dyke, one may bring pillows and bedding so it does not perish. If it is not in danger, food and water instead may be brought until the end of the sabbath. The avoidance of suffering of dumb animals is a law which overrides the interdicts of the rabbis' (b.Shab. 128b); 'One must remove debris to save life even on the sabbath. A child who has fallen in the sea, or into a pit, must be rescued even using a net though work is done and fishes may be caught in the net too' (b.Ket. 84b).

* * *

G 16. The Temple tax - Mt. 17:24-27.

The Temple tax was one levied by the Temple authorities on professing Jews. It was a Jewish tax, not a Roman one, laid on Jews for the upkeep of God's residence, the Temple in Jerusalem. The collectors were not the infamous gatherers of Roman taxes, but respected persons, specially commissioned to collect the tax during Nissan, the month before the Passover, and it was a privilege for Jews to contribute.

Since the collection was for the upkeep of the Temple, the priests, being part of the Temple household, were exempt. In later centuries the rabbis and renowned holy men were also exempt, and it is very likely this was true at the time of Jesus. '...we certify that priests, ... ministers of the house of God shall not have imposed on them tribute, custom or toll.' The collectors were perhaps uncertain of the status of Jesus and whether he was exempted too.

The collectors of the Temple tax came to Peter and asked if the teacher paid this tax. Peter confirmed this was the case, and afterwards, when he entered the house where they were staying in Capernaum, Jesus said to him, "Simon, do monarchs of this world take toll or poll-tax from their own sons or from others?" "From others", Peter answered. "Quite so," said Jesus. "But then the sons are exempt! However, we do not want to be a stumbling-block for these collectors. Go to the sea and catch the first fish that takes the hook; you'll find a shekel in its mouth to pay the tax for me and you."

This story appears only in Matthew, and relates to the collection of the offerings made by the people of Israel after Moses came down from Mount Sinai. The tax of a half shekel was levied on every male Jew over twenty years of age each year, and payment had to be made in Temple shekels: 'The Lord said to Moses, "When you take the census of the people of Israel, each shall give a ransom for himself to the Lord ... each shall give half a shekel, according to the shekel of the sanctuary ... Every one who is ... twenty years old and upwards shall give the Lord's offering"' (Ex. 30:12-13). Other money had to be changed into Temple-shekels and a surcharge was made for this service, unless a whole shekel was paid for two men together, or if one half was charity for someone without personal resources.

The priests were exempt because they were servants of the institution for which the tax was collected; in the secular world too, although a king may pay his own taxes to encourage his citizens to pay theirs, his employees, his servants, and his family were exempt. Jesus draws the obvious conclusion. He and his disciples ought to be exempt too. They are servants of, employees of, God and *they* should be exempt rather than the priests of the Temple.

The situation was very awkward. It was necessary not to compromise the principle that God's servants should not pay, but it was also imperative not to provoke a situation in which the collectors, under orders from Jerusalem, would be expected to coerce Jesus and his disciples to pay. This could cause the collectors to sin, and that was worse than taking the way of peace and paying the required shekel. With a typically Jewish mode of thinking, the solution to this kind of dilemma is illustrated by the following story.

It was forbidden for a Jew to have any (financial) transactions with a pagan during one of their festivals. One day, during such a festival, a rabbi was brought a gold coin from a pagan which he ought not to receive. Equally he ought not to deviate from the way of peace by refusing the gift. His friend solved the problem for him: 'Take the coin, but drop it at once into a well. Then you have received it and not received it.'

Where were they to get the shekel from? No doubt they had some funds collected from well-wishers but they could hardly use those against their understanding of the unrighteousness of the tax for themselves. If they could find a coin which was lost, that would be fine, since such a coin was in no man's ownership. The solution to this problem given in the passage - catching a fish and finding the money ready in its mouth - is clearly convenient, but it may be capable of a reasonable explanation. Some think that certain cat-fish, which were unclean in Jewish eyes because they were without scales, were very attracted to anything bright and shiny. If a coin dropped from the quay, one of these fishes would snap it up.

Others think it is more in the nature of a typical folk-tale, and in a rabbinical passage there is a similar story in which a fine pearl is found in a fish: 'Joseph-who-honours-the-Sabbath lived near a Gentile who owned much property. He was told Joseph would consume all his property so he sold all and bought a fine jewel which he put on the front of his turban. One day the wind blew it off and he lost the stone. A fish which swallowed it was later caught and taken to Joseph. He bought it and found in it the missing jewel which he sold for many pots of gold coins. An old man heard of it and remarked, "He who uses his wealth to honour the sabbath, the sabbath repays him"' (b.Shab.119a).

In any case, it is irrelevant to the main lesson of the passage. Out of regard for the ways of peace, that is, to avoid provoking another to sin, Jesus is shown to agree to something which was not based on a true understanding of the situation.

Some groups of Jews refused to pay the tax more than once in a life-time, for example Samaritans and the Qumran community; they followed the law: 'Each one ... from twenty years old and upwards, shall give the Lord's offering. The rich shall not give more nor the poor less than the half shekel ... to make atonement for your lives' (Ex. 30:14-15). In the laws laid down by Nehemiah after the return from exile, the Temple tax is one third of a shekel per man per year. The reason for this discrepancy remains obscure.

* * *

G 17. Caesar's due - Mt. 22:15-22. Mk. 12:13-17. Lk. 20:20-26.

It had been a matter of fierce disagreement whether Jews should pay Roman taxes or not. Some thought it was proper to do so since the foreign power was there with God's permission and maybe was his instrument of punishment for the sins of the Jews. Certain of the Pharisees agreed with the zealots that paying taxes in Palestine to the Roman Caesar was wrong. Taxes to the local king were approved, and paying taxes to Rome among the Jews outside Palestine was all right, but otherwise they objected to paying Roman taxes.

Yet other Pharisees were against the use of the Roman coin, in which the tax had to be paid, because it had on it the image of the Emperor and this was therefore a graven image and idolatrous. The Herodians on the other hand thought taxes ought to be paid to Rome, because Herod was kept in place by Roman power, and someone advocating that Roman taxes should not be paid was suspect in their eyes.

Some of the Pharisees and also some of Herod's party agreed on a plan to send some agents to Jesus to try to trap him with a question. "Master", they said, "you are a truthful man and you pay deference to no one, nor show partiality, but teach the way of God. Is it in accordance with the Law for us to pay taxes to Caesar?"

Seeing how sly their question was Jesus said to them, "Why are you putting me to the test? Show me a denarius." They found one and showed it to Jesus. "Whose image does it bear and whose superscription?", he asked.

"Caesar's", they replied.

"Then", said Jesus, "pay Caesar what is due to him, and pay to God what is due to God."

This answer surprised them and they went silently away.

The question was aimed at putting Jesus on the spot, since to suggest that Roman taxes were not to be paid was tantamount to insurrection, while to advocate that Jews should pay without concern was looked upon by some as treason to the Jewish cause.

The spies first flatter Jesus. They mention that he does not 'raise up the faces of men'. In a personal appeal to the king, the petitioner would kneel down and press his face to the floor and if his petition was granted his face would be lifted up. Here it implies that Jesus is a righteous judge who does not doctor his teaching to suit the importance, prestige and status of the enquirer. 'You (judges) shall not pervert justice; you shall not show partiality nor take a bribe, for a bribe blinds the eyes of the wise and subverts the cause of the righteous' (Dt. 16:19); 'The Lord sees not as man sees; man looks on the outward appearance, but the Lord looks on the heart' (I Sam. 16:7). Jesus sees the trap they have created for him and avoids either of the alternatives offered. It is not a question of either/or, but of both.

The problem of the relation between the Roman state and the Jews was difficult. There had been attempts to solve similar problems earlier: 'Amariah, the chief priest, is over you in all matters of the Lord; and Zebadiah ... in all matters of the king' (II Chr. 19:11), but in the time of Jesus in Palestine, there were strongly differing opinions amongst the Jews. They had their own kings, courts and assemblies, and only for major matters did Rome determine the outcome.

The question put to Jesus had no obvious answer, since the Law does not mention the difficulty and it is significant that they asked Jesus if it is in accordance with the Law that they should pay taxes to Rome. Jesus perhaps thought of other O.T. and I.T. passages, none of them in the Torah: 'By me kings reign and rulers decree what is just; by me princes rule and nobles govern the earth' (Pvb. 8:15-16); 'Do as the king commands you and if you have to swear by God, do not be precipitate' (Ecc. 8:2); 'Hear then, you kings, take this to heart ... It is the Lord who gave you your authority; your power comes from the Most High' (W.S. 6:1,3). Ultimately, the king and the Roman emperor were under God's authority and it is to his will they must submit in the end. It was not the foreign power which was contrary to the rule of God, but that of ungodly powers in the lives of men. One must not use the covenant with God to usurp the king's authority, yet, should the command be directly against God's rule, it cannot be obeyed. If one obeys God and thereby denies the ruler, one must accept that persecution may be the result. This happened to Nebuchadnezzar's three provincial governors, and rather than obey the king's demand to worship his idol, they ended up in the furnace.

* * *

G 18. Seven times married - Mt. 22:23-33. Mk. 12:18-27. Lk. 20:27-40.

The law of levirate marriage is: 'If brothers live together and one of them dies without leaving a son ... the husband's brother shall have intercourse with her (the widow); he shall take her in marriage and do his duty by her as her husband's brother. The first son she bears shall perpetuate the dead brother's name so that it may not be blotted out from Israel' (Dt. 25:5-6); and: 'Go in to your brother's widow and perform the duty of a brother-in-law to her, and raise up offspring for your brother' (Gen. 38:8). It was the maintenance of the family name which was crucial for the Jew: 'Do not remain unmarried lest you die nameless' (P.Ph. 175).

Some of the Sadducees who deny the resurrection of the dead came to him. They put a question to Jesus. "Master, Moses said that if there are brothers and one dies leaving a widow but no child, another brother should marry her and carry on his brother's family.
Now there were seven brothers. The first married and died without issue and his widow married a second brother. He also died without issue and the woman married the third brother. This was repeated until all seven had been her husband, and eventually she died too. When the resurrection comes, whose wife will she be, since in life she had married all seven?"
Jesus replied, "Are you wrong because you know neither the scriptures nor the power of God? The sons of the present world marry, but after the resurrection people neither marry nor are given in marriage. They are immortal, like angels in heaven. That the dead rise is shown by the book of Moses. At the bush, God said to Moses, 'I (am) the God of Abraham, Isaac and Jacob.' God is not the God of corpses, but of the living."

The story seems artificial and intended to test Jesus, apparently, although there is said to have been such a case, which is discussed in a rabbinical work. (The woman was considered too dangerous to marry again!)
In Judaism, one idea was that the body remained in existence for a year after death and the soul ascends to heaven and descends to the body again more than once. At the end of a year the body ceases to exist and the soul ascends to heaven permanently (b.Shab. 152b). In another passage the treatment of the soul was discussed. There were supposed to be three categories: righteous, unrighteous and those halfway between. The righteous go to paradise at once; the unrighteous go to Gehinnom, while the middle group also go to hell but only for a year. After that, about one third are raised up and admitted to heaven (b.R.H. 16b). There are three O.T. passages which may be relevant to this story. The first is that of Samuel, who, under God's guidance, rejects the first seven of David's brothers, sons of Jesse. The second is that of Tobias and his marriage to Sarah, whose previous seven husbands had died on their wedding nights (see Tobit, ch. 6). The third is the story of the martyrdom of the seven sons and their

mother, told in the book of Maccabees. In this story, the seven brothers are put to death one by one, so each one died childless and their mother was then put to death and died a widow and childless (see II Maccabees, ch. 7).

This story is one which Jews still remember. Martyrs were usually regarded as immortalised, and received directly into God's heaven as Abraham, Isaac and Jacob had been. In one version, it is said that those who '... with their whole heart make righteousness their first thought, these alone can master the weakness of the flesh, believing that they do not die to God, but are as our patriarchs, Abraham, Isaac and Jacob and are alive with God' (IV. Mac. 7:18-19); and: 'They (the seven sons) themselves knowing well that men dying for God are alive with him, as Abraham, Isaac and Jacob and all the patriarchs live with God ...' (IV. Mac. 16:25). In several other I.T. passages eternal life with God is promised for the righteous: 'The spirits of you who have died in righteousness shall live and rejoice ... before the face of the Great One' (I En. 103:4); 'The righteous live for ever' (W.S. 5:15).

The last paragraph of the passage uses Jewish phraseology: 'In the world to come there is no eating and drinking nor procreation and child-bearing, no trade or business, no enmity and strife', and the quotation is from the book of Exodus: 'I am the God of your father, the God of Abraham, the God of Isaac, and the God of Jacob.' (Ex. 3:6). In I.T. books also: 'You were spiritual [beings] living the eternal life ... and therefore I have not appointed wives for you ...' (I En. 15:6-7).

That one group of Jews did not believe in a future resurrection of the dead shows it was not stated in the O.T. in a way which compelled acceptance. The idea does not occur in the Pentateuch but is found elsewhere: 'They that sleep in the earth will awake and shout for joy ... and the earth will bring those long dead to birth again' (Is. 26:19); 'God will ransom my life, he will take me from the power of Sheol (hell)' (Ps. 49:15); 'The Lord rescues me from the pit of death and surrounds me with constant love' (Ps. 103:4). Another passage, 'The Lord, the God of your ancestors, the God of Abraham, the God of Isaac, and the God of Jacob, has sent me to you' (Ex. 3:15), was taken to mean that God has a continuing relationship with Abraham, in spite of his having died. As all other Jews follow Abraham, it follows the resurrection is to come, although it was believed that only those who died within the land of Israel would rise from the dead (b.Keth.111a).

The Sadducees wanted to find out Jesus' opinion of what heaven was supposed to be like, and in particular what would happen to human relationships after the resurrection. That angels do not marry and are without gender also seems to be something more common in Jewish writing other than the O.T. Life after death is portrayed as being spiritual and full of rejoicing like angels: 'You will have great joy as the angels of heaven ... you will be companions of the hosts of heaven' (I En. 104:4,6); 'They shall behold the world now invisible to them, and the time now hidden from them, and time shall no longer age them, and they will be made like angels ...' (II Bar. 51:8-10).

The point for Jesus was that in the next world all would be God's immortal children and therefore there was no need for sons to carry on a name, nor for marrying in order to do so. The whole idea is meaningless after the resurrection.

* * *

G 19. Divorce and remarriage - Mt. 5:31-32; 19:1-12. Mk. 10:1-12. Lk. 16:18.

The background for this passage is the disagreement about divorce among the different sections of Judaism at the time of Jesus. The spectrum of views ranged from no divorce at all to very easy divorce. It seems likely that Jesus seeks in this passage to make the Law on this topic applicable equally to men and women.

The idea that two became one in marriage may be due to the opinion of the day that before men and women are born, God had created them in couples, a man and his mate, as he had created Adam and Eve, so that to separate them was to undo God's work. This was partly based on: 'God created man in his image ... male and female he created them' (Gen. 1:27); and: 'Therefore a man leaves his father and mother and cleaves to his wife and they become one flesh' (Gen. 2:24).

The same idea occurs in other O.T. and I.T. books: 'God is a witness between you and the wife of your youth. You have been unfaithful to her, though she is your partner and your wife protected by contract. For God hates a man to pronounce separation and cover his cloak with outrage' (Mal. 2:14-16); '... they shall be caught by fornication by taking two wives during their life-time. But the fundamental principle of the creation is "Male and female he created them". They who went into the Ark, went in two by two. And ... it is written, he shall not multiply wives to himself' (Zad. 7:2-3); '(God made Eve from Adam's rib.) Therefore shall man and wife be one, and therefore shall a man leave his father and mother and join with his wife and they shall be one flesh' (Jub. 3:7).

These texts do not necessarily mean that the marriages are indissoluble, although God may determine who shall marry whom. Indeed the Law demanded that a man divorce his wife if she was immoral in her conduct, so that to remain within the Law Jesus did not dispute that divorce in such cases was necessary. Any woman who had had sexual contact was defiled and no man could avoid polluting himself if he had contact with her, except within their married union, so that the objection was less to divorce than to remarriage leading to polygamy.

Jesus was visiting Peraea when some of the Pharisees asked him a question, testing him: 'Is it allowed for a man to divorce his wife for any reason?"

Jesus replied, "Did not God make them male and female from the beginning of creation, so that a man leaves his father and his mother and clings to his wife and these two become one flesh? They are no longer two but one body. What God joined together, man must not separate."

The questioners said to him, "Why then did Moses permit a man to divorce his wife by a note of dismissal, and send her away?"

Jesus answered, "Yes, because of your hard-heartedness, Moses allowed you to put away your wives, but it has not been so from the beginning. I tell you this: the one who sends away his wife without cause and marries another, commits adultery."

Later the disciples said to Jesus, "If that's how
it is with husband and wife, it is better not to marry."
"That is something which not everyone can accept
but only those for whom it has been given," said Jesus.
"Some are eunuchs because they were born so, some were
made so by men, but others have made themselves eunuchs
for the sake of the kingdom of God. Let those accept it
who can."

It was a strange question for a Pharisee to put to Jesus. The Pharisee would certainly have known what the scriptures say, and that they followed the rule given in Torah. He would be very foolish to suppose Jesus did not also know the appropriate texts and could not be said to test Jesus by this question.

The justification for divorce was the wife's 'indecency'. It is not certain just what was meant by this word, but some extended it to include any attribute the husband found undesirable! Its meaning could in fact range from indecorous or indecent behaviour, incestuous relationships, sexual relations outside the permitted sanguinary ones (but see below), mixed marriages with a non-Jew, to prostitution, or if one of the pair had no intention of marrying the other.

It is unlikely to mean simply adultery. For one thing there is another Greek word which the evangelist uses when he wishes to specify adultery, which was punishable by death. It could mean incest since this is clearly forbidden in the Torah: 'No man shall approach anyone near of kin to uncover nakedness' (Lev. 18:6); 'Do not profane your daughter by making her a harlot ...' (Lev. 19:29), and the question put to Jesus refers to the Law. It was sometimes a practical problem because the great frequency of polygamy produced many half-siblings.

In addition, any non-Jews becoming converted to Judaism were thought to be born anew, to have broken all contacts with their previous existences. The new Jew could then take up a new relationship which might be within the forbidden degrees of blood relationship. The religious leaders seemed to have turned a blind eye to this situation. Since it is so difficult to be sure just what was meant, the term 'unchastity' is perhaps the one best to use.

This passage involves difficulties with languages and translation of the Hebrew or Aramaic underlying the Greek text. For Jews, sexual intercourse even before the marriage ceremony with an intention to marry was sufficient in Jewish law for the pair to be considered as married. Also whereas for Greeks, prostitution always meant payment to the woman, in Judaism it was still prostitution even when no money or payment of any kind was involved.

In Judaism, improper sexual behaviour was a sin. The usual text of the Torah concerning divorce is: 'If a man takes a wife but he dislikes her because of her indecency and he writes her a bill of divorce and puts it into her hand and sends her away; and she becomes another's wife, but the second husband also despises her and gives her a bill of divorce and sends her away, or if he dies; then her former husband cannot marry her again. She is defiled and that is an abomination before the Lord ...' (Dt. 24:1-4).

This does not state divorce is permitted, it requires it. Any sexual contact was defiling except that within marriage: 'If any man's wife goes astray and acts unfaithfully against him, if a man lies carnally with her ... she has defiled herself ...' (Num. 5:13); 'You shall not lie carnally with your neighbour's wife and defile yourself with her' (Lev. 18:20). If a woman was unchaste, she could not continue to be a righteous man's wife. Originally this rule applied to all, but later it became limited to the priests: 'They shall not marry a harlot or a woman who has been defiled; neither shall they marry a woman divorced from her husband' (Lev. 21:7).

Betrothals and marriages were often arranged and dissolved in order to accumulate and preserve wealth and dynasties. Marriage in Judaism is a contract, not a sacrament and a divorced woman is forbidden to her husband as she has become unclean (m.Sot. 5:1).

Jesus' teaching was similar to that of the Essenes and a reaction against the trivialisation of the marriage bond in his society. He maintains not only that divorce is not as God would have it but that the rules apply to both men and women. Many think he advocated the same standard among his followers as among the priests of the Temple, with strict monogamy, although the evangelist appears to have considered celibacy as at least acceptable. This view is quite contrary to most Jewish thought. Rabbinical passages make clear some other ideas: 'Any Jew without a wife is not a man, as it is written, "Male and female he created them", and he blessed them and named them mankind when they were created' (b.Ket. 8a, on Gen 5:2); 'Among those whose life is not life is the man who is ruled by his wife' (b.Betzah 32b); 'A bad wife is like leprosy to her husband ... Let him divorce her and be cured (b.Yeb. 63b).

Self-mutilation was strongly condemned in Judaism, and castration of men and animals was forbidden: 'Any animal that has its testicles bruised or crushed ... such you shall not do within your land, nor accept any such animal from a foreigner ...' (Lev. 22:24-25). Castration and celibacy here have to be taken figuratively: a man may give up marriage for the sake of God's kingdom, but it was not to be for its own sake.

* * *

G 20. The Law - Mt. 5:17-20. Lk. 16:17.

The Law comprised the instructions of the Torah. These were unalterable since the Torah was conceived as being engraved in stone. Such writing was unlike writing in other media which could be erased or destroyed. Incised writing was part of the stone, and could not be changed without destroying the whole. Thus the Law was unalterable but the interpretations and the rules which humans had evolved since were not the same and were subject to modification.

Jesus did not wish to annul the Law. He upheld it spiritually, making selective use of it, and also acted as rabbis have done before and since, using one part of scripture to reinterpret, extend, or limit more strictly, the accepted conventional meaning of another part of scripture.

In rabbinical literature, to abolish the Law meant also to misinterpret it. One 'cancels' Torah when it is misunderstood. To fulfil the Law is to interpret it correctly.

Jesus revered Torah, given by God and therefore to be obeyed. What Jesus is said to teach is the correct interpretation for those aspiring to enter the kingdom, and is not intended to make the Law redundant. The greater righteousness of his followers is specified: 'You shall be blameless before the Lord your God' (Dt 18:13); but he protects himself from the charge that he wants to reduce the importance of the Law and the Prophets.

"Do not suppose that I have come to abolish the Law and the Prophets," said Jesus. "I did not come to abolish, but to uphold and fulfil them. I tell you this, until heaven and earth pass away, not a letter, not a jot will disappear from the Law, or lose its force, until all that must happen has happened. If any man therefore sets aside even the least of the Law's demands, and teaches others to do likewise, he will be called the least in the kingdom of God; whereas anyone who keeps the Law and teaches others to do so, will stand high in the kingdom of God. It is certainly true that unless you show yourselves more righteous than the Pharisees and doctors of the Law, you can never enter the kingdom of God."

The evangelist, Matthew, tells us that Jesus came to fulfil the Law, to understand and interpret it correctly, to practise it fully and to become its ultimate end, that is to follow its observances as in the Jewish prayer which has come down to us from that time: 'O put it into our hearts to understand and to discern, to mark and learn and teach and heed, to do and to fulfil in love all the words of instruction in your Law.' In the community of Matthew, the leaders were called prophet, sage, martyr or scribe. They were accepted as fulfilling the scriptures, not destroying them.

The Law would remain for ever and for the Jew, keeping to the exact performance of the Torah was the source of light in a man's life. It was one way in which the Jew expressed his love of God: 'My heart stands in awe of your words; I rejoice at them like one who finds great spoil ... Great peace have those who love your

Law, and nothing can make them stumble' (Ps. 119:161-165). Any suggestion that the Torah was to be tampered with would arouse strong resistance. This was apparent also in I.T. writings: 'The people bade them pronounce a curse ... upon any who should make any alteration by adding or changing in any way ... the words which had been written, or making any omission' (L.A. 311); 'For to you and your fathers the Lord gave a Law more excellent than to all peoples' (II Bar. 77:3); and in rabbinical teaching: 'In the book it is written, "I came not to destroy the Law of Moses nor to add to it"' (b.Shab. 116b); 'When you walk, the Torah will lead you (in this world); when you lie down, it will watch over you (in the grave); and when you awake, it will talk with you (in the next world)' (m.Avot. 6:9).

Jesus used the scriptures of his day to proclaim to all, his insights into God's will, some of them typical of a mystic. Jesus used the Law as the mould from which to form his own teaching, demanding a performance based on God's standards not man's, so that his followers could become 'perfect': 'I am God Almighty; walk before me and be blameless' (Gen. 17:1). He promoted selflessness for God's glory similar to that Job proclaimed (Job 31), but his teaching was for the New Era. The covenants of Adam and Noah were archaic, and even that of Moses hung from a nail which would give way when the new Adam arose (see H 6).

In rabbinical literature the story of king Solomon is given as a warning. The Torah said a king should not take many wives because they could distract his heart from God (Dt. 17:17). Solomon took the view that in his case his heart would nevertheless be faithful and therefore he could take many wives. He rewrote the verse with the word 'not' to suit his own desires but God intervened and said, 'Solomon and a hundred like him will pass away but a *yod* in thee [the scriptures] will never pass away' (Cant.R. 11:3).

It was not only the written Torah which was of importance. There were the traditions which were kept alive by being memorised. They were thought of as a protective layer: 'The tradition is a fence round the Torah; tithes are a fence around riches; vows are a fence around abstinence; a fence round wisdom is silence' (m.Sot. 3:14).

* * *

G. Summary.

In this section the thrust of most of the passages was to make the religious leaders aware of how far they fell short in their calling and how misleading they were for others. They made no attempt to help and heal those who were sick and full of guilt and misery over their sins, or imagined sins, and they even added to their burdens by teaching that without propitiation and penance, God would not forgive them. The synagogues were useless!

Some of the leaders had substituted human rules such as the vow of Korban for God's rules, or had become idolaters rejecting the sanctity of God and his altar. They were like corrupt tenants of God's vineyard trying to take over Creation, and they would be removed. They thought they had built the true Temple, but they had rejected the crucial key stone for their building.

They put on a fine show of piety but God was not fooled. They were blind guides with the silliest judgements. Unfortunately the Israelites were taken in by these wolves in impressive garments, showing how rotten they too had become. God's punishment would fall on them on the day of Judgement which was near. The times were ripe; the abuses of the priesthood, the 'sons of the fathers', all the leaders of the Israelites, did not follow God's purpose. The old Temple and its abuses would be destroyed, and a new one built in the New Era.

These leaders concentrated on external show. Like tombs and bowls they were clean outside and full of putrefaction within; they thought it was the uncleanness of foods which produced a person's wicked thoughts. Like the rich man who held on to his wealth, they gave rein to their senses, their 'door-keeper' was dismissed and their bad inclination had taken over.

It was not Jesus who wished to destroy the Law. Far from it; he wished to see it practised as it had been intended. Its understanding and practice was what needed reform; the sabbath law was not defied nor contradicted. It was a righteous act to heal on the sabbath, it was permitted for the poor and hungry to take grain from the part of the field set aside for them, and rinsing of hands did not remove evil inclinations. Even those who did a good deed by force of circumstances realised that God's way was the best and were approved while those who proved themselves trustworthy in small matters could be given great responsibilities.

A few passages show how some of these leaders tried to trap Jesus with arguments about various dilemmas, which he answers with reference to O.T. teaching. Kings rule under God's authority and with his permission; there were no family names needing to be handed on to the next generation in heaven; marriages were not to be contracted for dynastic purposes and polygamy was contrary to God's will.

Even though he did not agree with the Temple tax system, Jesus was willing to pay it to the collectors rather than lead them into a greater mistake - provoking them to anger and aggression.

The whole of Jesus' ministry can be perceived as the embodiment of Judaism as it should be. The endless complications imposed by the scribes elders, sages and other religious leaders meant that only the most single-minded dedication could hope to bring a person to salvation. By returning to the relative simplicity of the Law, based on the commandment to love God and other people, Jesus cleared the way for all but the recalcitrant to live in God's realm and obey his rules.

The invective towards some of the Pharisees reported in the gospels may seem unduly harsh today, but was nothing out of the ordinary in the time of Jesus.

Throughout all Judaism, it was only the men of the society to which all the rules applied. Women for example, were exempt from the commandments which required observance at a particular stated time, because it might be that they had to attend to a child or other duties which could not be left. (m.Kid. 1:7).

* * *

H. Jesus as portrayed by the evangelists.

H 1. The feeding of the multitude, I - Mt. 14:13-21. Mk. 6:30-44. Lk. 9:10-17.

This story, like most of the miracle stories, seems to have been used by the evangelists to proclaim Jesus both as the New Moses, the one who would renew Israel, and a new Joshua who will reconquer Canaan for God. The text uses words which refer to 'rations' and the leek beds mentioned were in Canaan.

It is not necessary to establish whether it was an historical event or not, although it probably had its origin in an event in which many gathered and their hunger was stilled by Jesus' teaching. The miracles stories cannot have been recorded to promote someone who set his face so strongly against giving signs but they proclaim Jesus and his message as the means of redeeming Israel from its defection from God.

There are many associations with O.T. stories. Elisha feeding the multitude is one: 'A man came ... bringing ... twenty barley loaves and cakes of figs of the first-fruits. And Elisha said, "Give to the people and let them eat" But his servant said, "Why should I set this before a hundred men?" Elisha repeated, "Give them to the people and let them eat, for thus says the Lord: "They shall eat and leave""' (IV Kgs. 4:42-44 LXX).

Another is the story of Ruth and Boaz: 'Boaz passed to her dried grain and she ate until she was satisfied and she had some left over' (Rut. 2:14), but in Jewish literature, there was a belief or legend that food in the hand of the truly righteous would multiply. Ruth was thought to have received only as many grains of corn as Boaz could hold between the tips of his fingers, yet she was satisfied.

Again Abraham sent Hagar and Ishmael out into the wilderness with no more that a loaf and some water but because they belonged to his household, the bread and the water remained plentiful (PK 6:2).

The main O.T. basis for this passage is the story of the Exodus from Egypt. During the period in the wilderness, the Israelites were supplied with bread and quails from God: 'And the Lord humbled you and let you hunger and fed you with manna, which you did not know; ... that he might make you know that man does not live by bread alone, but that man lives by everything that proceeds out of the mouth of the Lord' (Dt. 8:3).

Then they were tricked into making a covenant with the pagan Gibeonites after sharing their bread: 'When the inhabitants of Gibeon heard what Joshua had done to Jericho and Ai, they acted with cunning, and made ready provisions, and took worn-out, patched sandals on their feet, and worn-out clothes; and all their provisions were dry and mouldy. They went to Joshua in the camp at Gilgal and said to him and to the men of Israel, "We have come from a far country ... because of the name of the Lord your God. ... Make now a covenant with us ... Here is our bread; it was still warm when we took it from our houses as our food for the journey ... but now it is dry and mouldy. These wine-skins were new when we filled them, see they are burst, and our garments and shoes are worn-out from the very long journey."

So the men partook of their provisions and did not ask directions from the Lord. And Joshua made peace with them, and made a covenant with them, to let them live; and the leaders of the congregation swore to them' (Jos. 9:3-15).

Ever since, the Israelites had been idolaters, sinful and wicked to a greater or lesser degree, while the Gibeonites became hewers of wood and drawers of water.

After their mission, Jesus said to the disciples, "Come away with me to a lonely place where you can rest", for they had had no chance even to eat, so many were coming and going.

They got into a boat to cross the Sea of Galilee to go to a deserted spot, but the people saw what was happening and rushed round by the shore and gathered from all the areas nearby to meet them.

When Jesus saw the great crowd, his heart went out to them. They were like sheep without a shepherd, and he began to teach them many things and heal the sick.

Time went by quickly and soon nightfall approached. "These people cannot remain here without food, and there is nowhere in this desolate place where they could get any," said the disciples. "Should you not send them to the farms and settlements round about so they can buy themselves something to eat?"

"You feed them," said Jesus.

"Feed them ourselves! Two hundred denarii would not be enough to buy bread for all these people."

"Go and see how many loaves there are," said Jesus. The disciples came back with five loaves and two fishes.

"Have them recline in companies on the green grass, a hundred groups, each of fifty, and let me have the loaves and fishes," said Jesus. He looked up to heaven and said the blessing, broke up the loaves and fishes and gave them to the disciples to distribute.

Everyone had enough, and the uneaten fragments were collected up, together with the remains of the fishes, and filled twelve baskets.

The disciples are offered the chance to rest, but the crowd nevertheless followed them and assembled in a a desolate place in the mountains, of which there were many in Galilee. 'He that walks in righteousness ... hating transgression and iniquity ... his refuge (is) a fortress among the rocks; bread and water shall be given him and never fail' (Is. 33:15-16). The people were like sheep without a shepherd, a crowd without any organisation or leadership, in chaos.

'Jesus had compassion for them'. This expression is strong: it means Jesus was so full of compassion that his bowels were churned up. He taught them about God's kingdom, which satisfied their hunger because it was from God: 'They asked and he brought quails and gave them bread in abundance' (Ps. 105:40). To a Hebrew of the day, bread and fishes would remind them of manna and quails, and however little one obtained, heavenly food was sufficient, as it had been for Elijah: 'An angel touched him and said, "Arise and eat" ... And there was a cake ... and a jar of water.

And he ate and drank and lay down again. And the angel came a second time ... and he arose and ate and drank, and went in the strength of that food forty days and forty nights to Horeb, the mount of God.' (I Kgs. 19:5-8).

Such manna was also remarkable: 'Moses said to Jethro, "In this manna, which God has given us, we can taste ... the taste of all the delicacies of the world"' (Mek.Ama 3); 'A great miracle was performed for the Israelite with the cake which they had been told to bake; they kept on eating it for thirty days until manna come down for them' (Mek.Pis. 14).

The crowd is organised by Jesus. The imagery is of soldiers, like beds of plants, probably leeks, arranged in groups of fifty, and the disciples are sent to them to get them ready to be campaigners with Jesus in conquering Canaan again, this time without being tricked or seduced into idolatry. It is possible to find analogies in the stories of the O.T. with this passage which are remarkably comprehensive. For example, Joshua had five thousand men with him when he took Ai at the beginning of the conquest of Canaan. Like the fish of Egypt, the two fishes were free: 'We remember the fish we ate in Egypt for nothing' (Num. 11:5), and the five loaves represent the five books of Moses, which Jesus reinterpreted and redistributed to those willing to accept them. They were the parts of Jesus' gospel, given out to the people by his disciples.

Jesus is shown as following the usual ritual before having a meal. He looked upwards and pronounced the Jewish grace or blessing: 'Blessed are you, O Lord our God, king of the universe, who brings forth bread from the earth', and then he broke the food and had it distributed. The crowd was satisfied: 'You shall eat and be full' (Dt. 8.10).

The residual fragments are those given to the servants of the Lord after the cereal offering has been made to God: 'If your offering is a cereal offering baked on a griddle it shall be of fine flour unleavened ... and you shall break it in pieces ...' (Lev. 2:5-6). The baskets into which the fragments were collected, represent the twelve tribes of Israel, reconstituted, perfected, and fed with the rest of the holy cereal offerings like the priesthood of Aaron and his sons.

There was no need for money. The bread they needed was not bought with money: 'Everyone who thirsts, come to the water; and he who has not money, come, buy and eat. Come, buy wine and milk without money and without price. Why spend your money on that which is not bread?' (Is. 55:1-2). In this case, the servants of the Lord were the disciples.

The N.T. story shows Jesus offering his bread, that is his word and teaching, to the Israelites: 'Your words were found and I ate them, and your words became to me a joy and delight of my heart' (Jer. 15:16); 'I will abundantly bless Zion's provisions; I will satisfy her poor with bread' (Ps. 132:15); 'The poor shall eat and be satisfied' (Ps. 22:26).

This was in order that they could revert to the purity of their forefathers before these had entered Canaan. Then they always had had enough and wanted for nothing. It is a picture of paradise, and is used by the evangelists to show that Jesus offers to the Jews a similar perfection in the kingdom of God in the New Era. To share bread or food with another was a symbol of having fellowship with one another and thus this story of sharing 'bread' with Jesus has similarities with the story of the Last Supper in which Jesus and his disciples share a meal. Some even think that this story was modelled on the Last Supper.

In rabbinical literature food and drink are understood as instruction in the Torah: 'If your enemy is hungry give him bread to eat and if he is thirsty give him water to drink. For you will heap coals of fire on his head and the Lord will reward [you]' (b.Suk. 52a).

For the Jews, the manna in the desert tasted of whatever the eater wished it to, except melons, cucumbers, onions and garlic, which the Israelites longed for but could not taste!

* * *

H 2. The 'apparition' - Mt. 14:22-33. Mk. 6:45-52.

Jesus sent his disciples on ahead to go by boat
to Bethsaida, while he himself sent the crowd away and
went off alone up the hill to pray. He remained there
until it was quite late. The disciples were well out on
the water, but made only slow progress against the wind
and the waves, so that it was in the fourth watch of the
night, between three and six in the morning, before they
approached their destination. Jesus came towards them
walking on the water. He was going to pass them by, but
they thought he was a ghost and cried out in terror.

He called out to them, "It is I, do not be
afraid." He climbed into the boat and immediately the
wind dropped. They were totally dumbfounded because they
had not understood the feeding sign. Their hearts were
hard, and their minds were closed.

There is a satisfactory solution to the physical facts of this story and the evangelist's purposes have also been elucidated. Some have suggested that the original text means that Jesus walked 'beside the water' rather than on it, but in all probability, he walked in it. The area of sea between the hill-side and the site of Bethsaida on the Sea of Galilee is very shallow, especially with a north-east wind, and it has been known even in recent times for people to cross the area on foot or by camel. On aerial photographs the shallows are clearly visible on both sides of the tongue of water from the Jordan river, which extends into the Sea of Galilee there. A north-east wind would also have hindered the progress of the boat which the disciples were struggling to row upstream, against the wind and current.

The passage says that Jesus was going to pass by the disciples but it is more than likely he had not expected them to be there at all. If conditions had been normal they would have reached their destination long before Jesus got there, but realising who they were, he waded over towards them. They were not expecting this at all and they were terrified. Jesus climbed into the boat and the head-wind dropped.

The last sentence of the passage would be puzzling and inexplicable if the above were the whole story. The evangelist sees the incident as echoing the crossing of the Jordan under Joshua to conquer the promised land (Jos. 3 and 4), although their hardness of heart reminds one of the condemnation of the synagogue, in the case of the man with a withered hand (G13).

Jesus is portrayed as moving over the water as God's spirit had done: 'The Spirit of God was moving over the face of the water' (Gen. 1:2); '(The Lord), who alone ... walks on the sea as on firm ground ...' (Job 9:8 LXX); '(The Lord answered Job) "Have you descended to the springs of the sea or walked in the unfathomable deep?"' (Job 38:16); 'Your way was through the sea, your path through the great waters' (Ps. 77:19); 'He pursues them and passes on safely by paths his feet have not trodden' (Is. 41:3); 'In the depths of the abyss I walked and ... over the waves of the sea ... I held sway' (Sir. 24:5-6).

The disciples thought they had met a spectre or a portent, it being a common

266

belief at the time that evil spirits could be abroad at night looking for suitable persons to occupy: 'They were haunted by monstrous apparitions and were paralysed by their soul's surrender, for fear sudden and unlooked for came upon them' (W.S. 17:15). The evangelists say Jesus told the disciples not to be afraid, or to have courage, again repeating O.T. and other texts: 'Fear not ... nor be dismayed ... for I will save you from afar' (Jer. 46:27); 'Have courage ... do not fear, the eternal Lord has sent us to you ...' (II En. 1:8).

The phrase 'It is I' in the text actually says, 'I am', and this is a pointer to the evangelists' purpose. It is used of God in the O.T., and the evangelists used the story to show Jesus beginning a new conquest of Canaan as judge, king and commander. In the new kingdom there will be peace and security: 'There the Lord in majesty will be for us a place of broad rivers and streams, where no galley with oars can go ... For the Lord is our judge, ruler and king; he will save us' (Is. 33:21-22). He will bring them to quiet and a place of safety: 'They were glad because they had quiet and he brought them to their desired haven' (Ps. 107:30).

The evangelist shows the disciples as not understanding the significance on the feeding of the multitude story: 'He satisfies him who is thirsty and the hungry he fills with good things' (Ps. 107:9), and describes them as dull-witted and hard-hearted. Hard-hearted does not always mean callous; it often means inability to understand, lack of an open mind to see the new.

Matthew alone adds a passage which most authorities think is designed to show Jesus as the Son of God. In such an area there would likely be hollows and irregularities in the sea bed into which someone wading across to Jesus could easily fall and appear to be drowning.

> **Peter called out to Jesus. 'Lord, if you be he, tell me to come to you over the water.' Jesus did so, and Peter stepped out of the boat and walked over the water towards Jesus. But when he saw the strength of the gale he was seized with fear, and beginning to sink, he cried, "Save me Lord,!". Jesus reached out his hand and held him and said, "Why did you doubt? How little faith you have!" Then he climbed into the boat and wind dropped.**
>
> **And the men in the boat worshipped him, exclaiming, "Truly you are the Son of God."**

In this passage, some have seen Peter challenging Jesus to perform a miracle to show he was divine. He puts Jesus to the proof by saying, "If you are the Messiah, tell me to walk over the water to you". Such testing of God or his Messiah was absolutely forbidden and Peter begins to sink into deep water. But Jesus, acting like God, puts out his hand and saves him: 'God drew me out of many waters' (Ps. 18:16); 'Though he fall ... the Lord upholds him by the hand' (Ps. 37:24).

* * *

H 3. Feeding the multitude, II - Mt. 15: 32-39. Mk. 8:1-10.

The background to this story of feeding the four thousand is similar to that discussed in the story of feeding the five thousand. It seems possible that whether or not this story is based on the same event which underlies the feeding of the five thousand, the evangelists had a particular purpose in mind in telling it.

In this story there were seven loaves and some think this may have a connection with the seven Noachide laws (see below) which determined whether pagans, that is non-Jews or Gentiles, could be admitted to Jewish fellowship. If they accepted these rules they could attend the synagogue services, although they remained Gentiles and, not being full Jews, were not reckoned as equal children of the house of Israel.

If this were correct, the feeding of the five thousand may be intended to show Jesus drafting Jews into his 'army', and the feeding of the four thousand in this passage, that he was happy to have Gentiles to help him in his battles: 'The friendship of the Lord is for those who fear him, and he makes known to them his covenant' (Ps. 25:14); 'The foreigners who join themselves to the Lord to minister to him ... and to be his servants ... and hold fast to my covenant - these I will bring to my holy mountain and make them joyful in my house of prayer ... I will gather yet others to him besides those already gathered' (Is. 56:6-8). The Gentiles were fewer in number than the Jews, which the evangelist may have meant to suggest that Gentiles had to be a minority in the kingdom of God.

Alternatively, the seven loaves could be associated with the seven nations with whom the Israelites mixed when they entered Canaan. God's instructions were that they should be eliminated: 'When the Lord your God brings you into the land you are entering to take possession of it and clears away any nations before you, the Hittites, the Girgashites, the Amorites, the Canaanites, the Perizzites, the Hivites and the Jebusites, seven nations greater and mightier than yourselves ... you must utterly destroy them. You shall make no covenant with them and show no mercy to them' (Dt. 7:1-2), but the Israelites disobeyed and allowed enclaves of them to remain. The passage suggests that although the descendants of these resident aliens could not become true Jews, that did not mean they could not obey God and participate in his kingdom: 'I will give you as a light to the nations that my salvation may reach to the ends of the earth' (Is. 49:6); 'Behold, you shall call nations that you know not and nations you knew not shall run to you' (Is. 55:5).

There was another occasion when a large crowd had been with Jesus for three days and he began to feel sorry for them. He called his disciples to him and said, "I feel sorry for these people. They have been here three days and have nothing to eat. If I send them away hungry to their homes, they will faint on the way; some have come from afar."

The disciples said, "How can we find bread enough for all these people in this desert place?"

Jesus said, "How many loaves have you?"

"Seven", they replied, "and a few small fishes."

Jesus commanded the crowd to recline on the ground, took the seven loaves and the fishes, and, after giving thanks to God, he broke them and gave them to the disciples to distribute to the people. They all ate and were satisfied and seven baskets were filled with fragments left over.

There were about four thousand people there and after he had dismissed them, he immediately got into a boat with his disciples and set out for the district of Dalmanutha.

Jesus wants the Gentiles to know that they, too, have the chance of repentance: 'He (the son of man) shall be a staff to the righteous whereon to stay themselves and not fall, and he shall be a light of the Gentiles and hope of those who are troubled' (I En. 48:4); 'From your root shall arise a stem and from it shall grow a rod of righteousness to the Gentiles, to judge and save all who call upon the Lord' (T.Jud. 24:5-6), despite the condemnation of some writers: 'But regarding the Gentiles it were tedious to tell how they always wrought impiety and wickedness and never wrought righteousness' (II Bar. 62:7).

Jesus aims to achieve what Joshua was tricked by the Gibeonites into spoiling, a perfect Israel (see H 1), and he recruits Jews and Gentiles for his mission. His few 'crumbs' were enough to satisfy the righteous - they have no need for luxurious excess. The blessing of Deuteronomy applied: 'If you obey the words of the Lord your God ... he will set you high above all nations of the earth. All blessings shall come and overtake you ... You shall be blessed in the city, in the field, blessed shall be the fruit of your body, the fruit of your ground, the fruit of your beasts, the increase of your cattle and young of your flock. Blessed shall be your basket and your kneading-trough' (Dt. 28:1-5).

The period of three days, during which the crowd had been without food, is significant, because it was believed it was the maximum period which God would normally allow the suffering of the just to last. After that period he would provide help: 'After two days he will revive us; on the third day he will raise us up' (Hos. 6:2); 'Gather all the Jews to be found in Susa and hold a fast ... and neither eat nor drink for three days, night and day' (Est. 4:16); 'Early in the morning Joshua rose and set out from Shittim with all the people of Israel. They came to the Jordan and lodged there before they passed over. At the end of three days the officers went through the camp and commanded the people' (Jos. 3:1-2); 'And the Lord appointed a great fish to swallow up Jonah; and Jonah was in the belly of the fish three days and three nights' (Jon. 1:17). In each case God's help came at the end of the three days.

A detailed examination of the language of these passages, H 1 and H 3, suggests that the evangelists wanted to show that those recruited by Jesus were to be either prophets or priests or both. This would also be in accord with O.T. teaching: 'Would that all the Lord's people were prophets, and the Lord would put his spirit upon them' (Num. 11:29); 'You shall be to me a kingdom of priests and a holy nation' (Ex. 19:6).

Noah was not regarded as a Jew, because he lived long before Abraham and Moses. There was no Israel in his day, but God made a covenant with him after the flood. The Noachide laws in the rabbinical literature are given as follows: The children of Noah enjoined concerning seven things. The first six were prohibitions against: idolatry, incest, murder, theft, cursing the divine name, and tearing flesh from a living animal (that is before the blood has drained from it). The seventh precept was the duty to promote justice.

* * *

H 4. The sequel to the feeding of the multitudes - Mt. 16:5-12. Mk. 8:14-21. Lk. 12:1.

The disciples were going by boat with Jesus to the other side, but realised that they had only one loaf of bread with them. Jesus began to warn them: "Beware of the evil influence of the leaven of the religious leaders and Herod."

The disciples thought he made this remark because they did not have several loaves of bread with them.

"Why do you talk about not having brought several loaves of bread with you?", asked Jesus. "You have eyes; can you not see? You have ears; can you not hear? Do you not understand even now? Are you so hardened in your hearts? Remember what happened when we fed the five thousand. When I broke the five loaves and gave them to the people, how many baskets of fragments did you collect?"

"Twelve", they replied. "And how many baskets of fragments did you collect after I broke the seven loaves to give to the four thousand?", asked Jesus

"Seven", they said.

"Do you still not realise that I was not speaking about bread? Be on your guard against the leaven of the Pharisees and the Sadducees, their blasphemy and false teaching."

Jesus once again is shown quoting from the O.T.: 'Hear this, O foolish and senseless people, who have eyes but see not, who have ears but hear not' (Jer. 5:21); 'Man, you dwell in the midst of a rebellious house who have eyes to see, but see not; who have ears to hear, but hear not' (Ezk. 12:2).

It seems likely that the point of this passage is that only one loaf of God's bread is required. God's word was not to be subdivided so that some parts were suitable for the Jews and some for others.

Leaven, or putrefaction, was a metaphor for sin or the evil inclination which Jesus warns against. It was the religious leaders' misleading interpretations of Judaism, and their concern for patriotic supremacy for Israel, as well as the Herodians' lack of principles and their time-serving desire for political and social power, which Jesus condemned.

The numbers used could very well refer to those numbers beloved of the Jews of the time: five thousand, the Israelites; five, the books of the Torah; twelve, the twelve tribes of Israel; seven, the seven Noachide laws, and four thousand, the Gentiles. Jesus will do away with these divisions and bring the practice of both the Jews and the Gentiles back to God's word.

* * *

H 5. The stilling of the storm - Mt. 8:23-27. Mk. 4:35-41. Lk. 8:22-25.

One day, towards evening, Jesus suggested to his disciples that, like several other boats, they cross over the Sea of Galilee to another place. Jesus was tired and went to sleep in the stern of the boat on a cushion.

A heavy squall blew up, the waves came into the boat and they were in danger of sinking. The disciples woke Jesus up: "Master, we are sinking! Don't you care if we all perish?"

Jesus aroused, rebuked the storm: "Be silent! Be muzzled!" The wind dropped and in the calm which followed Jesus said, "Why such fear, 'little-faiths'?" They were awe-struck and talked among themselves. "Who can this be? He even orders the wind and waves about and they obey him!"

The whole point of this story is missed and the evangelists' purpose is betrayed by concentrating on whether it really happened or not. The suddenness of storms and calms on the Sea of Galilee is notorious and no doubt similar events often occurred. The evangelists tell the story not to impress their readers with another wonder story but to show the kingdom of God being present and Jesus as the Messiah, using contemporary conventional metaphors.

The wind of the storm was thought by some to be the spirit of the storm and like other natural forces it was seen as part of God's activity on earth. The wind was the breath of God from his nostrils which could create great storms: 'At the blast of your nostrils the water piled up. You blew with your wind, and the sea covered them [the Egyptians]' (Ex. 15:8,10); 'The Lord drove the sea back by a strong east wind all night' (Ex. 14:21).

Others believed that during a storm, the wind and the waves were disturbed by demons. Only God's power could calm them down and this event could have been told to show that the kingdom of God is near, when evil powers will be subdued: 'O God ... who stills the roaring of the seas and the roaring of their waves ...' (Ps. 65:7); 'O Lord God of Hosts ... you rule the raging of the sea; when its waves rise, you still them' (Ps. 89:8-9).

Jonah experienced such a storm too, until he accepted his fate and gave up his plan to flee from the presence of God: 'The Lord hurled a great wind upon the sea and there was a mighty tempest so the ship threatened to break up. Then the sailors were afraid and each cried to his god ... But Jonah had lain down and was fast asleep. The captain came and said to him ... "Arise, call on your god!" ... Then the men were very afraid ... for Jonah had told them he was fleeing from the presence of the Lord' (Jon. 1:4-6,10).

Just as Jonah had been rescued by God, so were the disciples by Jesus. God stilled the storm, 'Then they cried to the Lord in their trouble and he delivered them from their distress; he made the storm be still and the waves of the sea were hushed. Then they were glad because they had quiet and he brought them to their desired haven.' (Ps. 107:28-30). Jesus was called by the disciples with words very like those of the psalmist: 'Rouse yourself! Why do you sleep, O Lord? Awake! Do not cast us off for ever ... Rise up, come to our help!' (Ps. 44:23,26).

David and his descendants had been promised that they would rule the sea and the wind, so that of course the Messiah had similar powers, being of David's line. Like God himself, he could create storms and still them and God had promised, 'I will set his hand on the sea and his right hand on the rivers. I will extend his rule over the sea and his dominion as far as the river. He will say to me, "You are my father, my God, my rock and my safe refuge"' (Ps. 89:25-26).

Rabbinical literature includes a similar story about R. Gamaliel, who by his prayer also is said to have caused the storm to cease: 'He stood up (in the boat) and cried, "Ruler of the Universe. It is revealed before you that it was not for my honour that I do this and not for the honour of my father's house, but for your honour, so that dissenters should not multiply in Israel." And the sea calmed from its ragings.'

* * *

H 6. Who is Jesus? - Mt. 16:13-19. Mk. 8:27-30. Lk. 9:18-21.

This passage is often seen as the turning point of the ministry of Jesus. Before this moment, the disciples are portrayed as not realising that Jesus was, or claimed to be, the Messiah; after it they are deemed to know. Whether this usual interpretation is correct, that Jesus' warning was to pre-empt any attempt to create a rebellious movement, must be left undetermined. It could be that Jesus forbade his disciples to spread abroad the statement that he was the Messiah, because he did not make that claim and did not want to lead others away from his primary concern: that they should follow the commandment to love God and one another.

Many at that time believed the promised messiah had already come in the form of king Hezekiah: 'There will be no Messiah for Israel since they have already enjoyed him during the reign of Hezekiah' (b.San. 98b). It was widely accepted that the Messiah in any case would not be a divine deliverer but a divinely appointed human being. Some thought that one of David's descendants would be the Messiah (Lam.R. 1:51 on Ps. 18:50) others that another king like David would come and be the Messiah (b.San. 98b on Jer. 30:9).

> One day Jesus was with his disciples and he asked them, "Who do people say that I am?" They replied, "Well, some say you are John (the Baptiser), others say you are Elijah or another of the prophets come back to life."
>
> "Who do you say I am?", asked Jesus. Peter replied, "You are the Messiah son of God of the living. Then Jesus sternly admonished them, that they tell this to no one."

[Matthew adds]:

> "You Simon, son of Jonah, are favoured indeed. You did not learn that from men but from my heavenly Father. You are Peter, the rock on which my church shall be built, and gates of Hades will never conquer it. I will give you the keys of the kingdom of God."

These passages have given rise to much controversy. They are unique because they refer to Peter as the rock on which the church will be built, whereas in other passages it is either God or Jesus who is referred to as the foundation stone (see G 6).

The famous pun on Petros (Peter) and petra (rock) is also odd. It is often asserted there is a pun on the Greek words for Peter (petros) and rock (petra), but Simon Barjonah is Aramaic, and there is an Aramaic word kephas, meaning Peter and rock, which could have been used. It is likely that when putting this into Greek, the Greek play on words was utilised instead. In the O.T., the Hebrew words used for foundation stone, bedrock and precious stone are different, but in Aramaic, the words for these are so alike as to cause confusion. This is made worse because the word for foundation stone could also mean the core group of the truly righteous on whom the future of the congregation would depend.

It was Jewish belief that when the Messiah comes, there will be a new Zion built of precious stones: 'Behold, I lay in Zion a stone - a tried stone, a precious corner stone, a settled foundation' (Is. 28:16). It is God who will provide the foundation stone: 'Of old you laid the foundations of the earth' (Ps. 102:25); 'Where were you when I laid the foundations of the earth?' (Job 38:4), and the new Jerusalem will be covered in gemstones: 'Behold, I will set your stones in antimony and lay the foundations with sapphires. I will make your pinnacles of agate, your gates of garnets, and your borders of precious stones' (Is. 54:11-12).

The name Peter could also mean gemstone and thus when Simon is called Peter it is more likely that he was being called a jewel of the kingdom than anything else. All the righteous, the sons of Zion were precious jewels, and according to Matthew, Peter will be the foundation stone of eternal, not earthly, structures, the first of the sons of the new kingdom, acting as gate-keeper.

Simon says Jesus is the Messiah, and Jesus reciprocates by calling Simon, 'Peter'. Yet he is also called 'son of Jonah' which has some interesting implications. Jonah avoided God's command to go to Nineveh because he saw that God was merciful enough to redeem even that place of evil if the people there repented. He could not accept that they could be more responsive than his own nation of chosen people. That would never do! The passage suggests Peter had been guilty of the same attitude of mind and it criticises any idea that non-Jews should be excluded from the Kingdom.

The disciples are told the 'Gates of Hades', the 'powers of death' would never conquer the church. The meaning of this statement is not easily discerned. The gates of Hades or Sheol cannot conquer but the evil forces they keep in can be let loose when Satan opens them. Then Peter will open the gates of heaven and the powers of God will come out to do battle with Satan's forces. It is in the church that the battle will be fought until God is triumphant and the strongholds of evil are plundered: 'The Lord shall open the gates of paradise and remove the sword threatening mankind. He shall give fruit from the tree of life to the saints and the spirit of holiness shall be upon them.' (T.Lev. 18:10-11).

From this may have arisen the statement that the disciples will bind evil spirits and make them harmless, thereby freeing, or loosening those who had been subject to them (see E 12a).

This passage is a good example of the richness in the gospel texts. The name, Peter, son of Jonah, could remind those listening to Jesus of a jewel, a foundation stone of the new kingdom, God's messenger, and one who still had not reconciled himself to the teaching that there was place in the kingdom for all who lived under God's rule.

Many thought the messiah would be: 'A man of the house of David with divine gifts but still human. He shall be a righteous king ... over them ... all shall be holy and their king the anointed of the Lord' (P.S.17:35-36; 18:6,8); '... he is God's anointed who shall be potent and mighty on earth' (I En. 52:4).

* * *

**H 7. Handed over into the power of men - Mt. 16:21-23; 17:22-23; 20:17-19.
Mk. 8:31-33; 9:1; 9:30-32; 10:32-34. Lk. 9:22, 43-45; 18:31-34.**

Jesus and his disciples were on their way to
Jerusalem and Jesus began to teach them. "The son of
man will be handed over into the power of men. He will
undergo great suffering, be rejected and handed over
to the elders, the chief priests and authorities. They
will condemn him to death, hand him over to pagans to be
mocked, spat upon, flogged and killed, but on the third
day he will rise again. I tell you this: some who are
standing here will not taste death before they see the
kingdom of God come."

Peter took hold of him and began to rebuke him:
"Far from it," he said. "This must never happen to you,
Lord."

Jesus said, "You I must ignore; you are a trap to
ensnare me. You think as men think, not as God thinks."

In this passage Jesus is shown as foreseeing his fate. Peter (another Jonah, see
H 6) tries to rescue him, but Jesus' response is clear. Many have attempted to soften
the harshness shown by Jesus' reply to Peter's concern for him in the last paragraph.
The passage suggests that Jesus felt Peter's attitude to be a temptation to avoid what
he believed was necessary to save Israel from God's wrath. Jesus' answer is partly a
quotation from the O.T.: 'For my thoughts are not your thoughts, nor your ways my
ways, says the Lord' (Is. 55:8). Some scholars put it more strongly and suggest that
Jesus was in fact speaking to himself and rejecting the temptation which he felt Satan
was putting before him.

There has been much discussion of the end of the first paragraph and, in
particular, 'he will rise again on the third day' or 'after three days'. The word 'rise'
could in Aramaic mean either resurrection or immortality.

For Jews, today was day one, tomorrow was the second day and the day
after tomorrow was the third day. That this is the meaning intended is confirmed by
reference to the O.T.; it was the longest period a righteous person would be left to
suffer: 'Come, let us return to the Lord; for it is he who has torn, and he will heal us;
he has struck down, and he will bind us up. After two days he will revive us; on the
third day he will raise us up' (Hos. 6:2). A period of three days could also mean a short
interval and it was the period during which it was believed that the spirit remained in a
person after death. Others thought that the soul hovered near the body of the deceased
for three days before an angel came to take it to its next abode. Others, however, said
this period lasted seven days.

Thus the implication would be that after a short period the day of Judgement
would occur and there would be a general resurrection. In this passage Jesus clearly
expected God to vindicate him after his atoning death by a general resurrection or by
his coming in power with his disciples in the kingdom of God on earth. (See also E 2,
C 9, E 14 and F 11)

It was believed by some that anyone put to death was abandoned by God and that only by resurrection would the person be vindicated, and it is clear that the passage has been added to and elaborated by the writers of the gospels or later editors. It is, however, in agreement with O.T. prophecy: 'Yes, I hear the whispering of many ... as they scheme together against me, as they plot to take my life.' (Ps. 31:13); 'The Lord, I say, is all I have; therefore I will wait for him patiently ... Let him give his cheek to the smiter and be filled with insults. The Lord will not cast him off for ever. He may punish cruelly, yet he will have compassion in the fullness of his love, he does not willingly afflict or punish any mortal man' (Lam. 3:24,30-33).

It also has echoes from the story of David who was in flight from king Saul: 'Then said David, "Will the men of Keilah surrender me and my men into Saul's hand?" And the Lord said, "They will surrender you"' (I Sam. 23:12). (See also H 10)

In rabbinical writings, it was believed that the righteous of any community were punished first and that the death of a righteous person was accepted by God as an atonement for the sins of others (b.M.K. 28a), as Moses offered himself for the Israelites (Ex. 32:32; b.Sot 14a).

The last verse of the first paragraph is slightly different in the three gospels. Luke's version is given above, while Mark adds 'with power'. Matthew modifies it to suit his ideas and writes: '... before they see the son of man coming in his kingdom.' It is uncertain where this verse originally belonged. According to some bible scholars, it may have originally been the beginning of the story of the transfiguration (see H 10).

* * *

H 8. Jesus' power and authority - Mt. 21:23-27. Mk. 11:27-33. Lk. 20:1-8.

As Jesus was walking and teaching in the Temple
one day, some of the members of the Sanhedrin, the chief
priests, doctors of the Law and elders, came to him,
and said, "By what authority do you do what you do? Who
empowered you to do these things?"

Jesus said, "Tell me one thing first. If you answer
me, I will explain to you who empowered me. Was the
baptism of John from heaven or from men?"

They began to argue amongst themselves.' If we say
from heaven, he will want to know why we did not believe
and accept him. If we say from men, we shall be in
danger, because the people take John to be a prophet.'
So they claimed not to know the correct answer.

"Exactly", said Jesus; "If you do not know that, I
will not tell you by what authority I do what I do."

After 70 C.E. no one could be a legitimate, authorised rabbi without being
ordained by pressing on of hands from another rabbi. Unfortunately it is not known if
this was true at the time of Jesus, before the destruction of the Temple in the war with
Rome.

It was the custom for a teacher to cite other teachers as authority or legitimation
for what he taught, but Jesus asserted that in any case Moses and the prophets were
empowered by heaven without any help from men. It was quite possible for others to
receive the same power directly from God.

There are other allusions in the passage. Again a parallel in the O.T. suggests
itself. Jesus will not explain who empowered him any more than Saul would tell his
uncle the words of Samuel: 'His uncle said, "Tell me what Samuel said." "He told us
that the asses had been found," said Saul; but he did not repeat what Samuel had said
about his being king' (I Sam. 10:15-16).

God does not give answers and signs, especially to questions and demands
put by the unfaithful: 'This is the word of the Lord God. "Do you come to consult me?
As I live, I will not be consulted by you'" (Ezk. 20:3) and Jesus, like Saul, remains
silent, even when some treat him with disdain: 'There were scoundrels who said,
"How can this fellow deliver us?" They thought nothing of him and brought him no
gifts' (I Sam. 10:27).

* * *

H 9. The Messiah, the son of David? - Mt. 22:41-46. Mk. 12:35-37. Lk. 20:41-44.

As he taught in the Temple, Jesus asked the Pharisees who had been listening: "How can the doctors of the Law say the Messiah is the son of David? Did not David himself, inspired by the Holy Spirit say, 'The Lord said to my Lord, "Sit at my right hand until I put your enemies under your feet." David calls him 'Lord;' so how is he his son?'
No one was able to answer a word.

The quotation is from Psalm 110: 'The Lord says to my Lord," "Sit at my right hand until I make your enemies your footstool'" (Ps. 110:1) which is changed in the gospel because it is conflated with: 'You have put all things under their feet' (Ps. 8:6) and 'The Lord has sworn and will not change his mind: "You are a priest for ever of the order of Melchizedek'" (Ps. 110:4). In rabbinical writings God did not make plain the narrative. David did, saying, 'The Lord said to my Lord, sit at my right hand' (Midr.Ps. on 110:1) and the Messiah is more beloved than the righteous priest (Aaron) (ARN 34 on Zch. 4:14). Some believed that this passage referred to king Hezekiah of the O.T.

By this passage Jesus is said to have disclaimed the title of Messiah as understood by most Jews of the time, a national political liberator and restorer of the Davidic throne. The enemies who will be subdued under the feet of God were the ungodly leaders of the Jews. Israel had forgotten its covenant with God, and the religious leaders were more concerned with the trappings of office, and rituals of the Temple, than God's primary commandment. When the enemies of God were subdued the Messiah will bring in a kingdom over the whole world 'not of this world'. Jesus implies that the Messiah is not David's son but God's son.

The passage is difficult. There were different opinions in Judaism about the Messiah from God. In the O.T. that he would be (a) a son of David, a conquering king, who would inaugurate a golden age of righteous rule after his military victories; (b) that the Messiah would be a son of Aaron, a true priest superior to any king; and (c) that he would be a Righteous One who would be slain as a sacrifice for others. At first the Righteous One was also thought to be of the house of David, but later, Christians claimed he was son of Joshua (Joseph). In I.T. books there is a picture of the Messiah being the king, the son of David: 'He will purge Jerusalem from Gentiles who trample her to destruction. He will purge Jerusalem and make it holy as it was even from the beginning' (P.S. 17:24-25).

In rabbinical literature, there were other theories, one of which is: 'There were four craftsmen who would measure [i.e. assess] Jerusalem. They were the Messiah, son of David; the Messiah, son of Joseph; Elijah; and the righteous priest [Melchizedek]' (b.Suk. 52b). Melchizedek was the king of Salem: 'Melchizedek king of Salem brought food and wine. He was priest of God Most High, creator of heaven and earth ... who has delivered your enemies into your power' (Gen. 14:18-20). It is interesting that at Qumran, Melchizedek was thought of as a heavenly being, anointed by the Spirit, who will reign and execute judgement against Satan, bring relief to captives, the poor, and the downtrodden.

In Judaism it was not considered blasphemous to claim to be any of these Messiahs, except the one who, on the last day would be God's messenger, his son, his Messiah on earth. It has been suggested that the background to this passage is the Passover ritual during which four questions were traditionally put, the fourth by the youngest child, or by the father if the child were too young to do so. In Mark the previous questions were about tribute to Caesar, the woman seven times married and which is the greatest commandment; Jesus' question is the fourth.

* * *

H 10. The transfiguration - Mt. 17:1-13. Mk. 9:2-13. Lk. 9:28-36.

After six days, Jesus took Peter, James and John up into the mountains to pray. They were alone and Jesus said to them, "I tell you this certain truth: there are some standing here who will not taste death before they have seen the kingdom of God having come in power."

Jesus was transfigured. His clothes became dazzlingly white, and his face shone. Then Elijah and Moses appeared and they were conversing with Jesus and spoke of his departure, which he was about to accomplish in Jerusalem. The disciples had been half asleep at first, but now, fully awake, Peter said, "Rabbi, how good it is we are here. Shall we build shelters for you and Moses and Elijah?" (They were terrified, and he said the first thing that came into his head!)

Just then a cloud came over and a voice was heard saying, "This is my son, my beloved, the chosen one. Listen to him." At that moment they saw that Jesus was alone. He came over to them and they went down from the place.

On their way down from the mountain Jesus told them not to mention to anyone what had happened, until the son of man had risen from the dead. They fastened on to this word, wondering what 'risen from the dead' might mean.

They asked Jesus, "Why is it the scribes say that Elijah must come first, and where has it been written about the son of man, that he must suffer much and be treated with contempt?"

Jesus replied, "Yes, Elijah does come first to set all right. I tell you this, Elijah has already come, and they did as they wished with him, so also will the son of man suffer at their hands, as it is written about him."

This passage has given rise to much more speculation than insight. The differences between the accounts given by the three evangelists cannot in this case be fully reconciled. Luke says after eight days, that the disciples were burdened or weighed down with sleep and it was only when they woke up properly that they realised what was happening. Matthew and Mark do not mention this. Nor do they say with Luke that Elijah spoke of Jesus' 'departure' which he has to fulfil in Jerusalem.

There is little doubt that the passage has been altered and modified, but it is intended perhaps mainly to show the efficacy of the kingdom in power, and that it is full of force. Bible scholars think that the statement that the kingdom will come before the death of some of those present, belongs here as well as in F 11, and may be a link with the events in Gethsemane too.

There are many references to the O.T. in this passage. The obvious one is the story of the six days Moses spent on the mountain. He had with him Aaron and Hur, and God called to him: 'The glory of the Lord settled on Mount Sinai, and cloud covered it six days; and on the seventh day, God called to Moses out of the midst of the cloud' (Ex. 24:16); 'Then the Lord came down in the cloud and spoke to him ...' (Num. 11:25); 'The Lord said to Moses, "I am coming to you in a thick cloud that the people may know that I speak with you"' (Ex. 19:9). Moses' face was changed: 'When Moses came down from the mountain, he did not know the skin of his face 'shone' because he had been talking with God' (Ex. 34:29), and he had to veil his face before the Israelites could look upon him: 'The people of Israel saw ... that the skin of Moses' face 'shone;' and Moses would put the veil on his face again, until he went in to speak with the Lord' (Ex. 34:35).

Similar statements are also found in I.T. books: 'Blessed are the righteous ... for they shall shine forth more than seven times brighter than the sun' (II En. 66:7); 'I saw the holy sons of God ... their garments were white and their faces shone like snow' (I En. 71:1); 'Their faces are destined to shine as the sun' (IV Ezr. 7:97). Only in Matthew is there reference to the 'son of man', that is Jesus, suffering in the last line of the passage, and it is not improper to see in this passage the evangelists' view of Jesus, based on the current ideas about the Messiah and the end of the era.

According to later books, 'The raiment with which God will clothe the Messiah will shine from one end of the world to the other. And the Israelites will make use of this radiance and they will say, 'Happy the hour in which the Messiah was created, happy the womb from which he came; happy the generation which sees him; happy the eye that is worthy to behold him' (PR 37:1) and as High Priest Elijah must anoint the Messiah at his coming' (MDR 10:1).

Shining garments were a sign of purity, and white garments were a sign of repentance: 'The angel said, "Remove the filthy garments from him." And he said to Joshua, "Behold, I have taken away your iniquity ..."' (Zch. 3:4); 'The Lord your God will raise up for you a prophet ... from among your own people: you shall heed such a prophet' (Dt. 18:15).

Both Moses and Elijah were rejected by their contemporaries. 'Now the sons of Reuben took men and rose up against Moses and Aaron and said to them, "You have gone too far ..."' (Num. 16:1-3); 'So Moses cried to the Lord, "What shall I do with these people? They are almost ready to stone me"' (Ex. 17:4). As for Elijah, 'Jezebel sent a message to Elijah, saying, "So may the gods do to me ... if I do not make your life as the life of one (of the prophets you have killed) by this time tomorrow." Then he was afraid and fled for his life ... And he asked that he might die saying, "It is enough now, O Lord, take away my life ..." And behold an angel touched him and said, "Arise and eat"' (I Kgs. 19:2-5).

Elijah and Moses were heroes: Moses had brought Israel out of Egypt and Elijah will repeat the rescue from the slavery of evil on the day of Judgement. They are thought to have been vindicated by God by being taken up directly to heaven. In rabbinical literature Moses and Elijah will be forerunners of the Messiah. Elijah was thought to have been without sin (Lev.R. 27:4) and such people would never die: there is no suffering without iniquity and no death without sin (b.Shab. 55b); and, as High Priest, Elijah must anoint the Messiah (MDR 10:1).

There were many occasions recorded in O.T. and I.T. literature when the heavens opened and God's voice was heard; the son of God was a traditional designation of the king of Israel: 'The Lord said to me, "You are my son; today I have begotten you. Ask of me and I will make the nations your heritage and ends of the earth your possession."' (Ps. 2:7); (the baptism story has the same message, see A 2); 'The heavens were opened and I saw, and power was given to me and a voice was heard from on high ...' (II Bar. 22:1); 'The heavens shall be opened to him to pour out the spirit, the blessing of the Holy Father' (T.Jud. 24:2); the Most High shall send forth his salvation in the visitation of a beloved, only begotten, prophet' (T.Ben. 9:2); 'They were both troubled and fell on their faces, and they were afraid. And Raphael said to them, "Be not afraid; peace be unto you ... All these days I appeared to you, and neither ate nor drank but it was a vision you saw. Now give God thanks because I ascend to him that sent me and write in a book all the things which have happened to you." And they got up and saw him no more' (Tob. 11:16-21).

Transfiguration of garments was a sign of royalty and thus the kingship of Jesus and the coming of the kingdom of God. At Qumran, '... all who walk in this spirit, it shall be joy in life without end, a crown of glory and a garment of majesty in unending light.' (DSS CD 4:7-8), and it is said in a rabbinical book: 'The righteous would be transfigured after death' (Sif.Dt. 10-11). For the evangelist, the transfigured Jesus shows the glory of God heralding the coming of the kingdom in the new world to come.

There has been much disagreement over the last section of the passage, and the order of the verses has been changed here to make them more comprehensible. Elijah could be the forerunner promised in O.T. and I.T. passages: 'Behold I send my messenger to prepare the way before me ... the messenger of the covenant in whom you delight, behold, he is coming ...' (Mal. 3:1); 'I will send you the prophet Elijah before the great and terrible day of the Lord comes. He will turn the hearts of parents to their children and the hearts of children to their parents, so that I will not come and strike the land with a curse' (Mal. 4:5-6). 'Elijah will come at the appointed time with warnings, to allay the divine wrath before the final fury, to reconcile father and son, and to restore the tribes of Israel' (Sir. 48:10) and in rabbinical teaching: 'R. Joshua said, "I have received as a tradition ... that Elijah will not come to declare clean or unclean ... but to remove afar those that were brought near by violence..." R.Simon said, "To bring agreements where there is matter for dispute." Some sages say neither to remove afar nor to bring nigh but to make peace in the world, as it is written [in Malachi]' (m.Eduy. 8:7).

The disciples question about Elijah's coming first must refer to his coming before either the rising of the dead, or the rising of the son of man from the dead. Jesus is shown as believing that just as the Messiah has to suffer and be rejected, so also must Elijah, and that he had come and had suffered martyrdom in the form of John the baptiser.

Not all scholars accept this idea, because in the O.T. the resurrection of the dead occurs on the 'day of the Lord', with no mention of Elijah coming first: 'At that time your people shall be delivered. ... And many of those who sleep in the earth shall awake, some to everlasting life, some to shame and everlasting contempt' (Dan. 12:1-2). At any rate one thing was clear: 'Those are the two anointed [Moses and Elijah] who stand by the Lord of the whole earth' (Zch. 4:14).

The passage almost certainly has connections with the story of Jonah. Peter had been called the son of Jonah, that is, he was like his predecessor, who sat and passively awaited the effect of God's message to Nineveh. Having given the message, he thought his job was finished. He was mistaken and was reproved. The booths of David had been cast down: 'How the Lord in his anger has set the daughter of Zion under a cloud! He has cast down ... the splendour of Israel' (Lam. 2:1). They will be rebuilt permanently in the New Jerusalem. The three key disciples had to realise that they must continue to spread Jesus' message, even if they suffered punishment or even death.

In this passage Peter, James and John are shown that there was to be no passivity. Booths to sit and wait in were not required. What was required was to continue to spread Jesus' message about God's will. This could entail even giving up one's life or self as Jesus would do, and could not include the O.T. solution for recalcitrant tribes, namely slaughter. The time for booths would be when the O.T. prophets, and those who had chosen to live under God's rule would sit down together for the messianic banquet in the New Era.

* * *

H 11. Jesus is tempted - Mt. 4:1-11. Mk. 1:12-13. Lk. 4:1-13.

Then the Spirit sent him away into the wilderness, and there he remained for forty days and nights fasting, tempted by the devil. He was with the wild beasts and the angels ministered to him.

Afterwards he was hungry and the devil tempted Jesus further: "If you are the Son of God, tell these stones to become bread!" Jesus refused: "Man shall not live by bread alone, but on every word from the mouth of God."

The devil took Jesus into Jerusalem and set him on the parapet of the Temple. Again Jesus was tempted. "If you are the Son of God, show us that God's angels will look after you. Throw yourself off this Temple pinnacle - the angels will see that you come to no harm! For it is written, 'He has commanded the angels concerning you and they will bear you up on their hands, lest you strike your foot against a stone.'"

Jesus answered him: "No; you are not to test the Lord your God."

Then the devil left him until the time when he showed Jesus all the kingdoms of the world in a moment, and tempted him once more. "I will give you authority over all the kingdoms of the whole world - all the glory of mankind will be yours if you will worship me."

"No", said Jesus, "scripture says, 'You shall worship the Lord your God and serve him alone.'"

Once again the passage is full of references to the events described in the O.T. and it immediately manifests its apocalyptic character. It begins with the idyllic paradise of the Garden of Eden, where angels ministered and the wild beasts were as gentle as lambs.' I will make for them a covenant on that day with the wild animals, the birds of the air, and the creeping things of the ground; ... and I will make you lie down in safety' (Hos 2:18). This was the time of the first Adam who succumbed to temptation. It was also the vision of the world after the day of Judgement in I.T. books: 'Both men and angels shall bless you, and God shall be glorified among the Gentiles through you. The devil shall flee from you, the wild beasts shall fear you and the Lord will love you' (T.Nap. 8:4).

Later, 'Moses was on the mountain forty days and forty nights ... He was with the Lord, and neither ate bread nor drank water' (Ex. 24:18; 34:28). It is usually thought that Moses also refused to turn the stones into bread: 'The Lord humbled you and let you hunger and fed you with manna ... that he might make you know that man does not live by bread alone, but that he lives by everything that proceeds out of the mouth of the Lord' (Dt. 8:3). God would provide the bread that was needed: 'The Lord said to Moses, "Behold I will rain bread from heaven for you"' (Ex. 16:4). The language, however, suggests that Jesus refused to ask God to change stones into bread. Jesus was not to be understood as a miracle worker, and just as he refused the request to assign places in heaven to some of his disciples (see E 2), his temptation was to deny God's ordinances for him.

Moses was shown all the land: 'Moses went up from the plains of Moab to the top of Pisgah ... and the Lord showed him all the land' (Dt. 34:1), or, as the rabbinical literature says, God gave power to the eyes of Moses, so that he could see the world from end to end; and in I.T. literature, the Messiah would come after Baruch had been shown all the land: 'Go up, therefore, to the top of that mountain, and there shall pass before thee all the regions of that land ...' (II Bar. 76:3).

Joshua, Jesus' namesake, conquered Canaan with all authority and glory. Jesus was tempted to imitate him, perhaps thinking of: 'The Lord said to me, "You are my son; today I have begotten you. Ask of me, and I will make the nations your heritage, and the ends of the earth your possession ..."' (Ps. 2:8); but he followed another path: 'You shall have no other gods besides me' (Dt. 5:7). The Israelites would hurt Moses with stones because he refused to provide the proof they wanted to show that he spoke truthfully when he said the Israelites were God's elect: 'The people found fault with Moses ... and Moses said to them, "Why do you put the Lord to the proof?"' (Ex. 17:2); 'He called the ... place Massah ... because of the fault-finding by the Israelites and because they tested the Lord by saying, "Is the Lord among us or not?"' (Ex. 17:7).

Jesus is tempted to provide proof of his being God's chosen by showing that stones would not be allowed to hurt him either: 'For he will give his angels charge of you to guard you in all your ways. On their hands they will bear you up, lest you dash your foot against a stone' (Ps. 91:11-12), but he refused this too. 'You shall fear the Lord your God; you shall serve him and swear by his name' (Dt. 6:13); 'You shall not put the Lord your God to the test, as you tested him at Massah' (Dt. 6:16). In rabbinical literature, there are similar stories. One legend is that Rabbi Kahana was selling baskets when a woman made immoral demands of him. He was so offended he climbed up and threw himself off the roof of the Temple but Elijah caught him. (It was thought Elijah remained on earth and would come to help good people in emergencies.) In addition, it was believed that 'When the Messiah appears he will stand on the Temple roof' (PR 36:2).

The idea of a man being tempted in order to test his resolution was not unusual: 'You shall remember all the ways which the Lord your God has led you these forty years in the wilderness ... testing you to know what was in your heart ...' (Dt. 8:2); '... God left Hezekiah to himself in order to try him and to know all that was in his heart' (II Chr. 32:31); 'The Lord God demands pure hearts, not bread nor candles, not meat nor cattle, but by these means he tempts the heart of men' (II En. 45:3).

In rabbinical writings, Abraham was also thought to have been tested ten times without succumbing: 'With ten temptations was Abraham our father tempted and he stood steadfast in them all ...' (m.Avot. 5:13). There is considerable similarity between the many miracle stories in rabbinical literature and those in the gospels and many examples show that there was quite commonly an opposition to the miracle-worker by the religious establishment.

* * *

H. Summary.

This group of passages demonstrates how the evangelists have used their descriptions of events to portray Jesus in particular ways. In some passages he is the New Adam, who does not succumb to temptation as did the first Adam. In others he is another Moses. In yet others, he is seen as Israel's anointed king and judge over Israel - the common Jewish understanding of the term 'messiah'. Jesus is also shown as the Messiah-son-of-God. In some passages Gentiles as well as Jews are shown to be acceptable in God's service.

I. Healings.

I 1. The demon-possessed - Mt. 7:28-29. Mk. 1:21-28. Lk. 4:33-37.

Jesus was in the synagogue at Capernaum one sabbath and taught the congregation. The people were astonished at his teaching. Such a note of authority he had, not like the regulars, scribes and teachers of the Law!

There was a man there, possessed by a demon. He shrieked wildly: "What is there between us and you, Jesus the Nazarene," he shouted. "Have you come to exorcise us? I know who you are - the Holy One of God."

"Be silent, be muzzled!", said Jesus, "and get out of him." Then, after throwing the man down without injuring him and with a loud cry, the demon left him.

Those present were dumbfounded. "Here's a new kind of teaching with authority and power. When he gives orders even the demons submit to him!"

So the news spread about and soon he was spoken about over the whole of Galilee.

There are different opinions about the words recorded here. Some suggest that 'Nazarene' (of Nazareth) and 'Nazirite' are so similar that the latter was what was meant. Nazirites were specially devoted Jews, and in the Greek version of the O.T. are called 'Holy Ones of God'. Others have said Israel was the 'Holy One of God', and yet others that it was a way of referring to God's Son, that is the Messiah.

Many similar stories are told in rabbinical writings, and words identical to those used by the afflicted man in this passage have been found on an Aramaic incantation bowl.

Jesus is said to teach with power. In rabbinical literature God is thought to have given Moses the first commandment directly, that is from God's mouth with God's power. Thus those who teach with power, like Jesus, are for the evangelists a second Moses.

* * *

I 2. The possessed son - Mt. 17:14-20. Mk. 9:14-29. Lk. 9:37-43.

This passage describes a boy with symptoms of an epileptic fit, who is described as being 'moon-struck', similar to the meaning of 'lunatic' in English. It is the same word as in: 'The moon shall not smite you by night' (Ps. 121:6). The O.T. passage which is echoed here, is the inability of Gehazi to revive the dead son of the Shumanite woman. Elisha had to do it: 'Gehazi ... laid Elisha's staff upon the face of the child but there was no sound or sign of life. He returned to Elisha and said, "The child has not woken."

When Elisha came in to the house, he saw the child lying dead on his bed. So he went in ... and prayed to the Lord. Then he ... laid on the child ... and the flesh of the child became warm ... and the child opened his eyes' (II Kgs. 4:31-35).

Jesus, with Peter, James and John came upon his other disciples arguing with several of the scribes. They all came to meet Jesus and he asked them what they were discussing. A man cried out, "Master, it's my son. He is possessed by a dumb demon that dashes him to the ground. He screams, foams at the mouth, grinds his teeth and becomes dried up[1]. I asked your disciples to help but they could do nothing."

Jesus exclaimed, "What an unbelieving and perverse generation! How long shall I have to put up with you? Bring your boy to me."

When Jesus saw him, the demon convulsed him and he fell down and rolled about. Jesus enquired of the father how long he had suffered like that. "Since childhood," said the father, "and the demon has often thrown him into fire and into water. If it is possible for you to do something, please take pity on us."

"If it is possible!" said Jesus. "Everything is possible to those who have faith."

"I have faith," said the man. "Help me with that I lack."

Jesus saw that bystanders were rapidly gathering round from all directions. He spoke sternly: spirit of dumbness and deafness, come out of him and never go back."

The boy was convulsed for the last time, and he lay as though dead, which indeed many thought he was. Jesus took him by the hand and raised him up and restored him to his father.

Afterwards, the disciples asked Jesus, "Why were we unsuccessful and could not cast out that demon?" Jesus replied, "Your faith was too weak. There is no means of casting out that kind except by prayer."

This healing story concerns the initial lack of faith of the father and the innocence of the boy. Like many others at the time, the father was unresponsive to the claims of Jesus at first, and the passage denounces the religious leaders and the old Israel, Jesus' generation, those he lived amongst, as corrupt. They were under God's curse: 'And the Lord said, "I hide my face from them ... They are a perverse generation, children who cannot be trusted"' (Dt.32:20); 'If you do not obey the Lord your God by diligently observing all his commandments and statutes ... then all these small curses shall come upon you ... The Lord will smite you with madness and blindness and confusion of mind ... you shall be driven mad by the sight you shall see ...' (Dt. 28:15,28,34); 'They mingled with the pagans and learned to do as they did. They served their idols, which became a snare to them. They sacrificed their sons and daughters to the demons, they poured out innocent blood, the blood of their sons and daughters' (Ps. 106:35-38).

Only when men understand they must change, can they have faith and be healed. 'Nevertheless, the Lord regarded their distress when he heard their cry. He remembered for their sake his covenant and, in his boundless love, relented' (Ps. 106:44-45); 'Behold, I am the Lord, the God of all flesh; is anything impossible for me?' (Jer. 32:27).

A dumb demon is an idol in another form: 'The workman trusts in his own creation when he makes dumb idols' (Hab. 2:18), but those who are innocent are precious and protected: 'When you pass through the waters I will be with you ...When you walk through fire you shall not be burned ... You are precious in my eyes and honoured and I love you ...' (Is. 43:2,4). So in this story, the boy survived in spite of his father's sins, until Jesus came to heal him and raise him again to life, after the demon had left him for dead.

The symptoms described are like those in a passage in an I.T. book: 'Demons afflict, oppress, destroy, attack, work destruction of the earth and cause trouble (some translations give: 'casting men on the ground making them mad'). They take no food but nonetheless hunger and thirst and dash themselves about. These spirits shall rise up against the children of men and women' (I En. 15:11-12). An Aramaic inscription from about 150 B.C.E. is for exorcists to help those afflicted by demons causing raging madness, convulsions, and deaf-and-dumbness. It gives the proper form of words to order the demon to cease plaguing the victim, and Jesus used the same phrases.

This passage is one which indicates Jesus could be irritated at times. His exclamation is one found in the O.T.: 'How long shall I bear with this evil congregation?' (Num. 14:27).

It is unlikely to be accidental that Mark mentioned that Jesus hastened to heal the boy because a crowd was gathering, but its significance is obscure.

---

[1] That is paralysed or rigid. See G 13.

* * *

I 3. Jesus exorcises a legion of demons - Mt. 8:28 - 9:1. Mk. 5:1-20. Lk. 8:26-39.

The area written of in this passage is sometimes called Gadarenes or Gergasenes. The latter lies about thirty miles from Galilee, while Gadera, lying about six miles from the southern end of the sea of Galilee, has the requisite landscape and was inhabited by Gentiles keeping pigs. These were used in sacrifices in parts of the Roman and Greek burial rituals; they were reviled by Jews as unclean, being supposed to be associated with the spirits of the underworld, and they were thought by Jews to be used by Gentiles for strongly forbidden sexual practices.

When they came to the country of Gerasenes, they met a man possessed by an unclean spirit, living in a cemetery. He was naked and uncontrollable, for even fetters could not hold him. He cried out constantly, and inflicted injuries on himself in his wildness.

Jesus, seeing him, ordered the unclean spirit to come out of him, but the man fell at Jesus' feet and said, "What have you to do with me, Jesus son of the Most High (God)? You shall not torment us before our time."

Jesus asked the name of his demon.

"Legion", the man replied, "there are so many of us! Please do not send us into the Abyss, but let us go into those pigs feeding over there," they said.

So Jesus gave them permission, and they entered into the pigs, and bunches of them ran over the edge of the cliff and fell into the sea, where they drowned.

The men in charge fled to the town and the district round about, and told what had happened, and a crowd gathered. They found the man cured, sitting quietly by Jesus, clothed and in his right mind. They were afraid, so they begged Jesus to leave the district. As he was preparing to depart in the boat, the man asked Jesus to allow him to go with him.

Jesus refused: "Go home to your own people and tell them what has happened and what God in his mercy has done for you," he said. The man went off and spread the news in the Ten Towns and they were all amazed.

This passage has many layers of meaning and whatever the real historical event which lies behind it, the language shows that the writers of the gospels have included it, not simply as another wonder tale, but in order to point to several conclusions.

A cemetery was an 'unclean place' and a habitation for demoniacs or in rabbinical works, 'imbeciles': 'One who goes out alone at night, one who spends his time in a cemetery, and he that tears his garments' (b.Hag.3b). A demon which could not be fettered was considered to be very strong and difficult to overpower.

The idea of possession by a demon is not unknown today and its exorcism is a kind of psychotherapy where nothing better can be offered. Some are undoubtedly more skilled than others in persuading someone who believes himself to be possessed that he can be helped. In principle, it is necessary for the subject to be convinced that the spirit of the exorcist is stronger than the demon. In the religious situation, it is that the Holy Spirit can overcome Satan's demons. This is the situation in this passage. In Jewish and other legends of the time, a similar story is found in which demons are overcome by a righteous exorcist.

It is to be noticed that Jesus had told the demon to come out of the demoniac before the demon assailed Jesus with cries of fear: 'Before they call, I will answer, while they are yet speaking I will hear' (Is. 65:24). The man's demon did not obey at once, but shrank from the effect of Jesus. Again Jesus took the initiative and asked the name of the demon, giving him power over the demon. The name 'Legion', well-known from Aramaic inscriptions concerned with magical incantations, showed numerous demons were to be removed and they bargained with Jesus. To be sent into the pigs was a solution; demons like pigs, or so Jews believed, and Jesus approved of the suggestion.

Jewish belief was that even demons would not be punished before the day of Judgement; hence their remark, 'Do not torment us before our time.' Because they recognised Jesus as harbinger or plenipotentiary of that day, they were afraid. They wanted to postpone that moment, when Satan would be conquered and they would have to return to Hades for ever. They begged Jesus not to send them into the Abyss, that is, Satan's realm. The evangelist implies that the powers of evil recognise Jesus as the Messiah, but that the time of the end of the era had not yet come.

Why the pigs went off in groups into the sea is not stated, but the man came to his right mind fully convinced Jesus had removed Satan's plague and freed him from his trouble. The pigs could have been frightened by the antics of the man in the last throes of his possession, if they were feeding close by on the hill-side, which is stated to be the case in some versions of this passage.

The cured demoniac then asked to accompany Jesus, but Jesus refused. Jesus does not seem to have been anxious to have a great number of disciples. He selected only a few, the evangelists say twelve, probably to represent the twelve tribes of Israel, and he sometimes sent would-be disciples away. It may be significant that not only did Jesus visit the Gentile area of the ten towns, but he told the man he had cured to proclaim what God had done for him among the Gentiles there. The man became an evangelist telling the people of his cure, which to some extent gave him an outlet for his exhibitionist gifts. 'Some sat in darkness and in gloom, prisoners in affliction and in irons ... some were sick through their sinful ways ... and they drew near to the gates of death. Then they cried to the Lord in their trouble and he delivered them from their distress. He sent forth his word and healed them ... Let them offer sacrifices of thanksgiving and tell of his deeds in songs of joy' (Ps. 107:10,17-22).

The purpose of Jesus was to relieve the possession of the man, freeing him for a useful life. That the man wished to show his gratitude was turned by Jesus to good account, by sending the man to preach to his own people rather than importing a Gentile into the group of disciples.

* * *

I 4. The deaf man with a speech impediment; the dumb man with a demon.
Mt. 9:32-33. Mk. 7:31-37.

Jesus was returning through Decapolis from his visit to the Tyrian area, and came through Sidon to the sea of Galilee. They brought to him a deaf and dumb man and they asked Jesus to lay his hands on him. Jesus took the man aside away from the others, put his fingers into his ears, spat and touched his tongue. Jesus groaned inwardly, looked up to heaven and said to the demon: "Ephphatha" ('Be opened').

The man was deaf no longer, the bond on his tongue was gone and he spoke correctly. Jesus told them to say nothing to anyone about what had happened, but the more he enjoined them to say nothing, the more people did just the opposite, so his fame spread far and wide. They said of him, "All he does, he does well! He even makes the deaf hear, the dumb speak."

Another time a man was brought to him, who was dumb and possessed of a demon. The demon was cast out and the man recovered his speech. Filled with amazement the onlookers said, "Nothing like this has been seen in Israel!"

To put a finger on the part which needed healing was an accepted part of healing, as was the use of saliva, which many believed had magical, curative powers. Jesus released the sufferers from their demons, prising open their grip: 'In that day the deaf shall hear ... and out of their gloom and darkness the eyes of the blind shall see' (Is. 29:18); 'Then the eyes of the blind shall be opened and the ears of the deaf unstopped' (Is. 35:5). The passage shows that the end of the old era was near and the day of Judgement at hand.

The translation given of 'Ephphatha' is a guess and it is possible that this word and the words 'Tabitha koum' in the passage of I 7, were not translated from Aramaic into Greek in the N.T. because they were magical, or words of a spell. It is known that such words were believed to be ineffective when translated into another language.

* * *

I 5. The man brought by his friends - Mt. 9:2-8. Mk. 2:1-12.
Lk. 4:31-32; 5:18-26.

Some time later, Jesus returned to Capernaum and the news spread like wildfire. Outside his house, a large crowd collected from everywhere round about, including Pharisees and teachers of the Law.

Jesus was addressing the crowd when some men appeared carrying a paralysed man on a mattress, with the idea of asking Jesus to cure him. The crowd, though, was so great that it was impossible to carry him in to Jesus, so they carried him on to the roof and let him down on his couch or mattress beside Jesus. Jesus saw the faith of the paralytic and his friends and said, "My child, your sins have been forgiven."

The doctors of the Law and Pharisees, observing this, began saying to themselves: "Only God can forgive sins and this fellow blasphemes when he pretends to forgive sins."

Jesus knew their thoughts and remarked, "Why do you reason in that way in your hearts? What is easier, to say to the man, 'Your sins have been forgiven', or to say, 'Rise, take up your mattress and go'? But in order that you know that the son of man has the authority on earth to forgive sins, (he turned and addressed the paralytic), I say to you, 'Rise, take up your mattress and go home.'" Thereupon, the man got up and went home.

The crowd were astounded and praised God. "Never before have we seen such things", they said.

The man is not stated to have expressed any repentance; perhaps he was so paralysed that he was unable to do so, or the determination of his friends convinced Jesus that he could be healed.

The passage shows Jesus stating that the man's sins were forgiven. In Judaism, only God can forgive sins and the Messiah was not able to do so. Sin was a kind of illness; and was seen also as susceptibility to injury, such as snake bites, but the patient is not healed of his sickness until his sins are forgiven. It was thought that God has given a part of his glory or wisdom to the sons of men and perhaps originally the words included: 'Blessed be he ... who has given a portion of this power to the sons of men'. This would parallel similar ideas in Judaism, with God giving some of his wisdom to sages, glory to a king and power to a wonder-maker.

It is often taken to mean Jesus himself had forgiven his sins, but this is not a necessary inference. Jesus did not transgress the Law; forgiveness of sins could be pronounced, as it was here, without implying it was not God who had forgiven them. No blasphemy was involved. Moreover, in the O.T. it was the priest who brought the repentant Israel before God so that she could be forgiven: 'The priest shall make atonement for all ... the people of Israel and they shall be forgiven' (Num. 15:25). The man of total faith helped the one with little or none, as he had done on several other occasions.

Even though he denies the relevance of the Pharisees' objection, Jesus uses a sacred formula, "Rise, take up your bed and walk", to encourage the man become well again. For Jesus the two modes of relieving a sinner's guilt were equally effective. The important thing was to convince the subject of this forgiveness. Once the man got up and walked away, no Pharisee could deny his sins had been forgiven! Jesus was recruiting for the passing of the spiritual Jordan into the promised land.

In this passage it seems as if it was Jesus' purpose to proclaim that the time of God's punishment was over. The New Era had begun and God was forgiving those deformed and diseased by their sins, so that they could become as the Israelites had been while in the wilderness, before they had polluted themselves with Canaanite idolatry. Jesus had authority to proclaim this on earth too, and he wished all to have faith that this was the case, so that they could bring the kingdom of God ever more fully into the world.

There is an intriguing aspect to this story which is of interest. In the culture of India and China, it was widely believed at the time that evil spirits could dwell within a house if they came in through a door or window. On the other hand, the spirit of a dead person, or a demon cast out of a person, would have to leave if there was a hole in the roof. Given the degree of contact between the Middle and Far East, even in those days, it is quite possible this belief lies at the root of this story. No doubt if the evangelists did not wish to promulgate this peculiar belief, they would invent a good reason for the action of the man's friends, such as a crowd preventing access except through the roof. The idea was also known to Goethe who refers to it in *Faust*.

An Aramaic inscription on an incantation vessel has a similar point: the demon is ordered to leave the house without harming those living there

A story found in the rabbinical literature says; 'One of the Roman emperors, Antoninus, had heard one of the rabbis telling his disciples that all of them were able to revive the dying or resurrect the dead. Some time later one of Antoninus' servants was at death's door and his master sent to the rabbi asking for one of the disciples to come to revive the dying man. The disciples found the man lying down, and said to him, "How is it that you are lying down while your master is standing?" Immediately, the man shook violently, broke out in sweat, and got to his feet.'

* * *

I 6. Simon's mother-in-law - Mt. 8:14-15. Mk. 1:29-31. Lk. 4:38-39.

On leaving the synagogue, Jesus went to the house
of Simon and Andrew together with James and John.
Simon's mother-in-law was ill in bed with fever,
but when they told Jesus about her, he came and,
rebuking the fever, took her by the hand. The fever left
her, and she got up at once and waited on them.

To take someone by the hand was a usual mode of healing and it is recorded in
several of the healing stories. Rebuking a fever is the method recorded on an Aramaic
incantation bowl, and refers to "God will rebuke you, Satan" (Zch. 3:2).

* * *

I 7. The daughter of Jairus, the leader of the synagogue - Mt. 9:18-19, 23-26. Mk. 5:21-24, 35-43. Lk. 8:40-42, 49-56.

Jesus was welcomed one day by the people, when he stepped ashore after crossing the Sea of Galilee, and among the crowd was Jairus, one of the leaders of the local synagogue. He threw himself at Jesus' feet and begged Jesus to come to lay his hands on his only daughter, a girl of about twelve years of age. "She is at death's door," he said, "but if you will come and lay your hands on her, it will save her life."

At this moment, a messenger arrived from Jairus' house: "Your daughter is dead; do not pester the teacher any further."

Jesus heard this and said, "Do not fear - only have faith."

They arrived at the house to find a great commotion of dirges and weeping. "Stop weeping and lamenting," said Jesus, "she's not dead, she's asleep." They ridiculed him, but Jesus put them all outside. Only the mother and father and Peter, John and James were allowed to go into the room where the girl was lying.

Jesus took the girl by the hand and spoke to her in her own tongue, "Talitha koum" (Little lamb, come!). She stood up at once, and walked about. They were all amazed by something so totally unexpected. Jesus told them to tell no one about it, but to give her something to eat.

The mourners wept and wailed. They were a reminder of O.T. teaching that God had withdrawn his favour. 'For this, gird yourselves with sackcloth, lament and wail' (Jer. 4:8, LXX). But the Philistines, that is unbelievers, shall be swept away. 'Behold, waters ... shall sweep away the land ... and men shall cry and all that dwell in the land shall howl' (Jer. 29:2, LXX). The evangelist wants us to understand that the girl's family and friends were lacking in faith, when they made so much commotion.

The Hebrew word which probably lies behind the word 'girl' in this passage, indicates she had reached, or was about to reach, marriageable age (13 years and one day old). She was due to be betrothed. Girls normally had no contact with men outside their immediate family circle, and many were terrified at the prospect of betrothal and marriage. A psychological reaction in which she lay rigid and without apparent feeling, could well have been her mode of putting off the awful day.

Her father is said to have been one of the leading members of the local synagogue, but this is strange, since at least in Palestine, each synagogue had only one leader. He asked Jesus to lay his hands on her, which may be a sign that he thought his daughter was suffering from possession by an evil spirit, the contemporary explanation for such situations.

When Jesus and his disciples arrived and went into the girl, Jesus took her hand and addressed her in words appropriate to a little child, far too young to be threatened by betrothal: 'Little lamb, arise.' When she realised it was not her prospective bridegroom come to claim her, she could get up and eat. Her fear was removed.

There are other intriguing aspects to this story. There are associations with the Song of Solomon, where twice the girl is called: 'Arise, my love, my fair one and come away' (S.S. 2:10,13). While Jesus puts himself far from being any earthly bridegroom, even with the presence of the parents and the three essential male witnesses, there are hints in the text that the evangelists want us to think of Jesus as a heavenly bridegroom who restores the 'dead' to life, that is, he brings lost ones back to the kingdom: 'For I, the Lord your God, hold your right hand; it is I who say to you, "Fear not, I will help you"' (Is. 41:13). Nothing is more expected than that those entering the kingdom of God should get something to eat at the heavenly banquet: 'If you are willing and obedient you shall eat the good of the land.' (Is. 1:19). They were not bereft and lost; 'My heart is smitten ... and withered; I forget to eat my bread' (Ps. 102:4), but restored to life: 'The Lord brought them out of darkness and gloom and broke their bonds asunder' (Ps. 107:14).

By her recovery the girl had returned to normality; in effect she had become fertile again, one of the conditions of ideal Israel. (See also I 8).

It is notable that Jesus ignores all the taboos about pollution from a possible corpse. If the mourners had been correct, and a corpse had lain within, the house would have been prohibited to any priest, but Jesus, not a priest, was sure it was 'sleep' not death, and dismissed the mourners and their crying.

For comment on 'Tabitha koum', see I 4; for a similar story in the secular literature, see the summary of this section below.

* * *

I 8. A woman with haemorrhage - Mt. 9:20-22. Mk. 5:25-34. Lk. 8:43-48.

Among the crowd was a woman who had suffered from haemorrhages for twelve years, and no one had been able to help her. She had long ago used up all her resources, but she had heard about Jesus, and wanted to seek his help. She came up behind Jesus and took hold of the hem of his cloak. "If I can touch his cloak, I shall be cured," she thought to herself.

Jesus stopped and turned and saw her and she came trembling and fell at his feet and confessed the truth of what she had done. "My daughter, your faith has cured you. Go in peace, you are made whole and free from your trouble", said Jesus.

This passage assumes acquaintance with the Jewish emphasis on fertility. It is concerned with a woman who had lost all hope of marriage and all hope of bearing children, because of constant bleeding. It is not to be assumed that her complaint was necessarily menstrual bleeding though it probably was; any form of haemorrhage would apply and Mark speaks of it as a sign of divine displeasure. She was deemed by the Law as unclean and a sinner, showing God's punishment: 'The Lord will bring on you ... afflictions severe and lasting and sickness grievous and lasting' (Dt. 28:59).

Any contact with a woman in this condition was unclean, and this uncleanness could then be passed on to others who came into contact with the first person affected. The woman should not have been near others, and to touch Jesus' cloak was enough to pollute him according to the strict levitical purity regulations. It is no wonder she was apprehensive when Jesus stopped and discovered who had done so, yet Jesus did not draw away from her. God had promised that there would be no barren women in Israel: 'You shall serve the Lord your God, and I will bless your bread and your water, and I will take away sickness from the midst of you. None shall abort their young or be barren in your land' (Ex. 23:25-26), so that those who were cured of their problems by their faith were sure that their supposed sins were forgiven.

Ezekiel's comment comes to mind: 'Thus says the Lord God to Jerusalem: "Your origin and birth are of the land of Canaan ... On the day you were born your navel cord was not cut, nor were you washed ... nor swathed with bands ... And when I passed you by and saw you lying in your blood, I said to you, 'Live and grow up like a plant of the field' ... When I passed by you again ... I spread my skirt over you and covered your nakedness. I ... entered into a covenant with you, says the Lord God, and you became mine"' (Ezk. 16:3-6, 8). God came and saw Israel in total uncleanness yet had cared for her, and made a covenant as in marriage with her. Yet this woman had been excluded from every synagogue, let alone the Temple, whereas in her distress this was just where she ought to have been to get spiritual help. Jesus accepted her faith had cured her.

Once again Jesus removed the fear of divine punishment as the cause of illness and sought instead to restore sufferers to wholeness. The woman had suffered a long time and a true healer was necessary: 'Bless the Lord, O my soul ... who forgives all your iniquities, who heals all your diseases' (Ps. 103:2-3); 'My son, if you have an illness do not neglect it but pray to the Lord, and he will heal you. Renounce your faults, amend your ways and cleanse your heart from all sin' (Sir. 38:9); 'Go in peace and may the Lord God go before you ...' (Jud. 8:35).

The woman came up behind Jesus and held the hem of his garment, which was thought by many to have the power of healing: 'You have been my helper and in the shelter of your wings I will rejoice. My soul keeps very close behind you ...' (Ps. 63:7-8). This was an action by which one sought a holy man's help, as Saul did after asking Samuel for forgiveness: 'As Samuel turned to go away, Saul laid hold upon the skirt of his robe ...' (I Sam. 15:27).

There was a danger in doing so though, too: 'The Lord will come down upon Mount Sinai ... You shall not go up into the mountain or touch the border of it ... No hand shall touch him, but that he shall be stoned or shot with arrows' (Ex. 19:12-13). While touching God would bring death, touching the border of the cloak of his prophet would bring life.

The evangelists show that Jairus (I 7), who was Moses' successor, was the official responsible for bringing the house of Israel into God's realm, but he is unable to do so. Jesus by his behaviour and actions does so. He ignores the supposed pollution by blood in favour of relieving the woman's guilt. He walked among people in spite of their 'uncleanness' and 'indecency', not as in the O.T.: 'Because the Lord God walks in the midst of your camp ... it must be holy, that he may not see anything indecent among you and turn away from you' (Dt. 23:14).

It may be that the evangelist put this passage in the middle of the story of Jairus' daughter (I 7), in order to point up the faith of the woman and lack of faith of the leader of a synagogue. He needed to be encouraged to have faith and not despair.

* * *

I 9. The young man at Nain - Lk. 7:11-17.

Jesus, his disciples and a large crowd walking towards Nain met a cortège. The only son of a widow lay on the bier and his mother and many from the town were with her.

When Jesus saw it his heart went out to them, and his bowels were churned up with compassion for them, and he said, "Weep no more". He laid his hand on the bier and stopped it and spoke to the young man, saying, "Young man, be risen." He sat up and began to talk to them and Jesus restored him to his mother.

They were all awe-struck and said, "God has sent a great prophet to care for us. He has visited his people." The story of what Jesus had done spread through all Judaea and the whole surrounding area.

The story is very similar to the O.T. stories of prophets who did miracles. Elijah and Elisha are examples, both of whom were instrumental in the revival of an apparently dead boy. That of Elijah may be quoted. 'The son of the woman ... became ill and his illness became so severe there was no breath left in him. Then she said to Elijah, "What have you against me, O man of God? You have come to bring my sin to remembrance and to cause the death of my son" ... And Elijah took her son ... into the upper room and laid him on his own bed ... He stretched himself three times upon the boy and cried to the Lord, "O Lord, my God, let this child's soul come into him again." And the Lord hearkened ... and the soul of the child returned to him and he revived. Elijah took the child ... and delivered him to his mother and said, "See your son lives." And the woman said, "Now I know that you are a man of God and the word of the Lord in your mouth is truth"' (I Kgs. 17:17-24).

The stories in the O.T. and N.T. have various differences and one which is significant is that the mother in the O.T. story upbraids Elijah for reminding her of her sins which she believes must be the cause of her son's illness and death. No such remark is found in the N.T. story. Here Jesus takes the initiative and stops the funeral procession, his compassion overpowering all other considerations. He demands no pious penitence but causes the boy to wake, sit up and talk.

In this way, Luke presents Jesus as leaving behind the concept of illness or death as God's wish and punishment for sin, and advocating the other aspect of Judaism - God's desire for unblemished people and his willingness to love all who will let him.

A more detailed analysis of the passage can demonstrate many other ways in which Luke fashioned his story. Although based on the O.T. stories, yet it was made to show Jesus as the prophet through whom God comes to visit his people. In this connection it seems likely that Psalm 88 was another O.T. passage which Luke may have had in mind: 'Do you work wonders for the dead? Shall their company rise up and praise you? Will they speak of your faithful love in the grave, of your sure help in the place of destruction?' (Ps. 88:10-11).

Once again the important point is not whether, or how, such an event could occur; there are plenty of alternative explanations which can be employed - but that Jesus showed God as the redeemer from sin and its consequences. No one should be upset by the idea that the evangelist imitated another well-known story to proclaim his message about Jesus. Imitation and emulation were the two principle criteria for good literature in the ancient world and it was only much later that originality became more valued.

It should not be supposed that stories of the revival of dead persons are unknown outside the bible. They are quite common in ancient literature and some are given here: 'Varro records that .. at Capua a person being carried out on a bier to burial returned home on foot. Also at Rome ... Corfidius came to life again after his funeral had been arranged with an undertaker, and he himself superintended the funeral of the relative who made the arrangement. There were two brothers ... the elder of whom appeared to have expired and when his will was opened the younger brother was read out as his heir, and began to arrange the funeral. In the meantime, the elder brother ... summoned his servants by clapping his hands ...' (Pliny, Nat. Hist., Bk. 7:176-177).

* * *

I 10. The centurion's boy - Mt. 8:5-10, 13. Lk. 7:2-10.

When Jesus came to Capernaum, a centurion came to him to ask his help. "Sir", he said, "my boy (or servant) lies paralysed and in great pain at home."
Jesus said, "I will come and heal him[1]."
The centurion said, "Sir, who am I to have you within my dwelling? Just say the word and my boy will be well. I know how it is, for I am a man under authority myself, with soldiers under me. I say to one, 'Go' and he goes; to another 'Come' and he comes; to my servant I say, 'Do this' and he does it."
Jesus heard him with astonishment and admiration and said to those following, "One thing is quite certain: from no one, even in Israel, have I found such understanding."
To the centurion he said, "Go. As you believed, so let it be." At that hour the boy recovered.

The centurion was the king's military representative, and he had understanding and humility before Jesus as God's representative, who could eject evil spirits. He knew about Judaism and reckoned that there was a hierarchy in the spiritual sphere as there was in the military.

Originally in Israel, too, there had been an hierarchy: Jethro had suggested to Moses that officers be appointed to help him to govern the people: 'So Moses gave heed to the voice of Jethro and did all that he said. Moses chose able men out of all Israel and made them heads over the people, rulers of thousands, of hundreds, of fifties and of tens' (Ex. 18:24-25). The centurion could give orders and they were obeyed; God did the same: 'The Lord said to Moses, "Go back to Egypt" ... So Moses ... went back to the land of Egypt' (Ex. 4:19-20); 'The Lord said to Moses, "Come up to me on the mountain and wait there. So Moses arose ... and went up into the mountain' (Ex. 24:12-13).

In an hierarchy, the chief has authority, and from that power and dominion. The centurion believed Jesus had dominion and that he could, if he would, heal a Gentile as he had healed Jews. His word was as good as God's and such a word had power: 'My thought is my counsellor, my Wisdom and my word is my deed ...' (II En. 33:4); 'Let all creation serve you; for you spoke and they were made ... and there is none that can resist your voice' (Jud. 16:14); 'O God of the fathers ... who made all things by your word' (W.S. 9:1). Such words could heal: 'They cried to the Lord in their trouble and he delivered them from their distress; he sent forth his word and healed them, and delivered them from destruction' (Ps. 107:19-20). There was no need for Jesus to visit the house. Such faith in Jesus' status and authority was rare and Jesus was surprised.

A subsidiary reason for the centurion's anxiety over Jesus visiting his house could have been that Jewish holy men normally would not enter a pagan house, nor any house where there was a risk of there being a corpse within, which might have been the case had the centurion's boy or servant died before he could be healed. This passage may also be a reflection on the experience of Naaman with Elisha. Naaman expected to be treated as an important personage, but Elisha simply sent a servant with a message.

This is another story in which Jesus is shown healing a Gentile, and one of two in which the healing occurred at a place at a distance from where Jesus was at the time. (The other is related in I 11.) A similar story is found in the rabbinical literature too: 'The son of Rabbi Gamaliel fell ill and he sent two disciples to Rabbi Chanina to pray on the boy's behalf. When Chanina saw them, he went up to an upper chamber and prayed for the boy. When he came down, he said to the two messengers, "Go, the fever has left him." They said to him, "Are you a prophet?" He replied, "I am no prophet, nor a prophet's son, but I know from my tradition that if my prayer is fluent in my mouth, it is accepted. If not, it is rejected."

The messengers sat down and noted down the time and when they returned home, they found that it had happened that at that very hour the fever had left the boy, and he had asked for water to drink' (b.Ber. 34b).

In the New Era, there would be no sick, wicked people in Zion: 'Look upon Zion ... No inhabitant will say, "I am ill", and the iniquity of the people who dwell there shall be taken away' (Is. 33:20,24).

[1] In some versions: 'Am I come to heal him?'

* * *

I 11. The Syrophoenician woman - Mt. 15:21-28. Mk. 7:24-30.

Jesus withdrew to the region of Tyre, hoping to remain 'incognito'. He found a lodging, but he was soon recognised.

A woman, whose little daughter was possessed by a demon, heard about him, and, coming to him, fell at his feet. (She was a Greek, a Syrophoenician by race.) She begged Jesus to drive the spirit out of her daughter, but he said, "Let the descendants of the house be satisfied first; it is not right to take the children's bread and throw it so the puppies can get it."

"Sir", said the woman, "even the puppies are allowed to eat the crumbs that fall under the children's table."

"Woman, what faith you have!", exclaimed Jesus. "Go home content; you will find your daughter cured." She returned home and found her daughter thrown on the couch - the demon had left her.

The story is not an attempt by the evangelists to show Jesus as a marvellous worker of wonders. It is concerned with the relationship between Jews and Gentiles and the acceptability of the latter in the kingdom of God in the New Era.

It has many features in common with the story of Elijah. He too went to the region of Tyre and Sidon where the inhabitants were opposed and resistant to Judaism: 'The word of the Lord came to Elijah: "Arise and go to Zarephath which belongs to Sidon and dwell there. Behold, I have commanded a widow to feed you' (I Kgs. 17:8-9). He then met the Gentile widow of Zarephath and asked for a crumb of bread. She showed her 'good inclination', her kindness, and shared her food with him, although there was really only enough for her child and herself. She thereby became worthy to receive God's help through Elijah, so that later Elijah was able to bring her son back to life. (This story is to be found in I Kgs. 17; see also I 9.)

There are other passages in the O.T. which show that Gentiles or pagans who were willing to accept God's rule were welcome into his protection and fellowship: 'So, too, with the foreigners who give their allegiance to me, the Lord, to minister to me and love my name ... them I will bring to my holy hill' (Is. 56:6); so it was not excluded for the woman to ask Jesus for help. She was doing what was advocated: 'Seek the Lord while he may be found, call upon him while he is near' (Is. 55:6).

Jesus at first takes up what may have been the accepted attitude of Judaism, in saying that the children of Israel must be fed until they are satisfied, before others can partake at the banquet in the kingdom of God. The bread, which also represents the word of God, was not to be cast to the young dogs or puppies under the table. In making this remark, Jesus could have had in mind: 'May their belly be filled with what you have stored up for them; may their children be fully sated ...' (Ps. 17:14).

The woman rebuts his argument. She takes up the reference to this Psalm, but points to the ending of the verse: '... may their children be fully sated, and may they leave something over for their babes.' She takes up the reference to young dogs, and says in effect that Gentile "puppies" are like the babies of the psalm, they too can receive some left-over crumbs from the table.

She was acclaimed for her faith. She was convinced God was able and willing to help her. He has promised to provide food for all creatures: 'He ... gives food to all his creatures' (Ps. 136:25); 'The earth is full of your creatures ... living things both great and small ... They all look to you to give them their food in due season' (Ps. 104:24-25,27); 'He gives the beasts their food, and to the young ravens which cry' (Ps. 147:9). Beasts included dogs which were classed as a kind of wild beast.

The woman relied on God's love. 'We will not keep away; to you we will come. For if I hunger, to you will I cry, O God, and you will give to me. You give rain ... that grass may spring up ... to prepare fodder for every living thing ... Who is the help of the poor and needy if not you, O Lord?' (P.S. 5:9-13).

Jesus is pleased and impressed by her faith in God's love which she clearly believed encompasses more than just Israel. Perhaps she reminded him of passages in an I.T. book: 'After these things there shall arise the Lord, the light of righteousness. He shall bring back all the Gentiles into zeal for him' (T.Zeb. 9:8); and, 'The Lord shall raise up a new priest, and all the words of the Lord shall be revealed to him ... In his priesthood the Gentiles shall be ... enlightened through the grace of the Lord' (T. Lev. 18:2,9). She received God's help through her faith.

The mother realised the Lord's house was free of demons and asked for an unprivileged position in order that she and her daughter may be accepted into it. (See also F 2).

In Matthew's version of this story, the disciples are said to have asked Jesus to, 'Send her away! She keeps crying after us." This odd sentence may be a mistranslation, and should read, "Send it away", that is, send the unclean spirit away, or release the girl from the grip of the demon in her. Matthew also says that Jesus answered at first, "I was sent to the lost sheep of the house of Israel, and to them alone". It was only after the woman persisted that Jesus helped her.

* * *

I 12. Bartimaeus receives his sight; Jesus cures two men of their blindness - Mt. 9:27-31; 20:29-34. Mk. 10:46-52. Lk. 18:35-43.

Jesus left Jericho and passed by the place where the blind beggar, Bartimaeus, sat, and, on hearing who was nearby, he began to call out, "Son of David, Jesus, have pity on me". He called out all the more when people rebuked him and told him to be quiet!

Jesus heard him, stopped and had Bartimaeus brought before him. "Take heart", the crowd said to Bartimaeus. "Stand up - he is calling you."

Bartimaeus threw off his cloak, sprang up and came to Jesus, who asked him why he was shouting. "Rabbouni, Lord, I want to be able to see again." Jesus said to him, "Your faith has cured you. Have your sight again." At once his sight returned and he followed after Jesus.

The name, son of Timaeus, suggests he might have been of a priestly family, and his blindness, cured instantaneously, presumably was of psychological origin. The main theme of the story is that a man who had considered himself a sinner became a follower of Jesus when reassured by Jesus that God had been able to forgive his sins.

The evangelist may have intended his readers to see the connections with several O.T. events. Moses and Gideon were called by God to his service, though both were sure they were unworthy: '(Then the Lord said), "Come, I will send you to Pharaoh that you may bring forth my people, the sons of Israel out of Egypt." But Moses said to God, "Who am I that I should go to Pharaoh and bring the sons of Israel out of Egypt?"' (Ex. 3:10-11); 'The Lord turned to him (Gideon) and said, "Go in this might of yours and deliver Israel from the hand of Midian; do not I send you?" And Gideon said, "Pray Lord, how can I deliver Israel? Behold my clan is the weakest in Manasseh, and I am the least in my family"' (Jdg. 6:14-15). They were the last people one would expect to do great works at the time of God's summons.

It was similar or worse with Bartimaeus. To be a beggar signified for Jews of the time that one was a sinner and cursed of God: 'May the children (of the wicked) wander about and beg ...' (Ps. 109:10). God would never allow one of his righteous to become a beggar: 'I have not seen the righteous forsaken or his children begging bread' (Ps. 37:25), but redemption was possible: 'The Lord raises up the poor from the dust and the needy from the ash-heap' (I Sam. 2:8). It must have been more than surprising that Jesus allowed one like Bartimaeus to follow him, and this is the only recorded occasion when one who had been healed was allowed to do so.

Bartimaeus cast off his cloak, a rather surprising thing for a beggar to do, since it would have been his only important possession probably. Garments have great significance in the bible, and this point could have been included to symbolise the repentance, change of heart and rebirth as a new man, which Bartimaeus underwent when he heard Jesus was near. He cast off the old order and his former sins.

Another possible association with the O.T. is with the fate of Eli, whose sons ran wild and did not follow the Lord. Eli became blind and his priestly line was abolished. 'Behold the days are coming, when I will cut off your strength, and the strength of your father's house, so that there will not be an old man in your house ... And this shall be a sign to you. Both your sons shall die on the same day. And I will raise up for myself a faithful priest, who shall do according to what is in my heart and in my mind; and I will build him a sure house, and he shall go in and out before my anointed for ever.' (I Sam. 2:31-35).

In the time of Jesus, it was believed that one of the signs of the New Era would be the beginning of a truly pure and righteous priestly caste. This would remove the curse on the house of Eli, who would be represented by one with defective eyes. There would be no more Temple sacrifices, no more priestly exploitation of the faithful, and no more of their blasphemy and oppressive burdens.

At first things were as God had wished, but later abuses crept in: 'The first to be anointed to the priesthood shall be great and speak to God as a father, and this priesthood shall be perfect with the Lord ... (Then) those who are idolaters, adulterers, lovers of money, proud, lawless, lascivious, abusers of children and beasts, shall become priests ... After their punishment by the Lord, the priesthood shall fall. Then the Lord shall raise up a new priest, to whom all the words of the Lord shall be revealed. He shall execute righteous judgement in all the earth. The heavens shall exult in his days and the earth shall rejoice ... The heavens shall be opened and ... sanctification shall come upon him with the Father's voice as from Abraham to Isaac ... The spirit of understanding and sanctification shall rest upon him ... In his priesthood the Gentiles shall be multiplied in knowledge and ... sin shall come to an end ... Satan shall be bound by him and he shall give power to his children to tread upon evil spirits.' (T.Lev. 17:2-18:12). In this New Era all good things can be expected.

There is a second story in Matthew's gospel on the theme of restoration of sight to the blind by Jesus, which many think is a variation on the story of Bartimaeus.

Passing on, Jesus was followed by two blind men who cried out, "Son of David, have pity on us." The people rebuked them and told them to be quiet. But they shouted all the more. "Lord, have pity on us, Son of David." They followed him into the house and Jesus asked them, "Do you believe I have the power to do what you want?" "Yes", they replied. Then Jesus touched their eyes and said, "Let it be as you believed it would be!" Their eyes were opened and Jesus told them sternly that they were not to let others hear about it, but they went off and told all they met.

Some see this passage as a creation by Matthew from other healing stories, intended as a contrast to the two disciples James and John, who were so blind they asked to have the best seats in the kingdom! (See E 2)

* * *

Jesus and his disciples visited Bethsaida and the people brought a blind man to him and begged him to touch him. Jesus took him by the hand and led him away to a spot outside the village. Jesus spat on his eyes, placed his hands on him, and asked him if he could see anything. The man began to regain his sight and said, "Yes, I see men: they look like trees moving about!"

Jesus put his hands on his eyes again; the man looked steadily and was restored. He kept on seeing all things clearly. Jesus sent him home and said, "Do not tell anyone about this."

The passage describes a healing by Jesus of a blind man using the traditional method with saliva which was thought to have healing properties. There is nothing necessarily mysterious about the event, since it is known that in severe cataracts of long standing, it is possible by pressing on the eye to push the useless lens out of the way, allowing some degree of sight to return. The man had had sight at one time in his life, since he knew what men and trees looked like, while those born blind cannot recognise anything in their vision if they become able to see. His restored vision would be a blurred, enlarged image and this accords well with his description of seeing men as trees, moving about.

An important point is that the passage says that Jesus pressed a second time and the man's sight became clear; but this time the word used means metaphorical sight, that is the man began, and continued, to have insight into Jesus' message. At the time it was thought that there was something stopping the light emerging from the eye and it was the removal of this blockage which allowed the man to see again. (See also F 9).

Jesus asked the man what he could see, just as God had asked Jeremiah and Amos among others: 'The word of the Lord came to me; "What is it you see, Jeremiah?" "An almond in early blossom," I answered. "You are right", said the Lord, "for I am early on watch over my word to perform it"' (Jer. 1:11-13); 'Then the Lord said to me, "The time is ripe to end my people Israel. Never again will I pass them by." In that day, says the Lord God, the singing women in the palace shall howl' (Am. 8:2-3).

There is a yet deeper underlying significance which would have been appreciated by Jesus' listeners. That which the man described, trees walking or moving about, repeated O.T. prophecies of the end of the world. Trees often represent men: 'The man is like a tree planted beside a watercourse which yields its fruit in season' (Ps. 1:3); 'They shall be called Trees of Righteousness, planted by the Lord that he may be glorified' (Is. 61:3); 'The paradise of the Lord, the trees of life are his pious ones. Their planting is rooted for ever' (P.S. 14:2-3). Trees could also represent soldiers carrying stakes (see F 11), and to see many trees moving, was tantamount to seeing an army coming to attack and destroy.

God might combine with the armies of Israel's enemies to subdue and punish her: 'Therefore thus says the Lord God: "Behold my anger and my wrath will be poured out on this place upon man and beast, upon the trees of the field ...'" (Jer. 7:20); 'I will encamp against you ... and besiege you with towers and raise siege works against you' (Is. 29:3); only a remnant shall be left: 'The glory of his forest and of his fruitful land will be destroyed, both body and soul ... the remnant of ... his forests will be so few that a child may write them down' (Is. 10:18-19).

In Jewish prophecy, when the end of the world came, the stones would cry out and the trees themselves be so afraid they would run away as fast as they could! These trees would be the fruitful ones standing outside a fortified town which it was forbidden to cut down even in a siege: 'When you besiege a city ... you shall not destroy its trees...; for you may eat of them but not cut them down. Are the trees in the field men, who should be besieged by you? Only the trees which you know bear no fruit may you destroy' (Dt. 20:19-21). The unfruitful trees, or those bearing useless fruit, would have already been chopped down and destroyed.

Jesus' followers would be terrified and would, like trees bearing good fruit, flee for their lives. Others would be like unfruitful trees welcoming an approaching army, assuming it would be one of Jews taking up arms against Rome and its puppet kings of Palestine.

There is a further point to be borne in mind. Healing the blind and deaf was one of the things which the Messiah would do when he came, according to O.T. prophecy: 'On that day, deaf men shall hear ... and the eyes of the blind shall see out of impenetrable darkness' (Is. 32:3). Thus Jesus is pictured as faced by a situation in which his healing was messianic, by the first touch the man's visions could suggest a military upheaval, or rebellion. By the second touch giving insight, the man is shown as recognising Jesus as the declarer of God's will.

* * *

I 14. A leper is cured - Mt. 8:1-4. Mk. 1:40-45. Lk. 5:12-15.

One day, Jesus was approached by a leper who prostrated himself and begged to be made clean (that is pronounced purified). "I know you can do this, if you will", he said. Jesus, full of compassion, stretched out his hand and touched him, saying, "I am willing; be clean again." The leprosy immediately left him, and he was purified. Jesus put him out and sternly admonished him: "Go and show yourself to the priest, and make the offering laid down by Moses as your testimony to them."

He, going out, began to proclaim and spread about the story, so that Jesus stayed outside the towns in the open country yet great crowds came to him.

The disease called leprosy in the bible was not the same as the disease known by this name in modern times. In Judaism, it included malignant skin diseases, discoloration of the skin, scabs, inflammation and scurf, as well as mould on clothes, fungus in houses, and reddish or greenish discoloration of buildings (see also J 3). It was thought to be one of God's punishments for lying and blasphemy: 'Miriam and Aaron spoke against Moses ... "Has the Lord really spoken only through Moses? Has he not spoken through us also?" ... And the anger of the Lord was kindled against them ... and, behold, Miriam became leprous, as white as snow' (Num. 12:1-2,9-10); 'King Uzziah was false to the Lord his God ... And Azariah the chief priest and all the priests looked at him and behold his forehead was leprous ... And he hastened to go out because the Lord had smitten him' (II Chr. 26:16,20).

Lepers were required to leave their villages and remain outside. 'He shall dwell alone in a habitation outside the camp' (Lev. 13:46); 'Command the people of Israel that they put out of the camp every leper' (Num. 5:2). 'The Lord said to Moses and Aaron: "When a man ... has a leprous disease on his skin, then he shall be brought to Aaron the priest or to one of his sons the priests. He shall examine the diseased spot on his body, and if it has turned white ... it is leprous disease ... He shall be pronounced unclean' (Lev. 13:1-3); 'All are qualified to inspect signs of leprosy but only a priest may pronounce them unclean or clean' (m.Neg. 3:1).

'Then the Lord said to Moses, "This shall be the law of the leper for the day of his purification. He shall be brought to the priest ... then if the disease is healed, the priest shall command him to bring for him two living clean birds and cedarwood and scarlet cloth and hyssop ... And he who is to be cleansed shall wash his clothes ... and bathe himself in water ..."' (Lev. 14:1-4, 8); 'Take heed in an attack of leprosy to be careful to do according to all that the levitical priests shall direct you. Remember what the Lord your God did to Miriam!' (Dt. 24:8-9).

Even after the first inspection by the priests has shown him to be clean, a leper has to remain outside the community for a further seven days. Only after a second inspection has shown him to be free from symptoms, can he return to his house: 'Let Miriam be shut up outside the camp for seven days' (Num. 12:14).

There are several interesting points in this story. It was a most extraordinary thing to do to touch a leper, since this automatically brought on a state of ritual defilement. Although the usual translation says Jesus was moved with passion, many manuscripts use a word which means he was moved to anger by the situation. The text also says that Jesus cast out the leper but it is not certain whether the next sentence refers to the leper or Jesus himself, who went out proclaiming what had happened. He remained in wild places where crowds gathered to listen to him. Perhaps the evangelists wanted us to see Jesus as beginning a new community of purified sinners in the New Kingdom away from the unrighteous community.

To be forgiven and healed was equivalent to being baptised with fire, and must be followed by washing in water: 'Everything that can stand the fire, you shall pass through the fire and it shall be clean. Nevertheless it shall also be purified with the water of impurity, and whatever cannot stand the fire, you must pass through the water' (Num. 31:23). The 'water of impurity' was the water in which 'impure' things were to be washed. It had nothing to do with cleansing but everything to do with ritual.

* * *

I 15. The grateful Samaritan - Lk. 17:11-19.

It was beside a village near to the border between Galilee and Samaria that Jesus was accosted by ten lepers. They stood some way off and called to him, "Master, take pity on us!"

"Go and show yourselves to the priests," said Jesus.

On their way to the priests they realised that they had been cured, and one of them, a Samaritan, turned back, praising God. He threw himself down before Jesus in deep gratitude.

"Were not all ten cleansed?", asked Jesus. "Where are the other nine? Could none of them be found to come back and praise God, except this foreigner?" And to the man he said, "Stand up and be on your way. Your faith has cured you."

In this passage, found only in Luke, ten lepers were cured whilst on their way to their priests, where they were to request purification. (Presumably, the Samaritan would go to a Samaritan priest.) Only after that would they be permitted to return to their communities.

One of them, the 'pagan' Samaritan, returned to praise and thank God. He was like Naaman, another Gentile who had been cured of his leprosy, and purified by the word of the prophet Elisha: 'Elisha sent a message to him saying, "Go and wash in the Jordan seven times and your flesh shall be restored and you shall be clean"' (II Kgs. 5:10). In other words, even Samaritans could enter God's kingdom.

Healing of lepers was a recognised sign of the coming of the kingdom of God (see C 8), and the other main points of this passage appear to be that the faith of the sufferer was the prerequisite for his cure; that the ceremonial as laid down in the Torah was not part of the cure but a social ceremony to mark the readmittance of the afflicted into normal society; and that God will cure Gentiles as well as Jews. The Samaritan's faith had been his salvation: his faith had saved him.

It was Jewish belief that if one did not thank someone from whom one had received a favour, all the merit belonged to the donor. Those like the nine Jews, who did not thank God with their praise, pay no attention to him and are no better than pagans. The ones like the Samaritan, who give thanks, reciprocate God's love for them and belong to his realm.

There are several O.T. passages which say that only a remnant will be spared: 'For though the people of Israel be as the sand of the sea, only a remnant will return' (Is. 10:22); 'Thus says the Lord God: "The city that sent forth a thousand, shall have a hundred left; that which sent forth a hundred, shall have ten left to the house of Israel' (Am. 5:3). What may be inferred from this remains uncertain.

* * *

I. Summary.

This section includes most of the miracles recorded in the gospels. They have evoked two main responses: they are fairy tales to boost the idea that Jesus was divine, or they can be rationally explained and they are therefore of little interest. Both points of view contain elements of the truth. They do indeed point to Jesus as being a very remarkable man, and there are reasonable explanations of most if not all of them. To treat them as exact accounts of the events they refer to, is to reduce Jesus' purpose to the level of superstition.

The passage of C 8 shows that Jewish teachers were little impressed by miracles. In Judaism it was considered that God's laws were not broken by God or anyone else, except where particular miracles are reported in the bible. In these cases, it was thought that these events were built into the world by God at the creation. God foresaw all that was to happen and what "special effects" would be required at certain times, and arranged everything at the beginning.

The evangelists portray Jesus as being anxious to help those who believed themselves condemned because of their sins, real or imagined. He will release them from their burden of guilt by encouraging them to accept God's forgiveness if they repent of their wrong-doing. Jesus was evidently an expert exorcist. His fame as a charismatic faith healer was so great that non-believers vied to use his name in their procedures, and the name of Jesus has been found among Aramaic inscriptions on vessels used in magical rites. Even in rabbinical writings it is acknowledged that Jews healed in the name of Jesus, although the rabbis disapproved of it.

Belief in spirit possession is quite common in times of distress, disruption and insecurity, and at the time of Jesus, belief that one of Satan's demons had taken up residence was a common explanation for personal set-backs and problems. If the subject had faith in the exorcist or healer, he could be persuaded that the demon had been sent away, or in other words, the removal of guilt leads to the relief of unconscious self-punishment. To help in this process symbolic actions and magic words are valuable; Jesus uses both. To spit, for example, was believed to drive away demons; and Jesus spoke certain 'magic' words which are left untranslated by the evangelists, because they thought they were only effective in their original language.

In several of the stories in this section, Jesus is said to have touched the person concerned or taken him or her by the hand. Healing with laying on hands was well known: 'So I prayed [for him] ... and I laid my hands on his [head]; and the scourge departed from him and the evil [spirit] was expelled [from him], and he lived' (DSS, 1QapGen. 20:29).

There are numerous miracle stories in the secular literature of the time, and two are given below. The first is from the 'Histories' of Tacitus: 'One of the common people of Alexandria, well known for his loss of sight threw himself before the Emperor Vespasion's knees, praying him with groans to cure his blindness. He besought the

Emperor to moisten his cheeks and eyes with his spittle. Another whose hand was useless begged Caesar to step and trample on it. Vespasion did as he was asked. The hand was instantly restored to use, and the day again shone for the blind man. Both facts are told by eye-witnesses even now, when falsehood brings no reward' (Bk. 4, 81).

The second is found in the 'Life of Apollonius' by Philostratus, a story in which a young girl, due to be married, "dies" and is restored, not to the bridegroom but to her father and her parental home: 'A girl died just in the hour of her marriage and the bridegroom was following her bier lamenting ... and the whole of Rome was mourning with him because the maiden belonged to a consular family. Apollonius, seeing their grief, said, "Put down the bier, for I will stop the tears you are shedding for this young woman." He asked her name ... touched her and whispered in secret some spell over her. At once she woke up from her apparent death, spoke out loud and returned to her father's house ... Whether Apollonius detected some spark of life in her or whether life was really extinct and he restored it by the warmth of his touch, is a mystery which neither I myself nor those who were present could decide' (Bk. 4,55).

J. Visions of the future.

J 1. Jerusalem - Mt. 23:37-39. Lk. 13:31-35; 19:41-44.

Some Pharisees came to warn Jesus. "Herod is out to kill you; you should get away while you can!" Jesus replied, "You can tell that jackal that I shall heal the sick, and cast out demons today and tomorrow, and the third day I finish my course. But now I must march for today and tomorrow and the day after, because it is not fitting for a prophet to perish outside Jerusalem."

When Jesus came in sight of the city, he wept over it and said, "O Jerusalem, Jerusalem, the city that murders the prophets and stones the messengers sent to her! How often have I longed to gather your children as a bird protects her brood under her wings, but you would not let me. Look, look; there is your house, the Temple, forsaken by God. And I tell you, you shall never see me until the time comes when you shall say, 'Blessed be he who comes in the name of the Lord.'

If you had only known on this great day the things that lead to peace! But no, it is hidden from your sight. You do not see that your enemies will besiege you, encircle you and hem you in, that they will raze you to the ground, you and your children within the walls. Not one stone will be left standing on another, all because you did not recognise the time of the visitation by God."

That some Pharisees warned Jesus indicates that not all of them looked upon him as an enemy. In referring to Herod as a jackal, Jesus obliquely reminded his listeners of O.T. ideas: 'I will make Jerusalem a heap of ruins, a haunt of jackals and the cities of Judah a desolation, without inhabitants' (Jer. 9:11); 'The precious sons of Zion worth their weights in finest gold - now they are counted as earthen pots, the work of a potter's hands. Even the jackals give the breast and suckle their young, but the daughters of my people have become cruel like ostriches in the wilderness' (Lam. 4:2-3); and from the Aramaic version of Isaiah: 'Wild cats shall cry in their castles, jackals in their pleasant dwelling-places; the time of the destruction of Babylon is near ...' (Tg.Is. 13:22). (Jackals and wild cats were symbols of the worst kind of impious hypocrites; see G 11). According to I.T. writing though: 'The city shall be delivered up for a time, and the people shall be chastened during a time [but] the world will not be given over to oblivion' (I Bar. 4:1).

It was a common metaphor to speak of Zion or Jerusalem as a mother: 'O Lord, my Lord, have I come into this world ... to see the evils of my mother? If I have found grace in your sight ... let me not behold the destruction of my mother' (II Bar. 3:1-2); 'How solitary lies the city once so full of people, once great among nations, now become a widow' (Lam. 1:1); 'Like birds hovering overhead so the Lord of Hosts will protect Jerusalem; he will protect and deliver it' (Is 31:5).

Jerusalem was the centre and focus of Israel, and the only place in which a prophet could be judged by the full Sanhedrin of seventy-one members. It had not found the things which promoted peace, and reduced the conflict, strife and tension between men. The city was in dire straits and the O.T. had described the fate Jerusalem and Israel would suffer: 'Remember O Lord, against the people of Edom the day of Jerusalem's fall, when they said, "Raze it, raze it, down to its foundations"' (Ps. 137:7); 'Zion's rulers sell justice, her priests teach for hire, her seers divine for money ... Therefore shall Zion become ploughed as a field, Jerusalem a heap of ruins and the Temple mount a rough heath' (Mic. 3:11-12); 'Son of man, set your face towards Jerusalem and ... prophesy against the land of Israel and say ... Thus says the Lord: "Behold I am against you and will draw forth my sword out of its sheath and shall cut off from you both righteous and wicked ... Sigh therefore, son of man, sigh with breaking heart and bitter grief before their eyes"' (Ezk. 21:2-3,6); 'The kings of the earth did not believe ... that foe or enemy could enter the gates of Jerusalem. This was for the sins of her prophets and the iniquities of her priests, who shed the blood of the righteous in the midst of her and wandered blind, through the streets, so defiled with blood ... that men cried out, 'Away, unclean!'"' (Lam. 4:12-14); 'O, that my head were a spring of water and my eyes a fountain of tears so that I might weep day and night for the claim of my poor people' (Jer. 9:1).

Israel had been warned: 'Take warning, O Jerusalem, or I shall turn from you in disgust and make you a desolation, an uninhabited land' (Jer. 6:8). Yet she was so blind she did not even take the opportunity to reform when the kingdom of God was beginning: 'For they are a nation without counsel and there is no understanding in them. If they were wise they would understand and discern their ... end. How could one man pursue a thousand, or two put to flight ten thousand ... unless the Lord had not handed them over' (Dt. 32:28-30). Indeed Luke, in the last sentence says that God had visited the earth, a comment similar to: 'What will you do on the day of visitation? Affliction shall come on you from afar; to whom will you flee for help? And where will you leave your reputation and glory?' (Is. 10:3, LXX).

It was such a pity because if only they had listened, they could have enjoyed heaven on earth, the kingdom of God as, for example, Isaiah had said, 'In that day, the plant of the Lord shall be glorious and beautiful, and the fruit of the land shall be the pride and splendour of Israel. Those left in Jerusalem ... will be called holy, when the Lord has ... cleansed the blood-stains of Jerusalem ... by a spirit of judgement ... Then the Lord will create over the whole of Mount Zion and all her assemblies ... a canopy and a pavilion, a shade from the heat of the day and refuge and shelter from rain and tempest' (Is. 4:2-6).

The picture of people gathered under the wings of God is well known in the O.T.: 'Hide me in the shadow of your wings' (Ps. 17:8), while the quotation at the end of the second paragraph is from Ps. 118:26. In the messianic era, when the new kingdom is fully established, Jerusalem would have no demons, no disease and perfect welfare.

The phrase 'today and tomorrow' meant a short period of time, and 'the third day' meant immediately afterwards.

Note on 'stoning'. Even in cases of capital punishment, which was avoided if at all possible, Judaism did not condone cruel modes of punishment, so that when a criminal was killed by stoning he was made to fall on a stone from a height, usually leading to fatal injury. If this was not sufficient to kill him, a stone was dropped on to his heart. In mitigating circumstances strangulation was used, being quicker and less cruel. The corpse could then be hung from a tree. Crucifixion was not a Jewish punishment and normally used by the Romans only for treason and rebellion.

* * *

J 2. Towns like Sodom and Gomorrah - Mt. 11:20-24. Lk. 10:13-15.

Tyre and Sidon were non-Jewish towns and Sodom and other places were infamous for their wickedness: 'Now the men of Sodom were wicked, great sinners against the Lord' (Gen. 13:13); 'The Lord said, "There is great outcry over the sins of Sodom and Gomorrah; their sins are very grave"' (Gen. 18:20). It was commonly believed that when God exterminated such places that was the end of them and their inhabitants: 'In this month the Lord executed his judgement on Sodom and Gomorrah and Zeboim and all the region of the Jordan and he burned them with fire and brimstone ... In like manner, God will execute judgement on the places where they have done according to the uncleanness of the Sodomites' (Jub. 16:5-6); 'On the day of turbulence, execration, indignation and anger, the Lord will burn his land and his city and all that is his, with flaming devouring fire, as he burnt Sodom' (Jub. 36:10). Many thought that there could be no hope for such sinners even to come to judgement on the last day, let alone to have any chance of entering into paradise.

Then Jesus spoke of the towns in which many great deeds had been performed. "Alas for you Chorazin and Bethsaida! If the works that were performed in you had been done in Tyre and Sidon, they would have repented long ago, in sackcloth and ashes. It will be more bearable for them than for you on the day of Judgement. As for you Capernaum, will you be raised to the skies? No, you'll be razed to the ground and end up in Hades. Sodom would have taken more notice than you of the deeds which have been performed in you, and it will be more bearable for that land than for you on the day of Judgement."

Jesus is shown here supporting those who disagreed with the comfortable notion that because the Jews are children of Abraham their sins will be more easily forgiven: 'If you hear of wicked ones in any of your cities who have led its inhabitants astray, by calling on them to serve other gods ... you shall put them to the sword ... You shall gather all goods as a complete offering to the Lord your God; it shall remain a mound of ruins, never to be rebuilt. ... Let nothing out of all that has been banned be found in your possession so the Lord may turn from his anger and show you compassion' (Dt. 13:12-17); 'The virgins of Jerusalem you profane, and with harlots ... you are joined. The daughters of Gentiles you wed ... Your union shall be like unto Sodom and Gomorrah. You are inflated with pride exalting yourselves against men and against the commands of God. You pour contempt on the holy things with mockery and laughter. Therefore the sanctuary chosen of the Lord shall be laid waste through your uncleanness and you shall be captives throughout all nations. You shall be an abomination to them and you shall receive reproach and everlasting shame from the righteous judgement of God' (T.Lev. 14:6-15:2).

Rabbinical writings show that the Jews thought Jonah did not wish to go to Niniveh for fear that the people there would repent, because the contrast with unrepentant Israel would be too obvious. In this passage the contrast between those who accepted and followed Jesus' teaching, and those who did not, is similarly emphasised.

Although Jesus did not await the results of his message at every place he visited as Jonah had done at Nineveh, that would be no excuse for Israel. There had been so many previous warnings: 'The Lord said to Moses, "How long will this people despise and provoke me? How long will they refuse to believe in me, in spite of all the signs which I have wrought among them? I will smite them with death and disinherit them"' (Num. 14:11-12). As for Capernaum, only this comment was possible: 'You said in your heart, "I will ascend to heaven; I will raise my throne above the stars of God; ... I will ascend to the tops of the clouds, I will make myself like the Most High". But you are brought down to Sheol, to the depths of the pit' (Is. 14:13-15).

There had been powerful deeds signifying the beginning of the New Era, and those who refused to recognise them must suffer the consequences: 'For the iniquity of the daughter of my people has been greater than the sin of Sodom, which was overthrown as in a moment, and no hand was raised against her' (Lam. 4:6). Their punishment would correspond to their sinfulness.

* * *

J 3. Events on the day of Judgement - Mt. 24:1-8,15-41. Mk. 13:1-8, 14-32. Lk. 17:22-37; 21:5-11, 20-33.

There are many apocalyptic passages in Jewish as in other literatures, purporting to reveal the fate of the world on the day of Judgement when the current state of things would come to an end and major changes would occur. The dispensations of men would be shattered by the coming of the kingdom in the New Era, and there are plenty of prophecies of calamities and destruction.

For example: 'At that time there shall arise Michael the great prince who has charge of your people and there shall be a time of trouble, such as never has been since there was a nation till that time' (Dan. 12:1); 'Behold the day of the Lord comes, cruel with wrath and fierce anger to make the earth a desolation and to destroy its sinners from it. For the stars of the heavens and their constellations will not give light, the sun will be dark at its rising and the moon with not shed its light. I will punish the world for its evil and the wicked for their iniquity' (Is. 13:9-11). 'I will throw my army round you like a wall; I will set a ring of outposts all around you and erect siege works against you ... And in an instant, suddenly, punishment will come from the Lord of Hosts with thunder, earthquake and great noise, with storm and tempest and a flame of devouring fire' (Is. 29:3,6).

In rabbinical works too: 'The people are brazen, dog-faced, without shame. In the year of the Messiah's coming there will be heresy over all' (b.San.97a). Nevertheless, it was not the total destruction of the earth which was awaited. Also it was believed that were the whole of Israel to repent of their sins, the Messiah would come immediately, and no doubt that must have been something Jesus himself could have wondered about.

Many other examples could be quoted from the O.T. The visions of O.T. writers like Daniel and the prophecies in I.T. books influenced N.T. writers. Compare for instance, 'As I looked, thrones were placed and one that was ancient of days took his seat. His raiment was white as snow and the hair of his head like pure wool ... I looked and behold there came one like a son of man with the clouds of heaven. He came to the Ancient of Days and was presented before him. He was given dominion and glory and kingdom, that all peoples, nations and tongues should serve him. His dominion is everlasting ... and shall not be destroyed' (Dan. 7:9,13-14); with: 'And there I saw One who had a Head of Days, and who was before time began, and his head was white like wool, and with him was another being whose countenance had the appearance of a man and his face was full of graciousness, like one of the holy angels.

I asked the angel who showed me all the hidden things who the son of man was, whence he was and why he went with the Head of Days. He answered, "This is the son of man who has righteousness, with whom dwells righteousness ... because the Lord of Spirits has chosen him and he has pre-eminence before the Lord of Spirits in uprightness for ever. This son of man shall put down kings from their thrones and kingdoms, loosen the reins of the strong, break the teeth of sinners, he shall put down the countenance of the strong and fill them with shame, and darkness shall be their dwelling and worms their bed"' (I En. 46:1-6).

Divine punishment was pictured in I.T. books much as in the O.T. Among numerous examples are: 'I will make the heavens tremble and the earth shall be shaken out of its place' (Is. 13:13); 'Calamity follows on calamity, wound on wound, tribulation on tribulation, and evil tidings on evil tidings, illness, evil judgements, snow and ice, fever, chills, torpor, famine and death, the sword and captivity' (Jub. 23:13).

From other books even more extreme terrors are promised: 'Concerning the signs, behold the days come when the inhabitants of the earth shall be seized with great panic, and the way of truth shall be hidden, and the land barren of faith, and iniquity shall be increased ... Then shall the sun suddenly shine forth by night and the moon by day; and blood shall trickle from wood, and the stone utter its voice, the peoples shall be in commotion and the stars shall change courses. One whom the dwellers on earth do not look for, shall wield sovereignty and the birds shall take to general flight and the sea shall cast forth its fish ... and the earth over wide regions shall open and fire burst forth for a long time; the wild beasts will desert their haunts and women will bear monsters' (IV Ezr. 5:1-2,4-8); 'The land shall cry out because of the calamity fallen upon the world, and all its deep shall howl. All upon it shall rave and perish amid great misfortune ... The heavenly hosts shall cry out and the world's foundations shall stagger and sway. The war of the heavenly warriors shall scourge the earth; it shall not end before the appointed destruction which shall be for ever and without compare' (DSS, H 5). 'For the Heavenly One will arise from his royal throne, and he will go forth from his holy habitation with indignation and wrath on behalf of his sons. And the earth shall tremble; to its confines it shall be shaken; the high mountains shall be made low and the hills shall be shaken and fall. The horns of the moon shall be broken and turned into blood and the sun shall not give light. The circle of the stars shall be thrown into disarray, and the sea shall retire into the abyss, the sources of the waters shall fail and the rivers shall dry up' (A.M. 10:3-6). 'Nations shall ravish nations, emperors and people ... All shall lie unburied and vultures and savage beasts shall devour the flesh. ... Then from the sunrise God shall send a king who shall give every land relief from the bane of war; some he shall slay, and on others he will impose oaths of loyalty' (S.O. 3:636, 643-644, 652-653).

'When the sun is darkened ... you women, pray not that you may bear, for the barren shall above all rejoice, and those without sons shall be glad and those with sons shall have anguish' (II Bar. 10:14); 'Time is divided into twelve parts and each one is reserved for that which is appointed for it. In the first part, there will be commotions; in the second, slaying the great ones; in the third, the deaths of many; in the fourth, the drawing of the sword; in the fifth, famine and no rain; in the sixth, earthquakes and terrors; ... in the eighth, many spectres and attacks of demons; in the ninth, fire; in the tenth, rapine and oppression; in the eleventh, wickedness and unchastity; and in the twelfth, confusion and a mixture of all of them' (II Bar. 27:1-13). (The seventh part is lost from the text.)

The day of Judgement would be a sudden event, after a period of general tribulation, sometimes called in Jewish literature as the birth-pangs of the messiah. Records had been made: 'Write the vision, make it plain upon the tablets, so he who runs may read it. For the vision is a witness to a meeting: it testifies to the end and does not lie. If it tarries, wait for it; it will surely come, it will not delay' (Hab. 2:2-3); 'The great day of the Lord is near, near and hastening fast ... A day of wrath is that day, a day of distress and anguish, ruin and devastation, darkness and gloom; a day of clouds and thick darkness, of trumpet blast and battle cry' (Zph. 1:14-16); 'On that day ... it shall be continuous day whose coming is known only to the Lord' (Zch. 14:7); and according to the prophecies of Ezekiel: 'Seven years preceding the advent of the Messiah would be years of famine or plenty; learning of the Torah or none; voices from heaven and finally wars everywhere: the wars of Gog and Magog' (Ezk. 38 and 39).

In I.T. books, also, prophecies about the day of judgement were common: 'Thus shall the Day of Judgement be: ... neither sun nor moon, nor stars ... neither darkness nor evening nor morning' (IV Ezr. 7:39-40); 'When a stupor shall seize the people of the earth and they shall fall into many tribulations ... and great torments ... - yea, it comes to pass when they abandon hope, that the time will then awake' (II Bar. 25:3-4).

After these disasters, many writers say that God's kingdom of heavenly perfection will begin on earth for those who have shown steadfast faith, while the great ones shall be cast down and the mighty fallen: 'All the kings and the mighty and the exalted and those who rule the earth shall fall down before him on their faces, and worship and set their hope on the son of man and petition him and supplicate for mercy at his hands' (I En. 62:9); 'In those days the Elect One shall arise, and he shall choose the righteous and holy from among them, for the day has drawn nigh that they should be saved ... In those days the mountains shall leap like rams and the hills skip like lambs satisfied with milk ...' (I En. 51:2,4); 'So are the times of the Most High; the beginning in portents and secret signs, and the end in effects and marvels. All who shall be then saved, those who shall escape on account of his works or his faith by which he has believed, these shall survive these perils and see my salvation in my land ... which I have sanctified for myself eternally' (IV Ezr. 9:7-9).

In many cases, the writers suppose that not only will the righteous be saved and given a place in the new kingdom but that sinners will be expelled, removed or exterminated: 'Those who died in grief shall arise in joy, and they who were poor for the Lord's sake shall be made rich; those who are put to death for the Lord's sake shall awake to life' (T.Jud. 25:4); 'I will cause my Elect One to dwell on earth, but sinners and evil-doers shall not set foot thereon' (I En. 45:4-5); 'When the Righteous One appears ... where then will be the dwellings of sinners? It had been good for them if they had not been born' (I En. 38:2); 'The dominion of the Romans shall come to an end and iniquity shall be vanquished leaving no remnant; for the sons of darkness, there shall be no escape' (DSS, WR:1); 'No evil will befall the one who fears the Lord, but in trials such a one will be rescued again and again' (Sir. 33:1).

In the N.T. several passages are found which together repeat much of what has been given above from the earlier literature and which describes what the day of Judgement is imagined to be like.

As they were leaving the Temple, the disciples pointed to the massive masonry of the Temple buildings and the votive offerings adorning them. Jesus said, "You see all these fine buildings? Not one stone will be left on another - all will be thrown down."

His disciples questioned him later, wishing to know when this event would take place. "Tell us, when will this happen? What will be the sign when this will be fulfilled and the day of Judgement is at hand?"

Jesus said, "Take care not to be misled. If anyone says to you, 'Look, here is the Messiah', or, 'There he is', do not believe it. Impostors will come claiming to be messiahs, or prophets, and they will produce signs and wonders to mislead God's chosen, if that were possible. If they tell you, 'He is outside', do not go out to find him; or if they say, 'He is in the inner room', do not believe it. Be on your guard: I have forewarned you of it all; 'Wherever the cadavers are, the vultures will gather.'

As it was in Noah's days, so will it be in the days of the son of man. Then they ate, drank and married, until the day that Noah went into the Ark and the flood came and made an end of them all. As in Lot's days too; they ate and drank, bought and sold, planted and built, but the day Lot left Sodom it rained fire from heaven and made an end of them all. That's how it will be when the son of man comes. There will be two men in the field, one will be taken, the other left. Or two women will be grinding corn, one will be taken and the other left.

When you hear the noise of battle near at hand, or reports of battles far away, or of wars and commotions, do not get alarmed and panic. Such things are bound to happen but the last day of the present era has not thereby come. Nation will war against nation, kingdom against kingdom; there will be earthquakes and famines in many places and, in the sky, great portents. These are the birth-pangs of the New Era.

When the desolating sacrilege is found where he has no right to be, standing in the holy place, or when you see Jerusalem encircled by armies, then those who are in Judaea must take to the hills. If a man is on his roof he must not go down into his house to fetch anything, or if he is in the field, he must not return for his cloak, for it is the time of visitation and vengeance. Remember Lot's wife! Alas for women with child in those days and those with babies at the breast. May it not happen in winter or on the sabbath! There will be great distress in the land such as has never been from the beginning and never will again occur. A terrible judgement will fall on this people. They will fall at the point of the sword and be carried captive into all countries. Jerusalem will be trampled down by foreigners until their day has run its course. If the Lord had not cut short those days of troubles, no one

324

could survive, but for the sake of God's elect the time will be shortened.

Portents will appear; the sun will be darkened, the moon will not give her light, the stars will fall from the sky and the celestial powers will be shaken. All the peoples of the world will lament, nations will stand helpless, not knowing which way to turn and men will faint with terror at the thought of all that is coming on the world.

When this begins to happen, stand upright and hold your heads high, because your redemption is nigh. When that day comes, the son of man will come like a lightning-flash or like the sun's rays at dawn that light up the whole earth, from east to west. He will come in the clouds with great power and glory and he will send out the angels and gather his chosen from the four winds, from the farthest bounds of earth and heaven."

The quotation at the end of the third paragraph of this passage is from Job: 'On the rock the vulture dwells and makes his home ... Thence he spies out the prey ... His young ones suck up blood and where the slain are, there is he' (Job 39:28-30).

To flee to the hills reminds us of the flight of Lot. 'They said, "Flee for your life, do not look back or stop anywhere in the valley, flee to the hills lest you be consumed"' (Gen. 19:17); and that of Mattathias and his sons: 'Follow me every one who is zealous for the Law and Covenant. He and his sons took to the hills, leaving all their belongings in the town' (I Mac. 2:28). Some have suggested that the idea behind this remark in the N.T. is the anxiety of the early community that the faithful should flee, taking the gospel with them so it would be preserved for posterity. (Compare also with I Mac. 13). The words are as in Hosea: 'The days of visitation have come, the days of recompense have come; Israel shall know it' (Hos. 9:7). The whole of this chapter in Hosea may underlie the N.T. passage; it is devoted to the consequences of Israel's sinfulness.

The sabbath was the worst day to suffer disasters and calamities because travelling was forbidden and fighting resistance was prohibited: 'They attacked the righteous on the sabbath and they died: they, their wives, and their children, and their cattle too' (I Mac. 2:38). Some supposed that God also had his rest day each sabbath so that he could not be expected to help when called upon until after sundown.

That one would be taken but not another, may reflect the separation of the Israelites from the Egyptians at the Exodus. It emphasises that the Kingdom of God could come suddenly and then the righteous and unrighteous will be swiftly separated.

The 'desolating sacrilege' is used in Daniel: 'Forces from the pagans shall appear and shall profane the Temple ... and they shall set up the desolating sacrilege' (Dan. 11:31); 'And from the time ... that the abomination that makes desolate is set up ...' (Dan. 12:11); 'Upon the wing of abominations shall come one who makes desolate, until the decreed end is poured out on the desolator' (Dan. 9:27). The use of this term in the gospels is thought by some to be related to the idolatrous altar to Zeus set up by king Antiochus to replace the altar in the Temple in 167 B.C.E. and which the Emperor Caligula's intention to place his own image there in C.E. 40, no doubt brought urgently back to memory.

That some would be spared because the Lord would cut short the time of destruction is found also in I.T. books: 'If you were not to receive mercy through Abraham, Isaac and Jacob our fathers, not one of our seed would be left upon earth' (T.Lev. 15:4); 'When the time draws near to visit the world, I will command the years and order the times and they will be shortened' (P.P. 19:12). Others have suggested that the meaning is that God would shorten the length of each day, that is bring on winter.

Yet others link it with Amalek the first enemy of Israel: 'Then came Amalek and fought with Israel ... And the Lord said to Moses, "I will blot out the remembrance of Amalek from under heaven ..." Moses said, "The Lord is at war with Amalek generation after generation' (Ex. 17:8,14,16). According to O.T. ideas, when Amalek is finally defeated in the messianic war, the kingdom of God will begin: 'Therefore when the Lord your God has given you rest from all your enemies in the land which the Lord your God gives you for an inheritance to possess, you shall blot out the remembrance of Amalek from under heaven' (Dt. 25:19). Then the vultures would come and remove the corpses of the dead - the unrighteous.

The last paragraph of the passage is based on the O.T.: 'I saw one like a son of man coming with the clouds of heaven' (Dan. 7:13); and 'Even if you are exiled to the ends of heaven, from there the Lord will gather you and from there he will bring you back' (Dt. 30:4).

There are good grounds for thinking that the description of the destruction of Jerusalem by Luke depicts his idea of the sack of Jerusalem by the Babylonians in B.C.E. 568, rather than an account of the conquest of that city by Titus at the end of the war of 66-70 C.E.

There has never been a time without someone or other claiming to be a prophet or the Messiah, and it has always been a problem to know which ones were false and which were not: 'There shall be many tidings and rumours ... and promises; some of them will prove to be idle' (II Bar. 48:34); 'If a prophet arises among you ... and gives you a sign or a wonder which comes to pass, and he says, "Let us go after other gods, let us serve them", you shall not listen to the words of that prophet' (Dt. 13:1-3). Many will deliberately comfort themselves with the belief that miraculous signs are from God and therefore no divine wrath can fall on them.

The introductory paragraph must be mentioned. It is laid down in the Torah that sometimes a dwelling can be smitten with a disease (in the bible often translated 'plague' or 'leprosy'. (See also I 14). It can be seen as reddish or greenish spots on the walls and by other signs: 'The priest shall examine the disease; and if the disease is on the walls of the house with greenish or reddish spots, and if it appears to be deeper than the surface, then the priest shall go out of the house ... and shut up the house seven days' (Lev. 14:37-38). If the priest finds though, that the disease is widespread, the whole house must be broken down and removed to a place apart: 'If the disease has spread in the house ... it is unclean. He shall break down the house, its stones and timber and all the plaster of the house and carry them forth out of the city to an unclean place' (Lev. 14:44-45).

At the same time, it was believed that devotion to mammon and the making of profit, of exploiting others for one's own gain, was exactly what was punished by smiting the house with 'leprosy'. It was no use supposing worldly wealth put one beyond God's reach; 'Woe to him who gets evil gain for his house to set his nest on high, to be safe from the reach of harm! You have devised shame on your house and forfeited your life. The stone will cry out from wall and the beam from the woodwork will respond' (Hab. 2:9-11). The last sentence of this quotation could also be translated: 'Blood and violence become the building materials, crying out against the ruler's injustice.'

Jesus, by his remarks, shows he considers the Temple to be so surfeited with wickedness as to be totally diseased and leprous, and that the whole 'building' will have to be pulled down, with no stone left on another. 'The holy stones lie at the head of every street' (Lam. 4:1).

Jesus continued with the following parable. "Consider the fig tree. As soon as its tender shoots appear, its leaves unfold and you know that summer is near. In the same way, when you next see these things happening, you can be sure that he is near. This truth I tell you: those who are alive now will be able to see this happening, but no one knows about the day or hour, not even the angels in heaven nor the Son. Only the Father knows. Heaven and earth will pass away, but my words will remain."

The apparently lifeless tree begins to awaken after winter and new shoots and leaves appear, and the tree turns green: 'Fear not, O Earth; be glad and rejoice for the Lord has done great things! ... The pastures of the wilderness shall be green ... the fig tree and vine give their full yield' (Jl. 2:21-22); 'The outcry of the Israelites has reached me; I have seen the brutality of their oppression by the Egyptians. I have come down to deliver my people out of the land of the Egyptians and to bring them into a fine wide-stretched land, flowing with milk and honey' (Ex. 3:7-8).

'God's reign is near, within the reach of the life time of those listening. The messiah will rebuild the sanctuary' (Tg.Is. 53:5); 'Joshua shall build the temple of the Lord, he shall bear the royal honour and shall sit and rule on his throne' (Zch. 6:13). Exactly when it would be completely present was uncertain.

In the O.T. and rabbinical books, the picture is of a utopia without restriction: 'Trees will grow fruit ready for use in one month, grain will be ready in fifteen days and garments will be of the finest quality wool. The moon will shine as bright as the sun and the sun will be seven times as bright as now and will heal all diseases' (Is. 30:26); 'Fresh water will spring out in Jerusalem' (Ezk. 47:9), ruins will be restored, Jerusalem rebuilt and the Temple covered in jewels' (Midr.Cant. 4:4); 'Peace will reign, with a new covenant between animals and Israel and weeping and wailing will no longer be heard' (Is. 65:19); 'There will be nothing but happiness and contentment' (Is 35:12; Ex.R. 15:21); 'there would be no illness nor deformity nor disease (Gen.R. 95:1) and death will be abolished' (Is. 25:7).

'The dead will resurrect and enjoy the new world if they were worthy of it but no proselytes would be admitted because they would only want to get the material benefits' (b.A.Z. 3b). There were some, though, who thought the only difference in the messianic era would be freedom from Roman occupation (b.Ber.34b).

It was not to be expected that the angels should know when all this would happen; they knew little about what went on in heaven according to Jewish belief. For example, '... not even the angels see the number (of the stars) ...' (II En. 40:3); 'Hear Enoch and take these my words, for not to my angels have I told my secrets ... nor have they understood my creating' (II En. 24:3).

The redemption promised by God at the time of the sacrifice of Isaac was about to be fulfilled: 'The Lord will bless you abundantly and greatly multiply your descendants until they are as many as the stars in the sky or the grains of sand on the sea-shore. Your descendants shall possess the cities of their enemies. All nations will pray to be blessed, as your descendants will be blessed, because you have obeyed me' (Gen. 22:17-18); 'It shall come to pass when all is accomplished that was to come ... the Messiah shall begin to be revealed' (II Bar. 29:3); 'The first heaven shall depart and pass away and a new heaven shall appear' (I En. 91:16).

How far this concept was shared by Jesus is difficult to know, but the last sentence of the passage reminds one of: 'Long ago you laid the foundations of the earth, and the heavens are the work of your hands. They will perish but you will endure, they will wear out like a garment, and you will throw them away. But you are the same and your years will be without end...' (Ps. 102:25-27); 'Lift up your eyes to the heavens, look at the earth beneath; the heavens grow dark like smoke, the earth wears out like a garment and those who live on it die like maggots; but my deliverance is everlasting and my salvation will never end' (Is. 51:6).

The fig tree was a symbol of God's realm, giving figs for the righteous in all seasons, and the righteous were also thought of as ripe figs - good fruit for those who would learn more of God's will. The disciples and followers of Jesus are to be encouraged by his words. The kingdom was becoming manifest, and the more they believed this and acted upon it the more quickly and fully they would experience it. (See also C 5).

* * *

J 4. The missionaries return - Lk. 10:17-20.

The seventy-two missionaries came back jubilant.
"Even the demons submit to us in your name", they said.
Jesus replied, "I saw Satan fall as lightning out of
heaven. I have given you authority to tread on snakes,
scorpions and on all the forces of the enemy and nothing
will ever harm you. Still, rejoice not that the spirits
submit to you, but rejoice that your names are recorded
in heaven."

Some of the ideas circulating at the time are strange: 'We demons fly up to heaven ... but we get exhausted ... some fall like leaves from the trees and men watching think stars are falling from heaven ... we drop like flashes of lightning to the earth. We burn cities down and set fields on fire' (T.Sol. 20:16-17).

The final overthrow of Satan was a vital part of Jewish belief. 'How has Lucifer ... that sent orders to all the nations, fallen from heaven and been crushed to earth!' (Is. 14:12 LXX). The seventy missionaries are symbolic of the Sanhedrin of the New Israel in the New Era, when Satan no longer had any powers and was cast out from heaven: 'The kingdom of the Lord shall appear throughout all his creation, and Satan shall be no more' (A.M. 10:1).

The time was near and the missionaries were on an urgent campaign to tell as many as possible before the cataclysm hit them: 'Fear the Lord and love your neighbour, and even though the spirits of Beliar [the prince of evil] afflict you with every evil, yet they will not have dominion over you ...' (T.Ben. 3:3); 'Then shall all the spirits of error be trodden under foot and men shall rule over wicked spirits' (T.Sim. 6:6).

At such a time, concern for wealth or status was equivalent to idolatry: just what God would not accept. But for those who were faithful and followed God's will, he will protect them as he had the Israelites in the wilderness: 'The Lord your God ... led you through the great and terrible wilderness with its fiery serpents and scorpions ...' (Dt. 8:15); 'You will tread on the lion and the adder; the young lion and the serpent you will trample under foot' (Ps. 91:13); 'Wild beasts shall come from the forest and minister to men. Snakes and dragons shall come forth from their holes to submit themselves to a little child. And women shall no longer have pain when they bear nor suffer torment when they yield the fruit of the womb' (II Bar. 73:6-7).

This is an apocalyptic passage, like J 3, modelled on, and strongly influenced by, earlier Jewish literature, both biblical and otherwise. It shows Jesus' apostles, his missionaries, under God's care, in accordance with the prevailing ideas of the day. Indeed, the passage may also mean Jesus points out to his disciples that the submission to them of the demons was because they, the demons, had seen Satan fall. They realised they no longer had a protector, and the disciples' success was the result of this.

* * *

J. Summary.

The passages in this section focus on an imagined future and show perhaps most clearly the influence of apocalyptic beliefs common at or before the time of Jesus. It was a strong belief in Judaism that destruction, tribulation and misery would come before the day of Judgement, the coming of the Messiah and the full development of the New Era. Then, in the New Era, Satan would be overthrown, all would follow God's will and everything would be perfect as God had always intended.

* * *

GENERAL CONCLUSIONS.

The gospels of Matthew, Mark and Luke are documents about Jews and are deeply embedded in Judaism. The literature available to Jesus and his contemporaries was extensive, including the bible in its Hebrew and Greek versions. There were oral traditions and practices probably transmitted by memory for the most part, the Oral Law, which had become by Jesus' day accepted by most Jews as more or less equal to the written mosaic law of the Torah in the first five books of the bible. Memorizing was a highly developed faculty among many people.

There were also numerous religious books written in the last few centuries B.C.E. many of which were never included with the canonical books of the bible. This literature I have called the 'intertestamentary literature' and I have included a few books which are thought to have been written in the first part of the first century C.E. It will be obvious from the numerous quotations that almost all of the teaching in the gospels is to be found in these Jewish writings.

The Jesus portrayed by the synoptic gospels was not interested in destroying Judaism. He adhered to its tenets such as the doctrine of the elected people, acknowledgement of the Torah as the supreme source of God's law, the words of the prophets as authoritative regarding divine truth. He believed God was the creator of the universe yet was Father in heaven. He observed the proper rituals of blessing the food, breaking the bread and sitting in groups. He wore a cloak with fringes, believed in reward and punishment, albeit in the world to come and he believed that all God's creation had to be looked after properly by mankind.

Some passages in these books portray Jesus as a new Adam or a new Moses and some describe events which it was believed would occur in association with the coming of the Jewish messiah, of which there were differing versions. Whether Jesus himself claimed to be 'Messiah' or worked on the basis that he was, remains arguable, but the fact that it is so unclear indicates how little importance, if any, the evangelists put on the idea which ought to reflect Jesus' opinion too.

It is uncertain just what was meant by 'the New Era', 'the World to Come' or 'the Messianic Age'. In some passages the emphasis is on its presence within those who obey God's laws and thereby enter his realm. The Kingdom will grow as more followers join the movement. In others, it is something which will follow the day of Judgement, when the Messiah will rule the whole earth and sin and evil will be eradicated: heaven on earth in fact. In yet other places, it is both internal and external, partly present and partly growing in the future.

Signs of the kingdom of God in the world are love, forgiveness, peace and reconciliation, and the kingdom is available to all who would become its citizens. The emphasis of Jesus' teaching is on positive qualities: freedom from sin; forgiving and being forgiven; trust in God; self-restraint in order to help others worse off than oneself; meekness; helping to avoid conflict; and mercy, which meant forgiving those doing wrong to oneself. All this was present in Judaism, as well as fasting, daily prayers,

331

the laws concerning food, purity and tithes, and prohibitions against various forms of sexual conduct. Those who would be fully God's servants would be without anger and hatred, but they would rebuke those with evil intent and especially those who misled the "little ones". Just as God provided for both the good and the bad, so must his servants be ready to do the same. God's servants would undergo suffering which was looked upon as God's punishment, but God would also heal those he punished, and they would become priests and prophets. They would heal others and have authority to settle arguments and resolve disputes.

For Jesus, the spirit of the Law rather than its letter was most important. His followers were people who examined their motives, were conscious of their true intentions and were perfectionists towards God's will. They would retain nothing in excess of their essential needs; they would not react with anger against attacks on themselves; they would not hate others; they would be pure in heart, that is, their 'good inclination' would be fully in control of their lives. Jesus seems to have maintained that God's promise of forgiveness would be valid for all who repented of their sinfulness and changed their underlying attitude of mind. To be forgiven by God assumes and requires that one forgives others without recompense or punishment, just as God did not exact retribution from those who returned to him.

The day of Judgement would come without warning. Satan would be finally overthrown and then the faithful workers, those who committed themselves to God's service in faith in his goodness, rather than calculating the disadvantages versus the rewards, would feast in God's kingdom. God would not impair his reputation for reliability: he would fulfil his promises and his servants could be sure of that.

It is not possible to transfer merit in God's realm. Each must stand or fall by the results of his or her own service, while pious words and devotions alone cut no ice with God. Even the best deeds receive no reward if they were performed from selfish motives. For Jesus the actions of healing, of exorcism, of preaching, of converting others, of calling on the name of the Lord, even by those claiming to be appointed by Jesus himself, or those who claimed to be his true descendants: all these were mockery and idolatry unless they came from a pure heart. Subscribing to 'proper' beliefs and creeds was of no importance and could count for nothing in the end. Jesus was a faith-healer and a faith-exorcist, too, like many others in his time but he always refused to provide signs or proofs of his claims, leaving people to evaluate his actions for themselves.

The rewards Jesus promised were mainly in the next life in the New Era but it is not clear if he thought of this as paradise in heaven after death; or as a purely spiritual heaven-like existence on earth for all, after the day of Judgement. It may be that he thought of it as a society on earth in which God's will would be obeyed, following judgement by God or the Messiah, who would come from heaven to earth.

Jesus seems to have taught several groups of people. There was the inner circle of disciples from whom Jesus expected maximum commitment to reach "perfection"; there were followers who would try their best but who would not fully measure up to God's standard. These were the country-folk, or peasant farmers; and there were the worst sinners, the tax-gatherers, prostitutes and evil ones. Finally there were the religious leaders, who so often ignored the true spirit of the Law and Prophets. They lacked true understanding and Jesus wanted the practice of God's instructions to be as God had intended. He wished neither to ignore nor to destroy the Law, but it was not the externals which mattered. The Temple authorities had arranged rituals and made rules which promoted idolatry, making God into a copy of themselves. They had corrupted God's world, and could only be rejected by God. They had substituted the show for the reality, words and rituals instead of deeds of love for God and mankind.

* * *

VERSES FROM THE SYNOPTIC GOSPELS

MATTHEW

3		18-22	F10	12	E7	**19**
1-12	A1	23-27	H5	18-23	C2	1-12
13-17	A2	28 -		24-30	C9	13-15
4		**9**		31-33	C4	16-29
1-11	H11	- 1	I3	34-35	E14	30
12-17	A3	2-8	I5	36-43	C9	**20**
5		9-13	D3	44-46	C1	1-15
3-12	E13a	14-17	G2	47-50	C10	16
13	F13	18-19	I7	51-52	F7	17-19
14-16	E11	20-22	I8	53-58	A4	20-28
17-20	G20	23-26	I7	**14**		29-34
21-24	E13b	27-31	I12	1-12	A6	**21**
25-26	C6	32-33	I4	13-21	H1	12-16
27-28	E13e	34	C12	22-23	H2	18-22
29-30	E3	36 -		**15**		23-27
31-32	G19	**10**		1-2	G7a	28-32
33-37	E13d	- 15	E15	3-9	G8	33-46
38-48	E13c	16	F 7	10-11	G7b	**22**
6		16-31	E16	12-14	G10	1-10
1-4	E12b	25	C12	15-20	G7b	11-14
5-13	E	32-33	F11	21-28	I11	15-22
13c		34-36	E16	32-38	H3	23-33
14-15	E6	37-39	F11	**16**		34-40
16-18	E12b	40-42	E15	1-4	C8	41-46
19-21	F5	**11**		5-12	H4	**23**
22-23	E11	2-15	A5	13-18	H6	1-7
24	G3	16-19	F5	19	E12a	8-11
25-34	F5	20-24	J2	20	H6	11-12
7		25-27	C14	21-23	H7	13-24
1-5	F9	28-30	C15	24-28	F11	25-26
6	F14	**12**			+ J4	29-36
7-12	E12	1-8	G12	**17**		37-39
13-14	B2	9-13	G13	1-13	H10	**24**
15	E16	22-28	C12	14-20a	I2	1-8
16-20	F7	29	C13	20b-21	C5	9-14
21-23	B2	30	E17	22-23	H7	15-41
24-27	D1	31-32	F12	24-27	G16	42-51
28-29	I1	33-37	F7	**18**		**25**
8		38-42	C8	1-10	E3	1-12
1-4	I14	43-45	D12	4	E10	13
5-10	I10	46-50	F1	12-14	D8	14-30
11-12	B2	**13**		15-20	E12a	31-46
13	I10	4-9	C2	21-35	E6	**26**
14-15	I6	10-17	E14			6-13

(chapters 19–26 codes, second part of the right-hand pair)

19		**22**		**24**	
1-12	G19	1-10	E4	1-8	J3
13-15	E3	11-14	F5	9-14	E16
16-29	F4	15-22	G17	15-41	J3
30	E10	23-33	G18	42-51	B1
20		34-40	F3	**25**	
1-15	D11	41-46	H9	1-12	B3
16	E10	**23**		13	B1
17-19	H7	1-7	G9	14-30	E7
20-28	E2	8-11	E1	31-46	B4
29-34	I12	11-12	E10	**26**	
21		13-24	G10	6-13	D5
12-16	G1	25-26	G7c		
18-22	C5	29-36	G11		
23-27	H8	37-39	J1		
28-32	D6				
33-46	G6				

MARK

1	
2-8	A1
9-11	A2
12-13	H11
14-15	A3
21-28	I1
29-31	I6
40-45	I14
2	
1-12	I5
13-17	D3
18-22	G2
23-28	G12
3	
1-6	G13
20-21	F1
22-26	C12
27	C13
28-30	F12
31-35	F1
4	
3-9	C2
10-12	E14
13-20	C2
21	E11
22-23	E16
24	F9
25	E7
26-29	C3
30-32	C4
35-41	H5
5	
1-20	I3
21-24	I7
25-34	I8
35-43	I7
6	
1-6a	A4
6b-13	E15
14-29	A6
30-44	H1
45-52	H2
7	
1-8	G7a

9-13	G13	9-13	E16	18	E7	45-46	G10	11-19	I15
14-23	G7b	14-32	J3	19-21	F1	47-51	G11	20-21	C8
24-30	I11	33-37	B1	22-25	H5	52	G10	22-37	J3
31-37	I4	**14**		26-39	I3	**12**		33	F11
8		3-9	D5	40-42	I7	1	H4	**18**	
1-10	H3			43-48	I8	1-7	E16	1-8	D10
11-13	C8		LUKE	49-56	I7	8-9	F11	9-14a	D7
14-21	H4	**3**		**9**		10	F12	14b	E10
22-26	I13	2-17	A1	1-6	E15	11-12	E16	15-17	E3
27-30	H6	19-20	A6	10-17	H1	13-34	F5	18-30	F4
31-33	H7	21-22	A2	18-21	H6	35-48	B1	31-34	H7
34 -		**4**		22	H7	49-53	E16	35-43	I12
9		1-13	H11	23-27	F11	54-57	C8	**19**	
-1	F11	14-15	A3		+ F14	57-59	C6	1-10	D4
	+ J4	16-30	A4	28-36	H10	**13**		12-27	F7
2-13	H10	31-32	I5	37-43a	I2	1-5	F8	41-44	J1
14-29	I2	33-37	I1	43b-45	H7	6-9	B5	45-46	G1
30-32	H7	38-39	I6	46-48	E3	10-17	G14	**20**	
33-37	E3	**5**		49-50	E17	18-21	C4	1-8	H8
38-40	E17	12-15	I14	51-56	E15	22-30	B2	9-19	G6
41	E15	18-26	I5	57-62	F10	31-35	J1	20-26	G17
42-48	E3	27-32	D3	**10**		**14**		27-40	G18
49-50	F13	33-39	G2	1-12	E15	1-6	G15	41-44	H9
10		**6**		13-15	J2	7-10	C11	45-47	G9
1-12	G19	1-5	G12	16	E15	11	E10	**21**	
13-16	E3	6-11	G13	17-20	J4	12-15	F6	1-4	E9
17-30	F4	20-26	E13a	21-22	C14	15-24	E4	5-11	J3
31	E10	27-36	E13c	23-24	E14	25-27	F11	12-19	E16
32-34	H7	37-38	F9	25-27	F3	28-32	C7	20-33	J3
35-45	E2	39	G10	38-42	E18	33	F11	34-36	B1
46-52	I12	40	E16	**11**		34-35	F13	**22**	
11		41-42	F9	1-4	E12c	**15**		24-27	E2
12-14	C5	43-45	F7	5-8	D9	1-10	D8	28-30	F4
15-17	G1	46	B2	9-13	E12c	11-32	F2		
20-24	C5	46-49	D1	14-15	C12	**16**			
25	E6	**7**		16	C8	1-15	G3		
27-33	H8	2-10	I10	17-20	C12	14-15	G4		
12		11-17	I9	21-22	C13	16	A5		
1-12	G6	18-28	A5	23	E17	17	G20		
13-17	G17	31-35	G5	24-26	D12	18	G19		
18-27	G18	36-50	D2	27-28	F1	19-31	G4		
28-34	F3	**8**		29-32	C8	**17**			
35-37	H9	4-8	C2	33-36	E11	1-3a	E3		
38-40	G9	9-10	E14	37-41	G7a	3b-4	E6		
41-44	E9	11-15	C2	42	G10	5-6	C5		
13		16	E11	43	G9	7-10	E8		
1-8	J3	17	E16	44	G7d	11	E15		

REFERENCES TO O.T. AND JEWISH LITERATURE

Genesis (Gen.).

1.2	H 2
1.27	G 19
1.31	F 3
2.24	G 19
3.21	E 13a
4.24	E 6
5.2	G 19
6.1-2	D 12
9.5	G 11
9.8-9	D 11
12.7	D 11
13.13	J 2
14.18-20	H 9
15.11	F 10
17.1	G 20
17.1-2	D 11
18	D 2
	D 4
18.1-2	C 4
18.6	C 4
18.20	J 2
19	D 2
19.1-2	E 15
19.17	J 3
20.4-7	B 1
22.11	E 18
22.17-18	J 3
25.11	E 13a
26.12	C 2
28.15-21	F 5
33.4	F 2
37.34	G 2
38.8	G 18
42.18	F 3
49.13	A 3
49.21	A 3

Exodus (Ex.).

2.14	F 5
3.4	E 18
3.6	G 18
3.7-8	J 3

3.10-11	I 12
3.15	G 18
4.12	E 16
4.19-20	I 10
5.1	G 2
10.16	F 2
12.11	E 15
	G 2
12.14	G 2
	G14
14.21	H 5
15.8	H 5
15.10	H 5
16.4	H 11
17.2	H 11
17.4	H 10
17.4-5	A 4
17.7	H 11
17.8	J 3
17.14	J 3
17.16	J 3
18.24-25	I 10
19.5	C 1
19.6	G 14
	H 3
19.9	H 10
19.10-11	A 3
19.12-13	I 8
19.17-18	A 1
20.5	G 11
20.10	G 12
20.12	F 2
	G 8
20.24	E 12a
21.17	G 8
21.23-25	E 13c
22.1	D 4
22.2-3	E 13c
23.20	A 1
	A 5
23.25-26	I 8
24.3	G 13
24.12-13	I 10
24.16	H 10
24.18	H 11
25.2	E 9

29.37	G 10
30.12-13	G 16
30.14-15	G 16
30.19-20	G 7a
31.14	G12
32.11-14	D10
32.32	H 7
33.4-5	G 2
33.11	C 14
33.13	C 14
33.16	E 15
34.28	H 11
34.29	H 10
34.35	H 10

Leviticus (Lev.).

2.5-6	H 1
2.13	F 13
5.24	D 4
6.14-18	G 12
13.1-3	I 14
13.46	I 14
14.1-4	I 14
14.8	I 14
14.37-38	J 3
14.44-45	J 3
16.30	C 6
17.13-14	G 7b
18.3-5	F 3
18.4	B 2
18.4-5	G 3
18.6	E 13e
	G 19
18.20	A 4
	E 13e
	G 19
18.24	E13e
19.2	E 13c
	F 3
19.3	F 2
	G 8
19.11-12	E 13d
19.14	E 13b
19.15-17	E 13b
19.17	E 12a

				I Kings (I Kgs.).	
	I 8	18.3-4	F 5		
23.15-16	G 3	23.10	C 7		
23.22-23	E 13d			3.5-14	F 5
23.24	D 11	Judges (Jdg.).		10.1	E 12c
23.25	G 12			13.4	G 13
24.8-9	I 14	3.14	G 14	17	G 7b
24.12-13	E 13c	6.14-15	I 12		G 13
24.14-15	D 11	6.19	C 4	17.8-9	I 11
24.16	G 11	9	F 7	17.17-24	I 9
25.5-6	G 18	9.45	F 13	18.44-45	C 8
25.19	J 3	14.12	E 14	19.2-5	H 10
28.1-5	H 3			19.5-8	H 1
28.12	E 13c	Ruth.		19.19-21	F 10
28.15	I 2			22.17	E 15
28.28	I 2	2.14	H 1	22.29	B 4
28.34	I 2				
28.47-48	C 15	I Samuel (I Sam.).		II Kings (II Kgs.).	
28.59	I 8				
28.60-61	G 14	2.8	D 3	1.8	A 1
29.2-4	E 14		I 12	2.13	F 10
	G 13	2.25	F 12	2.21	F 13
29.29	E 14	2.31-35	I 12	4.29	E 15
30.4	J 3	3.4	E 18	4.31-35	I 2
30.11-14	C 8	3.14	G 1	4.33	E 12c
30.15	G 13	9.13	C 11	4.42-44	H 1
30.17-18	G 13	9.21-22	C 11	5	G 7b
30.19	G 13	10.15-16	H 8	5.10	I 15
30.19-20	F 11	10.27	H 8	10.21-28	F 8
30.20	F 5	14.24	B 1	17.13	G 11
32.20	I 2	14.27	B 1	17.15	G 11
32.28-30	J 1	14.44	B 1	20.5-6	F 5
32.39	F 3	15.22	E 18		
32.41-42	C 7		F 3	I Chronicles (I Chr.)	
33.4	E 15	15.27	I 8		
33.9	F 10	16.7	G 17	12.32	G 5
34.1	H 11	21.3-6	G 12		
34.6	E 13a	23.12	H 7	II Chronicles (II Chr.).	
Joshua (Jos.).		II Samuel (II Sam).		7.14	F 2
				9.1-2	C 8
1.1-2	A 2	5.8	G 1	14.11	C 7
3.1-2	H 3	6.6-7	B 1	19.6-7	D 10
3.5	A 2	14.24	B 1	19.11	G 17
3-4	H 2	14.27	B 1	26.16	I 14
7 - 10	E 7	14.44	B 1	26.20	I 14
9.3-15	H 1	23.6	F 7	28.15	F 2
13.6-7	F 5			32.31	H 11

36.15-16	G 11		E 12c	35.13	E 15
			H 10	36.5	E 13a
Nehemiah (Nem.).		2.8	H 11	36.7	D 7
		2.11	A 3	37.10	C 9
9.21	G 15		D 2	37.11	E 13a
13.7-9	G 1	4.8	C 3	37.18-19	F 5
		5.9	G 7d	37.21-22	E 6
Ester (Est.).		8.2	E 3	37.24	H 2
			G 1	37.25	I 12
4.16	H 3	8.6	H 9	37.26	E 13a
		10.2-4	E 9	37.29	E 13a
Job.		10.6-7	E 9	37.32	G 13
		10.11	E 9	37.34	E 13c
1.21	F 11	11.7	E	38.12-15	C 6
5.17-18	F 3		13a	40.12	E 16
9.8	H 2	14.1	F 5	41.1	D 5
12.7-10	F 5	17.5	D 2	44.23	H 5
13.14-16	F 11	17.8	J 1	44.26	H 5
20.4-5	E 13a	17.14	I 11	46.1-3	C 5
22.2-3	E 8	17.15	E 3	49.7-8	B 3
22.6-9	B 4	17.23-27	B 4		E 2
24.2-3	D 11	17.35-36	H 6	49.7-9	F 11
24.9	D 11	18.6	H 6	49.15	G 18
24.15	E 13e	18.8	H 6	50.13-14	D 3
28.20	C 14	18.16	H 2	51.5-6	G 7c
28.23	C 14	18.50	H 6	51.10-12	F 9
31	G 20	19.1	C 8	52.7	F 5
31.1	E 13e	19.7	C 8	55.22	F 5
31.9	E 13e		C 14	55.23	G 15
31.11	E 13e	19.8	E 11	62.12	B 3
31.16-22		20.6-8	F 11		F 11
	E 13c	22.26	H 1	63.7-8	I 8
31.24	F 5	24.3-4	E 13a	65.7	H 5
31.27-28	E 13e	24.7	B 2	67.1-2	C 8
31.28	F 5	25.2-3	D 2	68.5	E 12c
32.17-19	G 2	25.4-5	E 1	69.1-2	E 2
38.4	H 6	25.14	H 3	69.1-3	G 15
38.4-6	G 6	26.6	G 7a	69.4	E 16
38.16	H 2	27.8	C 8	69.14	G 15
39.28-30	J 3	31.13	H 7	69.23	G 14
		32.3-4	G 13	72.11	C 10
Psalms (Ps.).		33.13	E 15	74.18	D 10
		33.15	E 15	74.22	D 10
		33.16	C 7	77.19	H 2
1.1	B 5	34.22	E 6	78.2	E 14
1.3	B 5	34.10	E 12c	78.7	E 14
	I 13	34.14	E 13a	78.35-36	G 7a
2.7	A 2				

80.8-9	G 6	107.30	H 2	3.16	B 4
80.14-15	G 6	109.6	C 12	3.27-28	D 9
82.1	E 12a	109.10	I 12	4.2	F 4
	E 13b	110.1	H 9	5.22	G 6
84.11	E 12c	110.4	H 9	6.6-11	F 5
85.2	F 12	113.7	G 14	6.23	E 11
85.9	E 15	116.3-4	F 11	7.27	E 12c
86.9	C 9	116.12	D 2	8.1	G 5
88.4	D 7	116.14	D 2	8.15-16	G 17
88.10-11	I 9	118.19-20	B 4	8.17	E 12c
89.1	C 5	118.21-23	G 6	8.27-30	C 14
89.8-9	H 5	118.26	J 1	9.2-5	E 4
89.25-26	H 5	119.46	E 16	9.4	C 14
89.26	E 12c	119.62	B 3	11.19	F 11
91.1-3	E 15	119.97	C 15	12.4	E 13e
91.4	C 4	119.105	B 3	13.1	D 6
91.11-12	H 11	119.130	C 14	15.19	B 2
91.13	J 4	119.161-5	G 20	16.5	G 3
91.16	B 1	119.165	C 15	16.7	E 13a
95.7	G 15	119.176	D 8	19.17	E 13c
100.5	E 13a	121.6	I 2		F 6
102.4	I 7	127.1	C 7	20.6	D 10
102.25	H 6	132.13	G 14	21.21	F 11
102.25-27	J 3	132.15	H 1	22.9	F 6
103.2-3	I 8	132.16-18	G 14	24.3-6	C 7
103.4	G 18	135.4	C 1	24.17	B 4
103.11	D 11	136.25	I 11		E 13c
103.13	F 2	137.7	J 1	24.29	E 13c
104.10-12	F 5	137.8-9	E 13c	25.6-7	C 11
104.12	C 4	138.6	G 4	25.21-22	E 13c
104.16	A 5	141.3-4	B 1	26.11	D 9
104.24-25	I 11	143.1-2	E 12c	27.1	F 5
104.27	F 5	145.9	G 15	28.2	C 6
	I 11	145.14	G 14	28.18	E 16
104.29-30	F 5	145.18	E 15	28.24	G 8
105.40	H 1	147.6	E 10	29.3	F 2
106.33-34	F 9		E 13a	30.5	G 3
106.35-38	I 2	147.8-9	F 5	30.8	E 12c
106.44-45	I 2	147.9	I 11	31.10	E 13e
107.1-3	B 2	147.11	F 5	31.10-31	G 5
107.9	E 13a				
	H 2	Proverbs (Pvb.).		Ecclesiastes (Ecc.).	
107.10	I 3				
107.14	I 7	2.4	D 8	1.15	G 4
107.17-22	I 3	3.9	G 8	3.4	E 13a
107.19-20	I 10	3.11-12	E 12a	5.2-3	E 12c
107.28-30	H 5	3.12	C 6	5.12	D 11

Reference	Code	Reference	Code	Reference	Code
57.18	G 15	4.8	I 7	48.7	F 5
57.20-21	E 15	5.20-21	E 14	50.34	D 10
58.1-8	E 12b	5.21	H 4	51.26	G 6
58.6	A 4	5.31	E 16	51.36	D 10
58.6-7	B 4	6.8	J 1		
	G 4	6.16	B 2	Lamentations (Lam.).	
58.8	G 15		C 15		
58.9	E 12c	6.27-30	G 1	Proem 2	F 14
58.10	F 5	7.2-7	G 1	1.1	J 1
	F 6	7.4	D 1	1.15	E 15
58.13-14	G 12	7.5-7	D 1	1.20	E 15
59.6-8	G 1	7.9-11	G 1	2.1	H 10
59.20	G 1	7.20	I 13	2.2-7	F 8
60.6	F 4	7.21-23	G 1	2.7	G 1
60.16-17	G 1	7.25-26	G 11	2.14	F 8
61.1-2	A 4	7.30	F 10	3.24	H 7
	A 5	7.33	F 10	3.25-26	B 1
61.2-3	E 13a	8.13	C 5	3.25-28	E 12a
61.3	I 13	9.1	J 1	3.30	E 13c
61.4	D 1	9.11	J 1	3.30-33	H 7
61.6	G 14	9.20-21	G 5	4.1	J 3
61.11	C 3	9.21-23	F 10	4.2-3	J 1
62.9	D 11	12.7	G 5	4.6	J 2
62.10	B 2	12.13	C 2	4.12-14	J 1
63.9-10	G 13	14.14	E 16	4.18	E 15
63.16	E 1	15.16	H 1	4.20	C 4
64.8	E 12c	17.5-6	C 2	5.3	E 1
	G 7c	17.8	B 5	5.5	C 15
65.13	E 5	17.18	D 2	5.7	E 2
65.13-14	E 13a	23.11	G 1	5.21	E 1
65.19	B 5	23.16-17	E 16		
	J 3	23.18	E 13b	Ezekiel (Ezk.).	
65.24	I 3	26.13	A 1		
66.2	E 10	29.2	I 7	3.17	B 1
	E 13a	29.12	E 12c	7.19	C 2
66.6	G 14	29.13	G 7a	8.8-9	B 1
66.13	E13a	29.17-18	G 11	9.4-7	F 8
66.22	G 1	30.9	H 6	11.19	E 1
66.24	A 1	30.17	F 3	12.1-6	B 1
		31.9	E 13a	12.2	H 4
Jeremiah (Jer.).		31.29-30	G 11	12.2-3	E 14
		31.31-32	D 11	12.6	C 8
1.11-13	I 13	31.33	C 8	13.13-14	D 1
2.20	C 15	31.33-34	E 1	16.3-6	I 8
2.21	G 6	32.27	I 2	16.8	I 8
3.4	E 12c	39.11-14	G 15	16.49	E 13a
4.3	C 2	46.27	H 2	17.2	E 14

1.14-16	J 3	4.1	C 9	30.2	E 10
3.9	C 7	4.5-6	A 5	41.3	C 15
3.9-13	C 15		H 10	44.13	E 13a
3.14-15	D 2			48.34	J 3
3.19	D 2			51.8	F 11
	G 1			51.8-10	G 18
				51.13	E 10

Haggai (Hag.).				62.7	H 3
				72.4-6	C 9
2.7-9	G 1	**Ahikar (Ahk.).**		73.6-7	J 4
		1.16	D 3	76.3	H 11
		1.18	E 13a	77.3	G 20
Zechariah (Zch).		1.22	E 13a		
		8.14	E 3		
2.8	E 11	8.20	E 3	**I Enoch (I En.).**	
3.1	C 12	8.25	B 5		
3.2	I 6	8.29	F 2	5.7	E 13a
3.4	H 10	8.34	F 2	10.4-6	E 5
4.14	H 9	8.38	G 15	10.13	B 4
	H 10			10.19	C 2
6.13	J 3	**Assumption of Moses**		15.6-7	G 18
13.4	E 16	**(A.M.).**		15.8	D 12
13.7	E 15			15.11-12	I 2
14.4	C 5	7.3-10	G 9	19.1	D 12
14.7	B 1	10.1	J 4	22.9-10	G 4
	J 3	10.1-3	B 4	22.11	E 5
14.8-9	C 10	10.3-6	J 3	25.4-5	C 4
14.16	C 9	10.10	G 4	38.2	J 3
14.20-21	G 1			44.5	D 3
		I Baruch (I Bar.).		45.4-5	J 3
				46.1-6	J 3
Malachi (Mal.).		4.1	J 1	47.2	E 2
		4.1-4	G 5	48.4	C 10
1.9	E5				H 3
2.7-8	G1	**II Baruch (II Bar.).**		48.8-9	E 16
2.10	E 12c			48.9	G 4
2.14-16	G 19	3.1-2	J 1	51.2	J 3
3.1	A 1	5.7	A 1	51.4	J 3
	H 10	10.14	J 3	52.4	H 6
3.1-2	A 5	14.12	F 5	56.8	G 4
3.1-3	F 8	22.1	A 2	62.9	J 3
	G 1		H 10	62.10-11	E 5
3.2-3	E 16	25.3-4	J 3	62.15	E 15
3.5	C 6	27.1-13	J 3	62.15-16	B 4
	D 11	29.3	C 5	63.10	G 3
3.10	E 13a		J 3	68.1-2	E 14
3.16	E 12a	29.5-6	C 5	69.4-11	C 12
3.16-18	B 4	29.6	A 5	69.27	E 5
	C 1				

71.1	H 10
90.8	E 15
90.11	E 15
90.28-29	G 1
91.16	J 3
94.6	D 1
94.8	F 5
95.4	F 12
96.4	E 13a
96.5	G 4
96.7-8	E 13a
100.1-2	E 16
103.4	G 4
	G 18
103.6-8	G 4
103.8	C 9
104.4	G 18
104.6	G 18

II Enoch (II En.).

Prolog.	A 4
1.8	H 2
8.7	C 5
9.1	B 4
14.1	C 15
24.3	J 3
30.8	C 14
33.4	I 10
34.1	C 15
40.3	J 3
42.6-14	E 13a
42.13	E 13a
44.1	E 13c
44.4	A 5
44.5	D3
	E 8
	F 9
44.15	A 5
45.3	H 11
49.1	E 13d
50.2-4	E 13c
50.5	F 5
51.3	E 13c
52.3-14	E 13a
52.11	E 13a
53.1	B 3

65.8-9	C9
66.7	H 10

II Esdras (II Esd.).

1.32	G 11

IV Ezra (IV Ezr.).

5.1-2	J 3
5.4-8	J 3
5.42	E 10
7.6-8	B 2
7.33-37	B 4
7.36	G 4
7.36-38	C 9
7.39-40	B 1
	J 3
7.83-84	E 13c
7.91-95	E 13c
7.97	H 10
7.102-105	B 3
	E 5
8.41	C 2
8.56	G 4
8.59	G 4
9.7-9	J 3
9.15	E 4
9.21	E14

Joseph and Asenath (J.A.).

11.18	E 13c

Jubilees (Jub.).

1.12	G 11
1.15	C 10
2.17	G 12
3.7	G 19
4.15	D 12
5.1-2	D 12
10.1	C 12
	D 12
11.11	C 2
16.5-6	J 2

21.11	F 13
23.13	J 3
23.19	E 16
32.25	E 16
36.4	E 13c
36.10	J 2
50.10-11	G 12

Judith (Jud.).

3.14	G 14
8.35	I 8
16.14	I 10
16.17	E 3

Letter of Aristeas (L.A.).

311	G 20

I Maccabees (I Mac.).

2.28	J 3
2.38	J 3
3.60	E12c
4.46	G 1
7.37	G 1
14.41	G 1

II Maccabees (II Mac.).

7	G 18
15.18	F 10

IV Maccabees (IV Mac.).

1.18	G 5
2.9-12	F 11
6.27-29	E 2
7.18-19	G 18
13.14-16	F 11
13.16	B 1
16.25	G 18
17.20-22	E 2

Prayer of Azariah (P.Az.).

18	C 8

Prayer of Manasseh (P.M.).

9.14	D 7

Psalms of Solomon (P.S.).

3.13	E 5
	G6
4.2-3	G 9
4.6-7	G 9
4.13-15	G 9
4.16-23	E 13c
4.28	E 13c
5.4	C13
5.6	F 5
5.9-13	I 11
5.17	E 12c
5.18-20	F 4
6.8	E 12c
6.8-10	B 2
8.11	G 6
9.9	E 13a
9.12	A 1
9.15	A 1
10.1-3	B 1
11.3	C 5
11.5-7	C 5
13.6-9	B 1
14.2-3	I 13
15.11	B 2
16.7-8	E 13e
17.17-22	D 10
17.23-27	B 4
17.24-25	H 9
17.32-33	G 1
17.33	J 3
17.35-36	H 6
18.6,8	H 6
18.4	F 2

Pseudo-Philo (P.P.).

11.1	D 11
19.12	J 3
23.10	B 2
28.4	G 6

Pseudo-Phycylides (P.Ph.).

8	G 8
19	D 11
22	D 11
24	F 6
52	F 7
175	G 18

Sibylline oracles (S.O.).

3.636	J 3
3.643-644	J 3
3.652	B 4
3.652-654	J 3
4.165	A 1
5.414	G 1
5.419-423	G 1

Sirach (Sir.).

1.4	C 14
3.8	D 6
3.9	E 3
3.18	E10
3.18-20	C 14
3.30	E 12b
4.4	F 5
4.21	D 9
5.1	F 5
5.5-6	E 6
5.8	G 3
5.13	F 7
6.24-25	C 15
6.30-31	C 15
7.14	E 12c
7.15	E 4
7.17	E 3
7.22	E 4
7.26	E 4
11.19	F 5
11.23	E 7
14.20-27	E 13a
15.14	F 11
15.14-17	G 13
17.5	E 12c
17.7	E 12c
17.25	A 1
17.29	A 1
19.13	F 9
19.13-15	C 6
19.17	C 6
20.2	C 6
21.5	D 10
21.10	B 2
23.2	B 1
	E12a
23.9	E 13d
24.5-6	H 2
24.19	C 15
24.19-21	E 13a
27.6	F 7
28.1-4	E 6
29.2	D 9
	G 3
29.8-12	E 13c
29.10	E 7
29.11-12	F 4
29.21	F 4
	F 5
31.15	E12c
33.1	J 3
33.19-23	F 2
33.30	D 11
34.19	G 1
35.14-17	D 10
35.18-19	D 10
35.24	D 10
36.17	E 12c
	G 5
37:22	G 3
38.9	I 8
40.15	C 2
42.1-5	E 7
48.10	H 10
51.10	E 12c

51.23	C 15
51.25-26	C 15
51.26	F 11
51.30	D 11

Susanna (Sus.).

59	B 1

Test. of Asher (TAsh.).

1.3	F 11
1.3-2.1	B 1
4.2	E 13b

Test. of Benjamin (TBen.).

3.3	J 4
3.8	E 2
4.2	E 11
6.1	D 12
8.2	E 13e
8.3	G 7b
9.2	H 10
10.5	C 10

Test. of Dan (TDan.).

3.2-3	E 13b
5.3	F 3
5.10-11	C 13
6.8	E 13c

Test. of Gad (TGad.).

4.1	E 13b
4.7	E 13c
5.3	E 16
6.1-7	E 13c
7.1	E 13a
7.6	E 13a

Test. of Issachar (TIss.).

3.4	E 11
3.8	E 11

5.2	F 3
7.2	E 13e

Test. of Joseph (TJos.).

1.5-7	B 4

Test. of Judah (TJud.).

18.2-3	G 3
24.2	A 2
	H 10
24.5-6	H 3
25.4	F 11
	J 3
25.4-5	E 13a

Test. of Levi (TLev.).

3.3	B 4
4.4	C 10
13.5	F 5
13.6	C 3
14.3-4	C 10
14.6-15.2	J 2
15.4	J 3
17.2-18.12	I 12
18.1-2	G 1
18.2	C 10
	I 11
18.6	A 2
	H 10
18.9	C 10
	I 11
18.10-11	G 1
	H 6
18.12	C 12
	E 15

Test. of Naphtali (TNap.).

2.10	E 11
8.4	H 11

Test. of Reuben (TReu.).

2.2	D 12
3.3-6	D 12
6.1	E 13e
6.9	E 13c

Test. of Simeon (TSim.).

2.12	G 13
6.6	E 15
	J 4

Test. of Solomon (TSol.).

20:16-17	J 4

Test. of Zebulun (TZeb.).

5.1	G 13
	G 15
5.3	E 12c
8.1	E 13a
9.8	C 10
	I 11

Tobit (Tob.).

2.2	E 4
4.7-10	E 9
4.15	
E12c	
4.16	F 4
6	G 18
8.3	D 12
11.16-21	H 10
12.8	E 12b

Wisdom of Solomon (W.S.).

1.6	F 12
2.22	E 14
3.7-8	F 4
4.3-4	C 2

4.15	E 14	Habb. 5.4	F 4	Bahodesh (Bah.)	
4.17	E 14	WR 1	J 3	2	D8
5.15	G 18	WR 10.5-6	F 4	3	B 1
6.1	G 17	WR 12	B 2		B 2
6.3	G 17	1 QapGen. 20-29	I summary		A 5
7.13	E 15	4QPs.ii, 9-10	E 13a	4	A 1
7.27	C 14	11QMelch.	A 4	5	E 7
8.3	C 14			6	E 16
9.1	I 10	Didache (Did.).		9	A 5
9.4	C 14			11	E 12a
11.23	A 1	12.1	E 16	Beshallah (Besh.)	
12.19	E 6	13.1	E 15	2	C 1
17.15	H 2			6	A 3

Oxyrhynchus papyri (P.O.)

Kaspa (Kas.)

Zadokite fragment (Zad.).

		3467	B 1	1	E 13c
		3351	G 3	2	C 6
7.2-3	G 19				F 2
8.15-17	G 12			3	A 4
10.3	E 13c				D 10
13.13	G 12	RABBINICAL.		Nezikin (Nez.)	

Dead Sea Scrolls (DSS)		Avot Rabbi Nathan (ARN)		1	A 1
				18	F 9
C.D. 4.7-8	H 10	12	B 3	Piska (Pis.)	
C.D. 4.15-19	B 1	14	F 6	1	C 14
C.D. 8.15-16	A 1	15	E 13b	12	F 7
C.D. 9.18	E 14	16	E 13b	14	H 1
C.Is. 2	D 6	24	E 13a	Shabbath (Shab.)	
CR 3.17-18	C 15	25	A 5	1	G 12
CR 3-4	E 11		F 3		G 13
CR 10	E 12a		G 3	Shirata (Shir.)	
DR 10	A 1	34	H 9	1	D 7
DR 15	E 13d	41	D 7	2	G 2
Hor.	E 11			Vayassa (Vay.)	
LF 4	B 2	Derek Erez Zutta (D.E.Z.)		7	D 2
H 1	C 7			Mishnah	
	C14	4.2	E 15	m.Avot.	
H 5	J 3			1.3	E 8
H 7	B 1	Mekilta		1.4	E 18
H 9	D 3	Amalek (Ama.)		1.6	F 9
H 10	C 7	3	A 5	1.13	G 2
	C 9		G 13	2.1	C 1
	D 1	4	D 10		F 3
H 11	C 7		D 11	2.5	F 9
	D 1			2.8	E 8
H 18.14-15	E 13a			2.15	D 11
					E 15
				3.13	E 13c

Tanna debe Eliyahu
(T.d.E.)
48   C 10

Targum Isaiah (Tg.Is.)
5.22-23   G 3
6.10   E 14
6.13   E 14
8.23   A 3
13.22   J 1
27.8   F 9
33.11-12   A 1
41.8   A 2
                     J 3
43.8   E 14
43.10   A 2
48.6   E 14
53.5   J 3
53.10   F 11
66.24   E 3

Targum Jeremiah
(Tg.Jer.)
6.13   G 11

Tosephta
Peah
4.18   F 5
4.19   F 3

Satan must be bound first - C 13
Sequel to the feeding of the multitudes
        - H 4
Separation of the sheep and the goats
        - B 4
Seven times married - G 18
Simon's mother-in-law - I 6
Stilling of the storm - H 5
Stripping ears of corn on the sabbath -
        G 12

Take up your cross - F 11
Ten lepers are cured - I 15
Ten maidens meet the bridegroom - B 3
The anointing - D 5
The 'apparition' - H 2
The barren fig tree - B 5
The beatitudes - E 13a
The centurion's son - I 10
The cleansing of the Temple - G 1
The coming of the kingdom - C 8
The deaf man with a speech impediment
        - I 4
The death of John - A 6
The demon-possessed at Capernaum -
        I 1
The demon-possessed son - I 2
The dumb man with a demon - I 4
The good Samaritan - F 3
The grateful forgiven sinner - D 2
The grateful Samaritan - I 15
The great feast - E 4
The greatest in the kingdom - E 2
The guest without the correct clothes
        - E 5
The light yoke - C 15
The lost sheep and the lost coin - D 8
The man brought by his friends - I 5
The man with a withered hand - G 13
The man with dropsy - G 15
The Messiah - the son of David? - H 9
The mission - E 15
The missionaries return - J 4
The mustard seed and the leaven - C 4
The narrow gate and closed door - B 2
The patient farmer - C 3
The Pharisee and the tax-gatherer - D 7

The prodigal son - F 2
The rich man and Lazarus - G 4
The right priority - E 18
The seine net - C 10
The sower - C 2
The Syrophoenician woman - I 11
The Temple tax - G 16
The tower-builder and the king facing
        the threat of battle - C 7
The transfiguration - H 10
The two sons - D 6
The (un)scrupulous bailiff - G 3
The use of resources - E 7
The wicked vineyard tenants - G 6
The widow's mite - E 9
The woman bent double - G 14
The workers in the vineyard - D 11
The young man at Nain - I 9
Towns like Sodom and Gomorrah - J 2

Vainglorious impostors - G 9

Weeds among the wheat - C 9
Who is Jesus? - H 6
Why parables? - E 14

Zacchaeus - D 4

Judgement - G 4
    lack of - C 6; E 6; F 2
    of another's sins - C 6; D 2;
    E6, 12c, 13b; F 2
    of one's own sins - C 2; D 2, 7;
    E 6, 12c; G 15; I 5
    relieves disease - G 13, 14, 15;
    I 2, 4, 5, 8, 11, 12, 13, 14
    repentance and - B 5; D 2, 7;
    E 12c; F 2; G 11; I 12
    seven times (seven) - E 6
    unforgiving satrap - E 6
Fornication
    forbidden - E 13e; G 19
Foundation(s)
    of earth - C 7; G 19; H 6; J 3
    good and bad - D 1
    Jesus' words - D 1
    stone - G 1, 6; H 6
Fourth year - G 6
Four thousand - H 3, 4
Fours - C 1, 2
Friend, friendship - D 9
Fruit(s)
    first - B 5; C 5
    from capital - D 5, E 4, 7, 8, 9;
    F 5, 6
    in messianic age - B 5; C 2, 3,
    5, 10
    known by - F 7; G 3
    lack of - B 5; C 5
    of righteousness - B 4
    of the inclinations - B 2; C 5;
    F 7
    of Wisdom - C 15; G 5

Garden of Eden - B 5; C 5; G 6
    fig tree symbol of - B 5; C 5
    tithed in fourth year - B 5
Garment(s)
    discarded - I 12
    hem of - I 8
    improper - E 5
    new or old - G 2
    of idolatry - E 5
    of mourners - E 5; G 1, 2
    of religious leaders - G 9

    of the redeemed - E 5; G 1
    shining - H 10
    sign of royalty - H 10
    taken from slave - G 6
    white - E 5; H 10
Gadera - I 3
Gate, broad or narrow - B 2
Gehinnom; see also Sheol
    the underworld, hell - B 4; I 3
Gem stones
    Peter - H 6
    Zion - H 6
Gentile(s)
    accepted - A 4; B 2, 4; C 5, 8,
    10; E 4, 13c; F 3; G 7b, 15;
    H 3; I 11
    baptism - A 1
    healed - I 10, I 11, I 15
    in heaven - E 5
    prayer - E 5
    rejected - C 10, F 14
    respond to Jesus - C 8
    to be taught later? - C 1
Gibeonite(s) - H 1, H 3
Girl(s)
    "dead" - I 7
    foolish - B 3
    step-daughter of Herod - A 6
    wise - B 3
God('s)
    above rulers and kings - G 17
    accepts the repentant - D 7
    approval - E 8
    army - C 7, 11; E 4, 5
    as creditor - D 2
    as employer - D 11
    as Father - E 1, 12c
    as friend - D 9
    as partner - E 7
    as teacher - C 14; E 1
    as tower of refuge - C 7
    benefits the bad and the good
    - E 13c
    bridegroom - D 2; G 2
    care - D 8; E 15; F 4, 5; I 11
    compassion - D 7
    covenant - A 4; C 7; D 11; E 1;

G 6

creation - E 3; F 5; G 6
creative power - C 4
debtor -E 8
demands righteousness - G 1
demands purity of heart - H 11
discipline - B 1; C 15; E 7, 12a,
13c; F 2
dwells with the righteous - D 1
elect - D 10; E 2, 5, 13a, 16
enemies of - D 10
face - C 8
food - H 1, 3; I 11
forgiveness - D 2, 7; E 6; F 2;
I 5
gifts - B 4; F 5; I 11
good - F 4
help - D 9
in war - C 7
Israel's bridegroom - B 3; G 2
Israel's redeemer - E 1
judgement and justice - D 10
kingdom of perfection - E 13c;
J 3
knows all - E 3
love - F 2
manna - C 2, 3; E 18; H 1, 3, 11
master - G 3
merciful - D 7
not to be tested - H 11
overlooks mistakes - C 3
overpowers evil spirits - H 5
overpowers storms - H 5
people (Israel) - D 11; E 11;
G 2; H 1
plan - C 3, 7, 9
plant(s) - B 5; G 6
possessions - C 1
power and authority - G 6, 17
protection - C 4, 5
punishment - A 4; B 1, 5; E 6,
13c; F 8;
G 11, 15; I 5, 8; J 2
punishment is over - I 5, 8
reciprocation - B 3; D 2, 9;
E 15
redemption - I 9; J 3

reign within - C 5
reliability - C 5
'reputation' - D 10
response to prayer - E 12c
rewards - B 2, 4; C 1; D 11,
E 8, 12b, 12c, 13a; F 11
saves - G 15
servants, slaves
cherished by God - C 1
Son, Wisdom - C 14; G 5
Son, Israel - C 14
summons to be obeyed - E 4, 5,
18
supplies all necessities - F 5
tempts men - H 11
trust in - C 7; D 9, 11; E 7; F 5
vengeance - C 6, 13; E 13c;
F 10; G 11; J 2, 3
vindication - D 10
vineyard - B 5; D 11; G 6
welcomes proselytes - D 8
wife, Wisdom - C 14
will - E 17, 18; F 11; G 20
wings - J 1
word - C 2, 14; D 9; E 12c, 18;
H 1, 3, 11
given to Jesus - C 12, 14
rejected - C 2, 9
yoke - C 15
Gnat - G 10
Golden rule - E 12c
Good Samaritan - F 3
Grain
with seeds and chaff - C 3
Grapes, in wilderness - B 5
Gratitude, of sinners - D 2
Grave(s) - A 2; D 9
Greatest in the kingdom - E 2
Great feast - E 4
Greed - F 5; G 3
Growth
in God's care - C 3
Guest(s)
invited - E 4
without correct garment - E 5
Guilt - F 8

Hand, source of sin - E 3
Harvest - C 2
     in due time - C 3, C 9
     of bad and good - C 3, C 9,
     E 15
Hatred - C 6, E 12a, 13b; F 2, 5
Healing
     by disciples - E 15
     demonics - I 1,2
     Elijah's - A 4
     faith needed - G 13, 14, 15; I 2
     to 15
     Gentiles - A 4; I 10, 11
     Jesus' - A 4; G 1
     of Samaritan - F 3
     on sabbath G 13, 14, 15
Heart, seat of mind - B 1; E 13a; F 11
Heaven
     first places in - E 2
     marriage in - G 18
     prayer in - E 2
     proclaims Messiah - A 2
     open to Gentiles - E 5
     Sadducees' question - G 18
Heavenly
     council - E 13b
     food - C 2, 3; E 18; H 1, 3, 11
     judges - F 4
     records - C 1, 3
     rewards - F 6
     treasure - B 1; C 1; D 5, 6; E 9,
     F 4, 5, 7
     voice - A 2; C 1; H 10
Heavy commandments - F 3
Hell: see Gehinnom, and Sheol.
Help
     for sinners - D 3; E 13c; G 13,
     14; I 5, 8, 12
     from a friend - D 9
     God's - D 9
Herod('s)
     a jackal - J 1
     and John - A 6
     oath - A 6
Hire
     of labourers - D 11
     payment for - D 11

     of Adam, Noah, Abraham,
     Jacob, Moses - D 11
Holy
     altar - G 10
     baptism of Spirit - A 1, E 16
     blasphemy against - F 12
     Jerusalem - G 1, 14; J 1
     overcomes demons - C 12, 13;
     I 3
     priests - F 3, 10
Home
     demons and - I 5
     for spirits - D 12
     for Spirit - D 12
House(s) - B 1
     destroyed - D 1
     foundations - D 1
     of Israel - B 1; C 7, 8
     survives - D 1
Hospitality - D 9; E 15
Honour - D 9
     to parents - F 1
Humility - E 10, 13c; F 9
     in repentance - D 7, F 2
     mark of God's servants - C 6,
     11; E 2, 8,12c
Hypocrites - D 6; G 7a, 9, 11; J 1
     condemned - D 6; E 12b, 12c

Idolatry - E 3; G 2; I 2; J 3, 4
     garments of - E 5
     Israel's - A 2; H 1; I 2
Ignorance
     mitigates punishment - B 1
Immersion G 7a
Imperfection - E 3
Incantations: see Magic
Incest - G 19
Inclination(s)
     checked by door-keeper - B 1;
     E 7; F 3; G 4
     fruits of - B 2; C 5; F 7
     good and bad - B 1; C 5, 15;
     E 3, 7; F 3, 7, 9, 11; G 4, 7
     ruled by reason - F 11
     servants - G 4
     under God's direction - D 10, 12

Inheritance - F 5
    laws of - F 2
Injury
    recompense for - F 3
Intention (see also Inclination) - B 1;
    D 6; F 7
Interdependence,
    characteristic of the kingdom
    - E 15
Interest, rates of - G 3
Intermediary - E 1
Insult(s) - E 13c
Investment, interest on capital - C 3;
    D 5; E 4, 7, 8, 9, 13a; F 5, 6
Involuntary sin - B 1
Isaac
    Jesus, a new - A 2
Israel('s), Israelites
    a bride - B 3
    a cedar tree - C 4
    a fig tree - B 5
    a house - B 1
    a plant - B 5
    a safe haven - C 4
    a vine - B 5
    covenant - A 4; C 8; D 11; E 1,
    11; F 10; G 6, 19; I 8
    destruction - G 5; I 13
    disobedient - B 1, 5; C 5; D 6;
    E 3, 14, G 1, 6
    Egypt's treasure - C 1
    fertile - I 7, 8
    food - H 1, 3
    gathered by Wisdom - C 15
    God's people - D 8, 11; E 1, 11;
    G 2; H 1
    idolatry - A 2; H 1; I 2
    in the wilderness - A 4; E 3, 15;
    F 5; H 1, 2; I 5
    laid waste - B 1
    like Adam - C 5
    must be perfect, complete -
    D 8; G 13, 14; H 1; I 7, 8, 9, 10
    must repent - A 1, 2, 5; B 5;
    E 15; F 8
    neglects covenant - A 4; G 6
    new - A 1; E 14, 15; G 2; I 5,

12
punished - B 1; E 3; F 8, 10;
G 14; J 2, 3
punishment stops - I 5
purifying - C 9
renewed - A 4; C 8; D 11;
F 10; G 2, 20
remnant left - I 15
righteous in - D 8; F 8
separation - C 10
sins atoned for - D 5
sins not more easily forgiven -
J 2
tempted - H 11
tricked by Gibeonites - H 1, 3
warned - J1, 2
wicked - A 6; B 2, 3, 4; C 8;
D 2; E 14; F 8, 10; G 2, 5, 6,
11, H 1; I 2, 13; J 2
without privileges - J 2
without sinners - C 9; H 1; I 9
without understanding - E 14;
H 4; J 1
yoke of - C 15

Jackal(s) - F 10; G 11; J 1
Jailers of heaven - G 10
James and John, seek first places - E 2
Jarius' daughter - I 7
Jerusalem
    a mother - J 1
    prophets die in - J 1
    to be destroyed - F 8, 10; J 1, 3
    to be holy - G 1, 14; J 1
    to be purged and punished -
    G 1; J 1
Jesus(')
    and the law - G 2, 20
    an 'apparition' - H 2
    anointed - D 2, 5
    as bridegroom - G 2
    as judge - G 17
    authority - H 8
    baptism - A 2; E 16
    bread - E 18; H 1, 3
    bridegroom - I 7
    brings divisiveness - E 16

King(s)
  authority - G 17
  benefactors - E 2
  bridegroom - B 4
  facing battle - C 7
  five captured - E 7
  Herod - A 6
  law versus God's - G 17
  Messiah - B 4
Kingdom of God
  admittance to, B 4, F 3, F 4
  after defeat of Amalek - J 3
  after defeat of Satan - J 4
  already begun - G 5
  a pearl - C 1
  a vineyard - B 5, D 11, G 6
  conditions in - F 10
  developing - C 3, C 4, C 7,
  E 14, F 5
  entry requirements - B 2
  forgiving - D 10, F 2
  for the obedient - E 17, E 18,
  F 11, G 20
  fruitful - J 3
  garden - G 6
  is near - C 8, E 14, E 15, F 5,
  G 15, J 2, 3
  its coming not observable - C 8,
  E 14
  life of - F 10
  new recruits to - D 11
  of supreme value - C 1
  open only to Israelites - C 12
  open to all - C 12
  open to repentant sinners - D 2
  peaceful - D 10, E 12a, E 13a,
  E 15, F 5, G 16, J 1
  perfect - J 3
  like Garden of Eden - G13, 14;
  signs of - A 3, 4, 5; C 4, 8;
  E 14; G 1, 3, 14, 15; I 12, 15;
  J 2, 3
  and the church - A 5
  treasure - C 1
  united - C 12; E 13a; F 5
  violence against - A 5
  with good and evil - C 2, 10

within oneself - C 8; G 18
without boundaries, barriers -
F 5
without sin or evil - C 9, 13;
  G 15; I 12; J 4
Korban - G 8
Known by fruits - F 7; G 3

Labourer(s)
  hire of - D 11
  wages of - D 11
Lamp
  eye as - E 11; F 6
  Hannukah - E 11
  symbol of God's word - B 3;
  E 11
  Torah - B 3
Last day: see Day of Judgement.
Law(s)
  a building - D 1
  all dependent on two - F 3
  a joy - G 20
  a yoke - C 15
  basis for judgement - D 10
  employment - D 11
  fig tree, symbol of - C 5
  God's v. king's - G 17
  hang on a peg - f 3
  in men's hearts - E 13a; G 20
  Jesus' understanding of - F 7;
  G 2, 20
  less than repentance - D 7
  light and heavy - F 3
  new - E 1; F 3, 7
  Noachide - G 10; H 3
  numbers required - D 8
  obeyed by Pharisees - D 7
  of divorce - G 19
  of inheritance - F 2
  of kings - G 17
  unalterable - G 20
  valued by Jews - C 15; G 20
  violence to - A 5
Lazarus - G 4
Leaven
  as fungus- E 16; H 4
  in bread dough - C 4

of Pharisees - E 16; H 4

Leper(s), leprosy - A 4; D 5; I 14, 15; J 3
    cured - C 8; I 14, 15
    grateful - I 15
    of buildings - I 14; J 3
    of Temple - G 1
    purification of - I 14

Levi, levite(s) - F 10
    avoid the dead - F 3
    called - D 3

Leviathan - C 10

Levirate marriage - G 18

Life
    blood - G 7b; I 8
    choose - F 11
    in kingdom of God - F 10
    less than kingdom of God - F 11
    self - F 11
    water of - C 10

Light
    commandments - F 3
    in a person - E 11; F 6
    for others - E 11
    of Torah - B 3; G 20

Little ones - E 3; G 5

Loan(s) - D 9; E 7, 13c; G 3

Log - F 9

Loosening - E 12a; G 12
    disciples - H 6

'Lord, Lord' - B 2; D 1; E 18

Lord's prayer - E 12c

Lost property - D 8

Love
    for all - E 13c; F 9
    of father - F 2
    of God - E 1, 7, 8; F 3
    of good and bad - F 11
    of money - G 2
    of neighbour - C 6; E 6; F 3

Magic
    parables - E 14
    words - I 4, 7

Maiden(s) - B 3

Mammon: see wealth.

Mankind
    blind - I 13
    choose good (life) or evil (death), - G 13
    deaf - I 4
    dependent on God - F 5
    one family - E 13b, 13c, F 1, 9, 11
    must work - F 5
    not as other animals - F 5
    to be clean inside and out - G 7c

Manna - C 2, 3; E 18; H 1, 3, 11

Marriage(s)
    in heaven - G 18
    levirate - G 18
    on earth - G 19
    priests' - G 19

Married seven times - G 18

Martyrdom - E 2; F 11; G 18

Mary and Martha - E 18

Master, God as - E 1

Material goods - F 5

Meal(s)
    sharing - D 3; H 1

Measure for measure - F 9

Melchizedek - A 4

Mercy
    God's - E 6, 12c
    to others - E 6, 12c

Merit : see also Treasure.
    as capital - D 5, E 7
    as service - B 3, E 7
    earned - D 5, 6; E 4, 8, 9, 13c; F 5, 6
    interest acquired - D 5; E 7
    not earned - B 3; E 8, 12b
    oil, symbol of - B 3
    transfer to others - B 3; E 2
    vicarious - B 3

Messiah
    anointed by Elijah - H 10
    as righteous king - H 6
    binds Satan - C 12
    brings perfection - C 5
    builds new Zion - H 6
    comes to Temple - G 1

Poor, poverty
  always here - D 5; E 9, 13c
  invite to party - F 6
  must be provided for - F 5
  need wages - D 11
  receive the kingdom of God -
  E 13a
  suffering - E 9
Portents of day of Judgement - C 5;
  E 16; I 13; J 3
Possession by demons - I 1, 2, 3, 4
Punishment of the wicked - E 5; G 15
Prayer
  for exorcism - I 2
  Gentile's - E 5
  God's response to - E 12c
  in heaven - E 2
  invalid and valid - D 7
  not a demand - C 5
  not prolonged - E 12c
  not repetitive - E 12c
  not to be incessant - D 9, 10
  numbers required - D 8
  of thanks - C 14
  Pharisee's - D 7
  private - E 12c
  tax-gatherer's - D 7
  Temple, a house of - G 1
  the Lord's - E 12c
Prepared for the day of Judgement - B 1
Priest(s)
  anointing - D 5
  attest leprosy cure - I 14, 15
  avoid the dead - F 3; I 7, 10
  corrupt - G 1, 6, 8, 10
  do not pay Temple tax - G 16
  holy - F 3, 10
  recalled to proper functions -
  G 1
  sabbath rules, and - G 12
Priesthood
  corrupt - G 1; I 12
  established by God - G 1
  marriage, and - G 19
  new - I 11
  purified - I 12
Primary commandment - F 3, 4; G 7a,

12
Proclamation of Jesus - A 3
Profane altar - G 10
Profit
  for God - B 5
  for Pharisee - D 7
  from business dealings - E 7
  from capital - E 7
  from slaves - E 7, 8
  from vineyard - G 6
  spiritual: see Merit.
Prophet(s)
  die in Jerusalem - J 1
  disciples as - H 6
  false - A 4; E 16; G 11; J 1, 3
  Jesus as - A 4; D 2; G 1; H 8,
  10, I 9
  John as - A 5,6; G 6
  killed - E 13a; G 11
  rejected - E 13a; G 11, 13
  to be obeyed - G 1
Promiscuity - E 13c
Proselyte(s) - D 8
Prospects for disciples - E 16
Prosperity
  of good - B 2
  of wicked - B 2
Punishment(s)
  collective - B 1
  deserved, undeserved - B 1
  flogging - B 1
  for fathers' sins - B 1
  God's - A 4; B 1, 5; E 6, 13c;
  F 8; G 11; I 5, 8; J 2
  Israel's - E 13; F 8, 10; G 14;
  J3
  Jerusalem - G 1, 11
  maiming - E 3
  mitigated - B 1; F 12
  not required after repentance
  - D 4; F 2; I 5
  of disciples - E 16
  of Israel - G 14; J 3
Puppies: see Dog.
Purifying
  Israel - C 9
  priests - I 12

symbol of God's realm - B 5;
D 11; G 6
tenants of - G 6
workers in - D 11
Violence
against disciples - E 16; G 6
against the kingdom - A 5
in families - A 5; F 16
Viper(s) - A 1; G 11; J 4
Virgins: see Girls.
Visions of the future - I 13; J 1, 2, 3, 4
Voice from heaven: see Heavenly voice
Votive offerings to God - G 8
Vow(s): see also Oaths
invalid - G 8

Wages(s)
for a day - D 11
for labourers - D 11
minimum - D 11
not to be withheld - D 11
Wakefulness
required - B 1
War
against sin, evil - C 7
excused service - E 4
God's help in - C 7
messianic - J 3
Warning against leaven - H 4
Washing
hands - G 7a
feet - D 2
Watch: see Door-keeper.
Watchers - D 12
Watches, of the night - B 1
Water
baptism - A 1, 6; E 16; I 14
of life - C 10
washing - G 7a
Way
broad or narrow - B 2; C 15
the Lord's - D 2
Wayfarer
care of - D 9; E 15
Wealth: see also Superfluity
corrupts - G 4
danger of F 4; J 4

on loan from God - E 9
to be shared - G 3
Wedding banquet, places at - C 11
Weeds among wheat - C 9
Welcome, Pharisee's - D 2
Why parables? - E 14
Wicked
afflicted - E 16
bailiff - G 3
functions of - F 8
in Israel - A 6; B 2, 3; C 8; D 2;
E 14; F 8, 10; G 2, 5, 6, 11;
H 1; I 2, 3; J 2
nations - E 15
rebuke - F 9
receive God's rain and sunshine
- E 13c
to be killed - D 1; E 13b
vineyard tenants - G 6
will not flourish - C 2
Widow(s)
fed Elijah - I 11
in Israel - A 4
justice for - D 10; G 9
mite - E 9
son revived - H 10; I 2
Wild animals
harmless - J 4
welcomed - D 8
Wilderness
Israel in - A 4; C 2; E 2, 3, 15;
H 1, 3; I 5; J 1, 4
John the Baptizer in - A 5
Will: see also Inclination.
God's - E 17, 18; F 11; G 20
man's - E 3
Wine
bottles or skins of - G 2
medication - F 3
new or old - G 2
Wisdom's - C 14; D 8; E 4; E 13a;
F 11, 12
characteristics - G 5
feast - E 4
fruits of - C 15; G 5
fulfilling the Law - G 20
gathers Israel - C 15

ERRATA

p. xv: Lindars B and Smalley SS
p. 97, line 10: insert: '(See also B1)'
       at the end of the paragraph.
p.216, line 2 up: change 'on' to 'no'.
p.259, line 8 up: change 'with' to 'without'
p.281, line 2 up: change 'F 11' to 'H 7'
p.349, col. 2: delete '/85.1??'